Contents

Figures and Table

Figures

Table

Acknowledgments

ON THE LONG AND WINDING PATH I TOOK to see this project to fruition, I have benefited greatly from the generosity and wisdom of many colleagues and friends. Some read chapters or early versions of the manuscript in its entirety. Others gave suggestions for sources or helped to refine my thinking in rich conversations. For their invaluable assistance, I would like to thank Marjorie Beale, Rose Beiler, Emmanuel Blanchard, Melissa Byrnes, Terry Burke, Elisa Camiscioli, Robert Cassanello, Marie-Claude Blanc-Chaléard, Helen Chenut, Hank Clark, Ray Clough, Muriel Cohen, Alice Conklin, Christoph Conrad, Carolyn Dudek, Angeline Escafré-Dublet, Patty Farless, Amy Foster, Emily Graham, Nancy Green, Jim House, Anna Maria Jones, Cathy Kudlick, Peter Larson, Jeanne Lazarus, Connie Lester, Claire Le Thomas, Mary Lewis, Neil MacMaster, Manuela Martini, Robert Moeller, Adlai Murdoch, Pap N'Diaye, Brian Newsome, Hakan Özoğlu, Paul-André Rosental, Nichole Rudolph, Philippe Rygiel, Dorothée Schneider, Daniel Schroeter, Paul Schue, Laura Sextro, Vladimir Solonari, Alexis Spire, Timothy Tackett, Ezekiel Walker, and the late Jim Valone and Larry Schehr. Their intellectual and moral support has strengthened this book in innumerable ways and made me a better scholar and a better person. In the final stages, Laura Frader, Eric Jennings, and Cliff Rosenberg carefully read the entire manuscript and offered insightful suggestions. All three put in an immense amount of time and effort, providing astute comments that forced me to think and rethink what I hoped to accomplish. I owe them a great debt.

I am incredibly grateful to both Monique Hervo and Nelly Forget for welcoming me into their homes. They taught me a great deal about the history of Algerian family services, the Algerian War, and most importantly about the courage of conviction. Writing this book enriched my life in countless ways; having the honor of meeting Hervo and Forget was one of its most precious gifts.

I cannot properly thank all the archivists and librarians who helped me in the past dozen years. In France, from Christine Pelloquin at CIEMI and Marie Poinsot at *Hommes et Migrations* to Henri Massenet and Valéry Bataille at the National Archives, I had help with every step I took. Director Chantal Hénocque and archivist Christiane Dujardin welcomed me at ASSFAM. This book simply would not have been possible without access to the archives of the oldest private charitable association serving Algerian families in France. It was a delight to work with the editorial staff at Stanford Press; I am grateful to Norris Pope, Stacy Wagner, Judith Hibbard, and Richard Gunde for all their work in the final stages of this process. Closer to home, I kept Sira Ambrosecchia, Carole Gonzalez, Jennifer Krolowitz, Jason Martin, Joanie Reynolds, Kristine Shrauger, and Kady Tran especially busy. I also learned a great deal from my students, particularly those in my graduate readings course on French imperialism and its legacies. I owe special thanks to Leanna Thomas and Michael Brooks for all the hours they spent helping with manuscript preparations.

Significant institutional support made this research possible. I wish to thank the Fulbright Commission, the University of Illinois and the Mellon Foundation, the Pauley Endowment, the Humanities Center at the University of California, Irvine, the Institut Français d'Amérique, the Association française des femmes diplômées des universités, and the University of California Center for German and European Studies for their generous support of my work.

My dear family followed my trajectory with love, patience, and encouragement; they deserve a great deal of praise. To my mother, Jacqueline; to my father, William; to my sisters and their families, Emily Lyons, Ryan, Paula and Grace Snyder, Anne, Christopher, and Austin Fedele; to my family through marriage, Kenneth, Susanne, and Timothy Bubar, Elizabeth Kozina, Patricia, Stephen, and Matthew Spear; to my aunts and uncles, especially Maryanne Occhiuto, Jane Patterson, and Marilyn Goris; and to my family in France, Claire, Xavier, Maryvonne, and Achille Maze-Colboc, I would have never gotten to this point without your genuine interest and your willingness to give me time to work.

For similar reasons, I want to thank friends who have consistently offered their moral and intellectual support. Bridget Pacholczak, Stephanie Conforti, Isabelle Couturier-Philippe, Brian O'Keefe, Wilson Wong, Susan Black, George Leubscher, John and Susan Van de Bogart, Jill Schmidle, Rick Mueller, Eric Filipink, Will and Sonia Saba, Mike and Heidi Primeaux and Greg McSwain read or talked about my work when I needed a sounding board and offered a glass of wine and time away when I needed a distraction. Among my close friends, who understand this work from the inside as historians and colleagues, I am most grateful to Carl Almer, Spencer Downing, Guadalupe García, Robert Johnson, Morag Martin, Michael Masatsugu, and especially Nichole Sanders. Nikki not only read everything I sent her, offering indispensible suggestions, but she also helped me stay grounded and prevented me from falling prey to self-doubt. I dedicate my book to the memory of Wiebke Ipsen, a great historian, taken from us all too soon. She only wanted the opportunity to work on her book, reminding me that seeing this project come to fruition is a great privilege. She continues to inspire me, helping me remember why I love what I do. I miss her so.

My final thanks go to Stephen, Leo and Mark Bubar. Steve has been a constant source of support for all my adult life. He read the manuscript multiple times and worked on every aspect of its construction. Together with Leo, Steve has made life a wonderful journey filled with happiness. I am so grateful to both of them. Leo does not fully understand why I spend so much time buried in books or at my computer. Nor does he fully grasp how much I appreciate playing with his latest Lego creation. He takes everything in stride. Steve, Leo and Mark, who just joined us, make life an absolute joy—I don't know what I would do without them.

I AM GRATEFUL to the editors for permission to use small portions of previously published material: "Genre et décolonisation: Le cas du service social familial Nord-Africain," in *Politique et administration du genre en migration mondes atlantiques, XIXe–XXe siècles*, ed. Philippe Rygiel (Paris: Editions Publibook, 2011), 137–55; "Social Welfare, French Muslims and Decolonization in France: The Case of the Fonds d'action sociale," *Patterns of Prejudice*, vol. 43, no. 1 (2009), 65–89; "Des bidonvilles aux HLM: Le logement des familles algériennes en France avant l'indépendance de l'Algérie," *Hommes et Migrations*, no. 1264 (2006), 35–49; and "The Civilizing Mission in the Metropole: Algerian Immigrants in France and the Politics of Adaptation during Decolonization," *Geschichte und Gesellchaft*, 23 (2006), 489–516.

The Civilizing Mission in the Metropole

Introduction

Imperialism still casts a considerable shadow over our own times.
—Edward Said, *Culture and Imperialism*

BEGINNING IN THE LATE 1940S and throughout the Algerian War for Independence (1954–1962), France offered a growing number of services to over 300,000 Algerian migrants living in the metropole. For about fifteen years, these services, which supplemented the nation's generous welfare state, exclusively targeted Algerians settled in France as part of the state's larger effort to maintain control over French Algeria. The overarching project brought together government agencies and private charitable associations to construct "an experimental laboratory" that sought to transform Algerian migrants.[1] The administrators and direct service providers built what became a network of services that sought to provide Algerians, families in particular, "a little something extra" to help them "grasp equality."[2] In doing so, the Algerian welfare network built upon and brought together two of the Republic's long-standing social engineering projects—the civilizing mission and the welfare state.

The central goal of this book is to show how the Algerian welfare network, by recasting and fusing these two projects, implemented a transformed civilizing mission, sometimes referred to as a modernization mission,[3] in the metropole. I explore the complex and often uneven ways social policy for Algerian migrants braided together compassion and coercion, service and surveillance, moralizing paternalism and generous material benefits. Why did the French government construct a well-developed network of social programs for this particular minority community during the tumultuous period of decolonization? Why, in the midst of a bloody anticolonial war that culminated in the loss of France's most prized imperial possession, did the state extend to Algerians the benefits associated with membership in the national community? Why did women and families, a small but growing minority of the Algerian population in France, play such an important role in the state's project?

In the unique circumstances of the post–World War II landscape, official policy made the Algerian welfare network a centerpiece of state endeavors to prove to Algerians, to the French, and to the international community that Algerians were part of the nation. France officially embraced Algerian migrants. The state framed Algerian migrants' access to welfare benefits in the principle of universal rights, granting them all of the metropolitan welfare state's services and encouraging families to settle and reproduce. At the same time, the architects of the network accepted and perpetuated the idea that Algerians had not yet "grasped equality"; Algerians would have to remake themselves, become like the French, if they were to succeed in adapting to life in the metropole. According to North African Family Social Service (Service social familial nord-africain, SSFNA), one of the most prominent private associations receiving government subsidies, Algerians had particular needs that required "specialized or complementary services." Organizations like North African Family Social Service, which became the network's backbone, insisted they did not replace regular welfare benefits available to all citizens. Rather their programs—from educational courses teaching gender-determined skills to housing assistance—intended "to affirm . . . and to valorize" the work done in regular services.[4] Furthermore, the welfare network's administrators and its direct service providers hoped to convince Algerians of the benefits of modern society—everything from the joys of consumerism to the advantages of embracing France's supposedly universal culture—while simultaneously weaning them of any attachment to Algerian nationalism.

Politically, establishing and funding specialized welfare programs provided concrete evidence that France—which saw itself as the birthplace of modern human rights—sought to establish equality. Reforms enacted in the 1940s officially afforded Algerians all of the rights and responsibilities of citizenship "without distinction of origin, race, language or religion";[5] Algerians, thus, had no need to seek independence. The reforms also reiterated Algeria's integral place in the nation; Algeria was not a colony but three French departments administered by the Interior Ministry. In the days after the Front de libération nationale (FLN) launched its initial attacks on 1 November 1954, Interior Minister François Mitterrand famously declared before the National Assembly, "Algeria is France."[6] A year later, he reiterated it was "indispensable that Algeria remain an extension of the metropole" and that the Republic remain "one and indivisible."[7] To support its soaring rhetoric, the state heralded the civilizing potential of specialized services, which allowed France to claim proudly that it did everything in its power to help Algerians adjust to life in the metropole, to restore harmony between compatriots from different parts of Greater France, and to uplift its charges. In this way, the welfare network was never wholly metropolitan or colonial, but grew out of techniques, institutions, and personnel that moved fluidly across the Mediterranean Sea. French social policy and action for Algerians provide concrete evidence of the interconnectedness of what Gary Wilder has called the French "imperial nation-state."[8]

The overall message underscored Algerians' place within the nation as special, particular citizens. Classified as *Français musulmans d'Algérie*, or French Muslims from Algeria, Algerians' status illustrated the tension between "principles of inclusion and practices of exclusion that have informed the republican project" for two centuries.[9] Although French universalism has long been associated with the principle of jus soli,[10] which has allowed anyone born on the nation's soil to claim legal membership, a number of cases, ranging from Jews, to women, to colonial subjects, have highlighted "the limits of universalism."[11] Extending citizenship, however flawed, to a particular category of citizens underscores this tension and provides a quintessential example of the complex and "fluid meanings of 'race.'"[12] The French grappled with Algerians' otherness by insisting that this particular, benighted group of migrants could be made compatible with French universal culture if everyone involved worked hard to help Algerians overcome their "handicaps."[13] Services addressed concerns about what to do with Algerian migrants, how to address their presumed backwardness, how to shield good migrants from the influence of Algerian nationalism, how to help them adapt, how to monitor them discreetly, and how to win their loyalty. In short, the civilizing potential of its services propelled the Algerian welfare network.

THIS CIVILIZING POTENTIAL depended on the ability of social services to address families and women in particular, extending the welfare state's "moralizing mission" to Algerian migrants.[14] The architects of the welfare network encouraged Algerian family settlement in order to ensure proper "integration"—a concept the French defined differently for male workers and migrant families. Beginning in 1948, French officials observed a shift in migration patterns. According to Jean-Jacques Rager, a University of Algiers graduate, colonial government official, and expert on emigration, "in recent years, [Algerians] have had a tendency to settle definitively in France with their wives."[15] In addition to witnessing migration patterns "changing, progressively" from temporary labor toward definitive settlement, experts, high-ranking government officials, and direct service providers afforded family settlement a disproportionate amount of attention and funding.[16] Even though the vast majority (over eighty percent) of Algerian migrants in France were male workers participating in the postwar economic boom, contemporary experts recommended "family immigration" since it was "in keeping with the natural order of things."[17] Long before most Algerians in France lived as families, the state encouraged Algerian family settlement for a host of reasons: to avoid giving "these French from North Africa the impression they were treated differently than the French from other departments,"[18] to prevent miscegenation, to infiltrate Algerian families through domestic outreach programs, to convert them to French ways, and to fight against Algerian nationalism.

These social policies and the violent dislocation of millions of people during the Algerian War made women and families the fastest growing and most politically significant segment of the Algerian population in France. The state attached great political importance to transforming Algerian migrants and to making them feel "almost at home."[19] Algerians, however, were not at home. Colonial discourses emphasizing Algerians' "absolute difference" influenced expert voices.[20] By qualifying Algerians' place in the metropole, these experts exposed their lingering concerns about the risks Algerian settlement posed to the nation's "vitality." Metropolitan France officially eschewed the legal discrimination and the highly organized system of surveillance embedded in the colonial regime and interwar policing. As Rager noted in his 1950 doctoral thesis, metropolitan authorities needed to avoid re-creating the "confusion between police work and social" services that had left Algerians in France during the interwar years with "a bad memory."[21] Instead, the state fostered a hybrid system, in which its agencies worked with local government offices and dozens of private, publicly funded institutions that became the motor of the specialized welfare network. Ideally, the range of programs and services worked together to reach coordinated goals. Yet, conflicting priorities inhibited the state's attempt to horizontally and vertically coordinate the welfare network and exposed divergent, often contradictory visions about how best to approach what became known as the "Algerian problem." Some administrators, especially those focused on ensuring that Algerians remained a flexible and unregulated labor pool, advocated vocational training programs, language courses, and single-sex dormitories for male migrants. Integration had a limited role in these programs, referring only to migrant workers' relationship to the industrial workplace. A growing number of officials, however, particularly those most concerned with saving French Algeria and with implementing an improved version of the transformative civilizing project (which they believed had been abandoned by the colonial lobby), developed services for women and families.

Algerian women played a vital role in this project to remake the entire migrant population. Welfare administrators and providers regarded women as the conduits of change. They built upon a tradition that had long constructed women as natural educators, vessels of social and cultural knowledge, who, nevertheless, had to be taught how to care for their families properly. Since the nineteenth century, male experts and middle-class female volunteers worked to instill values in women that embraced consumer society and allegiance to the nation.[22] These ideas migrated to Algeria (and other parts of the empire), where a wide range of colonial actors insisted "it is through the women that we can get hold of the soul of a people" and "bring frenchification to their hearth."[23] Frantz Fanon echoed these arguments in his well-known critique of French colonialism, written while he worked as a psychiatrist in Algeria at the height of the war. Fanon recognized Algerian women played *the* central role; the colonizer believed that if he could "win over the women . . . the rest will follow."[24]

French officials also encouraged Algerian family settlement in France because, as Ann Stoler reminds us, "the intimate" is an "embattled space."[25] The domestic realm, made a site of public intervention by the modern state in both the metropolitan and colonial settings, offered the promise of total transformation. For the administrators and social workers of the Algerian welfare network, its programs promised the kind of access to the household the colonizer had dreamed of but never attained. Using the gendered language that typified the hierarchical nature of conquest, metropolitan welfare network practitioners framed their mission as the need "to penetrate" the intimate family space.[26] If social workers could imbue Algerian women with a desire for the benefits of French society, they could influence men and the next generation. If Algerian women became proper, modern French housewives they could satisfy their husbands. By targeting women and families differently from male workers, welfare providers imagined their burdensome task would defeat Algerian nationalism and realize the elusive imperial dream of uplifting Algerian migrants.

During the Third Republic, the relationship between racial hygiene, eugenics, pronatalism, and social welfare kept Algerians and other perceived undesirables from the colonial empire on the edge of France's burgeoning welfare state.[27] France's demographic decline intensified French pronatalism, which fixed social policies on the control of women's reproductive function to ensure the nation's future.[28] To reinvigorate France, welfare programs promoted fecundity, immigration policies sought out "assimilable races," and the police closely monitored male colonial workers.[29] Colonial migrants received some segregated services, but the government limited the range of benefits, including family allowances, to those deemed capable of contributing to national reproductive growth.

After World War II, however, the threat of decolonization, coupled with the loss of status and the shame associated with Vichy collaboration, made it possible for Algerian women to become part of what Kristen Ross has called France's Cold War project of "hygiene and modernization."[30] Algerian women became a part of the solution in the 1950s because the future of French Algeria hung in the balance. In the new context, experts working in the Algerian welfare network advocated family settlement because it "humanized and normalized" this population and was preferable to "a mass of isolated, uprooted, and poorly adapted individuals," i.e., single men.[31]

Before the violence of the colonial war erupted in metropolitan France in the latter part of the 1950s, monitoring the Algerian migrant population remained a delicate operation. Since the rhetoric of keeping Algeria French centered on the idea of inclusion, most early monitoring happened discreetly, often behind the scenes. As part of the larger project to win hearts and minds, the state monitored Algerians through services, which played an important role in their "adaptation to our European life" while at the same time "separating them from any subversive propaganda."[32] The state also carefully framed Algerians' supplemental services as indispensable, partly to assuage concerns among local officials and the general population that these services amounted to special privileges only Algerians' received.

At the height of the Algerian conflict that ushered in the Fifth Republic in 1958, the state transferred policing techniques and personnel trained in Algeria to France to rout the FLN. Throughout the final years of the war, the welfare network's relationship to the fight against Algerian nationalism remained strong if complex. Some providers condoned state-sponsored violence, but most resisted police infiltration and became eloquent critics of repressive tactics. Nevertheless, the most knowledgeable experts and devoted service providers depicted "these poor people" as victims of the FLN and of their own deficiencies; they deserved pity not hatred.[33]

The welfare network relied on experiences and ideas drawn from both the colonial and metropolitan "laboratories of social modernity."[34] In both contexts, France predicated its mission on the need to modernize and transform society and on an unfaltering belief in the superiority of France's supposedly universal culture and its duties. Beginning in the nineteenth century, the civilizing mission rested on the notion of *mise en valeur*,[35] which evoked the need to bring out the best, to extract the colony's full potential using every tool that modern society and technology had to offer. And while it is most often associated with the development and exploitation of economic resources, as Alice Conklin has pointed out, colonizers also applied *mise en valeur* to the "social milieu." In both contexts, social reformers advocated "state intervention" in order to ensure "a healthy, efficient, and productive social order."[36] In the metropole, the regulation, strengthening, and improvement of society centered on what Jacques Donzelot, building on Michel Foucault's notion of biopower,[37] has called "the policing of families." Developing "the quality of a population and the strength of the nation" became the central goal, the *mise en valeur*, of the welfare state's protectionist family policies.[38]

By the 1950s, the work in the Algerian welfare network exemplified a melding of the metropolitan and colonial projects through a national mandate to integrate and monitor Algerians. The most dedicated advocates, many of whom came out of France's social Catholic tradition, vigorously worked to ensure the "adaptation and integration of these families in the French community."[39] Elisabeth Malet, for example, who first worked for a prominent social Catholic association and then became liaison for North African affairs with the Social Security office in Paris, argued that "French Muslims from Algeria" had particular needs and cultural preconceptions. Teams of nurses and social workers within the system needed special training to assist Algerians—and Algerian women in particular—and to prevent them from being left "on the margins of French society."[40] Experts, including social scientists, government bureaucrats, administrators, and direct services providers, agreed that Algerian migrants posed many problems and needed to be transformed to fit into modern, Western society.

At the same time, elements within the network perceived and responded to the Algerian problem in a variety of ways. The range of responses—from direct service providers, who spoke out against the war, to housing managers, who refused to accept Algerian residents in their apartment complexes—highlight the agency of groups and individual actors. The state's goals and political agenda, replete with internal contradictions, did not have absolute power or proceed as a monolith over Algerian migrants. The way agencies, experts, and direct service providers interpreted problems and possible solutions reveals when and why "discretionary power" made it possible for competing national, local, and colonial interests to pursue very different solutions.[41] The rivalries and distinctly different approaches to the Algerian problem allowed bureaucrats, police officers, social workers, and Algerians to navigate the system in ways that conflicted with one another and sometimes contradicted official policy.

Leading advocates spoke out against racial discrimination and residential segregation and made impassioned pleas about the need for solidarity between French citizens on both sides of the Mediterranean. Yet, the expert knowledge they disseminated perpetuated contradictory colonial notions. It reimagined elements of French racial thought by depicting Algerians as "pliant, as Orientals" while upholding France's commitment to "the fundamental unity of the human family."[42] The didactic literature, constructed to help service providers in their work, began with the presumption that Algerians came from a backward, premodern society governed by a collective mentality. Algerians had to be remade, had to become part of modern French society if an altered version of the civilizing mission might finally be achieved in the metropole. Advocates proposed services geared toward helping Algerians' to overcome a presumed natural inferiority, to turn away from Algerian nationalism, and to embrace modern life in the metropole.

To achieve Algerian integration, the network's architects hired housing managers and social workers with experience in the colonial setting. These reformers simultaneously endowed former colonists with the status of expert on Algerians' level of integration, criticized their predecessors for having abandoned the truly selfless mission to help their lesser brothers and sisters, and insisted that the lost endeavor would finally reach fruition in the metropole. In other words, the most dedicated advocates perpetuated colonial discourses about Algerians' presumed inferiority even as they *fought against* the numerous forms of discrimination Algerian migrants faced. In this way, service providers participated in a kind of soft racism that insists "on conformity to metropolitan norms [and] carries with it humiliations and the annihilation of cultural heritages" that Sue Peabody and Tyler Stovall have argued often has the same effects as "'harder' racism."[43]

A nation that has long claimed a tradition of color-blindness in law and social policy,[44] France also has a tradition of singling groups out for special treatment and for mixing police surveillance with welfare support. In this case, France afforded Algerians' services because the goals of routing the nationalist threat and patiently teaching Algerians how to become like the French interlocked. The seeming contradictions in the welfare network exemplify Etienne Balibar's contention that we must envision "racism as universalism."[45] When the welfare network fused with what Pierre Bourdieu and Abdelmalek Sayad called the "interventionalism" of colonialism, it attempted "to introduce a new political and social life."[46] In doing so it exposed the inherent and problematic place of the particular in the universalist framework. The two are at once incompatible and inextricably linked. Universalism makes it impossible to acknowledge difference and claim equality while at the same time defining the universal requires its opposite, the particular. Following the impulse to be inclusive, the French sought to convert the supposedly less fortunate to what was necessarily a better way. Like other state-led social engineering projects inspired by what James Scott has called "high-modernist ideology," the goals of the Algerian welfare network rested on Algerian advocates' hubris—on an "unshakable faith" in their ability to bring sweeping change to "all aspects of social life in order to improve the human condition."[47]

WHEN I BEGAN RESEARCH FOR THIS BOOK more than ten years ago, I planned to focus most of my attention on the period following Algerian independence in 1962. Scholarly literature pointed to the advent of family settlement, particularly in the 1970s, after Algeria (1973) and France (1974) closed their borders to immigration.[48] Despite popular support for these measures, public outcry that a total ban would permanently separate families prompted the French government to implement family reunification programs for male workers and their families. In the wake of these programs, immigration was said to have shifted from "the single man to the family"—from temporary worker migration to permanent settlement.[49] Professors, colleagues, and archivists reinforced this message, discouraging me from searching for evidence relating to Algerian families in the 1950s because the migration flow followed the *Gastarbeiter* model: male workers came to France temporarily to work in the massive post-war economic boom that became known as the "thirty glorious years."[50] I persisted; if there were no families, why had North African Family Social Service opened its doors and started providing services in 1951? I began working in archival collections from the period of the Algerian War to understand the origins of these services for an eventual first chapter.

What I discovered utterly transformed the project, making it possible for me to write a history of the Algerian welfare network from the immediate post–World War II era until Algeria gained independence in 1962. More than simply allowing me to analyze the importance of Algerian family settlement in metropolitan France during decolonization, my research demonstrates that gender played a more central role than scholars had realized. As Nancy Green has argued, the normalized image of the immigrant is "single, male . . . lonely" and mobile. In traditional immigration history, it is the men who move and the women who stay and care for the home.[51] Rethinking these assumptions did more than add women to the existing narrative; it allowed me to bring "metropole and colony, colonizer and colonized . . . into one analytic field" in order to explore social organization and relationships of power.[52]

In recent years, scholars inspired partly by Gerard Noiriel's call to end French "amnesia" about the importance of immigration in French history and by the need to examine how "modern colonialism was a republican project," have begun to investigate the effects of colonialism and migration in metropolitan France by studying, for the most part, the interwar era.[53] Popular memory and much of the scholarship on the post-1945 period and on Algerian migration in particular, however, have downplayed the uniqueness of Algerians' relationship to France in what Benjamin Stora has characterized as a yet another case of purposeful "French amnesia"—this time about the Algerian War and the history and legacy of colonialism. For Stora, the war without a name was (and is) at once omnipresent and France's great "shame."[54] Focusing on economic factors, scholarship emphasized both the masculine and the temporary nature of Algerian migratory patterns and downplayed the history of decolonization.[55] Yet, careful examination of the national obsession over the so-called immigration problem makes it patently clear the forgotten war "never disappeared."[56]

The recession of the 1970s exacerbated French antipathy against North Africans, other Muslims, and people of color in France. North Africans in particular became the targets of increasing scrutiny, hatred, violence, discrimination, and scapegoating at the hands of far-right leaders like Jean-Marie Le Pen.[57] The memory of French Algeria reared its head in national debates over immigration and nationality reform. In the 1980s and 1990s, public debate increasingly slipped back into the vocabulary of colonization, interchanging the word "immigrant" for "Muslim." Those from the "Maghreb (and particularly Algeria)" became synonymous with the problem.[58] As the Franco-Moroccan writer Tahar Ben Jelloun put it, "France doesn't have a problem with immigration as a whole. It does have a problem with its own colonial past in general, and with the Algerian past in particular."[59]

The work of Franco-Algerian sociologist Abdelmalek Sayad, the father of Algerian migration studies, has proved most useful to me in rethinking Algerian migration in the decade before Algerian independence. Sayad's influential model, which envisioned successive "generations" of migrants driven by economic push-pull factors,[60] came to dominate the field. Scholars who subsequently interpreted his work emphasized the economic factors and ignored the colonial context. Sayad, however, never lost sight of the colonial legacy.[61] He stressed the uniqueness of Algerian migration—he referred to it as "exemplary"—both because it created France's first, significant non-European population and because it resulted from the "most unequal balance of power." For Sayad, "the colonization of Algeria" gave rise to the economic push-pull factors that perpetuated what has been more than a century of Algerian migration to France.[62] Moreover, Sayad argued the treatment of an immigrant group derives more from whether a particular minority community is perceived as acceptable, as capable of integrating into the general population, than from the demographic composition of that population. As a result, certain groups are recognized as part of a permanent, "settler immigration," while others are imagined as temporary, "labor" migrants. For Sayad, the way these constructions have been used—to embrace certain groups and reject others—"borders on the nonsensical."[63]

In other words, discourses about Algerian migrants during the final decade of French control of Algeria influenced the perception of this minority. Since Algerians had to be treated as the equals of all other French citizens, they had to be depicted as possible settlers and to receive special services that facilitated their integration into French society and culture. Families played a central role in this process. Only the end of French rule in Algeria, not the demographic composition of the population, caused a major shift in representation. After 1962, the dominant discourse reinvented the Algerian population as a temporary male worker population whose right to be in France was tenuous at best.

Without dismissing the importance of economic factors, my book's examination of the Algerian welfare network contributes to scholarship exploring social policy for immigrants in the second half of the twentieth century.[64] In particular, it demonstrates, in concrete terms, how the politics of saving French Algeria dominated French policies and practices in regard to Algerian migration in the final years of colonial rule. It also highlights the links between colonial-era discourses and those of the contemporary period. Discussions of and responses to the urban unrest of 2005 and the on-going Veil Affair are framed in public perceptions of Muslims. As Joan Scott's work has aptly demonstrated, the national debate about the veil has not been about Muslim women as much as *it is about the dominant French view of them.*[65] Contemporary debates draw on assumptions analyzed in this book: the need to uplift and rescue women from a patriarchal culture and Muslims' incompatibility with modern, secular culture. The dominant discourse, now as in the 1950s, frames the discussion in universalism and exposes the "paradox of a civilizing mission aimed at the uncivilizable."[66]

TAKEN TOGETHER, these six chapters demonstrate how from about 1947 to 1962, when saving French Algeria dominated political life, France sought to teach Algerians how to become like the French even as Algerians' status as citizens remained problematic and the state employed surveillance and violent repression to destroy the FLN. Chapter 1 begins with a sketch of the history of the conquest to highlight Algeria's unique place in the French empire and to examine key colonial themes that influenced the architects of the metropolitan welfare network. Subsequently, it introduces the institutions that made up the social welfare network for Algerians in France during decolonization. It examines how the state and institutions that provided social services on both sides of the Mediterranean forged a new plan to remake the Algerian population. Through an exploration of the legal status and perceptions of the Algerian population in France after

World War II, Chapter 1 analyzes how contemporaries tried to control migration. When Algerian migrants were considered as candidates for family farm resettlement or seen by doctors to determine their fitness, French responses revealed both latent eugenic attitudes and conflicting priorities at various levels of the French bureaucracy.

To understand how France pursued its "conquest of hearts," Chapter 2 examines self-described experts' proposition for a more benign version of the imperial mission. It analyzes the knowledge produced by social scientists, government bureaucrats, and social reformers, some of whom had lived in the empire and many of whom had come out of France's social Catholic tradition. Through their research and direct contact with Algerian migrants, these experts believed they could unravel what they called the Algerian enigma.[67] They bolstered the notion of France's generosity, reinforced assumptions about Algerians' backwardness, and insisted the latter not the former was culpable for Algerians' predicament. These authoritative voices sought quantitative and qualitative data in order to serve openly and monitor quietly. Starting in about 1950, a growing number of influential experts began calling for Algerian family settlement in France. As an anchor of permanent settlement, the presence of women and children would prevent miscegenation and stabilize and depoliticize male workers. Particularly as concern about Algerian nationalism grew, family settlement became an avenue for welfare providers to redirect Algerians' supposedly collective mentality away from nationalism and toward loyalty to France.

Chapter 3 traces how social service providers depicted their vocation to overcome Algerians' apparently natural handicaps. All programs used the language of adaptation, but the ultimate goals service providers had for men and women diverged significantly. Male workers, considered temporary and flexible, required services to adjust to the labor market. This narrow view of integration translated into French language courses and vocational skills programs that sought to create disciplined, apolitical laborers who sent money home to their families. None of these services prepared male workers for permanent settlement. The small but growing family population, however, received disproportionate attention. The decision to allocate resources to Algerian families testifies to welfare providers' confidence in women's ability to help their families adapt to life in France. Yet, the confidence developed out of assumptions about Algerian women as apolitical and ready to embrace the supposed emancipation social workers offered. By analyzing home economics instruction, Chapter 3 assesses the social programs' goal to create modern, Western housewives who cooked French food, sent their children to school, and abandoned the veil.

Just as the general housing crisis affected more than a third of the metropolitan population after World War II, finding adequate housing characterized the most common and urgent problem facing Algerian migrants. Chapter 4 examines efforts to solve the Algerian housing crisis by using programs available to all citizens as well as specialized services addressing Algerians' particular needs. Given experts' belief that housing represented the ultimate destination of a long journey toward integration, Chapter 4 juxtaposes housing services for men and for families. Employers, the state, and charitable associations constructed single-sex dormitories, facilitated surveillance, and segregated Algerian men from the general population. The residential segregation of male workers, who sometimes lived with European immigrants, never raised concerns. Only when experts began to encourage family migration did integration begin to refer to permanent settlement.[68] Insistent that families could not be segregated from the general population, advocates resisted a national agency or system that might unwittingly create Algerian enclaves. Instead, charitable associations began to offer specialized help navigating the complex system of housing aid. Nevertheless, only a few Algerian families moved into rent-controlled apartments or into single-family homes.

When the Fourth Republic collapsed in 1958 and Charles de Gaulle took the reins of government, an expanded welfare network became part of the larger two-pronged solution to the Algerian quagmire. Alongside the expansion of military and police operations, which resulted in much bloodshed, the Fifth Republic emphasized its benevolent development project to save Algerians from "stagnation."[69] By examining the Constantine Plan in Algeria and the Social Action Fund in the metropole, Chapter 5 assesses the politics of expanding social services on both sides of the Mediterranean during the final years of the war. Welfare providers' actions defy simple characterization; some service providers participated directly and others tacitly in the system of state-sponsored violence and repression that peaked (at least in the metropole) with the police massacre of Algerian protesters in October 1961. Still others became among the most eloquent and persistent critics of violence and repression; they insisted their work was based in mutual respect and brotherhood. Yet, even ardent critics continued to fashion themselves as Algerians' guardians, believing nationalism represented the most egregious impediment to inclusion in French society. Right until the end of the war, some experts continued to insist only their hospitality and educational programs could help Algerians "overcome their difficulties."[70]

Since housing remained the most pressing problem—in terms of both Algerians' living conditions and the fight against nationalism—Chapter 6 opens with a critical analysis of the 1959 decision to liquidate the *bidonvilles*. This policy, which justified the violent destruction of Algerian shantytowns, rested on claims that the FLN victimized residents and that new housing would be built on the sites. Ending the bidonville problem required significant investment in family housing. Between 1959 and 1962 the Social Action Fund allocated as much as half of its metropolitan resources for this purpose. Even though worker-housing construction continued, family housing provided a more visible demonstration of the state's commitment to helping Algerians and to shaping and monitoring their behavior. To ensure families did not move into general housing prematurely, housing followed a two-step process. First, "un-evolved" families received training in transitional housing projects—mobile-home parks where they received gender-appropriate educational preparation for life in France. If women responded well to the transformation, social workers decided families could live in government subsidized rent-controlled apartments. A limited number of families moved into dozens of complexes built with money deducted from Algerian migrants' salaries. In the end, widespread discrimination allowed metropolitans and escaping French colonists to move into apartments earmarked for Algerians.

After independence in 1962, a radical shift took place in French policies targeting Algerians. The Conclusion briefly examines how concerns about Algerian settlement and an inability to come to terms with the colonial past translated into a reconfiguration of the specialized welfare network. Rather than dismantling it, leading administrators remade the network for multiple reasons—including safeguarding their own relevance and finding employment for former colonial bureaucrats. In a few short years, Algerians became invisible even as they remained eligible for many services. They became part of an undifferentiated sea of immigrants, disappearing from statistical analyses, annual reports, and mission statements. Even the names of both governmental agencies and charitable associations changed. Most organizations removed the word "Algerians" from their titles, replacing it with "migrant workers." Unable to come to terms with the Algerian crisis, France folded the origins and integrationist agenda of the era of decolonization into a larger, purposeful amnesia about Algerians' relationship to the nation. By 1966, the system created exclusively for Algerian migrants had become the foundation for all immigrant services in France—a system that has remained in place despite superficial changes into the twenty-first century. In recovering the complex history of the Algerian welfare network, we understand better the legacies of decolonization.

1

Civilizing "French Muslims from Algeria"

The master stroke of our work in Africa is colonization; it is this which should restore all the rest.

—Jules Cambon, Governor-General of Algeria (1891–1897)

JUST AS A GOVERNOR-GENERAL OF ALGERIA reflected on the righteousness of the colonial project, which rested on the superiority of French, universal culture and on the need to spread it among people whose "civilization" was "necessarily backward in comparison to our own,"[1] so too did the administrators and personnel of the burgeoning metropolitan welfare network herald their commitment to bringing Algerian migrants the benefits of modern, Western culture. If once and for all welfare providers could help France embrace its humanitarian obligations, administrators believed France could demonstrate its dedication to Algerians, repair the bond between France and Algeria, and restore the nation's place on the world stage. In many respects, what Governor-General Cambon called "the problem of colonization" was wholly different from what became known as the "Algerian problem" in the post-1945 metropolitan context.[2] Yet, the two problems were inextricably linked in countless ways.

To understand the interconnections, this chapter begins with an examination of the nature of the French conquest and colonization of Algeria by highlighting both Algeria's unique history and position in the French empire and by delineating some of the major and evolving themes in colonial discourse. Subsequently, it links the history of Algeria to the early history of migration in order to compare the status, perceptions, and treatment of the Algerian population before and after World War II. When placed alongside the history of colonialism and the "republican surveillance" of the interwar period,[3] the continuities as well as the distinct breaks in policies and practices regarding Algerian migrants during the era of de-

colonization come into view. Examining Algerians' juridical and social position during the Fourth Republic highlights the "paradoxical" nature of
Algerians' citizenship and of France's multiple, sometimes contradictory
objectives.[4] Understanding how contemporary thinkers imagined Algerians' place in France reveals much about the political landscape of the
post-1945 era, about the conflicting perspectives and priorities of experts
on both sides of the Mediterranean, and about the nature of the welfare
network itself. An initial sketch of the origins and the conglomeration of
institutions and experts that constituted the network shows how new priorities mingled with long-held beliefs about Algerians. This analysis reveals
how the welfare network developed as a hybrid system because of close ties
between the colonial and metropolitan governments. Institutions and personnel shared techniques, regularly interacted, and moved fluidly between
France and its empire.

Despite full agreement that Algerians would have to overcome their
own inadequacies if they were to adapt to France's universal culture, officials and direct service providers sometimes disagreed about the nature of
and solutions to the Algerian problem. Competing priorities and limited
resources hampered efforts to develop a consistent set of directives and to
reach an agreement about a unified approach. The architects of the welfare
network nevertheless aimed to reconcile the presence of a significant Algerian population in metropolitan France for both economic and political
reasons with lingering eugenic fears that Algerians' perceived racial and
cultural differences could constitute an insurmountable impediment to
their integration.

France and Algeria: A Brief History

From the moment the French arrived in Algiers in May 1830, brutal
violence characterized the conquest of Algeria. Military and later civilian
authorities on the ground and political thinkers from Marx to de Tocqueville justified the use of force as necessary to bring Algerians out "from the
dark night of superstition and ignorance" and into the modern era. They
advocated the introduction of education and modern techniques in industry, medicine, and social organization that would create a new society.[5] The
officer corps, populated with highly educated men from France's premier
schools and influenced by Saint-Simonian utopianism, viewed themselves
as scientists and educators. They envisioned the conquest as an obligation,

"a civilizing mission full of weariness and danger." Using the language of "pacification," colonizers believed that once Algeria had been conquered it could become "a vast field of study." As Marshal Thomas-Robert Bugeaud, governor-general of Algeria in the 1840s, famously put it, colonization occurred "by the sword and by the plough."[6]

In order to remake not only Algeria, but all of the empire, the French framed imperialism in the ever-evolving concept of a civilizing mission. The basic principle that the French should be "leading people to civilization" and "our superiority" had been central to developing conceptions of universalism and racial thought since the eighteenth century.[7] It continued to develop in the nineteenth century, with use of the term *mission civilisatrice* first appearing circa 1840 in reference to French actions in Algeria.[8] The concept took its most recognizable form during the Third Republic. One of France's most eloquent leaders, Prime Minister Jules Ferry, provided a well-known articulation of the civilizing mission's rationale in an 1884 speech. After outlining the economic, geopolitical, and nationalist reasons for pursuing the scramble for Africa, Ferry proclaimed that "the superior races have a right" and a "duty to civilize the inferior races." While other nations had failed to fulfill the task thrust upon them, France would not. Appealing to their sense of competition with European rivals, Ferry reminded his colleagues France would accept its calling with "generosity, with grandeur, and with sincerity."[9]

Decades before Ferry articulated France's imperial mission, proponents of conquest had already argued for a new kind of colonization, one devoid of excesses, particularly the reliance on chattel slavery associated with earlier periods of expansion. Algeria held a special place in the French imagination. If a significant settler colony implemented the new colonial model, it could solve France's "social question." Under the July Monarchy and after, proponents of colonization championed Algeria as a fertile territory upon which settlers could produce an ideal, hardworking, rural France devoid of metropolitan social problems. Proponents claimed that if the urban poor—especially those who might participate in revolutionary activities—could be motivated to emigrate, France could simultaneously provide a safety valve for domestic unrest and create a new class of yeomen farmers who, because of their ties to the land, could build a new society in Algeria.[10]

The idealization of agricultural labor meant the French set their sights on the acquisition of land. Through a willful refusal to acknowledge communal and other traditional types of property rights, the French military and later the civilian government effectively dismantled the centuries-old, locally regulated agricultural system. The French implemented property laws to confiscate and to cultivate common lands. In all, from 1830 to the end of World War I, Algeria's indigenous population lost 7.5 million hectares of land.[11]

The architects of French colonial expansion, like their counterparts constructing other European empires, claimed that this complete transformation, or *mise en valeur*, of indigenous society—through the introduction of private property as well as modern agriculture and other technologies to harness natural resources—brought progress.[12] Referring to the urban landscape of his hometown of Bône, one colonist basked in "the grandeur and the beauty of the task accomplished by the French," which could be properly understood only when one remembered the city had been "previously deserted, barren, and virtually without natural resources."[13] This triumphant assessment of conquest encapsulates the policy of assimilation, which became the "official objective" and "an ideal of republican dogma" that sought to reconcile the settler community's demands to assimilate Algerian territory and to maintain a strict racial hierarchy.[14] Frantz Fanon's 1961 indictment of colonialism summarized it this way:

A hostile, ungovernable, and fundamentally rebellious Nature is in fact synonymous in the colonies with the bush, the mosquitoes, the natives, and disease. Colonization has succeeded once this untamed Nature has been brought under control. Cutting railways through the bush, draining swamps, and ignoring the political and economic existence of the native population are in fact one and the same thing.[15]

Colonization, in other words, worked to assimilate Algerian territory, reimagining it not as a colony but as "one of the most beautiful provinces of France."[16] This utopian vision focused on French and other European settlement and made little space for the indigenous population.

From the initial conquest of Algiers until the implementation of a civil government in 1872, the French army, despite dissenting voices among Saint-Simonians and others, implemented a "system of extermination and repression."[17] As Dr. Eugène Bodichon, a committed republican and opponent of slavery who championed the rights of the poor and women—but not Algerians—explained, "Without violating the laws of morality, we must combat our African enemies with firepower joined to war by famine, internal strife, alcohol, corruption, and disorganization. . . . Without spilling any blood we can, each year, decimate them by attacking their food supplies."[18] Bodichon's description of commonly used techniques, including burning villages and crops, is representative of justifications of pacification as the natural or inevitable result of contact between modern society and one that was considered less civilized—with frequent references to Algeria as another American Far West as confirmation.[19] As demographer Kamel Kateb's research has shown, the violent war of conquest decimated the Algerian population. Although exact figures are impossible to determine, Kateb used colonial sources to estimate that in the first four decades of French rule over 800,000 Algerians died in military operations, with a roughly equal number of civilians falling victim to "pacification" tactics and the resulting droughts, famines, and epidemics.[20]

Even the Arab Bureaus, which the settler community criticized as evidence of the Second Empire's pro-Arab policies, participated in the pacification. According to Lieutenant-Colonel Eugène Daumas, a devotee of Bugeaud whom the latter appointed in the 1840s, the bureaus intended to "create pathways for our colonization [and] our commerce by maintaining public security, to protect all legitimate interests, and to improve the well-being of the indigenous population." Daumas continued that the men staffing the bureaus had to be prepared to use the "most expedient and least onerous" types of "military force in case of insurrection" and to be sure "the natives" accepted "our domination with as little revulsion as possible."[21]

In order to reconcile the desire to construct a utopian white settler colony with the irresolvable impediment of a permanent, if shattered, indigenous population, French experts postulated that the North African population was in a steady, if gradual, Social Darwinian decline.[22] In the French imagination, Algerians were not only backward, but also prone to violence and disease. Their social, religious, and cultural practices were either exotic and titillating or bizarre and frightening. Colonizers sought to emancipate Algerians from their recalcitrant adherence to a collective "Muslim mentality" that explained their penchant for idleness, brutality, and stagnation.[23] A state agent working in the 1850s acknowledged a surge in prostitution as "the saddest consequence" of "extreme poverty," but blamed it on "vices inherent in Islamic law." In particular, he noted the frequency with which Muslim judges allowed husbands to repudiate wives and concluded that this made prostitution the simplest solution for women who were "essentially ignorant, lazy, and unskilled."[24] Colonial officials generally placed responsibility for the problems of colonization on the Algerians' shoulders

despite contemporary evidence that the French knew the European presence—from the violence of pacification to the introduction of diseases like
cholera—caused much of the destruction.[25]

While the pacification stage of colonization officially ended with the
establishment of the civil regime, the settler community (which numbered
about 280,000 by the 1870s) sought to retain control in a number of ways.
In the wake of the Franco-Prussian War, the Commune, and the massive Algerian insurrection in 1871,[26] a settler brochure articulated French
anxieties: "The Arab must suffer the fate of the conquered; he must assimilate to our civilization or disappear. . . . European civilization is ruthless
when set against savagery."[27] Fear about Algerians' continued resistance
coupled with the perception that metropolitan authorities did not adequately support or protect the colonists' way of life inspired new strategies to implement a far-reaching system of legal discrimination that would
simultaneously control Algerians and strengthen the colonists' collective
voice in Paris.

The landmark reform of the French nationality law (1889), the
Native Code (1881), and in less straightforward ways, the Crémieux decree (1870) all eroded Algerians' status and further assured settler dominance. Adolphe Crémieux, the justice minister and the president of the
Alliance israélite universelle, sponsored a decree that partially abrogated
an 1865 law that had codified the primacy of the settlers as *citizens* over the
indigenous (Muslim and Jewish) *subjects*. By automatically naturalizing
Algerian Jews en masse, the Crémieux decree expanded the clear separation between the elite, which after 1870 officially included Jews, and the
majority of the Algerian population. Despite Crémieux's desire to increase
the number of citizens in Algeria while simultaneously championing Jews'
human rights, the decree fueled the anti-Semitism that made the Dreyfus
Affair a cause célèbre at the turn of the century.[28]

A decade after the massive insurrections of 1871, the newly enacted
Native Code regularized many of the repressive measures already in place.[29]
From 1881 until its repeal in the late 1940s, the code institutionalized racial segregation and discrimination by codifying crimes and infractions for
which only Algerians could be charged. It banned Algerians from holding
public gatherings and from leaving their villages without the permission
of French authorities. It also broadly defined the kinds of infractions for
which Algerians could be arrested to include any "disrespectful act" against
an agent of the French government.[30]

Still worried about insurrection and Jews' new influence, settlers sought a larger voice on the national stage. By passing the nationality reform law, the French parliament increased the number of registered voters in Algeria. Providing a path to citizenship, through the principle of jus soli, it stabilized the colonial regime and provided white settlers from places such as Italy, Spain, and Malta a greater voice in metropolitan politics. To highlight their identity, settlers began to call themselves *Français d'Algérie*, reserving the pejorative term *indigènes* for the Algerian population.[31]

Although the 1889 nationality law affected immigrants all over France, it had special significance in Algeria. It allowed Europeans to claim citizenship under a different provision, emphasizing Jewish otherness, and to align themselves racially with the French population. Legal interpretations of the new law decoupled citizenship and nationality and reinforced Muslims' status as national subjects, as established in 1865. Experts argued that since Algerian Muslims already had official status, they were not foreigners and therefore the new mass naturalization did not apply to them. Using religious and cultural language, the new rules linked race and status to expand the white settler community. Once naturalized, settlers became voting citizens, increasing the colonial lobby's influence in Paris and ensuring better control over Algeria's territory and inhabitants.[32]

Concurrently, the Third Republic marshaled a growing number of experts, including doctors, psychiatrists, statisticians, social scientists, and educators, who, along with others, including Catholics and feminists, set about remaking Algerian society in ways they believed would improve the wretched conditions most Algerians faced while simultaneously reducing resistance. Medical experts, including physicians and later psychiatrists, gave the developing discourses about the indigenous population a scientific veneer. Because they had the ability and authority to penetrate the areas of life normally off-limits to Europeans, medical experts became "indispensible agents of the civilizing mission."[33] An important example, Dr. Ricoux, led Algeria's Office of Population Statistics. His interest in learning as much as possible about the indigenous population provided a great deal of demographic information about birth, death, and marriage rates and played a key role in ensuring that the French stopped "ignoring that there are two different races" in Algeria: Kabyles (Berbers from the mountainous region of northwestern Algeria) and Arabs. By ensconcing it in supposedly disinterested empirical study, the knowledge that Ricoux and others constructed about Algerians solidified the myth that the problems facing Algeria and Algerians resulted from natural phenomena (including the supposedly natural differences between Berbers and Arabs) or Algerians' recalcitrance and not colonization.[34]

THE FIRST ALGERIANS migrated to France about the same time the French parliament passed nationality reform. The population grew slowly, however, because of Native Code restrictions. The first study of Algerians living in France, published in 1912, found that four to five thousand lived in small enclaves in Paris, Marseille, and Lyon.[35] Most were Kabyles, recruited to replace striking Italian workers in Marseille's maritime occupations because colonial, Orientalist discourse—what Patricia Lorcin has called the Kabyle myth—considered them the hardest-working and most dependable North Africans.[36]

The Great War expanded the Algerian population in France exponentially. During and even before the war, Algerian migration became part of the massive influx of manpower from France's vast colonial empire. In 1914, the French government rescinded travel visa requirements and circumvented the Native Code, allowing about 30,000 Algerians, mostly Kabyles, to migrate.[37] More came as part of the war effort. Algerians were among the over half million war workers and hundreds of thousands of soldiers from the empire serving France. Approximately 300,000 Algerians served France during the war, 175,000 in uniform and the rest as workers in various war-related and auxiliary capacities. Thirty-five thousand gave their lives in battle.[38]

Even though France won the war, it lost a larger percentage of its adult male population than any other belligerent. This massive loss of life bolstered the French pronatalist movement, which sought a two-pronged solution (fecundity and immigration) to demographic decline. As Elisa Camiscioli has shown, after the war a "wide range" of experts became increasingly devoted to "ameliorating the quantity and quality of the population" by managing immigration flows. Fears that colonial migrants from Asia and Africa would dilute the "race" inspired France to encourage immigration among Italians, Spaniards, and Poles, and to prevent or to control migration from the colonies since only the former could "reproduce with native women without substantially changing the 'racial composition' of the French people."[39]

The colonial government's desire to maintain control, coupled with metropolitan concerns about North African migrants' connections to communist politics and the burgeoning nationalist movements, exacerbated eugenic alarm.[40] All these fears translated into broken promises to extend rights to veterans and "led to novel forms of control in the metropole." Despite tight restrictions on migration—"including what amounted to internal passports" for Algerians—North Africans and others from the empire did become part of the massive migratory boom that characterized the 1920s.[41] While the vast majority of immigrants came from other European countries, according to the 1923 census roughly 60,000 Algerians, mostly single men, lived in France despite restrictions and efforts to repatriate all North Africans.[42]

Algerians officially had the right to claim unemployment and other benefits in the metropole as French nationals, but local governmental officials regularly excluded them from the benefits of the burgeoning welfare state. Instead, beginning in Paris, the French government established separate social welfare programs for North Africans. After a mentally disturbed and homeless Algerian man killed two women and injured several others in broad daylight in late 1923, the president of Paris' Municipal Council, Pierre Godin, used public hysteria to gain support for his plan to construct a system of services and police surveillance targeting immigrants. Godin defended his initiative, explaining "surveillance and protection give us the ability to penetrate into the intimate spaces of the population and control it; the best way for us to attract, to reassure, and to win over the North Africans is through assistance."[43] Underlining this view, which Godin had honed working in the colonies, in 1925 the prefecture of the Seine opened a special bureau on rue Lecomte that provided "surveillance, protection, and assistance."[44] Seeing the effectiveness of the rue Lecomte office, which provided a dormitory for about eighty and a medical and social service office, Interior Minister Albert Sarraut supported the expansion of the program, arguing this would prevent North Africans from being "left to themselves to fall into a state of destitution, engendering the most serious consequences."[45] Expansion included establishing offices in Marseille (1928), Lyon (1934), and other provincial cities, as well as the Franco-Muslim Hospital in Bobigny (1934).[46]

At the center of these services, Godin placed a special police brigade made up of what the communist daily L'Humanité called "thirty provocateurs, native spies . . . [who set about] terrorizing the immigrants."[47] To monitor North Africans effectively, the brigade kept individual identity files. As Clifford Rosenberg has shown, Godin made it an essential element of a much more extensive police network of immigrant surveillance that made Paris the "envy" of governments around the world.[48] Despite the brigade's draconian practices and the economic strains of the Great Depression, the Algerian population continued to grow. By 1938, official estimates counted over 90,000 Algerians, many of whom worked in France's most dangerous and undesirable industries, with nearly forty percent living in Paris.[49]

The shocking defeat in June 1940 interrupted all migration to France. Most Algerians living in France left, became POWs, went into hiding, or were officially unnoticed. One Vichy report counted about 14,000 in the occupied zone, but conceded "the numbers were certainly underestimates of the reality."[50] Algerians did not fit into Vichy's racially motivated National Revolution, but only Algerian Jews faced specific discrimination when the abolition of the Crémieux decree stripped them of citizenship.[51] The Vichy government never segregated Algerian migrants into work groups, as had been done during World War I, but it continued to monitor North Africans. The regime imprisoned Algerian nationalist leader Messali Hajj for refusing to collaborate and deported 35,000 Algerians in response to the sharp increase in unemployment after the armistice.[52] At the same time, both the Vichy regime and Charles de Gaulle's Free French movement understood courting France's colonial subjects throughout the war was necessary when making claims about legitimacy.[53] Hence, Vichy broke with interwar-era policies and extended, but never distributed, family allowances—welfare benefits with pronatalist objectives—to a limited number of Algerian workers in France.[54]

Imagining *Les Français musulmans d'Algérie* in the Metropole

At the end of World War II and in the wake of the new age of superpowers, the provisional government in Algiers and later the Fourth Republic sought to reassert France's position on the world stage. The nation's leaders understood France could not afford the financial strain or loss of international prestige that would accompany armed conflict with its colonial possessions. As the Cold War shifted the center of world politics away from the old European powers, the empire, and Algeria in particular, represented the clearest avenue by which France could maintain its traditional role as an international power and could retain a sense of national grandeur.[55] Particularly as the anticolonial rhetoric of the United States and the Soviet Union made it increasingly difficult to tout the benefits of imperialism, the French reimagined the empire. As part of this reframing, and in the hope of shoring up control over its vast overseas possessions, the provisional government recast the empire as the French Union in 1944. René Pleven, commissioner for the colonies and leader of the Brazzaville Conference, explained France would not relinquish control of the empire because "there are no peoples to liberate. . . . [They] do not want to know any other independence than the independence of France."[56] A new vocabulary—which included terms like the French Union, "modernizing" or "development" aid schemes—as well as a new legal status for colonial subjects, became central to the repackaging of French imperialism.

As early as 1944, French officials regularly used the term *Français musulmans d'Algérie* when referring to Algerians. This term, its acronym (FMA), and several others, including *musulmans, Français musulmans,* and *Français musulmans de souche,* became accepted nomenclature. The language symbolized the new approach and the promises de Gaulle and the Free French began making shortly after they arrived in Algiers in May 1943. The new terminology also moved beyond the confines of official state business, becoming increasingly common in the press and in popular discussions during the late 1940s. The language highlighted Algerians' relationship to France while distinguishing them from white settlers, who adopted the term *Français d'Algérie* in the late nineteenth century. The new terminology also maintained a clear distinction between *Français de souche* (a term referring to those with roots in the metropole) and their Muslim counterparts.[57]

These linguistic and juridical shifts are significant for a number of reasons. As Todd Shepard has argued, "the Republic broke with the post-1789 insistence that citizenship be one and indivisible, introducing . . . the possibility of both full political rights and the maintenance of local civil status."[58] In other words, by December 1943, the French National Liberation Committee (which became the provisional government) promised that thousands of Algerian men could become citizens without having to give up local civil status,[59] a legal distinction established during the Second Empire. The 1865 law made Algerians French nationals with local civil status, as opposed to French citizens governed by the civil code. Officially, local status protected Jewish and Muslim nationals' right to follow Talmudic or Koranic law and practices in certain personal matters, including marriage. In practice, the distinction conflated religious and ethnic identity, undergirded institutional racial discrimination, and played a key role in dispossessing the indigenous population of its property.[60] By creating a separate-but-equal façade, colonial jurists could claim France upheld the principle of color-blind universality, provided special privileges to subjects with different religious and cultural practices, and made Algerian equality possible, in principle. In practice, an Algerian who sought citizenship under French civil law had to renounce his local status, effectively requiring him to abandon Islam.[61] According to Patrick Weil, between 1865 and 1962 only 7,000 Algerians acquired French citizenship through this naturalization procedure.[62]

The reforms of the 1940s, articulated in the ordinance of 7 March 1944, and then made into law by the first National Assembly of the Fourth Republic on 20 September 1947, in what was known as the *Loi organique d'Algérie*, asserted that Algerians legally exercised all the rights and duties inherent in citizenship from equal access to public employment to the obligation of military service.[63] In addition, the 1947 law dismantled the Native Code, reaffirmed Algeria's integral position as three French departments, and ensured the right of unrestricted movement between Algeria and France. The nature of these reforms also demonstrates the challenges the French legislature faced in trying to address conflicting goals and constituencies. Supporters implemented reforms to deter Algerian elites' adherence to the nationalist movement by affording them citizenship without having to renounce Islam while sending the clear message that white settler privilege would be protected. On the one hand, one should not discount the significance of the government's decision to break with over a hundred years of overt legal discrimination in an effort to underscore France's commitment to Algerians and to keep Algeria French. On the other hand, the 1947 law and settlers' interpretation of it perpetuated Algerians' second-class status by making them a special group of citizens confined by limits that claimed to offer equality while actually maintaining a racial hierarchy. The legislature accomplished both by declaring Algerians had "effective equality" with all French citizens while simultaneously authorizing the new Algerian Assembly to determine how citizenship would be exercised.[64]

To ensure control by settlers, the Algerian Assembly (which had two houses, each with 60 representatives) continued to use the distinction between French and local civil status when determining the constituencies for each house. The upper house represented 532,000 voters with civil status,

63,000 of whom were Muslim. The lower house represented 1.3 million voters with local civil status.[65] Moreover, the Assembly had limited powers; the appointed governor-general disseminated bills and the colonial government, which had branches of metropolitan ministries, administered vital sectors of government, from defense and elections to the judicial system and local government. Beginning in 1948, the new governor-general Marcel Edmond Naegelen worked to diminish Algerians' participation further by handpicking Assembly candidates and by using widespread fraud and intimidation tactics against Algerian voters.[66]

The multiple contradictions in these reforms illustrate France's conflicting interests. To maintain its standing as a world power after 1945, metropolitan French officials had ample reason "to rally the Muslim population to the idea of autonomy within the French sphere of influence" without alarming Algeria's white ruling minority.[67] In this context, reformers secured Algeria's place in the French Union by invoking universalism—the tradition of pursuing "ideal . . . humanist principles"—and by constructing a particular category, the French Muslim from Algeria.[68] France then claimed Algerians were part of France, while maintaining discriminatory practices justified by the presumption that Algerians needed guidance. Furthermore, officials could argue France had a responsibility to remain in Algeria, even if Algerians did not understand they were better off with France's "liberal regime" than with a "tyrannical" one inspired by pan-Arab nationalism.[69]

The provision in the 1947 law reaffirming Algerians' freedom of movement held particular significance. The law clearly intended to highlight France's unique relationship with Algeria, as well as its commitment to the equality of citizens in the metropole. A 1953 guide to Algerian welfare programs published by leading experts explained that when Algerians "reside in metropolitan France, [they] enjoy all the rights associated with French citizenship and must submit to all the same obligations."[70] And even though the colonial regime worked to mitigate the impact of many reforms, settlers happily encouraged emigration in order to ease the indigenous population explosion.

Undoubtedly, the freedom of movement provision in the 1947 law made the migration boom of the postwar years possible. Unlike the interwar period, when Moroccans, Tunisians, and Algerians made up a frequently undifferentiated mass of North Africans living in France, Algerians constituted about ninety percent of North Africans in the metropole

during this period.[71] Nevertheless, into the mid-1950s the French continued to conflate the terms "North African" and "Algerian" when it suited
them. The slippage, it seems, built upon a tradition established in the colonial era. While colonizers differentiated among North Africans in order
to "divide and conquer," when it came to comparing North Africans to the
French, experts commonly collapsed differences between North African
groups to emphasize, as Richard Keller put it, the "rift between *l'homme
civilisé* and *l'homme primitif.*"[72] In the postwar metropole, this slippage
commonly occurred in newspaper reports that drew attention to problems—from criminal behavior to uncontrolled immigration—attributed
to North Africans.[73]

At the same time, experts and state officials did clarify Algerians'
unique status—that Moroccans and Tunisians were "protected" French nationals "not citizens like Algerians"[74]—when pertinent. Fearful that media
coverage would "provoke severe repercussions for the French Union plan,"
representatives of both the Union and the National Assembly called for a
concerted government drive to counter the media message.[75] The French
Union Assembly advised the government to launch a campaign to shape
public opinion by encouraging a "more welcoming" tone in media coverage and by convincing the public "to reject the prejudices and disdain" in
the press.[76] This continued for several years, with Interior Minister Léon
Martinaud-Déplat declaring in 1954 that "we must put an end to the misery and exploitation that North Africans suffer" and insisting that Algerians had "the same rights" as everyone else in the metropole.[77] Nonetheless,
newspapers openly worried the 1947 law forbade any monitoring of Algerians. Drawing on established stereotypes,[78] articles fretted this rapidly
growing population, without proper housing or surveillance, would turn
to crime.[79] Certainly, many top officials shared similar concerns, but to
counter nationalism and encourage an unregulated supply of flexible labor,
Algerian migration continued unfettered throughout the Algerian War.

Even though government officials rarely made this claim openly, it is
clear that long-standing support for pronatalist policies remained central
to concerns about Algerians' place in postwar France. In the aftermath of
the Holocaust, and in an era when the politics of saving French Algeria
trumped other priorities, openly racially motivated initiatives became increasingly indefensible, even for those who still believed France's vitality
was at stake. Reflecting the government's disavowal of eugenic programs,
France's immigration policies officially rejected the use of ethnic or racial

categories when selecting immigrants, even if, in practice, ethnic prefer-ences persisted.[80]

One small program, to settle Berber peasant families on abandoned farms, underscores the ways postwar priorities mingled with long-held beliefs. In 1946, officials in the Algerian Reform and Planning Office or-ganized a program to recruit "Algerian Muslim peasants" as agricultural workers in southwestern France. The southwest, officials reasoned, had a climate similar to that of Algeria and cultural elements that would facili-tate Algerians' adaptation. This idea, initially proposed during the inter-war period,[81] rested on the belief that Berbers made excellent farmhands and that their migration could ease population problems in Algeria, help France rebuild its economy, and "limit the demand for foreign workers."[82] Less than a year later, local residents and officials in the southwest, a region that had lost population and needed labor, complained the program had not produced "favorable results." According to the Agriculture Ministry, locals considered Algerian farmhands "unstable, elusive characters, who work 2, 3, or 4 days with the same employers, then emigrate toward the north to reach their final objective, Paris."[83]

Rather than abandoning the project, its coordinators decided to try family settlement by expanding a program the Labor Ministry had used with other groups since the interwar years.[84] To counteract the perceived "instability" of "certain elements" of the Algerian migrant population, the Agriculture Ministry worked with Algerian Services in the Algerian branch of the Interior Ministry to install Berber families with "peasant or herding" backgrounds in "depopulated" areas of France.[85] Kabyle or other Berber families, they reasoned, were more stable than single men and would fit into metropolitan life better than other Algerian ethnic groups because of their health, professional status, and "moral character."[86] Proponents sought Berber families because colonial wisdom had long held that they were more sedentary, more easily adaptable to Western civilization, and only superficially Islamic compared to the Arab majority.[87] Drawing on the Kabyle myth, the Interior Ministry's Algerian Affairs office proclaimed the program would create "a veritable peasantry" because rather than sim-ply being paid a salary, these families would be "anchored" to French soil through the cultivation of their own farms.[88]

Even if proponents touted the farm project as a solution to several problems, they anticipated two principal obstacles. It would be costly and local populations' resistance to "Berber colonization" might create "political danger."[89] As anticipated, most of the citizenry and local government officials in the affected departments, which included the Upper and Lower Alps, Gard (Nîmes), Hérault (Montpellier), Bouches-du-Rhône (Marseille), and Vaucluse (Avignon), bristled at the prospect of having Muslim neighbors. Regional government officials reported "unfavorable reactions" from the local populations.[90] In most cases, rather than rejecting the program out of hand, communities under consideration used delaying tactics, claiming that it would be too costly, that it would require more study, or that the appropriate abandoned farmland was (suddenly) unavailable. Some even pointed to significant differences in "religion and life style" between the Kabyle and metropolitan farming families, even if they considered Berbers "more evolved" than "the purely Arab population."[91]

Aware of the criticisms, proponents on both sides of the Mediterranean acknowledged and even agreed with most of the concerns while they simultaneously emphasized how the local impediments could be overcome. Most of the discussion recycled assumptions about Algerians that had long been central to colonial discourse, but proponents also argued the metropolitan residents of these communities would need "psychological preparation."[92] Preparing the local community involved convincing them that family settlement would be different, that the program offered symbiotic solutions, and that it served the interests of Greater France. Proponents insisted they would proceed with "restraint"—only families judged capable of adaptation would be allowed to participate.[93] In practical terms this translated into preferences for families that spoke French, knew metropolitan customs and agricultural methods, and could achieve "real adaptation" in about three years.[94] In terms of finding the land, proponents assumed these poor, rural communities would offer up abandoned parcels if the colonial government purchased land and invested in equipment everyone in the community could use. Officials also hoped locals could be convinced of the larger benefits. The "installation of rural Algerian families in depopulated regions of continental France" would ease overpopulation in Algeria and ensure the continued cultivation of France's rich farmland.[95]

As the colonial situation became increasingly turbulent, the political will and financial support for the family farm program waned. Proponents continued to advocate it even as they became resigned to its limited success.[96] Once aware it would only be implemented in a few places, proponents searched to justify the program's failure without calling attention to discrimination, prejudice, or Algerians' particularity. Most pointedly, in 1957, Algerian Affairs contended the project could not be realized unless the state allocated equal funds to "encourage interior rural migrations, [and] to facilitate the installation of French colonists from Morocco and Tunisia in the metropole."[97] In other words, the republican notion of equality, based on the principle that providing an advantage to some citizens amounted to privilege, called into question the program's uniform treatment of all those eligible for resettlement. If authorities intended to repopulate certain regions without relying on foreign immigration, the program had to be opened to the white settlers leaving Morocco and Tunisia after each gained independence in 1956. The program's failure had to be based on a defense of republican values and not depicted as resulting from racial or ethnic prejudices in the prospective host communities. Algerians, as citizens, could not be denied rights, nor could they receive special benefits denied other citizens.

SOME WELL-PLACED government officials agreed with local residents that Algerians did not fit in France. Among the most prominent, Georges Mauco, Alfred Sauvy, and Fernand Boverat had been influential in pronatalist and immigration politics in the interwar era and had successfully transitioned from the Third Republic, through Vichy, and into de Gaulle's provisional government and the Fourth Republic. Mauco and Sauvy, in particular, played instrumental, if subtly different roles, in developing the government's two-pronged population growth strategy, favoring immigration and raising birth rates.[98] As Philip Nord has recently shown, "the familist/pronatalist alliance" remained an influential voice in the postwar era. One of several pro-family institutions, the presidential advisory Committee on Population and the Family was created by de Gaulle in 1945 as a reincarnation of a similar body created under the Daladier administration in 1939. Despite their participation in Vichy racial policies, de Gaulle kept five of the committee's nine original members and selected Mauco, still considered the leading expert on immigration, as the new committee chair.[99] The same year, Michel Debré worked with Sauvy, a well-known statistician and population expert, to transform the Vichy-era demographic institution headed by the eugenicist Alexis Carrel into the National Institute for Demographic Studies (INED).[100] INED, also linked to Catholic and pronatalist institutions, made its assimilationist position clear from its first publications. It sought to control Algerian migration and to encourage immigration among those considered "ethnically desirable."[101] Sauvy also became the visionary behind France's National Immigration Office, established in 1945. The national office managed all immigration to France, maintained offices in certain countries to encourage suitable immigrants, and monitored immigrants in France. It did not have jurisdiction over Algerians or others from the empire because they were not "really immigrants, but subjects and eventually French citizens who, except for police and health regulations, circulated freely" in France.[102]

Mauco and Sauvy initially attempted to prevent Algerian migration altogether. When it became clear this was not politically viable, each called for limiting and segregating Algerian migrants and preventing them from marrying French women. Mauco had long contended North Africans, other Africans, and Asians could not be assimilated. His 1932 dissertation claimed these groups were "physically and morally undesirable" because their religious, cultural, and ethnic differences seemed wholly incompatible with French society.[103] While Mauco and Sauvy disagreed on several issues as they constructed France's initial postwar immigration policies,[104] they made similar arguments regarding North Africans. In a book published in 1945, Sauvy outlined a plan for ensuring French demographic health that explicitly excluded North Africans; he considered them inappropriate, neither "desirable" for repopulating France nor "assimilable." Sauvy conceded that male workers would eventually integrate by bringing their families or by marrying into the population. Since he did not want to risk integrating groups he considered racially inferior, Sauvy recommended isolating North Africans from the rest of the population.[105] According to Patrick Weil, Mauco placed an even greater premium on potential immigrants possessing assimilable ethnic origins than Sauvy,[106] but both men understood the politics of the postwar era. Sauvy, for example, expressed concern about the farm resettlement program and questioned the government's assertion that these families' "assimilation does not present any particular difficulties."[107] Yet, Sauvy, like Mauco, avoided making openly eugenic arguments in the 1950s in deference to France's larger political goals in Algeria.

Boverat, who had been president of the radical National Alliance against Depopulation in the interwar era and a member of the presidential Committee on Population and Families, also continued to express his concerns about France's vitality.[108] The least influential and most reactionary of the three, Boverat argued in the early 1950s that France "should only accept a carefully selected migration, consisting only of individuals who

accepted [French] morals and customs . . . [and who were] easily assimilated." He also explicitly indicated "Algerian Muslims did not correspond
to this definition in any way" because they were not "of the white race."[109]
Boverat was not only concerned about permanent family migration, but
like Sauvy and Mauco, he worried that male workers also posed problems.
Even if the majority of Algerian workers had Algerian wives who remained
in Algeria or joined them in France, some married or lived with French
women. In 1952, the Public Health and Population Ministry conducted a
survey that estimated 3,500 Algerian-European couples (both married and
not) resided in France.[110] By 1954, INED research estimated over 6,000 of
these mixed couples resided in France.[111] Boverat, believing mixed marriages might threaten the future of the "white race," advised that France
should encourage immigrants (from European countries) who would
make "acceptable marriage partners" for French women and implied that
intermarriage with Algerians was inappropriate.[112]

Long-held assumptions about the racial inferiority of nonwhites and
fears about miscegenation influenced experts even in the metropole's new
post–World War II political climate.[113] Aware of the stakes, however, none
of them publicly called for racial restrictions in the 1950s. Internal documents circulated among members of the High Advisory Commission on
Population and the Family (as the committee came to be called in the
mid-1950s) show a preference for immigrants considered ethnically appropriate as well as an awareness that eugenic language had to be carefully
masked.[114] Although the commission's influence waned, INED's increased.
Its researchers, who produced several important studies on immigration
throughout the period, officially shunned any hint of racial discrimination. At the same time, their research testified to the lingering desire to
monitor ethnic and racial minorities, which had been integral to republican policy throughout the colonial era. Indeed, INED's researchers played
a key role in the shift away from the language of "civilizing" and toward
"development."[115] Not only did the United Nations and other international organizations interested in demography seek out INED personnel,
but Sauvy and others influenced population politics and development
theory on a global scale, arguing for controls on "Third World" population
growth—and coining a new term in the process.[116]

The Labor Ministry led the first postwar program which "indirectly
put the brakes on immigration." Beginning in 1948, it tried to control the
influx of labor by "requiring Algerians to go through" recruitment offices

in Algerian cities.[117] French officials understood they had to proceed with care. In June, a representative of the governor-general's office in Algiers told a colleague at the Labor Ministry that the "reality of freedom of movement" had stifled the colonial administration's authority and warned the Labor Ministry would have to act with "prudence." Furthermore, he suggested part of the solution would come from the expansion of medical and employment contract services in the metropole because they would facilitate discreet surveillance.[118] Several years later, Emile Pelletier, the prefect of the Seine, explained how the policy was put into practice. The service centers "allowed [officials] to select the worthwhile elements [of the population] and to persuade the others that returning to their hometown [*douar*] is, for them, the only possible solution."[119]

Of the various programs, all focused on men deemed suitable for work in France. Officials who constructed orientation and transit centers, often called welcome centers, hoped to ensure only Algerians capable of "adapting" would remain in France. To justify these new control measures in the wake of sweeping reforms, administrators cast them in several ways. The centers, in Algeria and in metropolitan France, provided medical, orientation, employment placement, and repatriation services, and, eventually, job training and housing services.[120] All services monitored the population in some sense, even if the postwar atmosphere rejected the overt surveillance of the earlier periods. To compensate for Interior Minister Adrien Tixier's decision to dismantle the vast police surveillance apparatus immediately after the war, officials cast repatriation, an option stipulated in the 1947 law for Algerians "without resources," as state aid for the passage home.[121] It became *the* service state officials offered to Algerians deemed inapt, unhealthy, chronically unemployed, a danger to others, or a drain on the welfare state. The 1953 guide reminded service providers that the colonial government provided transportation to Algeria for the "unemployable, those on the dole for six months" or more, "released convicts, delinquent minors, or vagabonds," and the elderly, the infirm, and "children without family support."[122] In 1953, the Labor Ministry reported it had repatriated 2,152 Algerians, the vast majority (over 1,800) under the vague and eugenically inspired category "inapt."[123] Nevertheless, this policy was difficult to enforce for several reasons, even though the French continued to use it throughout the 1950s and even after Algerian independence.[124] Without systematic monitoring, Algerians fairly easily avoided repatriation. Some Algerians may have used this "service" to pay for a temporary trip home, and, by the time the Algerian War began, colonial officials discouraged repatriation for the unemployed out of fear that the policy would foment unrest and increase hostility toward France.[125] Even so, the threat of repatriation made Algerians' precarious lives in France even more uncertain. Justified as a way of ensuring that the expense of caring for the indigent would be borne by the colonial government rather than metropolitan taxpayers, in actuality repatriation became a way to circumvent the guarantee of freedom of movement and to control the most vulnerable migrants.

The centers' medical personnel often determined which Algerians were inapt for life in France. Fears of the spread of contagious disease in the Bouches-du-Rhône and other regions with significant Algerian populations inspired the Labor Ministry to hire fifty doctors to staff the welcome centers as early as 1948.[126] Concern primarily stemmed from long-held beliefs about Algerians' propensity to bring tuberculosis to France.[127] There were other fears as well, such as a sea of migrants, without work or housing, flooding France. Thus, in order to channel the best labor prospects to companies working with the Labor Ministry and to manage the flow of migrants into industry, state agencies encouraged Algerians to take a medical exam and obtain a work contract through the state so the infusion of migrants into industry could be managed. To get the word out, the colonial government sponsored an extensive media campaign, including radio broadcasts and posters, warning Algerians not to heed rumors that it was easy to find work and housing in France. They cautioned that only qualified workers who had obtained contracts could be assured of a better life in France.[128]

Overall, these programs did not succeed for several interrelated reasons. Algerians easily circumvented the voluntary controls, often aware—through friends or relatives already in France—they could find work without passing through these programs. It also became clear to prospective employers and workers that the medical examiners followed guidelines so stringent that they eliminated most applicants. Most companies preferred flexible labor—workers without the protections and restrictions that accompanied contracts.[129] As a result, the governor-general's office in Algiers worried it had more applicants than employment contracts while the Labor Ministry complained not enough Algerian workers were being granted contracts to work in France. It seems fairly clear the doctors working in these programs made racial considerations paramount in their decisions. In the fall of 1947, for example, none of the over 4,700 men who applied were accepted. By the following March, only one hundred men applied through these channels, despite estimates that about 24,000 Algerians had departed for the metropole (from October 1947 to February 1948).[130] The contradictory goals among those attempting to manage Algerian migration—from the doctors wanting to protect France's vitality to employers who preferred cheap and unregulated labor—made it difficult for the programs to work effectively. As a result, the Algerian population continued to grow because the political and economic incentives for maintaining Algerians' free access to the metropole trumped eugenic motivations.

Structuring a New Mission in the Metropole

In both direct and indirect ways, the people developing social services for Algerian migrants in France after World War II came out of traditions that had expanded French social policy throughout the imperial nation-state since the nineteenth century. In Algeria services for the indigenous population—whether the Arab Bureaus, missionary programs, schools, or others—had been part of the social laboratory of colonization since the first decades of conquest.[131] By the 1940s experts on social policy on both sides of the Mediterranean had long-established ties, even if they often disagreed about the nature of and the solutions to perceived problems. The institutions, personnel, and financial resources that grew the welfare network moved back and forth across the sea in numerous ways. The frequent and fluid connections between the metropole and the colony, encouraged at the highest levels of government, brought about increased cooperation and coordination even as differences in approach persisted.

Three ministries—Interior, Labor, and Public Health and Population—became the backbone of the Algerian social welfare network.[132] While other ministries provided some services, these three played the largest role in setting policies and funding the dozens of regional government agencies and private charitable institutions that worked directly with Algerian migrants. From the creation of the Fourth Republic until the decision to extend special powers to the colonial regime in 1956, the entire colonial government in Algeria fell under the jurisdiction of the Interior Ministry (because it was a part of France and not administered as a colony). As a result, significant coordination took place between ministerial offices. In fact, the Algerian and Overseas Departments Service of the Interior Ministry, commonly known as Algerian Affairs and headed by Pierre Damelon, had authority over most programs and policies concerning Algerians in metropolitan France well into the 1950s. Since 1949, the Interior Ministry had encouraged the state "to coordinate aid organizations."[133] According to the 1953 guide, the Interior Ministry oriented its work toward "moral aid . . . and the material needs of North Africans experiencing difficulty in their effort to integrate into the national community. Its vocation [was] rather polyvalent and polymorphous."[134]

To coordinate its many roles more effectively, the Interior Ministry opened a branch office of Algerian Affairs in Paris, which remained under the direction of its headquarters in Algeria.[135] In the early 1950s, this office coordinated most projects undertaken by the prefectures of the departmental governments. By the end of the 1950s, this office—which became the Muslim Affairs Service (Service des affaires musulmanes et de l'action sociale, SAMAS)—was arguably the most influential branch of Algerian Affairs overseeing the "principle problems posed by Algerian migration in the metropole" and doling out funds to most of the public and private social welfare programs that targeted Algerians.[136]

The Public Health and Population Ministry also played a key role in determining the network's priorities and in providing significant funding to direct service providers. Its intra-agency office, known simply as Bureau 10, dealt with "domestic migrations."[137] François Villey, an expert on the family wage and allowance system and immigration policy,[138] headed up Bureau 10 beginning in the early 1950s and came to have significant influence as the network expanded. Through this office and the ministry's advisory commission,[139] Public Health and Population allocated subsidies to health- and family-related government programs and to private associations whose missions fit under the umbrella of "social action." According to the 1953 guide, Bureau 10 dealt with all "health-related aid for North Africans as [it did] for metropolitans . . . [and it] put into place demographic, social, and familial policies. As such, it [was] especially preoccupied with the harmonious integration of North Africans into the metropolitan community." In particular, it dealt with "family problems . . . that [were] beginning to emerge with greater frequency among North Africans in the metropole."[140]

Although the Interior and Public Health and Population Ministries rarely coordinated programs, at least during the early 1950s, their programs and personnel often shared goals and attitudes about the future of and approach to Algerian migration. The Labor Ministry, on the other hand, had a different agenda. Rather than being concerned about Algerians' ability to adapt to life in France, the Labor Ministry gave priority to services that facilitated a flexible labor force at the disposal of the rapidly recovering economy. Its services focused on issues related to male workers. It organized or subsidized job placement offices, orientation centers, vocational training courses, and some dormitory housing. In 1949, it opened an office for the Social Supervision of the North African Workforce (Contrôle social de la main-d'œuvre nord-africaine), which employed social inspectors (contrôleurs sociaux) who dealt with labor issues. In 1950, it spent nearly 54 million francs on programs "in favor of the Algerian population" in France.[141] Two years later, it also began to manage the new Social and Sanitary Aid Fund (Fonds d'action sociale et sanitaire), created as a first attempt to respond to accusations of "discrimination" in the Social Security Administration's distribution of funds collected from Algerian workers' salaries. The Fund provided financial resources to private agencies offering housing and job training to Algerian workers (and eventually to families).[142]

Despite significant communication between ministries and agencies, approaches differed substantially. In particular, the Interior and Labor Ministries' long-standing rivalry over control of Algerian services, which had begun in the 1930s, continued. Beginning in the late 1940s, members of the National and French Union Assemblies urged these ministries to overcome their disagreements and territoriality over particular services in order to provide coordinated, efficient programs and services.[143] These pleas originated among those pressing for the new development-centered agenda that characterized the postwar era. A key figure, Abbé Paul Catrice, a priest from Lille, had worked in social Catholic circles before serving as a member of the Gaullist Mouvement républicain populaire (MRP) in the upper house of the French Union Assembly. According to Frederick Cooper, Catrice credited the Catholic Church and the MRP with bringing "social progress" to the empire when the Assembly enacted a new labor code.[144] Catrice likewise played a key role in advocating the expansion of social programs to Algerians, demanding the National Assembly provide the same welfare benefits (including family allowances and other social benefits under Social Security) to Algerians as enjoyed by citizens in the metropole. Unable to change the law, Catrice and his supporters raised awareness that the families of migrant workers were "clearly disadvantaged" if they remained in Algeria and won support among the French left and Algerian nationalists.[145]

In 1948, Catrice and twenty-five other French Union deputies also demanded that "a vast program of social improvements and education in favor of these workers" be implemented in the metropole to contend with the grave problems Algerian migrants faced. They reasoned that focusing on "civic, social, and vocational education" for migrants would also have salutary results in Algeria.[146] To make the imagined welfare network a reality, Catrice led a call for the state to create an interministerial commission to deal with North African questions in the metropole.[147] Within months, at the behest of the National Assembly, an interministerial decree created a national Interministerial Advisory Commission to study "the problem of North African immigration in the metropole and to propose a collective solution," inviting the prefects of regions with significant North African populations to sit on the commission. The deputies who proposed the Interministerial Advisory Commission for the Study of North African Questions argued that services offered by various ministries, municipalities, and charitable associations had to be coordinated to calm the metropolitan population's "unjustified" fears about all North Africans, and particularly about "French Muslims from Algeria," whom the deputies worried were not recognized as part of the "national community." These fears created a "situation" where North Africans became "victims," "brutally transplanted into a world completely different from their" homeland. Arriving in France without "professional qualifications" and living in "deplorable conditions," they became "veritable pariahs." The deputies' use of such strong language seems to have been intended to inspire quick and decisive action.[148]

Their language also reveals a great deal about what assumptions "public authorities" (*pouvoirs publics*) shared, even if they disagreed about how to proceed with the solution. Not only did the deputies presume that Algerian "fellow citizens" came from a backward society that shared little of the marvels of Western culture, but they also assumed that much would have to be done to uplift Algerians in the metropole. Moreover, the deputies understood that coordinating services for Algerian migrants had a larger goal—to prevent "severe repercussions for the French Union."[149] Ministerial staff also understood much was at stake. As a Labor Ministry official put it, only through the work of an interministerial commission could the state "realize the indispensable unity of opinion and action."[150] Yet, agreeing on the need for interministerial harmony was easier than enacting reforms to streamline the programs, especially when changes might be perceived as hindering one's own programs.

While there were ideological conflicts, most disagreement revolved around the allocation of resources. In one example, Algerian offices threatened to prevent the transfer of money for services in the metropole unless metropolitan offices agreed to begin contributing some of their own resources to these programs.[151] Initially, monies came from the Algerian offices at least in part to prevent any appearance that metropolitan budgets subsidized welfare for Algerian migrants (to avoid angering metropolitan taxpayers). And although preventing what was perceived as giving Algerians preferential treatment remained a concern, as the Franco-Algerian conflict took center stage, these ministries allocated growing sums from both metropolitan and colonial budgets.

In terms of ideological differences, one of the common themes that appeared in interministerial squabbling related to restrictive versus open migration. Much of the worry about restricting migration revolved around the supposed dangers migrants posed. Most administrators in favor of restrictions tried to veil the eugenic overtones of their arguments. For example, Dr. André Cavaillon, the director-general of Public Hygiene and Hospitals for the Public Health and Population Ministry, insisted that sanitary conditions, not issues of "race or of ethnic group," constituted the central problem of Algerian migration. He warned the Interministerial Advisory Commission's board of the dire consequences if Algerians were allowed to continue to live in squalor. The migrants' "tendency," he posited, to live in slums and to eat poorly in order to send more money home made them more susceptible to disease, which they would inadvertently spread among the general population. In developing his argument, Cavaillon made clear he was aware of the political ramifications of the freedom of movement policy. He began his report with an obligatory reminder that "Algerians are French citizens" and that limiting their access to metropolitan soil would be like distinguishing between citizens of "Seine-et-Marne and those of the Department of Seine-et-Oise." Yet, he bemoaned the decision to extend citizenship, pointing out that health problems had to be dealt with in different ways "north [and] . . . south of the border." Eliminating the controls, he claimed, had destroyed any legal approach to preventing the spread of disease. Although pessimistic, Cavaillon urged the Interministerial Advisory Commission to find a way to prevent Algerians from contracting and spreading disease.[152]

Damelon, who headed Algerian Affairs, provided the typical counterargument. Any programs, whether medical controls or others, would only work if Algerians did not view them as having "a discriminatory character." Rather than instituting restrictions, which he feared would result in "protests" among Algerians, Damelon argued the best way to protect greater French interests, while preventing the problems associated with Algerian migration, was to develop a "propaganda" campaign in Algeria that worked "to discourage excessive departures." In other words, Damelon and Cavaillon disagreed about how to deal with the Algerian problem even if they shared common ground. Damelon implicitly agreed with Cavaillon's assessment that Algerians' posed a danger. Yet, he rejected the restrictive solution and reminded his fellow board members of the larger geopolitical issues. For Damelon, restrictive measures had to be avoided because "national solidarity is at stake. North Africans had answered our call during the war and we must help them now, and we cannot lose sight of the decline France would suffer if it lost North Africa."[153]

Given the gravity of the situation and the Interministerial Advisory Commission's lack of real power, the state established a new Interministerial Commission for the Coordination of Muslim Social Affairs, which held some purse strings. Although individual ministries and agencies continued to allocate funds directly to programs and services, starting in 1952 the Interministerial Commission also had the authority to allocate some ministerial resources directly to programs and services, which required its board members to compromise.[154] In the first year, it allocated 56.5 million francs from the Interior Ministry's budget to direct service providers in the metropole.[155] Still, conflicts over both jurisdiction and objectives continued to plague the struggle to harmonize services.

A Public-Private Partnership

The desire to balance competing ministerial services and goals, the dearth of funding, and the widespread association of services with state surveillance fostered the Algerian welfare network's interest in public-private partnerships. Beginning in 1949, following the directives of the Interministerial Advisory Commission, the Interior Ministry implemented policies encouraging "the creation of private associations devoted to social welfare."[156] A desire to minimize the appearance of state surveillance stood behind the decision to use regional and municipal governments and private charitable organizations in the development of state initiatives. Yet, for this approach to succeed, Algerian Affairs had to convince departmental prefects that Algerian workers were needed in the metropole, that they were citizens, that they should be treated in accordance with "national solidarity," and that precious resources should be committed to facilitate their "adaptation to metropolitan life."[157] Since it was not clear if regional governments took advantage of the administrative infrastructure, Algerian Affairs made a "team" of experts available to the departmental governments. These experts worked "to facilitate the contacts between new arrivals, the [general] population, private organizations, and public authorities, [while remaining] in close contact with the appropriate administrations, that is the local branches of the Ministries of Public Health and Population and Labor and Social Security."[158]

The structure encouraged regional and municipal governmental agencies and charitable associations to work closely with the Algerian population. Programs sponsored by prefectures and municipalities or by private organizations generally received funding either directly from the Interior, Labor, or Public Health and Population Ministries, or through the Interministerial Commission. Some of the oldest charitable organizations that received subventions from the commission included Assistance morale aux Nord Africains (created in 1945), Service social familial nord-africain (1951), Maison de l'Afrique du Nord in Lyon (1951), Accueil familial nord-africain in Paris, the Nord, and Strasbourg (1952), Aide aux travailleurs d'outre-mer in the Bouches-du-Rhône (1949), Association d'aide aux Français d'Algérie de la région Lilloise (1951), and Union sociale nord-africaine de Lille (1951). These organizations, as well as dozens of others, offered a wide range of services, including orientation, emergency and permanent housing, vocational-skills training, and aid in navigating the bureaucracy. Moral Assistance for North Africans, the first organization established after World War II, received funding from the Interministerial Commission that grew from two to three million francs in the early 1950s.[159] Among the many services this social Catholic association provided in most regions with a significant Algerian population were dormitory housing, job training, and family services. Its founder, Father Jacques Ghys, subsequently established both North African Family Social Service and North African Social Studies (Etudes sociales nord-africains, ESNA), both of which played a central role in the welfare network. The latter published an important journal and a range of educational materials—for Algerians and those who worked with them—including the 1953 guide to services.

Ghys' organizations developed a national orientation, but most other organizations had a regional focus, even if their missions significantly overlapped. The Aid Association for French Muslims in the region of Lille, for example, opened an intervention office with social workers who provided assistance relating to emergency aid, clothing, medical referrals, repatriation, paid vacations, unemployment, housing and family issues including divorce and inheritance.[160] By 1953, in Paris alone a dozen private organizations exclusively served Algerians, and by 1956, the Interior Ministry partially funded 135 local governmental or private associations throughout the country.[161] This grew to 140 associations by 1958. Combined, these service organizations spent 400 million francs a year at the height of the war.[162]

One organization in particular, the Aid Commission for North Africans in the Metropole (Commission d'aide aux Nord Africains dans la métropole, CANAM), illustrates the fluid ties between Algeria and the metropole and the intimate intertwining of metropolitan and colonial endeavors. In the late 1940s, the Aid Commission took over the charitable services of the Vichy-era Comité Louis Morard (created in 1941). Georges Le Beau, honorary governor-general of Algeria and the first president of the Aid Commission, explained its mission was to provide "adaptation" services in "a spirit of fraternal solidarity."[163] As one of the first associations speaking on behalf of Algerians in the metropole, it addressed the French Union Assembly's recommendation to increase funding for programs that would mitigate the terrible conditions migrants faced in 1949.[164] By 1957, the Aid Commission's general administrative secretary claimed that for fifteen years it had "studied all aspects of Algerian migration to France, observed the effects of Western civilization on the adaptation of individuals and families, and researched all the appropriate avenues through which to facilitate the distribution of resources." Based on this research, the Aid Commission concluded that the following areas should be given priority: "orientation [*accueil*], placement, housing, general education, vocational training, feminine education, sanitary education, and help to those in hospitals and sanitariums."[165]

In the immediate postwar period, the Aid Commission received funding from the Algerian Office of Economics and Tourism.[166] As the welfare network began to grow, like most other organizations during this period, it received funds (which amounted to about 2 million francs annually in the early 1950s) through the Interministerial Commission.[167] Aid Commission board members reflected the organization's roots on both sides of the Mediterranean. It had representatives from the Interior, Public Health and Population, Labor, Foreign Affairs, and Education Ministries, as well as several highly placed colonial officials, including Le Beau, the secretary-general for Algerian Affairs, and a representative of the Bank of Algeria. The Aid Commission acted as a middleman; it distributed government funds to organizations that its board deemed worthy and it hired social workers and others who served as staff members in private associations or in regional governmental offices.[168]

In this way the Aid Commission sponsored a wide variety of programs, from housing and educational programs to radio broadcasts targeting Algerians. In 1951, for example, at the request of the governor-general of Algeria, the Aid Commission subsidized the operations of numerous charitable associations, including Aid to Overseas Workers in Marseille (to which it provided 600,000 francs), Friends of North Africans in Lorraine (200,000 francs), and Ghys' Moral Assistance for North Africans (800,000 francs).[169] It also worked with regional governments on specific projects including the instillation of a welcome center in Marseille (which cost 15 million francs).[170]

WHETHER IN CONSTRUCTING a network of services for Algerians in the metropole or in reforming Algerians' legal status, we see that despite divergent opinions about how to approach the Algerian problem, those working in the emerging welfare network shared a perspective informed by colonial discourses. Even if French priorities shifted significantly after World War II, a growing group of administrators, bureaucrats, and social scientists all began to implement new initiatives and to develop a system of services that was the product of an interconnected metropolitan and colonial government.

At no other time would it have been possible for the state to recruit Berber farming families to settle on abandoned land in southwest France to ease the overpopulation problems in Algeria, to ensure the *mise en valeur* of fertile French soil, and to prove Algerians were citizens like all others. Yet, even if the horrors of World War II had discredited racial sciences, Algerians' citizenship remained exceptional, circumscribed, and particular. Most French officials in this network agreed, even insisted, that Algerians had citizenship, but when examined critically their actions reveal even those who spoke up for Algerians' rights did not see them as French. To live in France, Algerians had to remake themselves. To use the language of the day, they had to "adapt" or "evolve" in order to be able to live harmoniously with the metropolitan population. Bureaucrats and experts were careful to avoid the expression most closely associated with the colonial project: the civilizing mission. Nevertheless, the colonial project undoubtedly affected their work and their goals. It seems clear that those who constructed this welfare network intended to "civilize" the Algerian migrants in their midst.

2

Instructing the Experts
Framing the Metropolitan "Conquest of Hearts"

IN 1955 North African Social Studies and INED jointly published *Les Algériens en France: Etude démographique et sociale*, the most comprehensive study of Algerian migrants to date. Its authors, Alain Girard, a department head at INED who had previously coauthored two INED immigration studies,[1] and Joseph Leriche, the director of North African Social Studies and editor-in-chief of the *Cahiers nord-africains*, built upon the most respected scholarship in the field and utilized the files of key administrators in Algerian Affairs, Social Security, and the Labor, Population, and Interior Ministries for their research. Their study also relied on, and even included, reports by direct service providers working in Marseille's most prominent private association serving Algerians, Aid to Overseas Workers.[2] It represents an important example of the production and dissemination of knowledge by influential social scientists and other experts working both inside and outside the state to find solutions to the so-called Algerian problem. It became part of an expanding body of literature that social workers, state employees, employers, and anyone else coming into contact with Algerian migrants had at their disposal, resources to which direct service providers in particular could turn for information and counsel.

Since experts like Girard and Leriche began with the assumption that direct service providers knew little about their new clients, they constructed this didactic literature to provide help. Girard, Leriche, and their colleagues insisted their research sought "to enlighten public authorities, to clarify opinions, to dispel harsh prejudices about an issue that is too easily sentimentalized." They sifted "through the options" to identify "apparent solutions" without intending to "dictate solutions" to the state or to charitable associations.[3] Nevertheless, there is no doubt the experts on Algeria and Algerians provided what they considered disinterested, scientific research in order to influence attitudes, policies, and actions.[4] Their work was part of a much larger postwar push toward professionalization through "new, quasi-governmental, quasi-academic institutions." They pursued what Luc Boltanski has described as research "intended to be both scientific and statistical, proscriptive and prescriptive."[5] An institution like INED, with its national scope, certainly never made the Algerian problem the only item on its research agenda, but it partnered with North African Social Studies to learn more and to find durable solutions.

The push for professional expertise also motivated the Algerian services' leadership, as part of its "Interministerial plan," to hire a growing cadre of functionaries to ensure that a unified message reached direct service providers. To work with experts constructing the didactic literature and to advise local metropolitan authorities, the Labor and Interior Ministries hired people with expertise in foreign languages and other fields gained in either military or civilian experience in the colonies.[6] Skirting the restrictions imposed by the 1947 law, the new bureaucrats also sought to manage and to control what appeared to be a massive new migration with staggering consequences for the metropole. In most cases they monitored direct service providers and Algerians from behind the scenes. Generally, the staff of private associations worked directly with Algerian migrants. According to both the Interior Ministry and North African Social Studies, social workers and others in charitable institutions were best able to provide "human contact," to approach Algerians "with respect" and "sympathy," while simultaneously collecting information to help "penetrate [their] mentality" and to remake them in ways that fit with metropolitan society.[7]

The most respected source for knowledge about Algerians among service providers was unquestionably North African Social Studies. It was not the lone voice of expertise on Algerians in France, but everyone in the field relied on and trusted its work. Its journals, *Cahiers nord-africains* and *Documents nord-africains*, brought together all sources its researchers believed anyone working with Algerians might need. The *Cahiers nord-africains* published original research, reprinted excerpts of influential studies, and provided bibliographic references to a great deal of literature by well-known social scientists, Orientalists, and other scholars educated in a variety of fields at France's premier metropolitan and colonial universities and whose impeccable credentials and research skills drew them to the Algerian problem, what North African Social Studies called a new "complex social problem."[8] The *Cahiers nord-africains* also published the work of social reformers, medical professionals, and social workers for their firsthand experience and expert knowledge of the Algerian "mentality."

North African Social Studies, as well as others working in the Algerian services network, grew out of several traditions of social analysis, including Le Playist, social Catholic, pronatalist, and other paternalist reform movements committed to social engineering in the metropole and in the colonies.[9] This tradition reinforced the notion that the Algerian mind held mysteries only they could unravel.[10] It exalted Marshall Hubert Lyautey as a shining example of a technocrat who reconciled his social Catholicism with a life in the service of France.[11] In view of his success in Morocco and his ability to cultivate "friendship between men" (in reference to his diplomatic rather than military approach to Sultan Moulay-Yousef), Lyautey embodied the idealized "man of action" who possessed the "qualities of the 'technician' and the man of learning."[12]

In the atmosphere of the postwar era, these researchers proposed a new approach. They wanted to avoid what they believed to be the excesses of imperialism and at the same time they intended to implement a new, more benign version of the civilizing mission in the metropole. These authoritative voices framed the new project as a "conquest of hearts," which could eschew "discrimination" and the "colonialist mentality."[13] Technocrats and service providers would, in the words of Girard and Leriche, encourage the citizens of France to accept the "responsibilities" thrust upon them. "History had linked the destiny" of these two peoples, the French and the Algerians, and had charged France with helping "a population less evolved than our own." As a result, the French needed to lead with "patience" in order to help Algerians give up their backward ways.[14] The prescriptive literature provided the advice service providers needed to assist "the Algerian Muslim population" by creating "a climate of welcome, comprehension, [and] education."[15]

To win Algerians over to the benefits of France's universal culture and to convince them to reject Algerian nationalism in any form, these experts implored the men and women working with Algerians to muster all their persuasive powers. If France was to succeed in helping Algerian migrants adapt, it needed "collective action . . . undertaken department by department, industrial region by industrial region, group by group, family by family, individual by individual: all of France should be 'sensitized' and made aware of their responsibilities in this immense educational task."[16]

After examining the private institutions that participated in the production and dissemination of information and the government agencies that coordinated and monitored direct service providers and Algerians, this chapter analyzes the quantitative and qualitative data produced about Algerians. Those data incorporated older stereotypes about Algerians' need for "integration into a milieu very different and much more evolved" than the one from which they came, and simultaneously extolled France's benevolence.[17] The didactic literature warned that in enacting France's universal mission, service providers should never "confuse social action with political and economic action." What they needed most was "patience."[18]

The Role of Private Institutions

The Interministerial Commission for the Coordination of Muslim Social Affairs fostered a public-private partnership to develop services for Algerian migrants in part because a core of private associations already had staff and programs in place. The Interministerial Commission subsidized private organizations' established relationships and relied on their special knowledge.[19] Yet, the state did not intend to fold the private organizations into the government bureaucracy; its agents supposed that private associations would attract much less suspicion than state-run services with which Algerians had ample previous, negative experiences in both Algeria and France. The Interior Ministry preferred to extend its reach, from 1949 on, through "the creation of private associations dedicated to mutual social assistance among these migrants." Five years later, fifty-eight mostly new associations had partnered with the state to solve the Algerian problem.[20]

Whereas the Interministerial plan was intended to "ensure . . . the coordination of social action," its authors determined that the most effective approach was "to decentralize action . . . by placing it as close as possible to the areas of established Algerian migration."[21] Too much coordination might backfire. Abbé Paul Catrice again warned that it would be "dangerous" if the Interior Ministry funneled metropolitan services through its offices because of its association with the colonial government. Citing the law of 20 September 1947, he argued that Algerians in France needed to feel they were like other French citizens, "under the jurisdiction of all ministries without discrimination, each according to its specialization, and not only [reporting to] the Interior Ministry" as they did in Algeria. Only by working together could governmental and private providers achieve what Catrice referred to as their "strictly social mission" to connect all Algerians to services.[22]

To emphasize the services' commitment to altruism and to distance them from France's history of surveillance and discrimination, private charitable institutions were made the backbone of the new welfare network. In general, private providers shared the state's mission, and for the most part their personnel worked closely with government staff, sharing resources and knowledge. The way the Interministerial Commission allocated its annual subsidies guaranteed the state's right to monitor service providers while simultaneously sidestepping the visible surveillance that had been the norm in the colonies and in interwar France. This arrangement also offered trusted experts in public and private institutions—many of which grew out of France's social Catholic tradition—an influential role in defining and transmitting the welfare network's goals.

As a movement, social Catholicism began as a response to the multiple crises in the nineteenth century. It provided a voice to citizens with deeply held religious convictions in the notoriously anticlerical Third Republic. Inspired by Pope Leo XIII's encyclicals from the early 1890s, social Catholics campaigned for "government intervention in social affairs" to improve conditions for working people and to prevent the spread of socialism.[23] Social Catholics sought practical answers to the "social question" by encouraging a new kind of leader, a technocrat and expert in social engineering who used his skills and authority to improve conditions for the lower classes and to promote social harmony.[24] Many found their voice in conservative, family-centered social initiatives, often inspired by the work of Frédéric Le Play, which sought the regulation and protection of families.[25] Social Catholics and other pronatalists advocated social reforms, a higher birthrate, and immigration limited to groups considered racially fit to reinvigorate the traditional French family. Due to their efforts and the expansion of employer-controlled family allowances, the interwar era became the golden age of employer-directed social welfare. By offering material benefits to workers who had sacrificed for the nation and by encouraging higher birthrates by tying allowances to family size, supporters made pronatalism patriotic.[26] After enjoying a significant role under Vichy, Catholics continued to be influential in creating family and population-centered institutions—including the High Committee on Population and the Family, the Population Ministry, INED, and the Institut national de la statistique et des études économiques (INSEE)—and in constructing family policy (including the way the Social Security Administration distributed family allowances) in the early Fourth Republic.[27]

Both Catholic and other social reformers also had a prominent role in France's expansion throughout the age of high imperialism.[28] Catholic missionaries played a critical, if contested, role in the construction and implementation of the civilizing mission. In Algeria, Monsignor Lavigerie became archbishop despite Napoleon III's reservations. To overcome doubts, the Sorbonne-educated Lavigerie, like other French Catholics, portrayed his work as part of France's destiny. Even though he intended to convert Muslims to Christianity—against state policy—Lavigerie framed his project in national rhetoric. In addition to encouraging white settlement in Algeria, he was, according to his biographer, "the advance guard of France" that would lead the nation to a "position of leadership" among the world powers.[29] This sometimes contentious yet often symbiotic relationship continued, especially as social Catholics sought to prove people of religious faith could be loyal, active citizens of the Republic. As J. P. Daughton has argued, even though anticlericalism pervaded the Third Republic, its leadership saw "no hypocrisy" in exporting a secular mission via Christian missionaries, who happened to be much less expensive than civil servants and in many cases had already developed relationships with indigenous populations. The Foreign Ministry frequently granted subsidies to Catholic charities—including schools, orphanages, and hospitals—seeking to "underwrite humanitarian services" even if that produced tensions between the state's secular project and the missionaries' evangelism.[30]

Entrusting missionaries to enact the state's goals is an important example of what many scholars have called the colonizers' treatment of the empire as a social laboratory.[31] Discourses about women reveal how ideas about social reform moved back and forth across the Mediterranean. Among a range of social reformers of all political stripes, a small, vocal group challenged dominant views about Algerian women and sought to improve their status. As Julia Clancy-Smith has shown, two static and contradictory visions of women—as over-sexualized objects of an imagined harem or as "servant or slave" to cruel, lascivious husbands—became "an inverted image or negative trope for confirming the European settlers' distinct cultural identity" that by the early twentieth century reinforced and legitimized France's colonial presence. The dominant colonial discourse, particularly after World War I, incorporated images of the maltreatment and inequality of women as proof of Algerian men's incompatibility with full French citizenship.[32]

In this atmosphere, prominent voices sought to improve women's condition. Hubertine Auclert, the radical feminist, and Marie Bugéja, the wife of a colonial administrator, represent two very different types of French women seeking social reform. In her book *Nos soeurs musulmanes* (1921), Bugéja argued that in "society, woman represents tradition; if one wants to modify tradition, that is, manners, customs, habits of feeling, thinking, it is advisable to begin with her." Advocating what Jeanne Bowlan called "maternal imperialism," Bugéja asserted that if the French could bring Algerian women "out of their ignorance, they would be precious auxiliaries for us."[33] Like Bugéja, Auclert was "a sincere, if self-appointed, advocate for Algerian women" whose arguments for Algerian women's emancipation—as part of her case for women's rights—largely failed and instead became "evidence for demonstrating the immutable difference of the indigenous population, especially when it came to matters of sexuality."[34]

Male reformers also called on French women to improve Algerian women's condition. The Musée Social, which brought together social reformers of diverse backgrounds beginning in the late nineteenth century to address the "social question," acted as a research center with a rich library collection. It embraced a social science model that combined a supposedly disinterested approach to social problems with the traditional moral values they regarded as lacking in contemporary society.[35] Its members, who included prominent social Catholics, developed programs in the Le Playist tradition, which viewed "mothers as the essential agents of reform within the family." In 1913, Georges Vabran argued that programs for working-class women in France—courses that educated them in home economics and child care—be extended to Tunisian women. In an address at the Musée Social, Vabran called on French women in the colonies to organize home economics classes for girls and to conduct home visits that would teach basic hygiene. The larger goal was for French women, through their traditional role as mothers, to extend the colonizers' reach into the family. As Vabran put it, "Only the hand of a woman can lift the veil which protects Muslim women"; it is "the mother [that] can help us accomplish and continue our educational and civilizing mission in the Islamic world."[36]

Despite the presence of missionaries and social reformers, calls for this type of social policy rarely translated into real programs in North Africa. As Neil MacMaster has recently argued, the settler population's concerns about the Algerian demographic explosion led to contradictory initiatives, including the introduction of "a discriminatory family benefits system" that limited access and made it difficult for the eligible to claim family benefits. As other colonies extended benefits beginning in the 1930s to curb nationalism, the settler lobby in Algeria implemented a program of "'negative Malthusianism' that operated through a failure to provide basic health care for the mass of Algerian poor." This approach frustrated some social Catholics in the colonies who wanted to reform the system and provide more benefits to the indigenous population.[37] On this issue, social Catholics broke with the settler lobby because they often remained staunchly grounded in a particular understanding of colonization that obligated them to uplift their colonial brethren and to bring them all the benefits of both Western civilization and Christianity.

Father Jacques Ghys, arguably the most influential social Catholic in the new welfare network for Algerian migrants, came out of this tradition. A member of the order of the Pères Blancs, founded in the 1860s to bring Western modernity and Catholicism first to Algeria and eventually to all of French-controlled Africa,[38] Ghys was convinced Algerians' could adapt to life in France if they would abandon traditional, Algerian ways. Trained in Oriental studies at the University of Tunis, Ghys brought his work and experience to the metropole after World War II.[39] Within the span of a few years, he founded Moral Assistance for North Africans, North African Family Social Service, and North African Social Studies, all three of which played a vital role in the new network. These organizations provided a great many services to Algerians, acted as role models to other associations and became *the* experts on the question of Algerians in France during decolonization and beyond.[40] Moral Assistance for North Africans began providing job training and housing services for adolescents in December 1947 and expanded its services to families in 1951.[41] North African Family Social Service, created in 1951, was the first metropolitan association dedicated to providing direct aid to Algerian women and their families; it played a crucial role in developing all educational and service programs for Algerian women and families. Ghys hired female social workers who either had experience in North Africa or agreed to accompany him to Algeria before starting work. Because the women who staffed North African Family Social Service became known for "their competence in everything concerning North Africans," other organizations sought their advice. Though most remained employed by North African Family Social Service, they were frequently loaned out to government agencies in localities without branch offices of the premier private association because of their "ability to maintain the role of liaison" with the state and because they were considered "specialists of unquestionable value and efficacy."[42]

In addition, Ghys' main legacy, North African Social Studies, published the *Cahiers nord-africains*. According to its first and long-time director, Joseph Leriche, the researchers who published in *Cahiers nord-africains* sought to "better 'arm'" the people responsible for Algerians' adjustment to life in France by using the only weapon they had: "persuasion."[43]

The journal, which published about six issues a year beginning in 1950, emerged as North African Social Studies' primary outlet for information to professionals working in the new network.[44] Ghys and his collaborators intended "to permit the man of action to situate his effort [in order] to find a solution to these vast problems through his day-to-day work for North African immigrants in the metropole."[45] Leriche explained that North African Social Studies' role was "to coordinate people whose jobs and vocations place them in contact with North African immigrants in the metropole and to find solutions to the problems posed by this immigration."[46]

North African Social Studies played the pivotal role in instructing private association and local government professionals who dealt directly with immigrants about their new clientele. According to statistics Leriche compiled in 1962, the *Cahiers* had over two hundred paid subscribers its first year and peaked with over eight hundred in the mid-1950s (in addition, about thirty had free subscriptions throughout the period). In the early 1950s, over forty-four percent of subscribers were individuals, with governmental offices and social organizations only ten and five percent, respectively. By 1961 state agencies and charitable associations accounted for more than two-thirds of paid subscriptions (with nearly forty-two and thirty percent, respectively). Businesses accounted for the final third, dwindling slightly near the end of the Algerian War, according to Leriche, because they had less need for workers. Moreover, the Labor and Public Health and Population Ministries had "multiple subscriptions" and numerous government agencies in France and Algeria—including "organizations affiliated [*dépendant*] with the army"—subscribed. Thirty percent of subscribers had addresses in Paris, and a quarter resided in Algeria.[47]

The Interministerial Commission underwrote its publications,[48] so that charitable associations, companies such as Renault, and government agencies could distribute supplemental publications, including a 1953 security manual (17,000 copies) and guides for employers and Algerians like "Du Douar à l'usine" from 1951 (31,000 copies). In 1953, when 25,000 copies of its guide to Algerian services flew off the shelves, the Interministerial Commission requested an additional 30,000 copies which the Interior Ministry distributed to ensure even those "not specialized in aid for North Africans" had access to the handbook.[49]

Each issue of the *Cahiers* revolved around a theme related to North Africa or Algerian migration to France. It made recommendations about how to reform the colonial regime in Algeria and how to build a better network of services for Algerians in France. The third issue, for example, published in March 1950, included articles entitled "Toward 'Social Services' or 'Social Action' Adapted for North Africans," and "About the Real Situation of North Africans" living in France. The latter recommended establishing services that would allow Algerian workers "to access the modern industrial lifestyle they could have among us" and went on to outline one of the first comprehensive plans for welfare programs dealing with Algerians' specific needs.[50] In the nearly ninety issues published before Algerian independence in 1962, it described life in Algeria, unraveled the apparently mysterious nature of "The Muslim Woman," sought to explain "Workers' Psychology," and addressed problems in education, housing, workplace safety, and women's issues in the metropole. All of these themes reinforced the high-minded, benevolent version of the civilizing mission that Ghys and his colleagues hoped to instill.[51]

As Patrick Simon has pointed out, even though North African Social Studies may have been peopled with experts in "the colonial world," it was "nevertheless the only thoughtful commentary" available during the period.[52] As a result, while in some sense the journal and the work of North African Social Studies and related organizations were part of the long tradition of Catholic missionary work, outreach, and publications for metropolitan audiences,[53] the journal distanced itself from its social Catholic roots and instead emphasized its reliance on "rigorous" research methods.[54]

Notwithstanding claims of a dispassionate approach, an issue outlining "who we are" examined the "heavy" burden on those promoting the welfare of Algerians by bringing "friendship [and] . . . education . . . [to] this portion of humanity that has to adapt to modern industrial and social life." In many ways, the *Cahiers* melded methods tested among the working class in France with those social reformers proposed in the colonies in order to reinforce traditional gender norms and to exalt the mother's role in the patriarchal family. This included, as Chapter 3 will explore in detail, home economics and child-rearing programs for women and girls.[55] Moreover, members of North African Social Studies recognized the failures of the colonial project, acknowledging that the "accusations of egoism and racism lodged against the 'colonial spirit'" had merit. Instead, they viewed the Algerian services network as their final opportunity to develop "social action" that "addresses the whole person."[56]

The *Cahiers*' approach echoed Lyon's Cardinal Gerlier's message to Catholics in the fall of 1951. In *La France catholique*, Gerlier urged the faithful to approach the North African "problem" in the "true spirit of Jesus Christ" by "respecting and comprehending [North Africans] and triumphing over prejudices that can arise from differences in language, dress, and mentality." He identified problems in the conditions North Africans faced, which seemed only slightly better than the life they left behind in a "land unable to support its population." For Gerlier, this could be solved by improving the conditions of life for North Africans and by eliminating misunderstandings resulting from prejudice. He asked Catholics to treat North Africans as brothers and sisters by helping them to find adequate housing, to work in "humane conditions" that paid a living wage, to understand the French language, and to accept guidance for their journey.[57]

Throughout this period, North African Social Studies adopted a similar tone. Its researchers made it clear they hoped the metropole would provide the fertile ground the colonies had been unable to offer. Using an approach that self-consciously rejected the negative politics and prejudices about Algerians' presumed recalcitrance that had become pervasive in the colonies, social reformers believed France could transform Algerians, finally making them modern citizens. They had high hopes that the "Algerian problem" could be solved if everyone in France would cooperate. North African Social Studies' goal was to use its diverse group of specialists to construct an army of "men of good will [who were] passionate about the ideal of justice and charity and who decide, in serving this ideal, to promote concrete solutions."[58] The *Cahiers* envisioned a gentler approach by combining themes from the reform movement in both France and Algeria. These specialists joined the social engineering skills needed to improve conditions among the working class, in the supposition that transforming women would end ignorance and modernize families, with a specialized knowledge that could decode Algerians' peculiar "mentality" and "backward" ways.

The experts at North African Social Studies and organizations like it probably received sustained government support and became influential in large part because their advice struck the perfect balance for the period—gently wrapping Algerians' naturalized inferiority into a benevolent French response. These reformers simultaneously denounced "all racism and ostracism" while perpetuating stereotypes about Algerian society's many "faults." In France, those working with Algerians had to tread lightly, helping Algerians adapt to "our legislation, our social and educational action, our attitudes" without brusquely or brutally upending their "patriarchal" traditions, just what "Lyautey dreamed" of doing in Morocco. They hoped to bring the true civilizing mission, lost in the colonial setting, and to see it implemented, not just among the specialists, but among everyone in France. To realize this dream, the *Cahiers* called on the state to take a more active role, arguing that all relevant branches of the government, from the governor-general in Algeria to the Labor and Public Health and Population Ministries, do their part to encourage and to create small "local teams" that could assist Algerians in their journey to become "modern," if they so desired.[59]

Government-Issued Expertise

In addition to relying on and encouraging the growth of private service providers, government-run institutions and agencies in key state ministries participated in the construction and dissemination of knowledge and policy concerning Algerians in France. The reliance on experts, and on a growing cadre of technocrats, fit into a much larger trend during the Fourth Republic. The 1950s witnessed a shift, which began during the Third Republic and Vichy, toward professionalization in state planning and a reliance on social sciences and "institutional architects" who worked to modernize the nation and its people by promoting "social evolution."[60] The collection of knowledge and its application in policies and practices grew out of a tradition of cross-fertilization among various institutions and other groups. The long-standing collaboration between North African Social Studies and INED is a revealing example.

It may not appear out of the ordinary for the *Cahiers nord-africains* to have cited research produced through France's national demographic institute, but it is significant that INED regularly cited the *Cahiers nord-africains* and relied on North African Social Studies' expertise when it came to this particular population. Moreover, four of INED's two dozen book-length studies published between 1947 and 1955, as well as a dozen or more articles in its journal, *Population*, examined Algerian migration in France or demography in Algeria.[61] One of them became the aforementioned *Les Algériens en France: Etude démographique et sociale*. Girard and Leriche's unfettered access to the files of government administrators in the Labor, Interior, and Public Health and Population Ministries speaks to what James Scott has called the "state's attempt to make a society legible."[62] Even though various government ministries, state agencies, and private associations had differing views on the so-called Algerian problem, all agreed that the collection and dissemination of expert knowledge about the growing migrant community would increase the state's ability to manage and to transform it.

Among the Interior and Labor Ministries' most regular outlets for the dissemination of information were dozens of circulars—to elucidate policies and inform service providers of procedural shifts—as well as orders and decrees that more precisely articulated its goals.[63] Besides encouraging horizontal cooperation among ministries, agencies, and associations, the leadership of these ministries integrated services vertically by assigning a growing number of bureaucrats to positions that facilitated subtle monitoring and the dissemination of information.

The Labor Ministry's Workforce Office hired the first cadre of experts to fulfill its objectives: to recruit Algerian workers for vacant positions in France and to act as "a kind of advocate" for North Africans. Its social inspectors approached businesses that might have openings and defended migrants' "interests" by making them aware of benefits available through their employers,[64] by finding "solutions to all administrative questions," and by facilitating their "observance of Muslim customs" and festivals.[65] Initially hired because of their experience in colonial affairs, the social inspectors also studied "the problems" posed by Algerian workers to prevent the duplication of services, "to ameliorate" workers' wages and conditions and to help them with orientation, job training, housing and other services.[66]

Abbé Paul Catrice gave official voice to Algerians' complaints about the social inspectors' lack of "sympathy" for their clients.[67] Algerians' frustrations stemmed from the inspectors' discretionary power, which disseminated and perpetuated colonial practices in the metropole. Inspectors had the authority "to follow" Algerian workers through orientation and work and to be certain they were absorbing the training "imparted to them." If inspectors determined Algerian workers had not met ill-defined standards, the state empowered them with "ensuring the repatriation" of the unemployed and those deemed "inapt" for life in the metropole.[68] To address these concerns and undoubtedly learn more about Algerians' worldview, the Labor Ministry hired more Arabic and Berber speakers, including at least five social inspectors of Muslim origin among the more than thirty working in twenty-six departments (including seven inspectors in the Department of the Seine) in the early 1950s.[69]

Algerian Affairs also responded to objections that the social inspectors did not have enough authority to address all aspects of the Algerian problem effectively by creating another bureaucratic position. Beginning in 1948, the Interior Ministry appointed "general administrative inspectors on special assignment" (*inspecteurs généraux de l'administration en mission extraordinaire*), known by their acronym IGAME, to preexisting military districts in order to extend ministerial, regional, and local governmental reach.[70] The IGAMEs had significant influence in the 1950s; they were "particularly competent" experts hired to help the prefectures organize "moral, material, and social assistance for the Muslim population."[71] To ensure the IGAMEs' independence from local politics and that the information they collected made its way to top administrators, the IGAMEs reported directly to the Algerian Affairs office in Paris.[72]

Several IGAMEs went on to hold even more powerful positions at the height of the Algerian War for Independence. Emile Pelletier, assigned to region five, which included Toulouse, later played a key role in developing housing services in Paris and its environs as prefect of the Seine and as interior minister for de Gaulle. His colleague Michel Massenet, like many of his generation, had graduated from the new Ecole nationale d'administration (ENA) before serving as an IGAME for region eight, which included Lyon. Massenet became, arguably, the most influential voice in the Algerian welfare network in the early Fifth Republic, reporting directly to Prime Minister Michel Debré. After Algerian independence in 1962, Massenet held several powerful positions and played a leading role in the network's shift from Algerians to all immigrants.[73]

The IGAMEs' mission expanded to Algeria in 1956, following the National Assembly's decision to extend the colonial government's special powers to crush what French authorities referred to as the insurrection.[74] Maurice Papon, one of three IGAMEs appointed in Algeria, headed the super-prefecture of Constantine and Bône. Long before his conviction for crimes against humanity in 1998 for the deportation of Bordeaux's Jews in 1942, Papon moved up the bureaucratic ladder after World War II. In addition to serving as head of the Algerian Affairs office in Paris under Interior Minister Adrien Tixier, Papon became an IGAME with significant influence over "civilian and military authorities" in order to better coordinate the campaign to put down the FLN.[75] The lessons Papon took from his twenty-year experience in policing ostracized groups served him well when he became Paris' police chief in 1958. Moreover, as James House and Neil MacMaster have argued, Papon's path was not unusual; it was emblematic of a pattern of repression that was "typical of a whole generation of government ministers, senior civil servants, army commanders, prefects, and politicians that sought to resolve the Algerian war" and whose career paths reinforced the intimate interconnections between the colonies and the metropole.[76]

To assist the IGAMEs in the metropole, the governor-general of Algeria appointed four technical consultants in Muslim Affairs (*conseillers techniques pour les affaires musulmanes*, CTAM) in 1952.[77] They were "Algerian civil service administrators, specializing in Muslim social questions" who reported directly to the IGAMEs.[78] Initially, the technical consultants assisted the IGAMEs in three principle areas: organizing social welfare services, keeping track of Algerians' radical political activities, and acting as a liaison with the prefects of each department.[79] These duties grew exponentially throughout France's war against Algerian nationalism, and by 1960, dozens of experts reported to the IGAMEs, including over thirty technical consultants, forty social inspectors, and twenty social counselors assigned to the prefect of the Seine.[80]

Officially, this structure intended to disperse specialized government employees into the decentralized welfare network in a way that allowed them to play a significant but low-profile role.[81] The IGAMEs regularly attended departmental meetings of the regional Advisory Commissions on North African Questions, led by the prefects of each department with a significant Algerian population. Like the Interministerial Commission, these regional commissions encouraged communication and coordination among various agencies in the network.[82] And, since most local officials did not report to the IGAMEs, regular, regional meetings provided a forum for discussion and an opportunity for the IGAMEs to be certain local officials upheld the larger political aims in the fight to keep Algeria French.[83]

The decentralized structure was also supposed to thwart accusations that this new network replicated the discriminatory practices common during the interwar years. Yet, by 1952, the program's coordinator in the Interior Ministry became increasingly aware that the IGAMEs' association with the colonial government jeopardized their mission. Algerians saw the IGAMEs as colonial agents who had infiltrated the metropolitan governmental and charitable organizations in order to monitor them. The coordinator worried that if Algerians perceived the programs implemented in France as employing colonial tactics it would undermine claims of altruism and would reduce Algerian participation in the expanding welfare network. To avoid any hint of impropriety, he explicitly instructed the IGAMEs to avoid all "direct contact" with the population they supposedly knew so well.[84] The IGAMEs continued to work with metropolitan service providers, monitoring indirectly and giving advice from behind the scenes about how to facilitate Algerians' "adaptation and promotion."[85] The IGAMEs may have kept a low profile among Algerian migrants, but they remained accessible to anyone in the welfare network who sought their expertise or connections. To ensure such access, the *Cahiers nord-africains* published the name of each region's IGAMEs in its 1953 guide.[86]

Algerians' suspicions about the IGAMEs were wholly justified. Records of the IGAMEs' quarterly meetings show they used their position to keep careful track of Algerians' activities in nationalist politics. As early as 1951, when Algerians participated in May Day parades, the IGAMEs worried about the influence that both the Mouvement pour le triomphe des libertés démocratiques (MTLD)—one of the Algerian nationalist groups inspired by Messali Hajj—and the French Communist Party had among Algerians. They feared that "police action" had driven Algerians into these "separatist movements" and that everything possible needed to be done to reverse this trend. Like other experts on Algerians, the IGAMEs stressed France's need to use social services not force "to integrate [Algerians] into the national community." The IGAMEs never doubted unrest among Algerians in France could jeopardize the stability of the empire. Nor did they imagine Algerians' protests as legitimate or as emanating from sustained, coherent political thought. Instead, the IGAMEs assumed that political groups sought to "influence" Algerians and exploited their "general malcontent created by unemployment and insecurity." By depicting Algerians as malleable, the IGAMEs also argued the French could persuade them to remain loyal through generous material benefits that made possible a "decent and normal life."[87]

Emmanuel Blanchard has carefully documented the police activities that the IGAMEs simultaneously called "indispensable" and worried would create "martyrs" for leftist groups.[88] While significant attention has been paid to the comprehensive system of police tracking put in place by Pierre Godin in the 1920s and to the systematic racial profiling and police violence Algerians endured at the height of the Algerian War, less attention, with the exception of Blanchard's work, has been paid to the Paris police and its tactics and coordination with other state agencies in the decade after World War II. At the war's end, Interior Minister Tixier, a Socialist and member of de Gaulle's provisional government in Algiers, sought the end of Godin's infamous North African Brigade and related services because they interfered with Algerians' access to the rights outlined in the March 1944 ordinance. Despite protests from Police Prefect Luizet and others who favored the rue Lecomte programs, Tixier disbanded the brigade, explaining to Luizet that Algerians needed to "know the government considers their well-being a top priority."[89] And even though Tixier dismantled the system of surveillance, most services remained in place with only cosmetic changes and with members of the old brigade integrated into the police ranks, working as experts on the Algerian problem and continuing to employ "exceptional practices." Using generic regulations to prevent delinquency and homelessness, the provision in the 1947 law that allowed for the repatriation of the chronically unemployed or inapt, and raids on nationalist organizations' meetings, the police continued to harass Algerian migrants.[90]

Luizet and his successors also tried to regain some of their previous authority through governmental channels and the press. Public perception of Algerian nationalists' participation in the 1953 Bastille Day protests, framed as a "riot," despite evidence that the police fired on peaceful protesters, killing six, opened the door to reorganizing specialized surveillance units. That summer, the police established a new Brigade against Aggression and Violence (BAV), which officially countered a rise in "nocturnal assaults" by criminals. The new brigade's focus on "the problem of North African criminality" was no secret. With half of its officers fluent in Arabic, Kabyle, or other North African languages, it increased Parisian authorities' ability to monitor, infiltrate, and break up gatherings of supporters of Algerian nationalism, which by 1955 included adherents of the new FLN.[91]

As the 1953 Bastille Day case exemplifies, the police blamed the victims of state violence for their own death and used the growing body of experts to draw attention to the presumed problem of Algerian criminality. The police and other authorities slowly increased surveillance and restrictions on Algerians without overtly circumventing the freedom-of-movement law. Furthermore, by focusing on Algerians' supposed inability to control themselves or to live in civilized society, the police drew on long-held stereotypes from colonial discourse.[92] And, as Blanchard has argued, "Algerian nationalists were not deceived" about the relationship between police surveillance and social work. Nationalists recognized the state underwrote most social services and the police had open lines of communication with many of the bureaucrats and charitable associations. As *L'Algérie libre* argued in 1954, the charitable associations' goals were "convergent with official organizations except that the latter were more humane." In fact, it argued the private associations did the work of "powerless officials."[93]

Quantity and Quality

To facilitate the conquest of hearts (and surveillance), experts in private organizations and government agencies set about collecting and disseminating detailed information about Algerian migrants. In the decade following World War II, numerous institutions conducted dozens of studies to learn as much as possible about the population. The new statistical data culled from these studies, combined with qualitative knowledge of Algerian society and culture, created a narrative about Algerian migration. Despite tensions between champions of France's overarching political goals, which required emphasizing Algerians' equality with other French citizens, and supporters of overt surveillance and repression, everyone agreed about Algerians' inferiority, about the "patriarchal character of the traditional Muslim family,"[94] and about France's tireless commitment to modernize Algerians. These and other themes played a pivotal role in the narrative experts constructed about Algerians' behaviors and the problems they faced in the metropole.

The government first attempted to count the Algerian migrant population just after the turn of the century and continued to do so into the

1940s when Vichy administrators conducted a census of North Africans in both the unoccupied and occupied zones.[95] Once the World War ended, the number of studies on the size and composition of the Algerian migrant population grew rapidly. Between 1945 and the start of the Algerian War in 1954, dozens of government agencies and private organizations commissioned such studies. In 1945 alone, five ministries conducted demographic studies on the Algerian migrant population.[96] Over the next decade, North African Social Studies, INED, INSEE, the Interior Ministry, and other state agencies, as well as lesser-known experts—who wrote doctoral dissertations, articles in targeted journals, and ENA internship reports—all added to the body of knowledge on the Algerian problem.[97]

Many studies from the late 1940s and early 1950s first set about explaining the causes of Algerian migration. Starting from the supposition that the new migration was a problem, the experts placed the blame squarely on the Algerians. According to Jean Despois, a geography professor at the University of Algiers, the terrible conditions most Algerians faced resulted from "natural conditions": North Africa's inhospitable geography and the cultural "limits" of North Africa's "indigenous societies."[98] Roger Parant, an administrator in the Algerian civil service, concurred and further argued "this Oriental society" had reached the equivalent of "our medieval society." It lacked a substantial, productive middle class that could bring the "unproductive mass" out of abject poverty. Without a middle class, Parant explained, Algeria's "anchorless mass" became vulnerable to "revolutionary doctrines" of both religious and pan-Arab nationalists.[99] He and others agreed that Algeria's problems "certainly predated the French occupation" and that it had become increasingly "poor and overpopulated" in spite of what experts insisted was France's tireless "service of the ideal."[100] They emphasized the "progress" France had brought to agriculture, industry, and the exploitation of natural resources.[101] Algerians, conversely, had become increasingly ungrateful "autochthones" who preferred "an authoritarian regime" to "our politics of emancipation."[102]

Contemporary understandings of Algeria's population explosion compounded concerns about migration. With the crisis in Algeria deepening, experts warned that emigration had become a veritable "necessity."[103] Aware that migration to France offered a safety valve for mounting problems, research on the Algerian problem always linked the dual crises—economic and demographic—in Algeria to migration. In the sixth volume of its influential series, INED commissioned historian, demographer, and social

Catholic Louis Chevalier to construct what became one of the most widely cited early studies.[104] In *Le problème démographique nord-africain* (1947), Chevalier analyzed Algeria's population explosion as well as the causes of migration. According to Chevalier's study, and many subsequent publications, the massive economic crisis and demographic boom in Algeria, and not colonization, had created a neo-Malthusian situation in which "the population suffers from an obvious lack of all basic food stuffs."[105] This massive crisis in Algeria caused much consternation in the French government. Academics and politicians alike worried Algeria's economy simply could not absorb the massive growth of the population. Vividly aware of Chevalier's study—and other, similar studies—Interior Minister Jules Moch warned the top fifty bureaucrats in the Algerian services sector that Algerians were arriving at the rate of 100,000 a year and that by 1953 a half million unemployed Algerians could be living in France.[106] Official estimates indicated the Muslim population expanded by about four million people within a thirty-year period (from 4.8 million in 1921 to about 8.8 million in 1954). Rager attributed this "high fecundity" to elevated marriage rates among the young.[107] Not only did these figures overestimate population growth, but the explanations failed to recognize that there was a general, if uneven, drop in mortality (since infant mortality rates remained relatively high) despite the massive social and geographical restructuring.[108]

Social scientists and bureaucrats inextricably linked economic and demographic problems and frequently presented emigration as the only plausible solution to the dual crises. Their work centered on the pull factors—Algerians emigrated for economic opportunity, better lives, and "psychological" reasons. Once in the metropole, Algerians found a "superior moral situation" because they could be more "independent and [could] escape the inferiority complex they experience" at home.[109] These types of explanations fit well with France's civilizing narrative. Migration provided both a safety valve for the Algerian pressure cooker and concrete evidence of France's benevolence. As a ranking member of Algerian Affairs remarked in 1957, migration represented "a decisive aspect of our politics of social emancipation in Algeria."[110]

Of course, tracking Algerians remained a priority, even if the 1947 law meant "no legal means exist to prevent them from coming if they wish."[111] Since openly admitting to tracking Algerians might further destabilize Algeria, improving the welfare network's ability to provide for Algerians' needs was the primary justification for the collection of data.

The government needed to accumulate as much demographic information as possible to assist bureaucrats and other service providers.

Early estimates about the size of the Algerian population in France varied wildly. According to Henri Bourbon's survey of statistics available between 1945 and 1952, the approximate size of the North African population in the metropole ranged from just under 200,000 to as many as 350,000, with the larger estimate first appearing in 1948.[112] Fluctuations often resulted from the way the statistics were compiled. In 1953, for example, the Labor Ministry used official employment records to estimate over 135,000 North Africans (nearly 130,000 Algerians, 6,500 Moroccans, and under 1,000 Tunisians) lived in the metropole. The Interior Ministry, on the other hand, arrived at much higher figures (nearly 235,000 Algerians, 11,000 Moroccans, and 2,100 Tunisians) by collecting data from the prefectures, airlines, and maritime companies.[113] While the numbers continued to vary slightly, most reports settled at about 300,000 North Africans.[114] At the height of the war, this number reached about 350,000, where it remained with some fluctuations—mostly a response to fear of invasion—even after Algerian independence in 1962.

The vast majority of North Africans in France were men (over eighty percent) between the ages of twenty and thirty-nine, a majority of whom (about sixty percent) were Berbers from the Kabyle region.[115] Most lived in large cities and industrial centers, although as Rager pointed out, there had been North Africans working "in all metropolitan departments" since 1949. Most studies estimated about a third lived in and around Paris, with significant communities in Lyon, Marseille, the Nord, and the coal-rich east, with smaller enclaves in about twenty departments.[116] They worked in numerous fields, with high concentrations in mining and in metallurgy in the late 1940s, before the construction boom overtook other sectors.[117] Rager estimated that by mid-1954 almost thirty-two percent worked in construction, about twenty percent in mechanical and electrical industries, thirty percent in metallurgy, and nearly six percent in mines and related industries, which correlated with other assessments that about seventy-three percent had regular employment, another seven percent did day labor or part-time work (without seeking public assistance), and a bit less than fifteen percent were looking for work.[118] The Interministerial Commission estimated that only about five percent were unemployed due to "illness or inaptitude" and only one percent received state unemployment benefits.[119]

These figures represented a significant drop in unemployment estimates from 1949 when experts believed nearly half of Algerians in France were unemployed.[120] Then, fears about the economy's slow recovery and inadequate employment opportunities for French men (especially returning POWs), as well as the desire to hire more qualified—read as white, European—workers translated into worries about a "floating mass" of 160,000 Algerians in France without work.[121]

By 1953 officials credited the new network of social programs with having successfully addressed the unemployment problem. Eugène Simoneau, who replaced Damelon as head of Algerian Affairs in 1951, attributed this to "the efforts of the state and government-supported private organizations" and to employers' sympathy for the "national interest in this human problem."[122] As the final citation illustrates, fears about Algerians shifted away from unemployment and toward the growing independence movement, though government officials rarely directly addressed Algerian nationalism. Following the violent repression of the 1953 Bastille Day protests, experts increasingly relied on discourses about hygiene, education, and delinquency to frame the problem.

As French experts tried to deal with the human problem, quantifying and discussing the benefits of family settlement became increasingly common. At first, many authorities noticed a shift from male migration to family reunification and settlement. Experts noted more Algerian workers, especially Berbers, brought their wives with them to settle in France or that women and children were "increasingly likely to join the head of household [already] in the metropole."[123] While not all saw this as a favorable development,[124] a growing number of government officials and members of the private associations considered family settlement the logical, "natural consequence of worker migration" and were cognizant that family settlement was "changing, progressively, the characteristics" of this migration.[125]

Building on older arguments about the vital role women played in modernizing the family, postwar experts insisted that the presence of women was necessary for Algerians to adapt and settle permanently in France. In his well-known 1932 report on immigration, the Orientalist scholar, social Catholic, and Collège de France member Louis Massignon insisted permanent settlement would not be possible if a migrant group consisted solely of male workers. His evidence indicated only seventy Algerian women lived in metropolitan France in the interwar period, which led him to conclude that "the absence of women, the preservers and anchors of displaced peoples, shows that the installation of [male] emigrants will not last." More than twenty years later, Henri Bourbon, referencing Massignon, argued the "new situation" indicated that families were more likely to migrate and to remain a long time or to settle definitively in France.[126] Experts commonly saw male migration as temporary, but once a man brought his family to France he "would not return to his birthplace."[127] Despite concerns about a permanent Algerian minority in France, most who saw it as inevitable argued family migration was invaluable.

For Rager and other experts, families represented the hope for Algerian integration in the metropole. Yet, their assessments of a family's adaptability often rested on thinly veiled references to race, class, and gender. In his influential thesis, Rager described "the moral and material situation" of migrant families as "satisfactory." He found them in good health, with "handsome, well-dressed, clean children." Moreover, unemployment rates among fathers was remarkably low. Even if mothers were "little or unevolved" (largely because they did not speak French), the families wanted to better themselves, with women learning to knit, sending children to school, and planning "to stay in France."[128] Experts expected Algerian women to help their husbands embrace French consumer culture and to reject Algerian nationalism. Specialists working at all levels of the welfare network predicted that Algerian women would change their families' situation dramatically, stabilizing and essentially depoliticizing men. As social workers in Douai put it, an Algerian man who found himself "in France with his family felt almost at home," and that, already so far away from his homeland, having his family at his side imbued him with dignity and made him less likely to stray down "wrong paths."[129]

With such high expectations and lingering trepidation about "this relatively new and appreciably growing"[130] segment of the population, the government wanted to know its size and composition. Yet, it proved much more difficult to quantify it than to observe it. From the earliest studies, whether of single men or the entire population, experts acknowledged "the relative fragility of official statistics."[131] Every attempt to determine the exact number of Algerian women and children in France throughout the 1950s acknowledged that the population experienced steady growth, but never produced precise figures instead only estimates.

While there had been regional estimates and Rager's national study of emigration, the first metropolitan studies to analyze the new family migration pattern occurred in 1952. The Public Health and Population

Ministry requested data from all the metropolitan departments to compile a national report on the state of this segment of the population. It determined that 3,400 Muslim women lived in France, 675 in and around Paris. The next year the Interior Ministry determined that 5,000 Muslim women and 11,000 children lived in France, at least one-third in the Paris area.[132] Officials became acutely aware that the number of families migrating was rapidly increasing. Between May 1952 and August 1953, an average of one hundred families migrated each month.[133] Based on its 1953 study of all metropolitan departments, the Interior Ministry estimated that of the approximately 180,000 Algerians (a figure that turned out to be lower than most contemporary estimates) in France, 4,851 were women and 10,057 children.[134]

In a detailed analysis of its 1953 findings, the Interior Ministry admitted its figures underestimated the actual number of Algerians in France. The functionaries who analyzed the information amended the final figures for the total population using other studies and entries recorded at border crossings. They felt confident in increasing the total figure by 115,000, to arrive at a more accurate figure of 330,000 Algerians. Even after the readjustment, however, the report still concluded that only about 5,000 Algerian women resided in France, about two percent of the population.[135] Despite neglecting to increase the number of women when it increased the total, the report provided details suggesting that women represented a higher proportion of the population than the final figures indicated. The authors explained that the family population was "extremely variable depending on the location." In the Bouches-du-Rhône, women made up over six percent of the population. They also suspected women constituted a larger portion of the population in rural areas. For example, a small village in Aude, a department in southwestern France, provided precise figures: women made up twenty percent of the Algerian population (17 women and 88 men).[136] Another small-scale study done in the Seine-et-Marne estimated ten percent of Algerian workers lived with their families (42 families and 421 men).[137] Yet, in other areas, experts believed the female population was practically nonexistent—for example, less than one percent (0.7 percent) of the population in the east. While regional variations must have existed, officials admitted that their figures likely overlooked pockets of the family population.[138]

Part of the reason bureaucrats reported inaccurate figures was that Algerians often resisted French record keeping. The Interior Ministry's analysis of its census concluded that "the enumeration of women and children with Muslim status is an extremely delicate operation. Muslims consider it indecent to pose questions concerning their marital status and the numbers provided constitute the most exact approximation possible." Algerians misrepresented the size of their families for cultural reasons; regional functionaries did the same for budgetary reasons. The Interior Ministry found that when it requested (through circulars) that departments conduct a census of Algerians, many prefectures either sent the same figures in response to each request or sent in their responses so quickly that officials, probably rightly, assumed the prefects never allocated precious funds or personnel to recount the local Algerian population. Additionally, the study's authors also admitted that figures remained inaccurate because they suspected some men had been counted twice, at work and at home.[139] Unfortunately, none of these issues inspired the Interior Ministry to update the final figures. No reports adjusted the number of Algerian women in France, which would have more accurately reflected the population's composition.

Regardless of the difficulty of determining the exact size of the Algerian family population, authorities recognized the number of Algerian women and children in France continued to grow. According to statistics Aid to Overseas Workers compiled by tracking Algerians' movements through the port of Marseille, even in months of negative overall migration—when more Algerian men were returning home—family migration into the metropole continued steadily.[140] Just before the outbreak of the Algerian War in November 1954, Girard and Leriche sifted through all the available figures in their landmark study and determined that about 20,000 Algerian women and children lived in France (6,000 families with 14,000–15,000 children).[141] In 1956, the Interior Ministry's Muslim Affairs Service compiled reports sent by the prefects of each metropolitan department and concluded that about ten percent of the Algerian population consisted of women (12,000) and children (18,000).[142] By the end of the decade, the family population had grown substantially. A 1959 report estimated 20,000 families (93,000 people) were part of the approximately 320,000 Algerians in France.[143] The 1962 census determined women made up as much as forty percent of the population in the neighborhoods outside of Paris with the highest concentrations of Algerians and, that overall, women made up twenty percent of the Algerian population in Hauts-de-Seine.[144]

Even members the High Committee on Population and the Family, who continued to harbor private concerns about protecting France's racial vitality, publically conceded that for moral and health reasons, to avoid instability and venereal diseases, family migration should be encouraged.[145] This litany of officially acceptable reasons to support family migration masked a more basic desire to stifle what some still considered a more pressing problem: miscegenation. Although few people ever overtly discussed this issue or supported legal restrictions, as Henri Bourbon noted, the French believed Algerian men came to the metropole because French women had a "reputation in Algeria for being easy."[146] The popular press also perpetuated colonial discourses about African men's "famous Oriental sensuality" and desire to treat women as "slaves."[147] With experts like Chevalier perpetuating the idea that Algerians were "latent syphilitics" and that over fifty percent of the population was infected, despite admitting his figures were "unverifiable,"[148] newspapers easily reinforced fears about Algerian men spreading venereal disease and stunting French women's ability to reproduce.[149] Moreover, the popular press described Algerian men as naturally "jealous" and prone to "premeditated" violence against women.[150] American Fulbright scholar Leo Bogart criticized the propensity of the French press to associate Algerians with crime even though their crime rates were "remarkably low" given "their situation."[151] Nevertheless, French experts thought they could prevent violence against women by quantifying biracial couples and discouraging intermarriage. To avoid interracial unions, experts predicted migrant workers settling in France would take Algerian brides.[152] Obliquely linking the desire to avoid race mixing and the assumption that women would depoliticize male migrants, a government journal with limited circulation outlined the official position in 1960: to fulfill the Algerian worker's need "to become a normal citizen," the "influx of families is desirable on a moral level" and will "finally allow these migrant workers to settle peacefully in France."[153]

To settle peacefully, Algerians had to embrace modern, French culture and had to reject their supposedly backward ways. Knowing as much as possible about the demographic and social nature of the Algerian migrant population would help social workers in achieving "mutual comprehension" and "North African [social] promotion."[154] The didactic literature provided what North African Social Studies called an "essentially constructive" description of North African culture and traditions,[155] with particular attention to Berber culture. Knowing about Algerians' way of life would inspire welfare providers to be patient. Once they understood how much Algerians had to overcome in order to live normally in modern society, social workers and others working in the welfare network could more easily create a "climate of trust" that would in turn establish "a fraternal bond that nothing could break."[156] This approach, which linked a number of themes covered in the quantitative analyses and the qualitative research emphasized Algerians' natural inferiority, France's benevolence, and the dedication required if the conquest of hearts was to succeed.

The *Cahiers'* first issue, a primer directed toward the often volunteer teachers of evening French classes, who apparently needed to be taught about the particularities of their new pupils, emphasized that Algerians "do not think like us . . . do not always reason like we do." To understand Algerians, they would have to know, above all else, that Algerians were "Orientals with a patriarchal mentality" and that these "Muslims with collective reactions" were "maladjusted proletarians."[157] Using language that drew on discourses about both the working class and the colonized, experts warned teachers that Algerians were ill-equipped for and generally "disoriented" by the modern, industrial workplace because they came from rural, isolated regions with ancient, stagnant cultures. When met with the shock of Western society, which thrust them "from the age of Abraham to the age of Taylor by traveling a thousand kilometers," Algerians preferred to maintain "their traditions and practices" and to "live on the margins of the French community."[158]

Over and over again, these experts insisted they espoused a new approach that rejected old eugenic views. As INED's director Alfred Sauvy argued, "no hereditary obstacle" prevented Algerians' "integration." Instead, he continued, "cultural differences constitute the most important obstacles" to Algerian "assimilation."[159] Sauvy and others, even as they distanced themselves from scientific racism, naturalized Algerians' otherness, insisting Algerians had a "static life regulated by the past" and that they needed to embrace the "transformation" offered them in France, if they had any hope of adjusting to French culture.[160]

The *Cahiers* explained that direct service providers needed to understand the "climate" from which their clients originated and to learn to be patient with Algerians' "indolence (which we quickly recognize in nonchalance and capricious laziness)."[161] When coupled with Algerians' sense of "inferiority" and their "rapid mood swings," the *Cahiers* warned that their "adaptation" to the metropole could be difficult.[162] Even though the researchers at North African Social Studies frequently acknowledged Algerians suffered greatly and often had the worst jobs, researchers fell short of accusing employers or institutions of structural discrimination. The *Cahiers* explained away discrimination in hiring and housing by presuming to know what Algerians wanted. Accordingly, Algerians were not given the worst jobs, passed over for promotion, or forced to live in squalid conditions because of systemic racism. Algerians, North African Social Studies claimed, simply preferred to do "repetitive" factory work, to send money home rather than think about long-term advancement and promotion, and to live in conditions reminiscent of their "nomadic" heritage.[163] Even though the majority of Algerians in France were Berbers from the Kabyle region, whom the Orientalist scholarship had long considered more sedentary than nomadic, these seemingly obvious inconsistencies in the stereotypical portrayal of Algerian society went unexamined.

Both INED and North African Social Studies researchers insisted that "indifference more than hostility" characterized metropolitans' opinions about Algerians in France.[164] Unable or unwilling to acknowledge the discrimination in hiring and housing, North African Social Studies' 1951 brochure "Du Douar à l'usine" subtly blamed Algerians who misinterpreted metropolitans' often unwitting "negligence" about their problems and jumped to the erroneous conclusion that "we despise them."[165] To educate metropolitans about the plight of their fellow citizens, experts from North African Social Studies participated in regional "public conferences" and smaller "private" information sessions organized in conjunction with charitable associations and local governmental officials. Between 1953 and 1954, conferences in Lille on "Islam and the Modern World," "North Africans at Work," and "North Africans and Families among Us" each drew audiences of about 200 people. In the same period, over 150 people attended nineteen private sessions held in homes, on college campuses, or in the facilities of charities such as St. Vincent de Paul.[166]

Despite acknowledging the need to transform metropolitans' opinions, the *Cahiers* and others consistently blamed Algerians, not racism, for the problems they faced in France. Algerians were "extremely susceptible" to thinking they sensed "racial discrimination in our attitude," which "pushed them to mistrust us."[167] To address what they regarded as Algerians' inability to accept French generosity, the *Cahiers* offered advice that echoed Rudyard Kipling's notion of the white man's burden. "To make France loved," employers and welfare providers had to remember to be "just" and "good" without forgetting "to be firm."[168] To carry out their mission, service providers had to treat their charges with "respect" and overcome or hide "metropolitans' instinctive belief in the superiority of their race," a "trait of our national character" shared with most in the West.[169] Providers had to remember to judge Algerians on their "abilities" and not their ethnicity, even if they were "clearly not as advanced" as "normal metropolitans."[170]

In keeping with claims that others could achieve equality if they embraced French universal culture, the *Cahiers* insisted that Algerians' deficiencies stemmed from a lack of "education" and not some kind of inherent quality.[171] Nevertheless, by emphasizing Algerians' need to become Western, the *Cahiers* sent the message that Algerians' differences were deficiencies. It told service providers to build Algerians' self-confidence by helping them "to develop characteristics appropriate for their race that fit in the framework of life in the twentieth century."[172]

Algerians could overcome their "'familial' mentality," considered common in North Africa and other parts of the Muslim world, if service providers were willing "to penetrate" the patriarchal structures and to offer modern alternatives.[173] Well aware that the French family had a long history of patriarchy—lasting until "the eve of the Revolution" and into the nineteenth century in some rural communities[174]—researchers emphasized how differently this basic social unit functioned in these two societies. The French family, described as "individualist" and as championing the independence of the nuclear family,[175] became a foil for the large and "complex" multigenerational North African family. In the latter even adult males were "minors, under the authority of the father or eldest" male relative.[176] The "absolute power" held by the head of the family had significant consequences, both in North Africa and among Algerians in France.[177]

This crude vision of family structure explained and justified Algerians' supposed inability to sustain independent thought. As in the colonial setting, experts insisted that Algerians resisted change and French advice in large part because the "sacred and religious" origins of patriarchal authority created a "veritable ancestor cult" in which Algerians could not question traditional authority. In the metropole, it provided an explanation for Algerians' refusal to submit to welfare providers' demands. Rather than acknowledging Algerians might consciously reject French recommendations for a variety of reasons, the *Cahiers* framed Algerians' behaviors as a recalcitrant inability to "arrive at an independent idea or attitude."[178] This assumption, coupled with the "human misery"[179] from which Algerians on both sides of the Mediterranean suffered, also provided the French with a carefully constructed rationalization for Algerians' adherence to national-ism. "Social contacts" with metropolitans might help with adaptation, but, even among people who had "adopted European customs," experts found "strongly anti-French Algerian nationalists."[180] Following this reasoning, Algerians could easily be convinced to follow "revolutionary doctrines" if nationalists infiltrated the minds of suggestible patriarchs who in turn would create a whole generation of young revolutionaries.[181]

The same suggestibility could be harnessed for France's interests. With the proper effort and patience, welfare providers could make Algeri-ans into "social leaders" in their communities.[182] Bringing "evolution" and France's "humanitarian ideal" to the Algerian migrant community could make them, upon their return to Algeria, "our best weapons against error, fanaticism, and hostile prejudices," according to Robert Laurette, an ad-ministrator in the Algerian Civil Service.[183] As the *Cahiers* told French language instructors, it is "our responsibility" to instill in Algerian pupils French ideas, preventing nationalism and making "modern workers."[184]

To create ideal, disciplined workers, the *Cahiers* argued that wel-fare providers had to understand the role and influence of "the Muslim woman" in North African society. Even if the vast majority of migrants were male workers, the family was the key to solving the Algerian problem. Social workers needed to learn about the place of women to understand the nature of North African society and to use women as a tool against men's propensity for immoral behavior and their attraction to Algerian nationalism. Since Algerian men working in France suffered from "psy-chological and occupational instability, hardship, sickness, moral distress, and the desire to revolt," which made them "search for distractions or un-healthy compensations," something had to be done. Encouraging family settlement would tie down "uprooted" men, who were depicted as highly "susceptible to subversive propaganda, abandoning their families in Alge-ria, hasty and poorly thought out mixed marriages, out-of-marriage co-habitation, [and] irrational hostility toward European civilization."[185] If these young men had the opportunity to live in "complete families," with-out creating the "unthinkable . . . 'family ghettos,'" an array of problems from open political dissent to miscegenation could be eradicated. This solution also placed significant expectations on Algerian women since a woman's touch, experts argued, could improve men's health and diet and could move Algerians from the margins of French society to a new stable "social level" and ultimately have "a regenerative" effect.[186]

The *Cahiers*, using what it called "real evidence" from everyday life, borrowed from deeply held and pervasive colonial assumptions about Muslim women that emphasized how "the woman is treated as an inferior" but actually wields significant influence in the home and over men. While insisting that Muslim women had "rights" and that marriage was not "a simple purchase agreement," the *Cahiers* emphasized the differences in North African and French attitudes about marriage. North Africa marriage was described as a legal contract normalized by "religious law," but "with us" it is a "mutual agreement between two people who spontaneously decide to unite their lives . . . with love and perfectly reciprocal respect."[187]

Furthermore, the *Cahiers* pointed out that Algerian women were treated as "minors" and that the "European and Christian presence" had brought education, social promotion, and "social security" programs forcing open this "closed society" and ending "Muslim women's suffering under [Islamic] matrimonial law." Through this portrait of the family, the *Cahiers* reinforced the notion that France had liberated Muslim women and that by doing so it had put a supposedly stagnant society "on the evolutionary road." It also implored social service workers to take up the burden of giving these women "all our attention, our love, and our intelligence." As more Algerian families came to France, the woman's role became increasingly essential because "it is at the mother's knee that an honest man is made."[188]

SOCIAL SERVICE WORKERS in both the public and private sectors received guidance from a range of experts with academic degrees or experience in the colonies. Their knowledge shaped and was shaped by this quantitative and qualitative information about Algerians. Ostensibly created to identify the problems associated with Algerian migration, to offer a "metropolitan solution" to those problems, and to help service providers understand and deal with their unfamiliar clients,[189] this new body of literature reinterpreted colonial discourses to fit the post–World War II atmosphere. Furthermore, the experts claimed that they offered incontrovertible evidence, obtained through scientific research, about Algerians' mentality, behaviors, and needs.

Some welfare providers became experts. Elisabeth Malet was a prominent example. She first worked for Ghys in the youth services section of Moral Assistance for North Africans. By 1953 Malet wrote for the *Cahiers* and other journals in her new role as special liaison for North Africans to

Paris' Social Security office. Professionals like Malet not only relied on the counsel of supposedly disinterested, neutral experts, but also themselves became voices of authority. Weaving their personal experiences with the lessons learned from colleagues and the didactic literature, service providers felt emboldened to interpret policy, to give advice, and to influence the lives of their Algerian clients.

3

Instructing a "Difficult and Delicate Clientele"
The Social Services Mission

Abdelhakim: Back home in the village life is not the same as in the metropole.
. . . Here . . . if a woman doesn't speak French she has to learn it as
quickly as possible. . . . Here, she has to do the shopping, to go out. . . .

His Friend: Yes, but what exactly do you expect from all this?

Abdelhakim: What do I expect? [I expect] her to adapt to the climate. . . .
I'm sure you already know that a veiled woman walking down the
street here will attract stares. . . . If you don't want anyone looking
at her the best thing to do is to make sure she looks like all the other
women, that first of all she is dressed like the others. . . . As her
husband, if you need to accompany her everywhere, lose a half-day's
work each time, that's just not possible.

His Friend: So you think that in the metropole women should live like the
French?

Abdelhakim: It's a question of good sense. They need to adapt in every
way. . . . To the food . . . to laundry. . . . In order for the woman to
acclimate she needs to observe the way her neighbors do housework
and be inspired.[1]

THIS DIALOGUE IS AN EXCERPT from an episode of a weekly radio
show that aired from the late 1940s through the mid-1960s on state-owned
radio in France and in Algeria.[2] Close collaboration between welfare network administrators and radio programmers ensured that the broadcasts
reinforced themes the welfare network sought to address. Its carefully
crafted message, like those of all the network's services, confronted "all economic, social and sanitary problems that the association administrators,
social assistants and social counselors know about and which motivate
their efforts on behalf of the North African workers and their families."[3]
Of course the radio broadcasts could never replicate the personal contact

of the other types of educational programs examined below, but radio provides a window onto the social programs' mission.

In many respects, the welfare providers' mission for Algerian clients shared features with the national project that for more than a century had been making "peasants into Frenchmen."[4] In constructing a social safety net, the state worked to instill middle-class values into clients depicted as backward, even foreign, as somehow neither fully modern nor fully French. To some degree the state had succeeded in creating a sense of shared identity and in developing a measure of social mobility for most of those French who participated in the burgeoning welfare state.[5] Administrators and social workers were also optimistic about Algerians' ability to adapt and to join their metropolitan compatriots in all that modern life offered. Yet their hope originated from assumptions about Algerians' otherness. The policies and practices developed out of the project to make peasants, the working class, and other immigrant groups French, but the architects of these programs believed they addressed the particular needs of a new "difficult and delicate clientele"[6] and hoped Algerians could learn to live like the French and become good, loyal "French Muslims."

When social workers and others envisioned their clients' successful adaptation, they began with the supposition that Algerians needed to uplift themselves, to overcome what were considered their handicaps in order to fit into French, universal culture. They worked diligently on behalf of Algerian migrants, tirelessly trying to improve their clients' material conditions and fighting against prejudices in the general population. Welfare providers were deeply committed to teaching practical skills and to providing access to a variety of goods and financial benefits that would help Algerians embrace modern, French culture. At the same time, they perpetuated racial and gender stereotypes by reinforcing widely held beliefs, including the notion that Algerians shared a collective mentality that supposedly ruled their stagnant, patriarchal society. By portraying their work as a burden, welfare providers subtly shifted blame for Algerians' precarious situation onto Algerians themselves.

The network's providers regularly used the language of adaptation when describing their goals. What adaptation meant, however, diverged significantly when it came to male workers on the one hand and women and families on the other. The Algerian welfare network addressed men as workers and heads of households and women as housewives playing a crucial role in their families' journey toward modern life. Just as Laura

Frader has shown for the interwar period, welfare programs for Algerians reinforced assumptions about gender and nationality and continued to embed political and social inequalities in the provision of welfare services.[7]

Social service administrators and providers defined male worker integration narrowly. They envisioned Algerian men's needs and adaptation in relation to the workplace. Male workers, considered temporary and flexible, required services to adjust to the labor market. Thus, this chapter begins with an assessment of educational programs for men that concentrated on vocational skills and on French language instruction. Alongside their continued interest in educational programs for men, a growing number of administrators advocated family settlement as the best solution to several interrelated problems. In addition to offering proof that Algerians were indeed French citizens, family settlement became a tool, particularly in addressing a persistent controversy about the inequitable distribution of family allowances to Algerians residing in Algeria. Since the French government gathered a surplus—when a significant portion of the deductions taken from Algerian migrant workers' salaries did not reach their families in Algeria—it used the surplus to fund social programs. Officials hoped that using the funds Algerians paid into the system but did not receive to offer services targeting Algerians would quiet critics and bring attention to France's magnanimous treatment of Algerians.

The heart of the controversy, the family allowance surplus, funded family services—as a way to respond to criticism that Algerians did not receive benefits other citizens received despite mandatory deductions and as a way to avoid giving families direct payments. Administrators reasoned that the best way to discipline male migrants was to make them accountable for the material well-being of their families. Workers who sent for their families cared more about their living conditions, became tied to the community in new ways through schools and other institutions, and were less likely to engage in risky behavior. Moreover, the decision to fund family services testified to a widespread confidence in the woman's ability to help her family adapt to modern life. As the final section of this chapter shows, social workers believed they could undo centuries of what the experts called clan-like patriarchy. Using a variety of programs that taught home economics and child rearing, administrators and social workers believed they could assist the Algerian woman to take her place as helpmate in the modern, nuclear family. She could imbue her children with loyalty and reverence for French culture and could create a haven for her husband that could contain his self-destructive behaviors, which ranged from drinking to nationalist politics. Social workers had great expectations about Algerian women that came, in part, from ingrained assumptions about women's apolitical nature and Muslim women's desire to embrace Western emancipation.[8] Service providers expected Algerian women, more than anyone else, to help their families fully adapt to French society.

Instructing Male Migrants

Vocational training programs (*formation professionnelle d'adultes*) and French language courses constituted the first and primary educational programs for Algerian men working in France after World War II.[9] The Labor Ministry, which ran these six-month training programs, opened the courses to Algerians for several reasons. First and foremost, these programs, much like the quota system implemented in 1958 to ensure ten percent of civil service jobs went to Algerians, intended to demonstrate France's commitment to integration.[10] Training addressed the "serious difficulties" Algerians had "adapting to life in the capital" due to their "ethnic origin" and ultimately helped with their "integration" into "the French economy."[11] According to one of the ministry's social inspectors, this training was important for integrating Algerians "into the company because once trained and promoted a worker generally does not wish to change employers."[12] Moreover, the programs' inherent "propaganda and recruitment"[13] fit into the larger project of integrating male workers into the French economy, in large part because stable employment, experts believed, would prevent Algerians' adherence to Algerian nationalism. Since the 1947 law gave Algerians "absolute equality . . . with metropolitan workers," the Labor Ministry insisted that employers had a responsibility to educate their workers in a way that would improve their skills.[14] As part of this, both employers and the vocational training programs also had to treat their "European and Muslim candidates" with "equality . . . [especially with] respect to everyone's religion." In practice this translated into simple accommodations, including offering late cafeteria dinners during Ramadan.[15]

Despite all of this, contemporaries considered the attempt to incorporate Algerians into the job-training programs a failure. Few Algerians actually qualified due to the French education system's admission requirements; they lacked the proper diplomas and language skills. To counteract this deficiency, experts used a supposedly social scientific "psychotechnical" method involving medical, psychological, and skills testing to determine aptitude.[16] This method, developed after World War I to evaluate and rationalize labor, perpetuated hierarchies based on ethnic stereotypes.[17] Algerians frequently failed the equivalency exams. In 1953, of roughly three thousand Algerians who applied, about a third failed the "psychotechnical tests," another third were admitted into programs, and the final third were channeled into "special centers" (three-month remedial programs) that fed back into the regular training programs.[18]

The Labor Ministry established an informal quota system that reserved between ten and fifteen percent of openings for Algerian men by the mid-1950s, but relatively few Algerians completed the courses.[19] Many left after being admitted because stable employment became available. Others avoided the government programs and instead relied on informal networks to find work. Once in a particular occupation, family members often trained the new arrivals. Employers also frequently, if quietly, undermined the Labor Ministry's policy. Most employers willing to hire Algerians preferred on-the-job training, for some of the same reasons they chafed at the government's role in recruitment in Algeria. They had more control and their workforce remained more flexible. Moreover, both the Patronat and some labor unions argued vocational training wasted six to nine months and could not replace real experience.[20]

Employers frequently kept Algerians in low-paying, unskilled, dangerous positions. They justified this by claiming Algerians were "maladapted" for work and accident prone, even though at least one study determined Algerians fared no worse than others, having accidents at the same rates as other workers when on the job for a comparable length of time. The study did concede that Algerians took longer to recover from accidents than most other workers, but argued this was because they did not have "a wife" in France to take care of them and to cajole them to return to work.[21] Some employers refused to hire Algerians at all. Job advertisements commonly included the phrase "No North Africans."[22] In these cases employers made hiring decisions based on widely held assumptions about Algerians' "indolence, susceptibility, poor health, lack of physical resistance, inability to adapt to industrial work [and] propensity for workplace accidents."[23] Despite the government's attempts to revamp its approach to job training, including an emphasis on specialized courses for young men ages 17 to 21,[24] these programs continued to be plagued by problems that intensified along with the Algerian War.

The state also supported remedial language courses that addressed what most viewed as Algerians' primary deficiency: their inability to read, write, and speak French well. Beginning in 1945, the National Education Ministry and a number of small private organizations sponsored language courses for Algerians in France. The Education Ministry first opened seven French classes in Paris, with more appearing in the suburbs of the capital and in the provinces.[25] By 1951, seventy-three centers around the country taught French to Algerian workers.[26] Nearly all classes took place at night, usually for several hours a couple of days a week, in order to accommodate men's work schedules. In the face of limited funds and trepidation that "the difficulties were great," Education Ministry officials praised the program and its students. Despite sporadic attendance due to exhaustion from long hours in manual-labor jobs or from problems with limited or inconvenient public transportation, the Education Ministry reported the program was a great success. "The sincere desire to learn and enthusiasm of many of our students" made it possible for most to learn to read French on an elementary level in about one year.[27]

The language classes also proved to be popular with Algerians and employers. Partly due to the Education Ministry's inability to meet demand, local, private initiatives filled the void, in some cases spontaneously and in others as part of a tradition that began in the interwar period. Social Catholics used a model developed in the early 1930s in the Paris suburb of Gennevilliers and in Lyon. Professor Louis Massignon and Dr. R. Barthe, chief physician for French Gas and Electric and president of North African Family Social Service, worked with Father Ghys to develop classes through Moral Assistance for North Africans. Based on the organizers' sense of "responsibility" towards Algerians, night classes intended to "establish human contact" and to help men adapt without interfering with the workday.[28]

Overseen by university professors and taught by volunteers with diverse backgrounds (from school teachers to graduate students in the *grandes écoles*), night classes imparted more than rudimentary language skills. North African Social Studies, which provided pedagogical advice to instructors in the first issue of the *Cahiers nord-africains*, urged that classes be "welcoming" by appealing to Algerians' "tastes" and providing a serious atmosphere while avoiding any "official, administrative" feel. Small classes encouraged "frank, sincere friendship" and allowed instructors to become "sponsors" who could listen to students' problems and could help them "without making them feel their inferiority."[29] Through this approach organizers believed that courses would help end segregation and isolation, would teach workers how to accomplish everyday tasks (like using a public phone, writing a money order, or sending a letter or a telegram), and would assist them with "integration into the leisure activities of the neighborhood."[30] By 1953, more than fifty private organizations held over 130 French classes for Algerian workers in thirty departments.[31] While exact figures for student enrollment are unknown, the Public Health and Population Ministry's request for enrollment figures yielded responses from nearly half the private classes and indicated about 2,300 students attended sixty-two classes.[32] Many courses assigned textbooks developed in Algeria or used North African Social Studies' brochures, including "Mémento de l'Algérien dans la métropole," as textbooks.[33]

At about the same time, Léon Rohet, an engineer with French Gas and Electric, enlisted the Red Cross and several humanities professors to help start a North African aid organization that offered evening classes in the alpine town of Annecy. For this small-scale initiative, Rohet developed a collection of thirty lessons that taught basic reading and mathematics in a locally published textbook called *Ali à Annecy*. Impressed with his approach, North African Social Studies adopted the Rohet method and published his revised text as *Ali apprend le français*.[34] In 1953, North African Social Studies distributed three thousand paperback copies of *Ali apprend le français* along with pedagogical support for instructors. Rohet's method quickly became the most commonly used approach and "significantly contributed to the development of courses in the local, private organizations."[35] In 1954, Rohet published a companion textbook for advanced students, and, by 1959, *Ali apprend le français* was in its fifth edition.[36]

In many respects the *Ali* series and North African Social Studies' other pedagogic materials drew upon French educational traditions, especially in terms of lesson plan structures and assignments. At the same time, assumptions about Algerians' mentality permeated all aspects of the texts. These materials constructed and reinforced a series of suppositions about what Algerians needed to learn, what type of work they did, and what language skills served them best. Introductions to these texts noted that the lessons had been carefully adapted to the students' "own psychological needs" and that the larger goals included providing an "apprenticeship to life in the metropole" to people who were "without culture and without preparation for life in the Occident, without any notion of hygiene or the dangers of industry."[37] The French classes taught an invaluable skill, generally with all-volunteer instructors who wanted to help men learn French. At the same time, these classes are an example of France's project to transform the Algerian population. Rohet and his colleagues, like others working in Algerian services, approached their work with a "high-modernist utopianism" that presumed Algerian inferiority and that improving the human condition meant embracing universal French culture.[38]

The texts used carefully chosen combinations of images, situations, and vocabulary that brought together aspects of Algerian culture, the experiences of migrant workers, and the benefits of French culture. To teach ordinal numbers, for example, lesson 23 told the story of one Algerian's journey in France. Having arrived in Marseille, where there was no work because "there are too many Algerians," he finally got a construction job in Annecy on the seventh day, which was fortunate since many of his friends did not find work until the tenth or twentieth day in France.[39] Most lessons had pictures of people dressed in what was clearly supposed to denote both French and Algerian styles, made reference to Algeria (regions, agricultural products, etc.), and taught pronunciation, verb conjugation, and basic grammar and mathematics through practical advice about how to live in France (see Figure 3.1). This included everything from food, weather, time, and hygiene to more complex lessons that explained how to buy new clothes, read a pay stub, get identity papers, and avoid and to recover from a workplace accident.[40]

Similarly, the advanced grammar text taught French cultural practices using a variety of brief, themed passages including how to bake bread (past tense), how to maintain proper hygiene (imperative tense), and how to define progress (conditional tense). In one telling example, Rohet used the search for employment to teach the conditional tense with sentences like: "I would find work if I were a skilled laborer."[41] Another seemingly forced passage taught vocabulary about France, describing it as "one of the most beautiful [nations] because of the richness of its soil and of the variety of its countryside."[42] At every opportunity the teaching aides professed France's greatness, reinforced its place as the pinnacle of civilization, and made clear that Algerians had to improve themselves if they were to adapt successfully.

All pedagogical resources created for the classroom, as well as others created for the workplace, reinforced pervasive stereotypes. Instruction materials assumed these men worked with their hands, depicting occupations such as construction, mining and factory work, as well as some

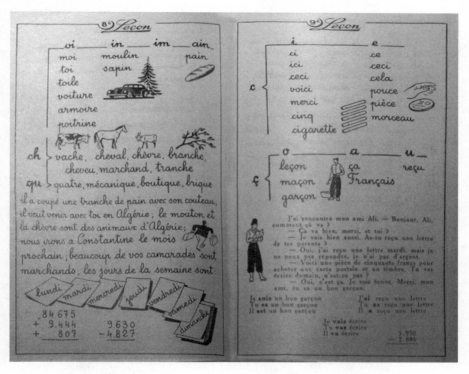

FIGURE 3.1. Lessons 8–9 in *Ali apprend le français*.
Source: Reprinted with the permission of *Hommes et Migrations*.

skilled labor such as welding and heavy equipment operation. A sample job application letter in *Ali apprend le français* (Figure 3.2) outlined the skills an employer in search of construction or factory laborers might need and implicitly reminded job seekers to identify themselves as Algerian, to be polite, and to make employers happy.[43] Pedagogical materials also frequently carried the message that workplace safety was workers' responsibility. A poster for display in the workplace counseled against drinking too much tea, because, like alcohol, it might be dangerous and habit forming. Furthermore, it advised that proper food and ample rest would prevent workplace accidents.[44] Similarly, a brief safety manual explained "accidents will not happen if you follow our safety advice." Prudence began at home, with proper accommodations, hygiene, and diet. A "good worker" used the right tools, stayed organized, and always made certain he worked in a safe environment before starting a task.[45]

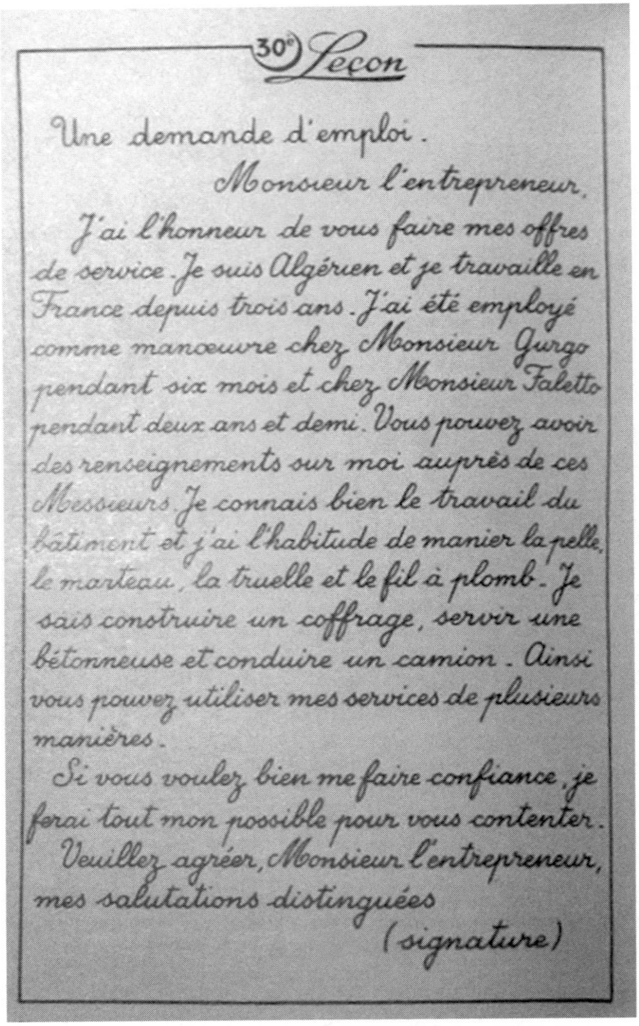

30e Leçon

Une demande d'emploi.

Monsieur l'entrepreneur,

J'ai l'honneur de vous faire mes offres de service. Je suis Algérien et je travaille en France depuis trois ans. J'ai été employé comme manœuvre chez Monsieur Gurgo pendant six mois et chez Monsieur Faletto pendant deux ans et demi. Vous pouvez avoir des renseignements sur moi auprès de ces Messieurs. Je connais bien le travail du bâtiment et j'ai l'habitude de manier la pelle, le marteau, la truelle et le fil à plomb. Je sais construire un coffrage, servir une bétonneuse et conduire un camion. Ainsi vous pouvez utiliser mes services de plusieurs manières.

Si vous voulez bien me faire confiance, je ferai tout mon possible pour vous contenter.

Veuillez agréer, Monsieur l'entrepreneur, mes salutations distinguées

(signature)

FIGURE 3.2. Lesson 30, a sample job application letter, from *Ali apprend le français*.
Source: Reprinted with the permission of *Hommes et Migrations*.

The manual attributed Algerians supposed higher rates of workplace accidents to carelessness or misplaced priorities. For the former, it never mentioned that what the employer did, including failing to provide proper tools or reprimanding or firing workers who complained about or tried to rectify unsafe conditions, could have played a role. Nor did it include information about how to file a complaint. For the latter, pedagogical resources attributed Algerians' poor hygiene, diet, and living conditions to a preference for living as frugally as possible in order to send every centime home to their families in Algeria.

The educational resources produced by the Labor Ministry, North African Social Studies, and their collaborators reveal tensions within the Algerian welfare network. The people behind these programs consciously worked to resolve the problems Algerians faced while they perpetuated contradictory stereotypes with historical referents. By conflating well-known stereotypes about the hardworking, stable Berber and the unreliable and careless Arab, the textbooks reinforced Algerian workers' circumscribed position. This essentialist, circular reasoning, like arguments made about working women and other immigrant groups, implied that Algerians were naturally drawn to or better suited for certain types of repetitive and low-paid work, which justified discrimination.

This is particularly important given that welfare providers, experts, and administrators routinely criticized employers and the general population for perpetuating unjustified stereotypes about Algerians and professed that their mission was to change the attitudes of the metropolitan French. The seeming contradictions are a reminder that, at base, the mission to help was fundamentally about transforming Algerians, making up for their deficiencies so they could adapt to life in France. Algerians were not to be feared, hated, or rejected. Instead, these "boys," as the materials frequently referred to Algerian men, needed to be shown compassion, pity and, above all, patience as they slowly made their journey. When it came to the materials for Algerians, the experts never mentioned prejudices in the general population nor openly addressed their efforts to change attitudes. Doing so might have jeopardized government subsidies or antagonized employers unwilling to disseminate materials that might confirm Algerians' complaints. It was one thing to offer an internal assessment of French prejudices; it was another to offer ammunition to Algerian nationalists. Finally, these programs, if unwittingly, further marginalized Algerians by offering only segregated classes. While remedial language courses could not be integrated within the general population, they might have been integrated into similar programs for European immigrants. Unable to justify the segregation because of concerns about Algerians' militancy, experts instead insisted that only specially prepared teachers could deal with Algerians' particular mentality.

Instructing over the Radio

Of all the educational programs the French government sponsored during the 1950s, broadcasts on state-owned radio had the potential to reach most Algerians.[46] The earliest shows, part of the Labor Ministry's efforts to control migration after the 1947 law, warned men that life in France would be difficult if they came without a work contract.[47] Broadcast in both Arabic and Kabyle, the program expanded its themes and reach in just a few years. A growing number of sources—including the Interministerial Commission and the National Security Office—committed financial resources to the radio program at least in part because several studies indicated that the broadcasts had significant "educative" influence over listeners.[48] Each week, the Editorial Board, which included representatives from Radio France, the Aid Commission for North Africans in the Metropole, and the Interior, Labor and Public Health and Population Ministries, met to determine program content. In 1953, the Interministerial Commission allocated over two million francs to fund weekly social and educational programs, with an extra 500,000 francs set aside to study "listener mail."[49] The Editorial Board hoped to make these programs a tool for disseminating information and advice. Programs had the dual propagandistic role of emphasizing everything France offered in the way of social rights and benefits and of attempting to control Algerian migration by offering friendly warnings about what to expect and how to behave.[50]

For over a decade, episodes simultaneously touted the richness of French civilization and cautioned about the problems Algerians might face if they failed to adapt. Programming encouraged certain Algerians to emigrate and discouraged anyone unwilling to change from making the trip. The preferred technique consisted of prepared "dialogues or little dramatic plays" that mimicked informal conversations between average Algerians rather than emphasizing that French experts wrote the scripts.[51] According to René Grinda, the director of Arab and Kabyle Radio Programs, the inspiration for the series came from Algerians, who, when questioned for a "vast study" on the "problem of emigration," expressed an interest in hearing more from Algerians living in France.[52]

The 1953–1954 seasons ran a series of episodes chronicling Algerians' experiences in France, which included everything from poems to testimonials about working with social service organizations, including Aid to

Overseas Workers. Programs tackled topics from cultural education, such as a visit to the Louvre, to practical advice, such as accessing "family allowance benefits if your family lives in the metropole."[53] The radio programming also acknowledged the transformation of the Algerian population in France and advised both male workers and female homemakers on how to make the adjustment.

Programs for Algerian women reached out to "the feminine audience that has a considerable influence on the family."[54] They echoed themes in the didactic literature targeting French women in the 1950s.[55] Even though French women had gained the vote and many worked outside the home, women's magazines and experts idealized the wife and mother. In her well-known book on the science of housework, Eva Compain reminded her readers "a woman is the soul of the home. . . . She creates the moral atmosphere of the family and thereby contributes to a great extent to the health and happiness of everyone."[56] Starting in 1950, Miss Hana, Miss Ghalia, and Miss Linda used themes from the discourse on domesticity to construct informal dialogues to teach Algerian women about everything from child care, laundry and ironing, to the benefits of doctor visits and how to access welfare benefits.[57] Within a few years, programs targeting women began to receive mail regularly, with listeners often requesting more information about particular programs. By 1959, women in France and in Algeria sent in over twelve thousand letters (nineteen percent of all mail received for broadcasts targeting Algerians), convincing program coordinators they had reached their target audience.[58]

The majority of programs directly addressed men as heads of households. Broadcasts explained how to bring families from Algeria and how to ensure they managed in the new environment. The dialogues provided basic information about how to apply for benefits, cut through red tape, and become part of the system. They also naturalized family reunification while simultaneously highlighting the inherent difficulties. In the episode excerpted at the beginning of this chapter, Abdelhakim acknowledged and supported his friend's desire to have his family join him. This was a natural step, if his friend had a stable job and proper housing. It would only work, Abdelhakim insisted, if families were willing to adapt to French customs, including Western, unveiled dress for women.[59] As with all the other social programs, radio broadcasts welcomed Algerians to embrace France's universal culture and to abandon any particularities that would attract attention.

The Family Allowance Controversy

Radio programs consistently addressed a controversy that dragged on throughout the period: the unequal distribution of family allowance benefits.[60] Echoing all official responses, radio broadcasts framed the discussion of family allowances as part of France's commitment to its Muslim citizens. Internal documents also revealed French fears; programmers felt compelled to undercut what they described as Algerian and pan-Arab militant nationalists' claims that the allowance system discriminated against Algerians.[61] This kind of regular attention begins to explain just how contentious the debate became and what role allowances played in the war to win the allegiance of Algerians.

The family allowance system, which began as part of the interwar era's employer-dominated welfare system, expanded significantly after World War II to become one of the largest components of the nearly comprehensive, national system and the heart of the modern French welfare state. According to Pierre Laroque, a member of the Conseil d'Etat, who oversaw the consolidation of France's welfare state as Social Security's first director, family allowance benefits accounted for half of all Social Security payments in 1946.[62] In the context of the so-called Algerian problem, this contemporary debate revolved around inequities built into the welfare system. Throughout the period, Algerian workers paid into the system at exactly the same rate as all French workers. If their families resided in the metropole, they received benefits "on the same footing as metropolitan workers."[63] If, however, dependent children resided in Algeria, they were eligible for a much lower "Algerian rate" of family allowances. In addition, the policy barred families in Algeria from receiving any related benefits, including prenatal, maternity, and housing allowances.[64]

These inequities highlighted the policy's dual demographic goals. From its earliest incarnations, the family allowance program represented an important pronatalist victory in the struggle to reverse France's declining birthrate.[65] The Algerian rate, on the other hand, clearly intended to curb what French experts imagined as the opposite problem in Algeria: an uncontrolled population explosion. In this way, family allowances simultaneously exposed the colonial regime's antinatalist goals and the fissures in the French state's approach to the Algerian problem. Moreover, both paternalist policy and French experts' responses to the controversy perpetuated disparities in France's social model.

One of the first instances of public outcry over the discrepancies in family allowance payments occurred in 1949 when Abbé Catrice and his allies in the French Union Assembly, in line with their promotion of social rights in the French Union, mounted a campaign to extend benefits to Algerians at the same rate as their metropolitan compatriots.[66] Rather than acquiesce to demands to reform the system, state officials justified the discrepancy. The Algerian rate was reasonable, they contended, not only because of Algeria's lower cost of living, but also because family allowances had always been limited to children living in the metropole.[67] In fact, Pierre Laroque viewed the extension of benefits to Algerian children as an exceptional privilege. Algerians, he insisted, should consider themselves lucky to be getting anything at all.[68]

Once Algerian and pan-Arab nationalists took up the issue, French counter-propaganda emphasized the program's "humanitarian" goals—to demonstrate how Algerians' "old mother country" carried out its "tutelary duty."[69] This agenda appeared most visibly in the state-run radio programs. By regularly providing practical information about Algerians' right to access the welfare system, the broadcasts reinforced France's benevolence while simultaneously undermining Algerian nationalist claims.[70]

Given that French officials could not openly admit the Algerian War influenced migration patterns,[71] family allowances became the only acceptable explanation for the rapid growth in family migration. Some reluctantly admitted the discrepancy in family allowances "could not help but encourage family emigration."[72] In most cases, however, researchers and bureaucrats offered a more positive explanation. As one put it, it was easy to understand why an Algerian would send for his wife and children: "it reduced expenses and reunited his family, which had access, in France, to higher family allowances."[73] Benefits probably played a role in some Algerian families' decisions to migrate. Yet, they were not the sole motivation. Families migrated, no doubt, for a variety of reasons. In particular, once the colonial regime implemented a massive program of forced relocations to break the FLN, fleeing families, when they could, joined relatives in France rather than live in the internment camps euphemistically referred to as "New Villages."[74]

Catrice and his allies were not alone in their criticism of the separate and unequal family allowance policy. In 1956, Andrée Michel, a young feminist sociologist at the prestigious Centre national de la recherche scientifique (CNRS),[75] published a comprehensive study of Algerians in France that argued the allowance policy amounted to legal "discrimination." Her work, which built on Rager's research, demonstrated the "amount allocated, the distribution of funds and . . . the notion of a dependent child" were all determined by an inherently unequal system.[76] According to Rager, this form of discrimination began in Algeria in 1932, when landmark metropolitan legislation made employer-controlled family allowance benefits mandatory. However, rather than implementing the new welfare policy in Algeria, colonial officials argued that providing benefits to "natives" (*indigènes*) encouraged higher birthrates, fraud, and polygamy.[77]

Twenty years later, the state extended the allocations to migrant workers' families in Algeria, but it still undercut pronatalism; families in Algeria received between one-third and two-thirds less than those living in and around Paris (see Table 3.1). The payment differential was intended to restrict Algerian family size. Moreover, although 73,060 families (with 172,945 children) in Algeria had registered for benefits by 1953,[78] they faced numerous obstacles when attempting to collect benefits. First, the governor-general's office handpicked union representatives in the local Family Allowances Bureaus, which excluded workers from the management and distribution of benefits. In addition, Algerian policy called for the quarterly distribution of payments (in contrast to monthly distribution in the metropole), required families to wait six months before receiving benefits, made it difficult for the unemployed and those on vacation to receive benefits, and limited dependents to biological children except in rare instances (a significant contrast to the flexible metropolitan policy, which allowed recipients to claim any dependent child). Finally, many families eligible for these benefits went without when local officials refused to provide birth

TABLE 3.1. Family allowance benefits in 1955.

Number of children per household	Metropolitan benefit amounts (Paris area)	Algerian benefit amounts	Algerian benefit as percent of metropolitan benefit
1	3,450	2,400	70%
2	11,794	4,800	41%
3	20,896	7,200	34%
4	28,273	9,600	34%
5	33,650	12,000	36%
6	43,027	14,400	33%

Data in second and third columns from Michel, *Les travailleurs algériens en France*, 145.

certificates or to register children, demanded bribes, or simply withheld payments altogether.[79]

The inherent contradiction between extending benefits as a nod to French universalism and generosity and the desire to discourage Algerian fecundity lay at the heart of the "family allowance problem."[80] Policy makers understood they could not openly admit that an antinatalist agenda informed the application of the otherwise pronatalist policy.[81] Those who did provide uninhibited responses had an openly colonialist perspective or limited themselves to voicing their concerns in publications meant for French experts for fear that "anti-French agitators" would use the issue to gain support in Algeria and beyond.[82] They argued the discrepancy simultaneously encouraged growth in France's long-stagnant birthrate and restraint among Algerians, whose population growth needed to be controlled.[83] A law professor at the University of Algiers, whose research advocated curbing population growth in the Muslim world, openly condemned the extension of family allowances to Algeria as "demagoguery of the worst kind" that no one had the courage to oppose.[84]

Since eliminating family allowances for Algerians ran counter to the goal of maintaining French-Algeria, government officials instead sought a solution to silence critics. When Catrice and others initially demanded an accounting for the millions of francs that went into the Family Allowances Bureau's coffers, Laroque claimed that Social Security had no surplus; all the money collected was equally distributed among the children in the system.[85] By 1952, criticisms forced Laroque to establish the Social and Sanitary Aid Fund, which distributed via social programs some of the millions of francs that Algerians paid into the system.[86] Then, in 1955, Social Security simultaneously extended benefits to metropolitan and Algerian workers in sectors of the economy (including agriculture) that had previously been excluded from the system.[87] The new policy made citizens in these sectors of the economy, regardless of origin, eligible at the same time. It also encouraged Algerians to seek employment in agriculture, which Algerian migrants rarely did despite the abandoned farms project. While it benefited French farmers more than any other group, the new policy offered evidence that the French government was expanding Algerians' access to its generous welfare state even if the discriminatory payment structure remained in place.

While the controversy never completely disappeared, the government's decision to funnel the surplus into services for Algerians quieted many critics. The government claimed it had resolved the problem. It also avoided lump-sum back payments to individual Algerians, which the French assumed would be confiscated by Algerian nationalists. The network of welfare providers benefited greatly from this solution since the family allowance surplus, including both financial support and staff, became available to private associations working with Algerian migrants. A growing portion of these resources, particularly in terms of staff, helped to expand services for Algerian women and families and to extend the reach of the family allowance system.

Welfare Services for Algerian Women and Families

Not all service providers approved of or encouraged Algerian family settlement. When a national survey in 1953 asked social workers about the desirability of family settlement,[88] a few argued that families would be better off "back home" because of difficulties finding employment and housing in the metropole. More social workers, however, assessed family migration positively. Echoing the experts, they argued that "family emigration was, in principle, desirable" for numerous reasons. Social workers thought that the woman's presence would be good for male workers. It was unnatural for a man to live without his helpmate; the family brought a sense of "balance and 'humanization'" to the household.[89] According to social workers in Douai, reuniting families helped men maintain their "dignity," relieved them of the "multiple worries" associated with managing a household from afar, and helped them avoid "shady characters, alcohol, debauchery, etc."[90] In addition, social workers argued that family migration "would accelerate the destruction of the patriarchal family" and create more "Europeanized" families.[91]

Social workers in Algiers also responded to the 1953 survey by focusing on the modernizing effects of emigration to the metropole. Not only did they consider family migration both more "normal" and "more stable" than male migration, but they also believed that it ended the long, unnatural separation of families which affected men and women, if differently. Men apparently faced a host of problems related to health and moral issues. One of these increasingly included the birth of children despite fathers' prolonged absences. Social workers in Algeria hoped that reuniting families would allow the migrant worker to fulfill his roles as "husband and father" and as primary "educator." The Algerian woman, apparently bereft of direction or initiative, could, in the more "evolved" metropole, "learn quickly how to raise her children, keep her home better, etc." Family migration then, as social welfare providers in Algiers imagined it, would "facilitate the evolution of the Algerian family because a real evolution cannot be achieved without the woman."[92]

The notion that the evolutionary progress fell squarely on women's shoulders had long been part of metropolitan and colonial discourse. In the 1930s, pronatalists argued the French woman was the natural "protector of the native language, mores, traditions and even of national prejudices. It is the woman who transmits them to future generations."[93] At the time, only a French woman, eugenically desirable and capable of transmitting French culture, could make her immigrant husband and children French. In the 1950s, metropolitan authorities optimistically charged Algerian women migrants with the important task of transmitting French values (even as they assumed women did not transmit Algerian nationalist ideals) to their families. Under the close supervision of specialized service providers, Algerian women could help their families adapt to modern Western ways, a task already assigned to them in the colonial setting. Renée Bley, the first and long-time director of North African Family Social Service, argued that "the evolution of women" constituted "one of the fundamental problems facing North Africa." Beginning with the assumption that traditional, stagnant North African society had never created a proper "place" for women, Bley praised the French civilizing mission, insisting that "diverse contacts with the Occident in the past century" had "penetrated the consciousness of the Muslim world in North Africa." The crowning achievement of this project was that "now nothing can stop the Muslim woman . . . in her march forward."[94] The specialized services Bley managed acted as more than a simple continuation of the colonial project. The metropolitan environment could do what the colonial setting had failed to do: provide "a good adaptation." And, as Bley noted, "if we help her become a free being, the Muslim woman" could accompany her husband in the creation of a "new society" built from the best in both.[95] Those working for other service providers echoed this hopeful, if qualified, language. According to the North African Study and Action Committee in Lille, "contacts" with Algerian women were of central importance because, despite being "courageous" and having "goodwill," their "poor adaptation to modern life" posed the main impediment to "their evolution."[96]

This focus on the woman's pivotal role in Algerians' "adaptation to the French way of life" also built upon themes in the metropolitan welfare state.[97] Since the Third Republic, pronatalists and their allies made protective services for mothers and children "the linchpin" of social welfare.[98] When the Fourth Republic incorporated the family allowance system into the postwar Social Security Administration, the state made the regulation of women and families "the cornerstone of the post-war welfare state."[99] As Kristen Ross has argued, the "prevailing logic" of the early Cold War centered on reinvigorating France through modernization and hygiene; "If the woman is clean, the family is clean, the nation is clean."[100] While women from the colonies, considered eugenically undesirable, had been explicitly excluded from these types of metropolitan services in the interwar period,[101] the political situation had shifted significantly during and after World War II. Algerian women could be included in the national home economics project, especially if they helped clean up the Algerian crisis. The belief that France could emancipate Algerian women provided evidence of France's commitment to its Muslim citizens. Moreover, France encouraged Algerian women to migrate, which in the eyes of many officials would forestall Algerian men's interest in both nationalist movements and procreating with French women.

As a result, Algerian women received all the benefits available to metropolitan women, including eligibility for medals as mothers of large families, a eugenic program the state resuscitated to stimulate the postwar baby boom.[102] Each Mother's Day local governmental officials honored women with bronze, silver, or gold medals (depending on fecundity) in a public ceremony. Beginning in 1945, Algerian women in France became eligible for these medals. As historian Sophie Lamri has shown, one Parisian suburb between 1945 and 1960 honored at least thirty-two Algerian mothers who imbued their children with "a sense of honor, love of work, attachment to home and respect for their social and patriotic duties." Such women were the epitome of motherhood: French, prolific, and civic-minded. The bureaucrats who selected awardees could have systematically overlooked Algerian women. Instead, the state publicly embraced a handful of Algerian women to display French hospitality and to encourage Algerians' loyalty in the fight against nationalism.[103]

Even if most Algerian women in France did not receive medals rewarding their fecundity, all Algerian women in France were eligible for an array of benefits that helped them adjust to life and undertake their maternal duties, while simultaneously making it easier for social workers to "penetrate" the intimate family spaces and gain their clients' "confidence."[104] Monitoring became increasingly important as fears about male migrants' allegiance to Algerian nationalist groups grew. Experts from the IGAME to the *Cahiers nord-africains* warned social workers that men without families were vulnerable to medical, social, political, and moral dangers. The problems that single Algerian men faced, they warned, had vast consequences. If left unchecked their behavior might damage the national body biologically and politically. If migrant workers had their families to look after, they would no longer have time for either depraved amusements or the politics of independence, making family settlement attractive to French authorities at all levels of the welfare network.

Direct service providers, responding to all these factors, worked to transform the Algerian household from the inside out. According to a prominent woman working in the field, they wanted to achieve more than "a superficial" transformation; they hoped "to make these women evolve in fundamental ways."[105] Many administrators believed that families could completely adapt to French society by fully embracing modern life, which required a willingness to forgo their own traditions. While the administrators and social workers in the direct service organizations had complex understandings of their clients, most had a fairly positive attitude about Algerians' ability and willingness to adapt.

The administrators and social workers who managed and provided these services generally viewed women as in need of significant assistance, but also as possessing both a desire and an aptitude for life in France. In her study of 92 families in the Seine-et-Marne, west of Paris, Elisabeth Malet excluded a dozen or more families that had been there "a long time," arguing that they had become so "completely integrated . . . and adapted" to life in this suburban community that they did not need specialized services. Malet, encouraged by how well families in her study had adapted to the community, reported that many had a good "rapport with neighbors."[106] Similarly, M.-L. Tournier, who worked in the Prefecture of the Seine (and not for a specialized service), found the Algerian women with whom she had contact were "intuitive and generally confident." She was equally impressed with their ability to learn quickly. After they received the attention she and her assistant offered, Tournier's clients managed "pretty well in French," went shopping on their own, and even attended breast-feeding classes.[107]

Another prominent woman in the field, Madame S. Belpeer, offered a unique perspective. Possibly the only woman of "Muslim origin" to have an administrative role in the social welfare network, she worked closely with her husband, Louis Belpeer, the director of Aid to Overseas Workers.[108] She conducted extensive research on two groups of families with which she did outreach in the Cap Janet neighborhood of Marseille and in Aix-en-Provence.[109] Given that the families in Cap Janet lived in seaside blockhouses built by the Germans (to repel an invasion), Belpeer emphasized that these women did the best they could "to make their interior clean and to put it in order." The structures provided little shelter, let alone the comforts of a normal home, yet the families coped with the situation and constructed a community. Despite living, literally, on the edge of French territory, Belpeer argued these women had made great strides. They not only kept up their homes, but also did everything they could to care for their children properly, including sending them to school and to the doctor when necessary.[110] Likewise, Belpeer reported the women in Aix attended school and were instrumental in the families' decision to move to the metropole. These women pushed their husbands, Belpeer insisted, because they knew the metropole would fulfill their "desire to evolve and to get to know our civilization."[111]

To help Algerian families in their transformation, specialized providers used three types of services: office hours, courses that taught gender-determined skills, and home visits. The specialized network used mostly female direct service providers, including both professionally trained social workers and volunteer family workers. The former, women with diplomas from specialized schools, were a relatively new phenomenon. The trend began in the late nineteenth century and expanded during World War I and the interwar period when the drive to rationalize work called for replacing charity workers, the often middle-class housewives who were the foot soldiers of the early welfare state, with a new "cadre of trained women welfare workers."[112] The state and private organizations in the Algerian services network during the 1950s employed women in both categories. In most cases, associations sought professionally trained social workers imbued with the state's commitment to "productive housework."[113] But social workers, often employed by the state or larger charitable associations, were in high demand and generally loaned out to smaller associations for just a few hours a week. Volunteer family workers, whose expertise rested on personal experience as women and as mothers, provided much of the training Algerian women received.

Given the demand for and initial scarcity of professionally trained social workers, numerous governmental offices and most service organizations created weekly office hours during which a social worker could offer practical advice. Most prominently, each week the Department of the Seine loaned fourteen of its social counselors—half of whom were Muslims—to the mayor's offices of arrondissements and suburban communities with dense Algerian populations.[114] The Seine's social counselors, like all those manning this type of help desk, assisted Algerians in cutting through bureaucratic red tape and pointed them toward private associations.[115]

Some associations had their own help desks. Others, unable to employ a full-time social worker, had professionals from either the public (Social Security, Family Allowances Bureaus, departmental offices) or the private (Aid Commission for North Africans in the Metropole, North African Family Social Service) sector help with everything from problems associated with male workers to those relating to family settlement.[116] Even though other services became more important later in the decade, office hours continued to play an essential role. North African Family Social Service reported that its social workers assisted 7,825 people in weekly office hours in 1957 and made nearly 44,000 calls to other services on behalf of those seeking assistance in 1958.[117] That same year the Aid Commission touted that its staff had held over 2,000 office hours during which time they had addressed over 20,000 "social problems."[118]

Organizations that could, expanded services to provide home economics courses. Starting with the assumption that "the family problem rests largely on women's efforts,"[119] courses taught housekeeping skills and child-rearing techniques. Early on, organizations held classes in the homes of well-established Algerian families. Eventually, courses became more formal, meeting in centers provided by the local branches of Family Allowances, private organizations, and eventually in the social centers of social housing complexes.[120] Most sessions lasted two to three hours and offered free babysitting so that women with small children could attend. Algerian women, often isolated from the general population, chose to attend classes to familiarize themselves with their new environment, learn about services, and meet their neighbors. These courses offered women a place to gather socially outside the home, often in comfortable facilities.[121]

While the Department of the Seine offered nine language courses, the equivalent of night courses for men, to Algerian women in Paris by 1956,[122] the vast majority of courses focused on women's supposedly natural burdens. According to Malet, the deaths of three nursing infants in the winter of 1951 inspired the creation of North African Family Social Service and its mandate to take up "family education" among Algerians.[123] The initial focus did not last. Apparently nursing mothers did not appreciate being lectured to about the hygienic and nutritional benefits of either breast- or bottle-feeding, particularly from "a single woman without children." As a result, North African Family Social Service shifted its emphasis to a wider range of practical household skills.[124]

In the early years, North African Family Social Service collaborated with the Red Cross, which had similar classes for European immigrants. Classes expanded quickly, and in less than a year, Family Allowances offered to provide North African Family Social Service salaried home economics instructors assisted by volunteers.[125] Other associations followed suit. In Aix-en-Provence and Marseille, Aid to Overseas Workers created among the earliest home economics programs outside Paris for "Muslim women and their families."[126] Sewing became especially popular because, as a social worker reported, only half the women she worked with in Marseille could sew.[127] In one sewing class organized by the Aid Commission for North Africans in the Metropole in Moselle, women met for four hours once a week. The registered home economics teacher from the Family Allowances Bureau led the class, and an assistant worked closely with pupils. Donated toys, baby bottles, and even pastries and tea created a convivial atmosphere that encouraged women to gain confidence in both sewing and French. The sewing materials, however, were not donated. Instead, students' husbands bought them (despite the instructor's desire that the wives shop). At first, they had only one sewing machine, donated by North African Family Social Service, which rotated through students' homes between classes. Eventually, several husbands bought sewing machines, which made it possible for women to make all their families' clothing and household linens.[128]

In addition to providing sewing lessons, courses taught women how to knit, wash, iron, keep a sanitary home, provide adequate child care, cook nutritious food, do household shopping, transmit French mores to the entire family, and speak French. According to Madame Belpeer, the "Course of Initiation to Western Life" was desperately needed because "the Muslim woman knows absolutely nothing of the basic skills requisite to balance her budget, care for her children, maintain her home, satisfy her husband and . . . behave normally in the metropole."[129] Nevertheless, she believed that "the Muslim woman [had] a curiosity, an extreme virtuosity, an acceptance of the effort and diligence [required in life] that we did not anticipate."[130] This particularly rich description underlines just how much service providers believed Algerian women needed to change in order to become modern housewives and how essential the presence of women were to Algerians' successful adaptation. Belpeer, clearly influenced by dominant discourses about ideal womanhood and the presumption that Algerian women did not work outside the home (despite her own work), advocated a typical emancipation, one that freed women from their presumed backward traditions and gave them the opportunity to be a helpmate. The social science approach, which treated housewifery as a profession, required that the Algerian woman, just like her compatriots, learn "it is her job to create a home." Since experts insisted that every "woman must create happiness,"[131] Algerian women had an even greater burden: to embrace a whole new way of life that would fulfill husbands and sons more than Algerian nationalist politics.

By the mid-1950s, a handful of associations in most of the regions with significant Algerian populations offered classes to Algerian women. The local Family Allowances Bureaus provided certified teachers who had also gone through a complex approval process that involved a regional social counselor assisting the IGAME and an inspector from the Population Ministry.[132] The program was expanded in 1955 as a result of a state subsidy that contributed 30 francs per student to associations that provided 200 hours a year of class time to verified family allowance recipients.[133] In its first years of operation, North African Family Social Service sponsored home economics classes with at least ten women in attendance in a dozen centers in Paris, Metz, Lille, and Lyon.[134] These classes expanded quickly, and by 1954 North Africa Family Social Service held 374 meetings attended by 2,259 women.[135] Aid to Overseas Workers had a course in Aix and four in Marseille to accommodate one hundred adult women and their daughters by 1953–1954 and planned to expand the enrollment by at least thirty families the following year.[136] In the first trimester the Family Allowances Bureau supported the program financially, Aid to Overseas Workers held over 8,000 hours of class time, with the expectation that each student would attend between six and eight hours a week for up to two years.[137] Impressed with its work, North African Social Studies heralded Aid to Overseas Workers as a "model" for other organizations.[138] Its work was worth emulating, at least in part, because, as the leading family organization in the Bouches-du-Rhône, Aid to Overseas Workers boasted a holistic approach, teaching not just cleaning, but true home economics, French, and civics.[139] These types of classes continued to expand throughout the decade. By 1957, former IGAME Michel Massenet estimated eight thousand Algerian women attended courses organized by the major private social service agencies throughout France.[140]

Home visits constituted the final technique the Family Allowances Bureaus and private associations utilized. Initially, with the expansion and professionalization of the welfare state, social workers assigned to all French families accepted Algerian families as part of their regular clientele. Yet, fairly quickly people working in both the public and private sectors believed this arrangement did not adequately address the problem. Social workers felt overwhelmed, citing both the growing number of families settling in France and the depth of Algerians' needs. Fearful that she simply could not address Algerians' needs adequately and attend to her regular caseload, M.-L. Tournier turned to North African Family Social Service for help.[141]

As a result, North African Family Social Service, Aid Commission for North Africans in the Metropole, Aid to Overseas Workers, and other, smaller regional associations expanded operations to include home visits.[142] According to Renée Bley, "family workers" assisted social workers who "knew the psychology, customs and often the families' language." They worked in "collaboration with the official services" to "help the Muslim family" achieve a "better life." Through this "coordination" they offered "individualized education" in both "slums" and "normal" housing to "families that wanted to make an effort."[143]

Social workers, trained in "teaching individualized housekeeping," had caseloads of up to two hundred families.[144] To manage so many families, they worked closely with paid assistants and unpaid volunteers who could "penetrate" families that lacked "a sense of household organization" and could offer "useful" advice.[145] In many cases, family workers spoke some Arabic or Kabyle (because they were former colonists). Others requested interpreters or asked that classes be set up at night so they could learn their clients' languages after work.[146]

The various types of welfare providers assigned to work in Algerian homes subscribed to "the tutorial action of government authorities" and viewed their work as a "supplementary" service.[147] To that end they acted as a "very precious" intermediary who helped regular social workers to inculcate in Algerian women the benefits of adopting Western ways of life.[148] According to Malet,

A family educator went from house to house to teach mothers how to care for their children and maintain their household, and give them a basic introduction to child rearing and housekeeping. These families are particularly appreciative for her presence; mothers come get her between visits for help or advice.[149]

Following long-held traditions and their domestic science training, French service providers believed that women were the heart of the family, that poor women had to be taught how to fulfill their natural role as wife and mother, and that their clients were grateful for and attentive to everything the educators had to impart. In many cases, social workers acknowledged terrible living conditions were to blame when families seemed willing but unable to remake themselves sufficiently, but they also held the Algerian woman responsible for her own "ignorance" and placed the burden of transforming the family onto her shoulders.[150]

Home visits offered several advantages over other types of services. Unlike radio programs, office hours, or even home economics classes, home visits allowed service providers access to individual homes. Even if clients initially reached out by signing up for family allowances or by coming to an association, social workers and their colleagues could learn much more about clients and their neighbors by conducting home visits. Entering Algerian enclaves to assist clients, social workers encouraged more participation in the welfare network. By making visible improvements to clients' material conditions, from painting and installing cupboards and shelving to helping them apply for benefits, social workers drew the attention of everyone in the community.[151] Additionally, home visits allowed social workers to survey Algerian neighborhoods, to estimate the size and growth of the population in a given area, and to insert themselves into the lives and homes of those who had not sought assistance.

The Belpeers, for example, with the help of one social worker, kept track of over five hundred families in thirty-five separate enclaves in Marseille as of June 1954. While Aid to Overseas Workers did not have regular contact with each family, it tried to keep an accurate count of Algerian families in the city and to maintain regular contact with several families in each conglomeration.[152] Overall, Aid to Overseas Workers made over seven hundred home visits in 1953–1954.[153] By 1962, it "followed, oriented and educated 1,600 families,"[154] and had knowledge of thousands more.

Similarly, North African Family Social Service made 2,455 home visits to 182 families in 1954 and began contacts with 54 new families it hoped to accept as clients in the first part of 1955.[155] By 1957, the association employed seventeen family workers and thirteen assistants who had made more than ten thousand home visits.[156]

Family workers, who had the most regular contact with clients, believed they established intimate bonds with and made a significant difference in their clients' lives. Regular visits provided "an excellent point of entry; the social workers and their assistants quickly became the family's friends, 'their French family.'"[157] The North African Friendly Society in Nanterre relied on weekly home visits to provide "very fruitful" information about its clients' difficulties and to teach the association's staff about the "North African mentality."[158] A family worker from North African Family Social Service reported that she and her assistant had transformed a family in just "three weeks of work." Everyone benefited. The husband, described as "an evolved man, a skilled worker," who wanted "a 'metropolitan' home," was happy about the changes. The children had proper beds (instead of sleeping on the floor), clean laundry, and a better diet with more vegetables. All this was thanks to the mother, who had begun with a "very Algerian mentality," but became "more relaxed, more open." By the end she was taking her job seriously. She woke up early, donned an apron to cook and to clean, served French dishes, and made sure dinner was "ready when her husband returned from work."[159]

This scenario, fairly typical in many respects, highlights a number of the themes that commonly appeared in social and family workers' assessments of their clients and their work. Although social workers and association administrators commonly deplored Algerians' plight and living conditions, they ultimately blamed Algerians and associated success with the acceptance of particular French cultural practices. To ensure that Algerian families would internalize French practices concerning everything from dress to child care, welfare providers built upon paternalist programs that since the nineteenth century had sought to transform the lower-class family.[160] These programs developed out of "the model for home-based maternal and infant social work" set up by the Paris branch of Family Allowances in the 1920s.[161]

Even if both French and Algerian women needed to be taught how to fulfill their natural role as wife and mother, providers in the Algerian welfare network saw their clients as different from other poor French women.

Whereas French mothers might work outside the home, Algerian women were not expected to join the ranks of French women in wage labor.[162] Colonial discourse regarded Muslim women as malleable, in need of emancipation, and as a "politically passive 'other.'"[163] Most frequently, social workers described Algerian women as backward in some way, as "uprooted," as "inferior" to French working-class women, as ill-prepared for modern life, and as posing "a major impediment to their [own] evolution."[164] Most social workers emphasized Algerians' otherness as well as their high expectations of Algerian women's ability to change. According to Claude Mothes, who worked with social service agencies to conduct three surveys of Algerians in the Paris area in 1953, women represented a segment of the population "particularly adaptable to our way of life."[165] Many women showed a facility in French, learning enough to understand and be understood. Younger women, some argued, could adapt more easily and rapidly.[166] Others pointed out that women from Algeria's urban centers were "more evolved" and less likely to have obligations to the "patriarchal clan" than their counterparts from rural areas.[167] To achieve success, social workers had to be patient. Malet warned that many of their clients would initially turn toward the "natural defense" of people confronting "the unknown" that required "a rapid evolution."[168] Bley concurred, pointing out that since Muslims from the "Orient" had an "imprecise notion of time," Algerian women needed to reflect before they could bring their husbands around to the new ways of doing things.[169] To ease their clients' journey, social workers like Tournier tried to discourage "dependence," to undo the "very passive submission" Algerian women had been taught since childhood, and to instill a sense of confidence.[170] Service providers also claimed to help clients move beyond the "tribal wars" they fled in Algeria and to let go of their "prejudices," which were attributed to Algerians' religious and cultural heritage.[171]

No one in the welfare network argued that Algerians had to give up religion; instead, they expected the new environment would transform their beliefs. Algerians, particularly women, often kept religious traditions, but experts believed they did so in private to avoid drawing attention to their differences.[172] In this respect, Madame Belpeer articulated a widely accepted view that religious practice remained sacred, but premodern. As with each generation before them, Algerians' customs would disappear as they adapted to Western life. While implying that this was both natural and necessary, she insisted that their "evolution" depended "greatly on our attitude." If only this could be understood as a "human and national problem" that required the French "to open our doors and our hearts" to Muslim compatriots, the century-long civilizing mission could finally be achieved in the metropole.[173]

Welfare providers pointed to outward signs to determine if their clients had begun to break with "their traditions."[174] Not surprisingly, a woman's willingness to embrace French fashion was paramount in her transformation, even inspiring some volunteers in eastern France to give Algerian women French fashion magazines.[175] According to a social worker from Le Havre, her client made huge strides in just one week because she had "abandoned the veil and quickly began wearing simple yet tasteful European styles."[176] In another case, an Algerian woman remarked that she had decided "to conform" to French styles to fit in better.[177]

When women did not accept French advice, social workers frequently infantilized them, assuming the refusal was due to the husband's absolute control or to "mental deficiencies" that prevented these women from taking care of their homes and their children.[178] Just as social reformers on both sides of the Mediterranean believed they brought progress, they also believed they opened "new horizons" by guiding clients toward their role as wife and mother.[179] Behaviors as diverse as throwing away clothes rather than laundering them (because they had no access to a washing machine) or having too many gold bracelets or tattoos elicited criticism about misplaced priorities. Rather than examining the origins of these behaviors, misunderstanding or unfamiliarity offered proof that Algerian women were "lazy" or "coquettish" and needed to be taught frugality and modesty.[180]

Discussions of diet and food preparation, like other cultural practices, also illustrated service providers' immense ignorance about Algerian culture, which they supposedly knew so well. Despite arguing that a man's life and diet improved with his wife's arrival in France,[181] social workers assumed that Algerian women were totally ignorant about how to prepare nutritious food for their families. Social and family workers usually insisted that Algerian women had no idea how to cook unless they prepared French cuisine and viewed the North African diet of "couscous, bread, [and] biscuits" as nutritionally inferior and inappropriate for the "metropolitan climate." Social workers encouraged women to breast-feed for the first year, but believed the "brisk" shift to a North African diet supplemented with canned milk after the first birthday put children's health at risk.[182] Unable or unwilling to acknowledge that Algeria had a rich culinary tradition, educators with the Aid Commission for North Africans in the Metropole viewed Algerian women's desire to share their own recipes as an obstinate attachment "to their traditions" rather than as a gesture of hospitality.[183] Only Madame Belpeer seemed to view the offer of mint tea as a welcoming gesture.[184] She understood her clients' desire to maintain culinary practices or refusal to prepare French dishes had complex motivations, including Islamic prohibitions against eating "impure food."[185]

Finally, Algerian women's relationships with husbands and children also played a central role in how social workers viewed the adaptation process. Assessments of men followed two contradictory themes: men were either the more evolved family member whose wife was an obstacle to the family's Westernization or the suspicious patriarch whose attempt to separate his family from metropolitans was "cruel, inhuman."[186] For the former, his evolution, spurred by his daily interaction with metropolitans in the workplace, helped him to discover "the advantages of metropolitan life." The well-adapted Algerian migrant brought his family members to France so they could escape "the hard life from another century" they endured in Algeria.[187] Social workers praised these men for not preventing women from going out and for encouraging wives to adapt "little by little to metropolitan mores."[188] They also reported when men requested services or expressed appreciation. One man had apparently called in Aid to Overseas Workers to reason with his wife, to teach her how to behave properly.[189] In another case a husband stopped into the Aid to Overseas Workers' office to report that he was "thrilled" about the change in his wife, in his whole family. Because of the social worker, when he "returned after a day of work," he felt the "harmony" brought to his home.[190]

Even if social workers praised some husbands' progressive attitudes, they also commonly viewed men as an impediment to women's emancipation. Social workers claimed that men saw classes as a distraction that took their wife's attention away from the home and frequently criticized men for cloistering their wives or for rejecting services out of fear that they would lose their "marital authority."[191] Social workers also reported that Algerian men expressed a preference for female social workers, nurses, midwives, and even doctors because of the possible threat "the masculine element" might introduce.[192] Despite concerns about husbands who "displayed discontent" and sometimes demanded that the social worker cease her visits, female social workers believed their special access to intimate family spaces helped them offer families a better life.[193]

Social workers' effort to liberate Algerian women had clear limits, circumscribed by French gender norms in the 1950s. Even though social workers intended to destroy the vestiges of "the patriarchal family,"[194] they never questioned the husband's place as head of the nuclear household. Even when husbands did all the shopping, kept women cloistered in the home, or only allowed them to go out "veiled and in a taxi," the women were labeled as "withdrawn" or refusing to "evolve."[195] Social workers acted with "great prudence," always getting "the husband's okay" before introducing a new idea or program into the family.[196] Social workers wanted to liberate women from the backwardness of Algerian society including its patriarchal home and veil. They did not, however, view her liberation as outside the male-headed household. Social workers wanted her to accept her place as helpmate to her husband in the nuclear family, which for Madame Belpeer included trading in her "role as servant" for a relationship characterized by greater balance in household relations.[197]

While social workers wanted women to take up their duties in running the household, they also chafed at the idea that some Algerian men thought the family worker could temporarily replace their wives' domestic labor. In one case, a family worker reported that she had to explain to her client's husband that she was not there to take care of the older children and to do the housework while his wife recovered from childbirth.[198] Despite these problems, social workers frequently reported that husbands "gradually accepted this menace that emancipated their women because they too realized they needed her."[199]

How the Algerian woman raised her children represented the litmus test of her ability to assume her proper role. According to Mothes, the future of the Algerian community in France depended on whether children could successfully adapt.[200] When social workers determined that a client did not take her responsibility seriously, they described her as playing all day, as buying anything that "caught her eye" rather than household necessities, and as generally unable to take care of her children.[201] Before family services developed, authorities required Algerian families to turn children over to protective services before parents could receive assistance.[202] Once family services developed in the early 1950s, social workers continued to persuade women to give up custody temporarily or involuntarily removed children from the home if Algerian women did not meet expectations.[203] Yet, Renée Bley, who had significant influence as director of the largest private association, argued that rather than risking the "innumerable repercussions" that resulted from separating families, social workers should do everything possible to keep families together. Even though some families continued to be separated, she advocated that social service agencies spend more energy doing their work: teaching mothers how to properly care for children.[204]

When children seemed to be well adjusted, social workers praised Algerian mothers as well as their own efforts. In one case, Madame Belpeer explained that "our Muslim" had made great strides with the help of Aid to Overseas Workers and the St. Vincent de Paul Society. She was "poor but clean, always happy, giving her children meticulous care" and effectively navigating the French bureaucracy, which included signing up for family allowances.[205] Giving birth in hospitals, taking children to the doctor, sending them to school in Western-style dress, seeing that they washed their hands before meals and wore an apron at home to keep clothes clean were all signs that women were doing their job effectively.[206] In the Seine-et-Marne, teachers reported Algerian students excelled in school. They were "studious, attentive and conscientious" and at the "head of the class" in some schools. For these teachers, Algerian children "fused perfectly with the metropolitan children" except in cases where the "attitude [of] little metropolitans" soured "integration."[207] Though rare, this final observation is indicative of how much metropolitans' attitudes must have colored Algerians' experiences. As well, it is a reminder that these kinds of attitudes inspired the welfare network to dispel prejudices and to reshape public opinion through educational events and the media.

INVESTMENTS IN RADIO BROADCASTS, vocational training, courses in language and home economics demonstrated France's commitment to Algerians while simultaneously providing a means to better track a population that became harder to monitor once the 1947 law reinforced their freedom of movement. Welfare programs promised social mobility in exchange for access to the intimate space of the home. If men became disciplined workers and women became modern housewives who lived frugally and with simple dignity, creating a haven for husbands, all could participate in France's postwar economic boom.

The staff working in the various social programs shared faith in Algerians' ability to adapt to life in the metropole. Yet their faith originated from assumptions about Algerians' otherness; French social workers began with the presumption that Algerians were not equal to their metropolitan compatriots and needed to uplift themselves, to overcome their handicaps, and to fit into French, universal culture. Social workers saw themselves as advocates for Algerians, working tirelessly to improve their clients' material conditions and fighting against the prejudices in the general population, but they nevertheless perpetuated racial stereotypes, reinforced discriminatory beliefs, and reinstated a new version of the civilizing mission in the metropole.

At most, Algerians could become like their French compatriots. Contemporary nomenclature spotlighted the immutable, racial difference that ultimately separated those rooted in the French soil—the literal translation of *les français de souches*—from French citizens who were always differentiated, identified by their particularity, as Muslims and as Algerians. Of course, one can point to examples of Algerian Muslims, whether Madame Belpeer or the families that Malet declined to study, who earned praise for having completely assimilated or for having given up their origins. The very existence of these exceptions reinforced contemporary beliefs about the ability of France's universal culture to absorb those who embraced its transcendent qualities and to reject those intractable enough to make simultaneous demands for equality and Algeria's right to independence.

4

From Dormitories to Homes
Housing Workers and Families
during the Fourth Republic

ALONG WITH MORE THAN A THIRD of the general population in France after World War II, finding adequate housing was Algerian migrants' most common and urgent problem. Given the dire situation, the new Reconstruction and Urbanization Ministry made the construction and rehabilitation of residential housing a crucial part of its massive postwar urban renewal project. Law or practice excluded the majority of immigrants from most of the policies and programs that afforded French citizens the opportunity to move from dilapidated slums into newly built, single-family homes and massive apartment complexes synonymous with the Cold War economic boom.[1] Just as they did with other benefits, Algerians officially had the right to "all the possible housing programs offered by our legislation."[2] Eugène Claudius-Petit, Minister of Reconstruction and Urbanization, explained in 1952 that the "problem of decent housing" for Algerians, "whether single men or families," could be solved using models already in place in French departments and municipalities that combined local resources with loans from employer organizations.[3] Yet, as in other cases, eligibility did not necessarily translate into access. Algerians received mixed messages due to contradictory goals and attitudes within the bureaucracy. To deal with the dire need and to counteract both Algerians' ignorance about housing programs as well as discriminatory practices at the local level, a variety of state agencies and private charitable institutions helped Algerians gain access to benefits open to all or developed specialized services addressing their particular needs.

Nearly all Algerians lived in precarious conditions, either in all manner of slums, where they were vulnerable to exploitative landlords, or in shantytowns known as *bidonvilles* where mud infiltrated homes and shoes, hundreds of people shared one water spigot, and stove fires threatened to set everything alight.[4] These conditions constituted what North African Social Studies called Algerians' "great misery."[5] Housing, the experts insisted, represented the "determinant factor" in Algerians' "integration" into "modern life."[6]

The ways contemporary experts understood the nature, meaning, and goals of integration differed significantly for single men and families. For the former, integration referred to Algerians' relationship to the workplace. Adapting to the demands of the economy required language and occupational skills and mobility. To meet the housing needs of male workers, employers, government agencies, and private organizations constructed single-sex dormitories. Dormitories incorporated Algerians into the workforce based on employers' changing needs, offered educational programs on site, and facilitated monitoring Algerians' behavior. Integration, at least for male workers, ended here. The residential segregation—from the general population and frequently from French and immigrant workers in similar facilities—Algerians experienced in dormitories never seemed to raise concerns until some experts began to argue that only "the basic social unit," the family, could ensure Algerian "integration" into "the French community."[7]

When it came to family integration, experts, advocates, and bureaucrats concurred the ultimate goal was for families to "evolve" enough to live side by side with metropolitan families. Families could apply for the same housing subsidies and loans as everyone else. Family housing advocates facilitated Algerians' participation in regular housing subsidy programs by offering specialized, supplemental services that helped Algerians navigate the system. Algerian housing advocates resisted the creation of a separate national agency, citing evidence that some "well adapted" families rented or bought apartments or single-family homes via the current system.[8] They feared a separate solution to the Algerian family housing crisis might result in permanent Algerian enclaves. Throughout the first half of the 1950s, high-level officials and experts repeatedly declared their primary goal: to avoid segregation and inequities in the allotment of housing. They expected the individualized and decentralized approach they advocated would slowly bring "well-adapted" Algerian families into French society.

This approach appeared to be effective, especially when only a few families needed housing.

The commitment to supplemental aid at the local level also facilitated discriminatory practices. As with other low-level bureaucrats, local housing providers, including city officials and housing managers, had significant discretionary power.[9] As the Algerian family population grew, experts noted "discriminatory treatment" at the local level.[10] Despite their frustration, advocates continued to hope, amid growing hostility in some communities about the possibility of Algerian neighbors, that they could overcome prejudice and bring more resources to bear on the housing issue. New resources, including those filtered through a national construction company for Algerians created in 1956, made it possible not only to build more housing, but also to hire former colonists and military veterans as housing managers and to rely on social workers and other service providers to determine when Algerian families had evolved enough to move into regular housing. Throughout, both those seeking to help Algerians find housing and those wanting to avoid having Algerian neighbors framed parts of their arguments in terms of Algerians' willingness or refusal to take specialized guidance and to overcome a "natural" desire to self-segregate. The social network's consistent message, that Algerians could adapt and transform themselves to fit into French society, also gave some providers ample reason to deny certain Algerians, those they deemed ill-prepared for life in the metropole, access to decent housing.

Dormitories for Algerian Workers

The vast majority of Algerian migrant housing came in the form of dormitories for male workers. This type of housing was certainly not a new phenomenon. Since the nineteenth century, employers offered worker housing, and the state subsidized regional, municipal, and private housing projects for workers in urban and industrial areas.[11] State agencies and some employers first made a limited number of dormitories available to North Africans and other immigrant groups in the 1930s. Some facilities remained open after the war. The dormitory on rue Lecomte, which had been the headquarters for Paris' police surveillance during the interwar years, continued to provide one hundred men food and shelter in the 1950s.[12] Yet, since dormitories offered a limited number of beds and had a reputation for monitoring residents, most Algerians found housing on their own. In 1948, an orientation center reported that 18,630 of the 20,000 Algerians that passed through its doors located lodging without assistance. For most, this meant sleeping wherever they could—in cheap hotels, cafés, and slums—and paying exorbitant rents for inadequate, over-crowded, and unhealthy dwellings. Of the balance, 960 lived in public facilities and 470 lived in dormitories financed through private (nonprofit and employer) initiatives.[13]

With so many Algerians living precariously, some experts proposed a variety of strategies in the first part of the 1950s. All accepted the male dor-mitory model, but suggested different, sometimes region-specific plans for financing and management. Just as with the expansion of other services, worker-housing policy developed among both horizontal and vertical fric-tions—conflicting priorities and tensions in the administrative hierarchy.

In 1951, the *Cahiers nord-africains'* Joseph Leriche made one of the first proposals to counteract the exclusion of Algerians from housing cen-ters built for the general population or immigrants. Leriche advocated small, employer-built housing centers. These, which he called "modern Medinas," would have adequate space for each resident, proper hygiene facilities, common rooms, and prayer rooms that made residents feel "at home." In order to respond to the needs of "their race," Leriche also pro-moted the inclusion of educational components facilitating Algerians' "social promotion."[14] His proposal imagined an expanded and idealized version of what was happening already, since companies that employed Algerians became the first to provide housing in the years immediately following World War II.[15] The Labor Ministry's social inspectors played a central role in coordinating and monitoring the dormitory system,[16] but overall the government's role remained limited not only because employ-ers hoped to retain control over a flexible workforce, but also because the government had other priorities and limited funds. Experts encouraged employer-sponsored housing by arguing that companies benefited from Algerians' labor and therefore should incur the costs associated with it. Persuading employers to house workers seemed the best solution. Large companies could build facilities on a scale that private organizations simply could not afford or manage.[17]

In keeping with Leriche's proposal, the Labor Ministry subsidized the first employer-built dormitories for Algerian workers on or near job sites. Some locations divided units into rooms for between two and six people, but most provided noisy, barrack-style facilities with no privacy. All had collective bathrooms, and many had a cafeteria or a kitchen as well. Like any housing of this nature, it "facilitated surveillance,"[18] making it unpopular with Algerians.

Large companies outside big cities or in regions with particularly acute housing shortages provided housing for their Algerian employees. To help businesses, the Patronat created a nonprofit construction company that built housing centers destined for Algerian workers. In order to receive state aid and low-cost loans, the employers' construction companies could not legally link housing to work contracts. Like nonprofit construction companies, they had to allow government oversight and to seek express permission to transform "collective [male] housing into family housing." By the late 1940s, this arrangement provided housing for thousands of Algerians. According to a survey of twenty companies in the Lyon area that Rager conducted for his dissertation, they employed 1,057 Algerians (including two Moroccans), of which employers housed 714. Families, both ethnically mixed and Algerian, had to provide their own housing. One company, St. Gobain, provided housing for all but thirty of its one hundred workers. About half of those who housed themselves were men with families, four Algerian men married to European women and ten married to Algerian women. In the eastern department of Moselle, Rager found that the coal and steel industries housed about half of the 4,659 Algerians they employed.[19] To help the economic recovery, the Patronat renewed its housing program in 1952. The initial announcement mentioned a thousand beds in five new Parisian centers and plans to expand to other parts of the country.[20]

Employers did not have a monopoly on Algerian worker housing. Since the interwar period, Paris and, to a lesser extent, Marseille had departmental and municipal housing. Paris had six dormitories, with the Prefecture of the Seine funding five and the Red Cross one. In addition, just over a thousand Algerians found shelter in facilities mostly located in the industrial suburbs west of Paris, including Nanterre, Gennevilliers, and Boulogne-Billancourt.[21] These facilities did not begin to address demand. In 1949, a survey by a small aid agency determined Paris had about five thousand homeless Algerians and the number kept mounting. This figure, though, excluded the undetermined majority of the population that reportedly lived in substandard conditions. Algerians often paid exorbitant prices (100–300 francs a night) to sleep in private, unregulated slums. Public dormitories had reasonable rents; the Prefecture of the Seine's dormitory fees varied from nothing to 16 francs a night, if there was room and if one accepted the significant trade-offs.[22] Many Algerians preferred overcrowded cafés and filthy slums to constant surveillance.

The Department of the Seine hoped that a collaborative project would resolve the problem. The Association of Dormitories for North African Workers in the Paris Region (Association des foyers nord-africains de la région parisienne, AFNARP) managed the existing facilities and built new dormitories in conjunction with other organizations. The association's board of directors included officials from the Patronat, the Labor and Public Health and Population Ministries, and the General Council for Family Allowances. By 1956, sixteen towns near the capital had a total of twenty-nine dormitories with seven more under construction.[23]

The port city of Marseille, Algerians' most likely point of entry, responded differently than the capital. It had more welcome centers than housing facilities, and most of its dormitories housed those under consideration for repatriation due to a medical condition or suspicion of being unfit to work in France. Few employers showed interest in providing housing.[24] As a result, Marseille had some of the poorest living conditions in all of France, breeding disease and discontent. In response, the departmental government in the Bouches-du-Rhône began to take advantage of national funds, starting with the construction of two dormitories.[25]

These initiatives began in 1950 as part of the state's first push to expand social programs for Algerians. The Labor Ministry's Social Security Administration, through its Social and Sanitary Aid Fund, initially committed 500 million francs for male worker housing.[26] By 1953, Social Security announced the Family Allowances Bureaus' distribution of funds to large housing projects in Nancy (30 million francs), Rouen (45 million), St. Etienne (50 million), Marseille (100 million), and Paris (200 million).[27]

Other ministries also participated in Algerian worker housing, but on a smaller scale. In 1950, the Interior Ministry urged departmental prefects, via the Patronat, to encourage companies to redouble their efforts "to ameliorate the housing situation of Muslim workers from North Africa, to improve their standard of living, to protect their health and, overall, to facilitate their adaptation to metropolitan life."[28] Two years later the Reconstruction and Urbanization Ministry, under the leadership of Claudius-Petit, proposed a massive housing project in conjunction with the Patronat.[29] Finally, many regional governments—departmental and municipal—built dormitories for Algerian workers with both public and private funds.[30]

Even as the Labor Ministry continued to encourage employers, together with the local branches of the Family Allowances Bureau and local governments "to develop collective housing for the Muslim personnel," the state took the lead. Beginning in 1953, the Courant Plan required employers to deduct one percent from all workers' salaries to pay for housing services, a portion of which employers kept to help defray the costs of housing their workers. Regional governments collected the bulk of these funds and used them to establish more local housing projects. This affected Algerians too. In 1954, the Labor Ministry sent a circular to all prefects reminding them that the deduction came from Algerian workers' paychecks too. They should be using it, other funds, and the reduced-rate government loans to build housing for the local Algerian population.[31]

As funding increased, dormitory housing remained the norm for male workers. The goal, according to a report compiled for the French Union Assembly, was "simply put, to see North Africans integrated into housing meant for the French proletariat."[32] Administrators consistently used the language of integration in reference to male workers, arguing that when "housing only workers from Algeria, a tribal atmosphere instantly developed. On the other hand, in centers where French of metropolitan origin and Algerians lived together, the climate improved and workers of different ethnic origins developed a better understanding of one another."[33] Correspondence called for a *brassage* or mixture of Algerians and foreigners and in some cases French workers.[34] In other words, Algerian workers in these government-sponsored dormitories lived with other workers, usually foreigners and occasionally French, but they remained segregated from the general population. This fit with contemporary understandings of integration; Algerian workers needed to interact with other workers, to speak French, to have a safe a place to sleep, and to acquire the skills industry needed. They needed whatever services employers deemed necessary for the workplace. And, even though government officials wanted Algerian workers' experiences to counter the FLN's message that France cared nothing for its colonial workers, the *brassage* never materialized. A Muslim Affairs Service study of sixty-three dormitories found that eight exclusively served North Africans, nine were authorized to house North Africans and foreigners, three actually housed North Africans and foreigners, ten housed metropolitans and foreigners (but not North Africans), one housed both metropolitans and North Africans, and thirty-three were, in theory, open to all workers without distinction of origin.[35] Moreover, workers lived in dormitories built near the industries for which they worked, away from the general population and under the watchful eyes of employers by day and dormitory managers by night.

Government officials touted these projects as a massive venture. The construction of dormitories, however, never kept pace with the growing number of migrants and was hampered by growing hostility from municipal government officials and local residents. Even if new construction tried to keep pace with migration, as Andrée Michel reported in 1956, both groups frequently dragged their feet when the Social and Sanitary Aid Fund proposed building a North African workers' dormitory in a given community. "Hostile petitions covered with signatures" from residents not wanting anything to do with Algerian worker housing compounded bureaucrats' evasions, which included slowing the purchase or transfer of land and losing permits in a sea of red tape.[36]

Even though local intolerance slowed the process, advocates urged more construction out of a concern for the practical as well as political consequences. North African Social Studies' 1953 guide estimated France had between 35,000 to 40,000 beds for Algerian workers, taking both public and private (nonprofit and employer) housing into account.[37] Despite ongoing construction, a 1957 report determined that seventy-seven percent of Algerian workers still provided their own housing. The vast majority continued to live in overcrowded slums with other Algerians from the same villages, regions, or extended families, isolated from the general population. For the rest, employers still provided the majority of housing—50,000 beds. Nevertheless, the public sector, which had 18,000 beds in seventy-nine dormitories nationwide, was the fastest growing sector due to another new initiative that took shape in 1956.[38]

The policy shift came out of calls for a new "politics of housing." In 1954, the French Union Assembly commissioned a study, following a particularly bitter winter, to determine Algerians' housing needs and to propose solutions. The resulting report "invited the government of the French Republic to develop a housing policy for the North African workforce in the metropole" that encouraged "cooperation" at all levels, including state, charitable, and professional organizations and brought together all the "various resources: loans, grants, subsidies, financing" already available with additional substantial resources to "resolve the problem."[39] Although the report was not too concrete, it represented the start of a movement to find a coordinated solution.[40] The existing arrangement, with its multiple layers of decision making, encountered a great deal of bureaucratic red tape, slowing construction. Social inspectors tried to promote coopera- tion, but charities, employers, and local and national government agencies hesitated to work together and could not meet the demand.

The Interministerial Commission reached an impasse. Ministries wanted to handle issues related to Algerian settlement in different ways, preventing the committee from coming together.[41] The Interior Ministry's leadership believed that the attempts to solve the problem had become a disorganized jumble of approaches. It began to take a greater interest in simplifying Algerian housing policy. Increasingly motivated by a desire to end the isolation and poor hygienic conditions Algerians faced and by a de- sire to monitor the population more closely as both the war in Algeria and the civil war among Algerian nationalist groups escalated in France, officials worked to find a unified solution.[42] The Public Health and Population and Interior Ministries recommended the creation of one centrally controlled organization that could oversee the building of housing for Algerians all over France. The new plan called for a reformulation of administrative structures in order "to harmonize efforts, to rationalize the types of construction, to justly distribute settlements [throughout France] and to accelerate the rate of construction."[43] In other words, proponents advocated a coherent solu- tion to a problem that had theretofore been handled haphazardly.

The proposed organization's most vocal supporter and first president, who remained at the helm until 1977, was Eugène Claudius-Petit. A so- cial Catholic of humble origins, Petit took the codename Claudius during the Resistance and was a member of the provisional government in Al- giers before his tenure as Minister of Reconstruction and Urbanization.[44] Claudius-Petit argued that a mixed-economy national construction com- pany would provide the most efficient solution. A collaborative, national response could draw on financial resources of both the private and public sectors to build ample new facilities. In this way the proposition built on models devised in the late nineteenth century, yet with a much grander, national scope. Claudius-Petit approached the problem as he had the gen- eral housing crisis; he considered it an issue of economies of scale. Just as it was more efficient to build apartment houses than single-family houses, it was more cost effective to coordinate construction at the national level than allow for inefficiencies and duplications to continue at the local level. A national construction company could build or renovate housing facili- ties more efficiently than businesses, local authorities, or private organizations could on their own.[45] The new company he and others imagined could also help local initiatives implement projects more quickly, provide access to more capital for investment, and circumvent obstacles—principally bureaucratic headaches—lesser organizations might encounter.

Claudius-Petit's proposal initially provoked controversy. Housing for migrant workers had long been the realm of the Labor Ministry. It coordinated public, private, and employer-sponsored dormitory housing for workers. Therefore, in initial discussions, Labor Ministry officials advocated revamping the process by focusing on construction by employers in conjunction with new local associations that would address Algerians' needs and secure additional funds from the Social and Sanitary Aid Fund. Retaining the current structure gave employers more control over the workforce's mobility. The Labor Ministry's proposal, however, did not persuade other ministries, which were ready for greater change. Leaders from the Public Health and Population and Interior Ministries convinced the reluctant Labor Ministry to support the creation of a new national housing organization.[46]

Christened the *Société nationale d'économie mixte pour la construction de logements destinés aux français musulmans originaires d'Algérie et à leurs familles* and known exclusively by its cumbersome acronym, the SONACOTRAL, which coordinated most construction projects for Algerian migrants, became synonymous with Algerian worker housing. Created in the fall of 1956, the state-subsidized, nonprofit company enjoyed the support and expertise of the public and private sectors.[47] To facilitate education and surveillance, the SONACOTRAL employed former police officers, army veterans, and other former colonial administrators as dormitory managers.[48]

The SONACOTRAL streamlined the financing of housing projects. Its nonprofit status made it eligible for low-interest loans guaranteed by the state. Its basic budget came from the mandatory one percent of Algerian workers' salaries that employers collected,[49] the same financing technique the Courant Plan used to amass general social housing funds starting in 1953. Subsidies from various branches of the government, contributions from local governments, charitable organizations, and employers, and substantial loans from the Crédit Foncier augmented its capital.[50] Unlike previous projects, the SONACOTRAL could break ground with only an average of ten to fifteen percent of the total construction cost in starting capital because it borrowed as much as seventy percent from the Crédit

Foncier.[51] Additional funds could be obtained through loans against construction sites' land value and contributions from private organizations and local governments for projects undertaken for them. Claudius-Petit named François Villey of the Public Health and Population Ministry liaison to the government for the SONACOTRAL in January 1957. Villey had high hopes, announcing that the SONACOTRAL would "construct 50,000 beds in 5 years," 20,000 in the first year.[52]

Male workers remained the SONACOTRAL's primary concern, but from the outset it also built housing for Algerian families. Villey, in particular, made it clear that family housing constituted "one of the company's missions." Even if the SONACOTRAL built fewer units for families than for male workers, he argued that the family population was "very important, from the human and social perspective" and that housing would make it possible for Algerians to integrate into the "metropolitan community."[53] This sentiment, however, was never accepted unanimously. A representative of the Labor Ministry protested. In a note to one of his colleagues, he insisted he did "not share the personal tendency of the Secretary of State for Public Health and Population who wants to encourage Muslim families to come to the metropole at any cost: the available funds are barely enough to carry out housing projects for solitary workers."[54] The Labor Ministry, not surprisingly, wanted to meet the needs of workers and employers, so it continued to reject Algerian family migration as a solution to current problems. For the Labor Ministry, maintaining maximum labor flexibility took precedence over other goals. Families promoted settlement and made it less likely workers could be shifted from one region to another as the economy required.

Other priorities partially trumped the Labor Ministry's agenda once again. From the beginning, localities had solicited SONACOTRAL funds for family housing even though they represented a minority of SONACOTRAL projects. In 1958, to reassure the Construction Ministry, Claudius-Petit reiterated that the SONACOTRAL reserved ten to fifteen percent of its funds for family housing. Rather than simply pointing to Algerian men's demographic dominance, Claudius-Petit provided a more complex, revealing explanation for limiting family housing support. Too many resources allocated to families might set a negative precedent for local authorities. He argued that if the national agency regularly dealt with Algerian families, local governments would forgo their obligation to assist new residents. If local officials associated the SONACOTRAL with Algerian families' housing, they might stop extending other housing services to this community. As a result, the de facto segregation of the slums would become permanent. Claudius-Petit also worried that providing housing would encourage more migration from Algeria than France could accommodate. If Algerians heard about unlimited, new housing in France the bidonvilles and slums would overflow, endangering public health.[55]

Claudius-Petit suggested a two-fold solution: better control of migration from Algeria and creating transitional housing for Algerian families. As Chapter 6 will examine in greater detail, the SONACOTRAL participated in the construction of transitional housing for Algerian families labeled as insufficiently adapted to life in France. In theory, they would live in these units a short time, receive educational services, and move into permanent social housing projects with the general population once they were ready.[56] This limited commitment to family housing grew as the SONACOTRAL leadership strove to accommodate what it saw as the Algerian population's changing needs. In late 1957, the director of the Interior Ministry's Muslim Aid Service sent out a circular hoping to determine future departmental needs for housing Algerian men through the SONACOTRAL. Each prefecture responded to questionnaires about housing male workers. The majority of respondents also furnished an unsolicited, urgent appeal for a greater commitment to housing the rising number of women and children coming to France to join husbands and fathers.[57]

Social Housing and Algerian Families

Before the creation of the SONACOTRAL and the explosion in transitional housing during the Fifth Republic, Algerian families—"French citizens like all others"—gained access to housing aid the same way as other citizens in the metropole, through what is known as *le logement social*.[58] Social housing, a term without a precise English equivalent, refers to all housing projects, publicly and privately held single-family houses and multiunit apartments, for which rental or purchase prices are controlled in order to ensure residents do not pay exorbitant prices in relation to their income. The term includes public housing constructed and managed by municipal authorities or other governmental agencies. It also includes housing built according to a mixed-economy model that brings together privately held companies eligible for special low-interest loans and other government subsidies when they agree to price controls.

The concept originated among social reformers who sought to improve conditions among the urban, working poor in the second half of the nineteenth century.[59] Two schools of thought, both of which continued to influence housing in the twentieth century, dominated the discussion of social housing in the nineteenth century. Both argued that having a decent place to live would transform the lives of working-class families and solve numerous social problems. One, led by Frédéric Le Play, argued in favor of the "moralizing and saving character of home ownership" for the masses. Le Play's work as a social theorist and reformer was instrumental in the development of a paternalistic, employer-centered, frequently Catholic social movement that produced the powerful Patronat.[60] Many contemporary reformers considered the Workers' City established in Mulhouse, based on Le Play's ideas, a great success because its residents lived as nuclear family units and women and children no longer had to work outside the home.[61] Others, who agreed on little else, doubted the need for workers to become homeowners in order to instill in them (bourgeois) morality and save them from (working-class) vices. Many Utopian thinkers, social Catholics, and industrialists disagreed with Le Play's supposition that renting posed a danger to society since workers without property had less to lose and consequently could be more easily enticed into political and social revolt. They believed the responsibility of housing fell on the government or on employers and usually advocated collective, apartment housing rather than single-family homes. Not wanting to give up control, conservative industrialist-philanthropists called for private investment in the construction of collective housing, while lobbying for government subsidies.[62]

By the turn of the twentieth century, the republican government accepted a more active role in social housing. In 1894, the Siegfried law entrenched this mixed-economy model by allowing private interests to build low- and moderate-income housing with substantial government support. The units, called *Habitat à bon marché*, or housing at a fair price, came to be known as HBM housing.[63] Over the next half century, France's tepid commitment to social housing continued,[64] but World War I and the Great Depression depleted France's housing stock quicker than units could be constructed. Throughout the period social housing facilitated the surveillance of residents. Social workers taught certain hygienic and social practices to working-class clients and reported lawbreakers to the police. The desire to facilitate the supervision of residents and the de facto segregation of the poor to peripheral locations characterized this era and influenced housing policies in the colonies and in France after World War II.[65]

After World War II, rebuilding the war-torn nation became a vital preoccupation of the Fourth Republic. Responsibility for the arduous task fell primarily on the new Reconstruction and Urbanization Ministry. Its first two ministers prioritized national infrastructure, industry, and public buildings.[66] The third, Claudius-Petit, prioritized residential housing. He took housing as his mandate, even trying to remove the "re"(construction) from the ministry's title. Although Pierre Courant replaced him as minister before the plan that drove France's postwar housing boom had been enacted, Claudius-Petit made an indelible mark on housing policies for the masses and left a legacy in the realm of housing for Algerian workers and families that outlived his three-decade tenure as president of the SONACOTRAL.

Despite a 1947 INED study that found most people in France preferred single-family homes to collective housing,[67] Claudius-Petit believed in the benefits of collective housing. A student of the modernist Swiss architect Le Corbusier and a devotee of the Bauhaus movement, Claudius-Petit wanted the administration to construct a new France inspired by modernist ideals. For Claudius-Petit, collective housing units were the only way to ensure that all those without housing could be provided with clean, low-cost accommodations. He urged the government to commit ten to fifteen percent of its annual budget to housing at a time when it allocated a maximum of two percent annually. To deal with past oversights, current problems, and the postwar baby boom, Claudius-Petit urged France to construct fourteen million new and rehabilitated (war-damaged or just dilapidated) dwellings in France. While this goal was not reached under his leadership, his vision, including shifting the HBMs to the *Habitat à loyer modéré*, or "moderate-rent housing," known as HLMs, colored the nature of social housing for years to come.[68]

Pierre Courant, who is most closely associated with the expansion of social housing in the postwar era, replaced Claudius-Petit as minister of Reconstruction and Urbanization in 1953. The plan he instituted became France's first long-term and comprehensive social housing policy. Unprecedented government intervention utterly transformed the nature of social housing in France by setting national standards for housing styles and sizes, and offering new incentives to HLM companies, such as bonuses, low-interest loans, and cash subsidies. Much of the funding came from a one-percent tax on wages in companies with ten or more employees. The Courant Plan had broad support. The 1954 census estimated thirty-six percent of the French lived in overcrowded dwellings; another study determined that as many as forty-two percent lived without running water, and even more, up to ninety percent, had no shower or bathtub. The plan gained even more broad-based support when housing-rights advocates launched a media campaign during the harsh winter of 1953–1954.[69] Under the leadership of Abbé Pierre, the resistance fighter (who, like Claudius-Petit, kept his nom de guerre after the war), Catholic priest, and founder of Emmaüs (the French equivalent of the Goodwill), activists publicized the homelessness crisis. They transformed the death of a French woman, found frozen and lifeless on the street after being evicted from her apartment, into a cause célèbre.[70] This kind of political pressure brought more attention to the plight of the poor through gendered, patriotic arguments linking inadequate housing to all manner of social ills "threatening French renewal and the birth rate."[71] As a result, the number of construction companies building and renovating housing for low- and moderate-income families grew steadily throughout the 1950s. Nearly 500,000 units were constructed between 1953 and 1962, with over 80,000 in 1959, the peak year. It made this the era of the *grands ensembles*, massive collective housing projects. People from various social classes clambered for a place in the new apartment homes because they offered every modern comfort on a budget.[72]

The large-scale commitment to housing did not, however, entirely resolve France's housing problems. The inability to meet growing needs due to the baby boom and immigration continued. A study published in *Le Monde* in April 1958 called housing "our shame."[73] In addition, the neediest did not become the first residents of new dwellings. The owners and managers of the new complexes preferred tenants with better, regular incomes to ensure the timely payment of rents.[74] Many residents with stable incomes may have initially found the new social housing complexes infinitely better than their previous dwellings, but the love affair eventually ended in divorce. Residents complained about enduring surveillance at the hands of managers, being isolated from city centers and public transportation, and subsisting in the smallest average living spaces in Western Europe.[75] The first beneficiaries of subsidized housing either resided in the most desirable locations or eventually moved into housing available on the open market. In some cases, white, French residents moved out of quickly and poorly constructed apartments made undesirable by decay and disrepair, leaving space for the working poor and immigrants. In other cases, housing projects built in poor, mostly European immigrant neighborhoods accommodated only those that had no other options. In both cases, the semi-independent *grand ensemble* neighborhoods of which social reformers dreamed often became de facto ghettos by the 1970s.[76]

Most immigrants, especially people of color from the empire who had been previously excluded from housing, moved in as the French moved out.[77] Algerians had been the one exception, the one minority that received housing aid throughout the Cold War housing boom. In fact, since Algerian families were eligible for "general housing aid," the Social Security Administration sent a circular to its personnel in 1953 pointing out that the 500 million francs it allocated through the Social and Sanitary Aid Fund for Algerian housing was only for male workers and specifically forbade distributing these funds to any Algerians who had "brought their family to France."[78]

Algerian families did not need the specialized funds, according to this logic; they already received regular housing allocations and other financial aid (subsidies and loans) from a number of public and private organizations that helped any family buy or rent a home. This included aid from the local Family Allowances Bureaus, from employer organizations like the Industrial Housing Committees (Comités interprofessionnel de logement, CIL), from the Patronat, and from Vichy-era cooperative centers known as Propaganda and Action against Slums (Propagande et action contre le taudis, PACT). These organizations supplemented the Crédit Foncier's low-interest loans. Some Algerians managed to navigate the system early on and moved their families into what social workers and other bureaucrats considered appropriate housing. Exact figures are unknown, but anecdotal references appear frequently in archival and published documents from the period. As early as 1950, a foyer manager in the Parisian suburb of Saint-Denis reported that six former residents had either bought or rented apartments for their families.[79] Following up on Rager's research which found that some Algerian families lived in "very well kept" if simple accommodations,[80] Claude Mothes reported that, of the eighteen families attending Ramadan events sponsored by the Aid Commission for North Africans in the Metropole in 1953, five were in "bad" housing, most were in a transitional situation, two lived in a "suburban home" (*pavillon en banlieue*), and two more lived in HLM apartments, a situation she found typical among Algerian men that had been in France since World War II.[81] Likewise, the dozen families Elisabeth Malet excluded from her survey because they were so well "integrated" into the neighborhood had probably been in France for a while.[82]

In certain areas and occupations, the proportion of Algerian families living in conditions similar to those of their metropolitan compatriots seemed to be growing. In June 1954, an Aid to Overseas Workers' intern reported that at least thirty of the over five hundred Algerian families estimated to be living in and around Marseilles had already moved into three-bedroom HLM apartments.[83] Two years later, Rager found that 9.2 percent of Algerians working for Les Charbonnages de France, the recently nationalized coal mining industry, had brought their families to France. He reported that "these families seemed well-adapted [and] healthy" and that each lived in an HLM apartment or "even a house."[84]

That even a few Algerians were able to ascend to the ranks of those living in decent housing or to become first-time homeowners was a significant feat, given the nature of the housing market and the multiple impediments to Algerians receiving the aid for which they qualified. In the first place, successfully navigating the system never happened in a straightforward manner. No unified method or central organization existed to simplify the process and to help potential candidates buy homes. From the start, the maze of services for the general population was fraught with obstacles that hampered any family's success.[85] It seems likely as well that the timing of a family's arrival in France played a key role in its ability to become a home renter or owner. Anecdotal evidence suggests that Algerians in France in the 1940s and those for whom a company, association, or other entity stepped in, particularly when it concerned a small number of families, received effective assistance.[86] Nevertheless, in 1952, Madame Belpeer predicted a lack of adequate housing would become the central issue facing service providers in the coming years.[87] North African Family Social Service reported that a well-known survey of Algerian families corroborated Belpeer's fear. It determined that housing was Algerian families' "primary necessity" (*première urgence*) because precarious living conditions had "provoked a rapid increase in hospitalizations."[88] To begin to address the problem, Madame Belpeer and others mounted a concerted intervention that avoided isolating Algerians in "family ghettos." Only proper housing could ensure Algerians would integrate into French society.[89]

Advocates began to articulate a new politics of housing for Algerian families in France at about the time the politics of the general housing crisis in France climaxed with the passage of the Courant Plan in 1953. Again, the timing of Algerian family settlement seems to have mattered. No doubt influenced by the national discussion, the *Cahiers nord-africains* dedicated an issue to housing in late 1953. The changing character of the population from single men to families struck North African Social Studies' researchers as their most important new concern. Leriche "could not insist strongly enough on what excellent family housing would do to encourage these people's development." Not only would it improve their economic situation, but it was a "social and moral" imperative. Since male-worker migration fostered "an unstable immigration of isolated uprooted masses ill-adapted to work life and life in general," the *Cahiers* argued that Algerian workers would be better off in the "humane and normal context" of the family than in "abnormal" collective housing for workers.[90]

Others concurred. The Aid Commission for North Africans in the Metropole, social counselors in the Prefecture of the Seine, and the French Union Assembly all worried about the "deplorable housing conditions" that most Algerian families endured and argued that a solution for Algerian family housing had to be made part of the larger solution for Algerian worker housing.[91] According to both the Aid Commission and social counselors, at least 800 Algerian families in the Paris area needed housing. At least 110 of these families (with 420 children) were in absolutely dire circumstances. In the worst cases, up to eight children lived with their parents in one room "without water or gas and in deplorable sanitary conditions."[92] The Aid Commission's president, keenly aware of the political stakes, took a bold proposal to the Reconstruction and Housing Ministry in January 1954. He urged the state to join the Aid Commission and other organizations in developing programs that underwrote low-interest loans for Algerian families to purchase homes. He recommended that ten percent of all emergency housing in the Paris area be set aside for Algerian families. These measures were necessary, he explained, "to facilitate the adaptation of these families . . . and to encourage their social promotion." He warned that they should not be segregated from the general population and argued "their integration . . . in the national community" was "desirable." The Aid Commission president implied that discriminatory housing practices had to be at fault since even Algerian men with "a normal salary" could not find adequate housing for their families. The combination of deplorable living conditions and bureaucratic runaround, he pointed out, could make these families "bitter" about "our institutions," which might create significant problems if they returned to Algeria with "a deformed image of France."[93]

The first issue of the *Cahiers nord-africains* dedicated to family housing outlined housing managers' reasons for accepting so few Algerian tenants. In some instances, managers, who had substantial discretion in choosing occupants, turned away Algerian families for the same reasons they rejected the poorest French applicants: concerns about their job security and their ability to make rental or mortgage payments. They also openly worried about accusations of giving Algerians preferential treatment if French families "who have waited for years" watched Algerian families settle into apartments. Underscoring the close relationship between housing managers and employers, other justifications revolved around the desire to assure Algerian workers' maximum flexibility in the workforce. Housing managers wondered "what incentive" they had to house the families of long-time workers. Would not families pose a threat to control over workers and make them less willing to follow the fluctuations in the job market?[94]

Social housing managers, recruited because of experiences in the colonial setting that apparently helped them understand their clients,[95] explained their reluctance arose from fears that Algerian families did not know how to maintain their homes or that they would bring in "relatives and friends," overcrowding dwellings and making life difficult for the neighbors.[96] Given the housing crisis and tradition, French families also lived in multigenerational households. Social workers, however, discouraged everyone from the practice, describing it as "tribal."[97] Housing managers also claimed that French families preferred to have people with similar social, cultural, and religious beliefs as neighbors. Despite legal assurances that Algerian families could apply for any housing aid, managers often made decisions about admittance based on the candidate's "quality and solvency."[98] Thus, Algerians had two strikes against them. They either shared or were believed to share the characteristics of abject poverty with parts of the general population that made both undesirable tenants. In addition, Algerians apparently lacked other qualities that landlords and neighbors found attractive.

Dissatisfied with this standard list of excuses, North African Social Studies' researchers provided another set of reasons, placing some blame on housing managers and the bureaucracy, but also perpetuating assumptions regarding Algerians' "natural" tendencies. Like their compatriots, many Algerians had trouble navigating the complex and unfamiliar bureaucracy. The *Cahiers* pointed out that even if some Algerian families had stable employment and sufficient resources,[99] many could not afford mortgage payments even with substantial financial aid.[100] Leriche argued that Algerians faced multiple practical and "psychological" difficulties in navigating the system. The former included everything from ignorance about "the nature and role of interest-bearing loans" to trouble understanding brochures and other printed materials too complicated for even North African Social Studies' researchers to follow.

These were minor issues, however, compared to what Leriche called the "real obstacle to integration." Algerians' "apathy" and the "circle of silence" perpetuated in the "para-patriarchal" family made them avoid "risks," an observation which ignored the perils of migration and, as in so many other instances, subtly placed blame for the housing shortage on Algerians themselves. This supposedly natural risk aversion, Leriche insisted, meant Algerians feared the specter of future unemployment or sickness so much that they hesitated to move into better, more costly housing.[101]

To assist Algerian families in overcoming all these obstacles, several associations, housing cooperatives, and friendly societies (that served veterans) worked together to help Algerian families find apartments and single-family homes. Small organizations provided supplemental services that might level the playing field by simplifying the search for housing in immeasurable ways: locating the right parcel of land or home for sale or rent, cutting through red tape, filling in financing gaps, and so on. They frequently acted as a guarantor for loans and negotiated low rates with the Crédit Foncier or other government-sanctioned institutions, allowing families that would have otherwise been denied mortgages the opportunity to purchase homes with reasonable payment schedules. Through these programs potential homebuyers could get loans at an interest rate of one percent to be repaid over ten years.[102] These organizations, inheritors of the ideas Le Play had advanced in the nineteenth century, made homeownership possible. Their advocates saw owning, not long-term renting, as the answer to housing and social problems.

Some regional centers for Propaganda and Action against Slums, which usually worked with organizations involved in procuring housing for the general population, collaborated with advocates for Algerian families beginning in the early 1950s. The center for Propaganda and Action against

Slums in Marseille worked with Aid to Overseas Workers to help Algerian families facing eviction buy apartments. Similarly, this cooperative's offices in the departments of the Nord and the Seine, respectively, worked with the North African Friendly Society of the Nord and the North African Union of Valenciennes, an organization managed by Algerians, along with other local lodging committees and social housing construction companies to help Algerian families buy apartments or houses.[103] Other associations also worked with Housing Committees and the following agencies: the North African Friendly Society of Roubaix-Tourcoing, the Aid Commission for North Africans in the Metropole, the Committee for Lodging North African Families in Lille, Moral Assistance for North Africans (one of Father Ghys' associations that also founded housing committees in Paris and Lille), and the North African Family Welcome Group, which had offices in Paris, the Nord, and Strasbourg.[104]

Another, large project involved the Algerian Muslim Cooperative for First Time Home Ownership. With financing from the Crédit Foncier, it sold 1,012 units in five apartment complexes in Lyon and its suburbs. It is one of the first important examples of the use of an informal quota system in allocating housing to Algerian families. Only twenty to thirty percent of the new apartment homes could be made available for Algerian families to purchase. Administrators wanted to avoid ghettoizing Algerians in enclaves that might encourage Algerian nationalism and insisted that units be "reserved" only for "stable and adapted Muslim families."[105] Social workers determined which families met these criteria. Only those that had shown sufficient progress in language and home economics classes could move into apartments side by side with the general population.[106]

In response to what Le Beau and social counselors saw as a mounting crisis in Paris and its environs, the Prefecture of the Seine intended to set aside 1,500 housing units for Algerian families in 1954 if it could get sufficient financial backing from the appropriate government ministries.[107] Two years later, Emile Pelletier, the prefect of the Seine, proudly announced—in a glossy brochure that depicted children in their new apartment—that his office had placed sixty-one Muslim families in "the same conditions as metropolitan families" (see Figure 4.1).[108]

These apartment homes were a model for the housing policy North African Social Studies proposed in late 1953. Most of the outline for this policy differed little from what was already underway; nevertheless, the *Cahiers* called its approach a "distinct effort—technically and socially—

FIGURE 4.1. Children, presumably doing their homework, from one of the sixty-one Algerian families living in apartments sponsored by the Department of the Seine in Paris, Bagnolet, and Ivry-sur-Seine in 1955.

Source: Emile Pelletier, *Accueil et hébergement des Nord Africains dans le Département de la Seine*, 15 March 1956.

[geared to produce] a better adaptation." The *Cahiers* emphasized that Algerian families could still apply for any new program under the Courant Plan, especially the economic lodging programs, known as Logec (from *Logement économique*). To assist them, Leriche proposed a new organization to help families navigate the system and to find appropriate land on which to build or even to secure an architect. Finally, Leriche recommended the restrictions that limited Social and Sanitary Aid Fund monies for male workers be lifted so some funds could be set aside for family housing.[109]

Despite calls for a better, more efficient use of resources, the *Cahiers* and others in the welfare network rejected the "systematic clustering" of Algerian families. They preferred loosely coordinated, supplementary services that worked with general housing aid programs over "a full unification of method" for fear that the latter would become arbitrary, discriminatory, or lead to segregation. Leriche argued Muslim families' complex needs made a one-size-fits-all solution impossible. Only a case-by-case approach could truly identify each family's needs. Helping families gain access to these programs would facilitate "adaptation and integration" and ensure that they "harmoniously melt" into France. The loosely organized approach could be overseen by a committee of people "interested" in Algerians' welfare. It could sufficiently coordinate services, ensure families' needs got met, and prevent the segregation that might result from another approach.[110]

Yet, as numerous examples cited above show, Algerians were not simply the victims of poor timing. The preference for former colonists in managerial roles and the persistent reliance on pejorative stereotypes about Algerians, even among those who proclaimed their commitment to eradicating prejudice, made discrimination more likely. The start of the Algerian War in November 1954, which increased the size of the general population as well as its awareness of this migrant community, no doubt also made many wonder if Algerians deserved special help.

To counteract the growing sense of frustration and Algerian nationalist propaganda, French administrators expanded the government's public relations campaign without directly confronting discriminatory practices. This took numerous forms. One of the most straightforward appeared in a radio broadcast that delicately balanced near contradictory messages. It emphasized France's deep commitment to its Algerian citizens and made it clear that Algerians had to be proactive and help themselves. Not only did the program highlight France's generosity, but it implied any problems Algerians had were their own fault, without acknowledging the existence of or proposing solutions to discrimination.

The broadcast in May 1956 followed the typical format, mimicking an informal conversation between the better-informed Abdelhakim and his friend. It opened with Abdelhakim's explanation that they had not previously discussed family housing in part because "it only concerned those who live with their families." With family migration more common, it was important to remember that "all heads of household" had the right to all benefits, including a housing allocation, which helped "families of modest means to acquire decent housing that corresponds to their needs." Abdelhakim told his friend that in order to qualify, families had to contribute a percentage of their income (four percent for a family of six). In addition, families had to show their apartment met minimum space and cleanliness requirements and ensure the cash subsidy was actually used for housing and not to supplement income. When asked how to apply and how much a family could earn, Abdelhakim explained his friend should go to the office where he received his regular benefits for more information. Mimicking a common stereotype, Abdelhakim claimed he was unable to give his friend an exact calculation because "I'm not good at math," but added he knew families earning between 1,000 to 4,000 francs a month had applied. Finally, when asked about the difficulties in finding housing, Abdelhakim explained the state created the program to "facilitate things," but only "perseverance" would help his friend find "the home of his dreams." To reinforce the message of Algerians' personal responsibility for their situation, the segment ended with an exchange of proverbs: as you make your bed, so you must lie upon it, and God helps those who help themselves.[111]

The message, that France provided benefits Algerians could enjoy if they gave it their all, also provided a justification for limiting social housing to a select group of Algerians: those whom social workers and other service employees decided had sufficiently evolved in the educational programs. When Prefect Pelletier announced that the Seine had housed sixty-one families, he insisted it selected the most "deserving" and that the program could not be expanded.[112] The apartments, Pelletier explained, were for the "families of French citizens," which of course included Algerian families. But, Algerians could not receive any privileges; they could not receive "special funds" beyond what metropolitan citizens received, "unless [the funds] are used to build temporary housing or for special education that would permit their integration into normal housing."[113] The Committee for Lodging North African Families in Paris and a local social housing company (an unnamed HLM) that worked together articulated similar goals. They argued the state should make family housing a priority—committing more energy to this problem than to housing for Algerian workers—because better housing would facilitate the "integration" of deserving families. Not all families could adapt, and social housing officials tried to quantify Algerians' limitations. They estimated there were 1,500 families in the region needing housing, but social workers had judged only half were ready to move into HLM apartments. More could eventually move into social housing if they continued their education. Yet the goal had never been "to provide all the North African families with accommodations . . . but to make it possible for adaptable North African families to integrate into French society." Like Pelletier, these social housing providers made sure to qualify their promises so as not to raise the ire of metropolitan French on HLM waiting lists. Given the continued general housing crisis, Algerian family housing advocates never wanted to appear to give their clients privileged access to housing that surpassed that which most "Parisian families" enjoyed.[114]

INTEGRATION, as we have seen, meant something wholly different for male workers than for families. Residential segregation remained the norm for male workers before and after the state's commitment to a national solution via the SONACOTRAL. Algerian families, in contrast, had a more complex experience during the Fourth Republic. For the experts, moving into decent housing was the ultimate sign of a transformed family capable of a more complete assimilation into the national community. To reach the goal, a growing number of advocates and experts urged the government to invest in specialized family housing with an educational component because it offered the best chance of helping Algerians "to integrate harmoniously into our social structures." By 1956, four issues on housing appeared in the *Cahiers nord-africains* in five years, proclaiming that family housing had to be made a priority. Always careful to avoid the perception that housing aid for Algerian families privileged them in some way, advocates insisted that only "adapted and stabilized" families would live side by side with the metropolitan French. Housing the right families would solve the Algerian problem, which a growing number of advocates believed had been "complicated and aggravated" by the unnatural male migratory flows. To avoid a flood of the wrong families, service providers and experts also advocated quality control of migrants and promoted the repatriation of any family considered incapable of adapting.[115]

Once the war's violence and the Algerian family housing crisis expanded in the metropole in the latter part of the decade, North African Social Studies and others inside and outside the government campaigned vigorously for more services and transitional housing. What essentially amounted to mobile-home parks, which in theory temporarily segregated Algerian families, appeared to be the most palatable compromise between permanently segregating Algerians and moving ill-adapted families into the general population too soon. Transitional housing sites immediately improved residents' material conditions, but did so in an environment tailored to their supposed educational needs. The instruction that transitional housing offered was crucial, the *Cahiers* declared, because "it is not just in handing out a home with a bathroom that these nomads of the Sahara . . . will transform into deep-rooted Parisians."[116]

Women, charged with making the home, again became the heart of policies for and judgments about Algerians' acclimation to French society. Since women either "facilitated or rendered integration more difficult," educational services for them were incorporated into the housing process in order to maximize "the chances for success."[117] This in turn created more opportunities for social workers and housing managers to use their expertise when deciding a family's fate. If Algerians, and especially women, failed to reach the goals social workers, housing managers, and others set for them, the failure was depicted as an Algerian shortcoming. As the Algerian conflict intensified in the metropole, leaders in the welfare network continued denouncing segregation and tried fixing problems in the system. Yet, the politics of the war made it nearly impossible to acknowledge systemic discrimination. Instead, advocates continued to be hopeful about Algerians' ability and willingness to embrace modern French culture, which had added political meaning at the height of the war. They concentrated on reminding Algerians they could reach the goal, if only they tried a little harder.

5

Services and Surveillance
Welfare, the Police, and the Algerian War

IN THE SPRING OF 1958, the Fourth Republic collapsed under the weight of the Algerian crisis. *Ultras*, right-wing settlers and members of the French military who no longer trusted the metropolitan government's willingness to safeguard French Algeria, took to the barricades on 13 May. Legitimizing their actions as part of the revolutionary tradition, Generals Salan and Massu refused to put down the revolt and instead created a Committee of Public Safety that proclaimed its mission to be "the maintenance of Algeria as an integral part of France."[1] Within weeks, President Coty, fearing civil war, agreed to allow General Charles de Gaulle to form a new government.[2] De Gaulle immediately announced his readiness to establish a new Republic capable of uniting France. Sixty-eight percent of the French polled supported this. The ultras, taking responsibility for bringing de Gaulle and the Fifth Republic into existence, were convinced the new regime owed them unfailing loyalty.[3]

In constructing his new government, de Gaulle developed a two-pronged approach to the Algerian crisis. On the one hand, he expanded military operations, resulting in some of the war's most intense bloodshed, particularly in metropolitan France.[4] On the other hand, he emphasized France's benevolence, creating the Constantine Plan for Algeria and, in the metropole, the Social Action Fund for Algerian Workers and Their Families (Fonds d'action sociale pour les travailleurs algériens en métropole et leurs familles, FAS). This approach underscores the tensions and contradictions inherent in all French policy and action for Algerians. In the particular circumstances of the early Fifth Republic (1958–1962), when close collaboration between colonial civil and military authorities and metropolitan civilian and police officials regularized discriminatory practices, arbitrary arrests, and even torture,[5] welfare programs became the quintessential material and rhetorical tool on all levels and on both sides of the conflict. Examined in historical context, these intertwined projects—the Social Action Fund financed Constantine Plan services in Algeria—illustrate just how closely linked France and Algeria continued to be in the shadow of Algerian independence. Policies, personnel, and social action moved fluidly as the state tried to monitor and to eliminate anyone suspected of subversion.

Announcing his plan to transform Algeria in Constantine on 3 October 1958, de Gaulle promised to develop human and natural resources so that every Algerian would have a "share in what modern civilization can and must bring to men in terms of well-being and dignity." His speech showed how the new language of development fit with the paternalism of colonialism and the expanding welfare state. He reassured his audience, which included the international community as much as the French and Algerian people, that France accepted its "duty" to help bring "evolution" and warned that if critics stood in the way of the plan France offered, with arms outstretched in "brotherhood," Algeria would remain stagnant.[6] In the metropole, de Gaulle's government recommitted to the metropolitan welfare network, creating the Social Action Fund and appointing a special delegate in charge of social action for Algerian migrants who reported directly to Prime Minister Michel Debré. An ardent supporter of French Algeria, Debré also worked closely with Algerian Affairs, Muslim Affairs Service, the police, and others to bring social services under the control of an elaborate system of surveillance and repression to counteract the FLN's power and to win suggestible Algerians over to France's side by employing all available forms of "political and psychological action."[7]

Many within the service apparatus condemned violence, even if they had not yet let go of the dream of French Algeria. When the prime minister's office asked key officials to provide suggestions about how to approach the Algerian problem, the Muslim Affairs Service director insisted that social action's "delicate task" was to counter "nationalist and anti-French sentiments" without encouraging Algerians' feelings "of isolation, maladjustment and inferiority." The "ultimate goal" of the welfare programs, he continued, was "to integrate" Algerians into the metropole by ensuring they had access to "normal" services offered to "all other citizens."[8] One of the central tensions analyzed in this book is how for some people the welfare network provided window dressing that enabled and hid the elimination of the Algerian threat, while for others it remained a deep-rooted calling. All actors, including Algerian recipients of services, made a range of choices within the constraints of this historical context. The work of certain service providers was intimately intertwined with police and military operations. Others shared the police's commitment to rout the FLN, but rejected repressive tactics and became, to varying degrees, eloquent and persistent critics of state-sponsored violence.

Advocates insisted their work was based on respect and "fraternity" and continued to fashion themselves as Algerians' protectors.[9] Believing Algerian nationalism was the most egregious impediment to Algerians' inclusion in French society, most characterized the majority of the Algerian population as disapproving of and without voluntary ties to the FLN. Instead, even as secret negotiations were underway to end the war, representatives of the social welfare network continued to insist Algerians had "diverse handicaps." Nationalists' power of seduction made it necessary for services "to multiply, reinforce and personalize the links between each migrant and the metropolitan population, [and] to neutralize the themes of propaganda preferred by the FLN."[10]

These assumptions about Algerians' ineptitude and vulnerability belie the complex ties Algerian migrants had to France and to Algeria. Many Algerians understood the system, signed up for family allowances, and lodged complaints using the language of citizenship to demand their right to social benefits. Algerians differentiated between services, avoided some and mitigated the intrusion of others while trying to improve their material conditions. Some service providers never considered the possibility that Algerians could manipulate both sides; Algerians told representatives of the French system and the FLN what they wanted to hear in order to survive.

The political realities also circumscribed the responses of the welfare network's actors. In many cases, the choices made by certain administrators and direct providers—including Michel Massenet, Germaine Tillion, Nelly Forget, and Brigitte Gall—illuminated the sharp contrast between their commitment to fighting repression and the state's widespread use of violence. At the same time, social service administrators and providers on both sides of the Mediterranean had to come to terms with their relationship to the war, particularly as the lines between civil and police/military action blurred. For most, their goals, their funding, their very existence depended on a commitment to undermining the FLN and to naturalizing France's civilizing mission. The infusion of government resources expanded services and reinforced the ties between the national agenda and private, local, and state programs.

With the stakes so high and the desire to break the FLN so strong, welfare providers could not avoid involvement in the war either directly or indirectly. Some dedicated providers were caught up in the war, becoming victims of FLN, police, or Secret Army Organization (Organisation de l'armée secrète, OAS) retaliations against suspected conspirators. Others, within the state, particularly those aligned with the military and the police, spotlighted the welfare network's activities because they still offered the best proof of France's generosity. Framed increasingly in new development aid language, services formed part of a campaign to show the world—the United Nations, the United States, and others paying close attention to Algeria's fight for independence[11]—that France did the right thing for its citizens.

Mounting Violence in the Metropole

Algerians, particularly in and around Paris, faced arbitrary, brutal treatment from both the FLN and the French police with growing frequency from 1957. Already targeted as undesirables by a police force that sought to criminalize their misery,[12] migrants got caught up in the bloody civil war between the French Federation of the FLN and Messali Hajj's Mouvement national algérien (MNA) when the former crushed its rival and took control of the metropole's lucrative resources.[13] Once it largely eliminated the MNA, the FLN required Algerian men to contribute thirty-five francs a month, or roughly five percent of their salary. Married couples paid fifty francs a month, a significant expense for single-income families. On top of these ostensibly voluntary contributions, the FLN required special contributions on holidays, such as the anniversary of the outbreak of hostilities in Algeria, 1 November 1954. Violence and intimidation compelled anyone who at first refused or felt they could not afford to contribute.[14] The FLN also collected significant revenue from prostitution. Already in 1954 the Labor Ministry estimated two thousand young Algerian women had "willingly come [to Paris] alone. Without any familial ties . . . they slip into prostitution."[15] Like all others, sex workers either willingly participated in the nationalist cause or were coerced to do so. By the end of the decade, prostitutes made significant contributions, often more than workingmen (sixty francs a month in Pigalle, eighty francs in Clichy, and as much as one hundred francs on the Champs Elysées). In addition, larger hotels, those with twenty or more sex workers, collected thousands of francs per month in sometimes forced contributions from male clients.[16] Ali Haroun, the French Federation's Minister of Information, reported that, all in all, roughly eighty percent (forty-seven million francs in 1960 alone) of the budget for the Provisional Government in Algeria came from Algerians living France.[17]

Although the French government's desire to coordinate police surveillance began early in the decade, the war provided cause and justification for the expansion of its multipronged approach to crush Algerian nationalism. Beginning with the extension of special powers in Algeria in March 1956, the Interior Ministry's role and powers on both sides of the Mediterranean grew exponentially.[18] Over the next two years, the state expanded its policing powers, opened internment camps to hold Algerian suspects, and, in March 1958, appointed Maurice Papon chief of police in Paris, all to eradicate the threat of the FLN.[19]

Papon implemented a system of programs and policies to break the FLN's financial and military strength, particularly once the seventh *wilaya*, the FLN's term for its military commands, opened in the metropole in August 1958.[20] This included special police brigades and information services staffed with people brought in from Algeria. Among the most infamous were the Technical Assistance Service and the Auxiliary Police Force. The former, led by several administrators of a similar program in Algeria, tried to establish paternal relationships through welfare services that collected information about Algerians.[21] The Technical Assistance Service's Commander Cunibile hoped to build trust among Algerians that would eventually inspire them to make "confessions" about FLN activities. Echoing Godin's surveillance program from the interwar period, by 1960 Cunibile's office had files on 70,000 individuals, nearly half the Algerians in the Paris region.[22]

When these tactics did not produce the desired effect, in September 1958 Prime Minister Debré gave the order to "to destroy" the rebellion.[23] To that end, in 1960, the Technical Assistance Service brought in indigenous Algerian army detachments, known as *harkis*, to deepen the state's infiltration of the Algerian population.[24] The new Auxiliary Police Force, made up of 350 harkis, along with other regular and special police forces, terrorized Algerians. The police profiled Algerians in public places such as buses; conducted bogus, humiliating searches; destroyed identification papers; and detained people at random. These practices reinforced stereotypes about Algerians' supposed savagery and, when only harki officers were involved, left the impression that the violence perpetrated was strictly intra-Algerian.[25] The harkis were particularly feared because, as one female militant remembered, "they beat [and] they burned everything that got in their way."[26] After raiding rooming houses in Paris' Goutte d'Or, the harkis set up torture chambers in basements, which further terrorized prisoners and neighbors who heard the cries until Debré ordered the harkis pulled back in June 1961.[27]

In October 1961, the Interministerial Committee approved Papon's proposal to impose an unprecedented curfew on the Algerian population.[28] The decision to so blatantly target this segment of the citizenry inspired protest among French politicians, unions, and the Algerian migrant community. The FLN responded by organizing a series of peaceful, public demonstrations over several days to protest years of humiliation and police brutality, including the curfew. Though the FLN usually embraced violence when bringing attention to its cause, this time it hoped to use peaceful methods to bring injustices to the attention of all Parisians and the international community.[29]

By all accounts, the protests, organized to begin on 17 October 1961, took Algerians from Paris' periphery to its center with demonstrations along Paris' main arteries: from the boulevards Saint-Michel and Saint-Germain to the National Assembly and in the area around the Arc de Triomphe and the Champs Elysées.[30] The FLN used coercion and peer-pressure to ensure all Algerians—including small children—marched.[31] As one woman put it, "We were obliged to march, but we wanted to march because we had nothing to lose."[32]

Official accounts insisted that two people died, but it is now clear that dozens were killed, and thousands more were arrested and detained, and many deported to unknown fates.[33] In the days that followed, women who participated in the initial demonstrations organized protests against the arrest and disappearance of male relatives (see Figure 5.1). To disband the protests, the police claimed they "accompanied" the female protesters to "social centers . . . open to serve them."[34] These women were not taken to social centers; most were bused to Nanterre, even if it meant they

FIGURE 5.1. From "1,000 Algerian Women and 550 Children Rounded Up Yesterday in Paris," an article in the Communist daily *L'Humanité*, 21 October 1961. The caption reads: "In the streets, in police vans, and even when they were crowded into internment centers, Algerian women protested."
Source: Courtesy of *L'Humanité*.

had to walk or to take public transportation to homes elsewhere in the region.[35] The official explanation, however, probably seemed plausible to many at the time since the French government had both prioritized social services and "distanced" (*dissociées*) them from police activities.[36]

The Social Action Fund and the Coordination of Services

The Social Action Fund, established by ordinance in October 1958, became the centerpiece of the Fifth Republic's initiative to prioritize welfare programs. It oversaw the vast majority of funding portioned out to organizations that provided services to Algerians on both sides of the Mediterranean.[37] Taking shape over the months that followed, the Social Action Fund developed organizational and financial structures that allowed it to coordinate all social services for Algerians. Its board of directors included the prime minister's representatives and officials from other key government agencies, such as the Labor, Finance, and Public Health and Population Ministries, Social Security, and the colonial government.[38] This original group expanded repeatedly during the final years of the Algerian War.[39] The first major addition came in January 1959 when Prime Minister Michel Debré named Michel Massenet, the former IGAME who had been working for Information Minister Jacques Soustelle since June 1958, as his representative in charge of social intervention for French Muslims from Algeria in the metropole. In addition to becoming the most powerful member of the board of the Social Action Fund, Massenet sat on the boards of numerous other pertinent government offices and organizations, including the newly reincarnated Interministerial Committee, the Interior Ministry's Muslim Affairs Service, the SONACOTRAL, and various association boards, including the Aid Commission for North Africans in the Metropole, to ensure support for the prime minister's programs and goals.[40]

Even before his official appointment as Debré's special representative, Massenet had been working behind the scenes. According to Massenet's recollections from nearly forty years later, de Gaulle summoned him to the Elysée Palace to oversee "the problem of Algerians in France." A dozen others had already rejected what was a thankless job, but Massenet believed it was his destiny.[41] Before the end of 1958, Massenet traveled to Nanterre, the first of many visits to assess the situation in a town synonymous with the Algerian problem.[42] And, even though the Fund's president, Jacques Doublet (a veteran of the interwar pronatalist movement, the Carrel Foundation, and Mauco's High Committee on Population and the Family),[43] and its director, Guy de Serre de Justignac, managed daily affairs and the laborious process of doling out subventions, Massenet had considerable control over decision making for both the Social Action Fund and the entire Algerian welfare network. The Social Action Fund archives demonstrate that welfare organizations applying for aid understood who made the decisions; in many cases association staff addressed letters directly to Massenet, referring to him as the director of the Social Action Fund.[44] At the June 1961 meeting, Doublet "paid homage" to the "essential role" Massenet played in day-to-day operations and in building consensus among ministries that often had divergent funding priorities.[45] The Labor, Interior (particularly through its Muslim Affairs Service), and the Public Health and Population Ministries continued to fund programs emphasizing what their leaders saw as the most pressing issues.[46] Yet, Massenet, representing the prime minister, never hesitated to remind colleagues that their work should always act as a "supplement" to that of the Fund.[47]

The power de Gaulle and Debré invested in social action as part of the war effort came in large measure from the purse. Even if there were internal controversies about exactly how to fill the Social Action Fund's coffers,[48] the Fund represented the Fifth Republic's final, concerted effort to put the long-standing family allowance controversy to rest. The Fund distributed money Algerians contributed to the system. Still unwilling to make direct retroactive payments to families in Algeria that might put cash into the hands of the FLN, de Gaulle's new government intended to use these funds as part of its two-pronged plan to end the crisis: buying goodwill and making France's commitment to Algerians clear to domestic and international detractors.[49]

The Social Action Fund built upon and continued the Algerian welfare network's objectives. The Fund insisted that it complemented the welfare state. Likewise, it worked to balance the "tensions" between assistance—by addressing Algerians' "handicaps" through transitional services that encouraged their "integration"—and what might be perceived as impulses to privilege Algerians over metropolitans. Instead, it encouraged a *brassage*, or mixing, of the two communities to eliminate discrimination. To achieve its mandate, the Fund addressed four areas the state (*les pouvoirs publics*) prioritized: ending the bidonville problem; promoting Algerians' "intellectual and professional" qualifications to benefit the economy; encouraging "evolution," especially among youths and families; and filling any "gaps in the existing social network."[50]

A brief examination of the organizations and projects the Fund supported clarifies its interpretation of these priorities. In all, it partially funded about 150 private associations, aided local governmental projects, and sponsored over two hundred social counselors who worked with various direct service providers.[51] These included nearly all the organizations examined in previous chapters, which benefited from "a larger and more diversified" commitment to "social action."[52] For its first year of operations (1959), the Fund split its budget of nearly 3 billion old francs between Algeria and the metropole. Just over a third, more than 1 billion old francs, went for metropolitan projects, and nearly two-thirds, over 1.7 billion old francs, were transferred back to Algeria.[53]

To respond to metropolitan priorities, the first annual budget allocated about fifty-eight percent of metropolitan funds to single male and family housing, twenty percent to job training, eleven percent to education, and nine percent to youth services. The final two percent, or 20 million old francs, went to North African Family Social Service. Even though all associations applying for funds had to submit applications, which the board used to make its determinations, North African Family Social Service and a handful of other organizations had special privileges. They included the SONACOTRAL and Father Ghys' other association, Moral Assistance for North Africans. The latter received 45 million old francs, which it used for a wide variety of its services, from specialized youth services and dormitories for young Algerian men to educational services including basic education for men and women, vocational training programs, and financial support for North African Social Studies, which published the *Cahiers nord-africains*. The board evaluated all projects individually (including all SONACOTRAL projects), but Ghys' organizations merited individual lines in the Social Action Fund's annual budget and essentially received pre-approval.[54]

When North African Family Social Service requested an increase in its annual subvention from 200,000 to 250,000 new francs in 1960,[55] Massenet preempted board members' questions by announcing that he had just met with and assured Director Renée Bley that it would be approved. The association's work was critical; Massenet considered it "a 'pilot service.' . . . Its action serves as a model for all services dealing with Algerians." Concurring, the representative of the Public Health Ministry described North African Family Social Service as a "motor" for the entire network.[56] The expertise and reach North African Family Social Service acquired in its first decade made it *the* association to which all others turned. By 1958, it had eight offices and touted that approximately two-thirds of the estimated 15,000 Algerian families (with 50,000 children) in France were within reach of a North African Family Social Service office or one of the twenty-six social centers it managed.[57] The next year, its social workers conducted 11,269 home visits and logged 43,771 calls to other public and private service providers on Algerians' behalf.[58] Moreover, it directly participated in programs managed by state agencies and many other associations, trained social workers, and decided if Algerians could be integrated into French society.[59]

North African Family Social Service's prominent role in the network demonstrates how vital building horizontal and vertical relationships was to the Social Action Fund's approach.[60] Massenet not only corresponded with agencies the Social Action Fund supported, but regularly traveled to regions with significant Algerian populations to reinforce his support for local leaders and programs and to monitor the progress of specific projects. He visited offices and projects in and around Paris and well beyond, traveling to Lyon, Marseille, and Algeria. Marseille received special attention. As a main port of entry, its problems were not "local but . . . national." And while some board members thought the city's request for an additional 35,000 new francs in June 1960 (to ease the burden on its overtaxed services) would set "a dangerous precedent," Massenet pushed dissenting board members to accept the request by invoking the authority of the prime minister.[61]

Massenet, who spoke for Prime Minister Debré in high-level meetings of the organizations that made up the Algerian welfare network, had less influence beyond these circles. The Algerian welfare network played a vital role in the war on Algerian nationalism, but its leadership held little sway with civilian and military leaders in Algeria or with the Paris police.

The Constantine Plan and Services in Algeria

The Constantine Plan, the Fifth Republic's massive project to remake Algeria, was part of a long tradition of programs the colonial government and private entities set up for Algerians. After 1945, Catholic missionaries continued to play a key role. In 1950, Abbé Scotto sent Marie-Renée Chéné, a social worker, to the Boubsila-Berardi bidonville of east Algiers' Hussien-Dey district. Within a year members of the Swiss-based Civil Service International and others joined her in work that Nelly Forget, a young French member of the Civil Service International, remembered as "improvised social-educative" programs implemented with "generosity and conviction" if few resources.[62]

These services, which provided remedial education, medical clinics, and other services, including some housing,[63] remained relatively obscure until 1955 when the new governor-general, Jacques Soustelle, implemented an integrationist agenda meant to pacify the "Algerian rebels" through a reform of the "sociopolitical administration." As James Le Sueur has argued, Soustelle used his credentials as a prominent anthropologist to counter the growing leftist intellectual protest against French policies and to legitimize a paternalistic reform he envisioned would champion France as the "bearer of progress and civilization."[64] A specialist in Latin American ethnography, Soustelle had done fieldwork in Mexico, became the assistant director of the Musée de l'homme in 1938, and joined de Gaulle in London during the war. Building on his experiences, Soustelle argued that educational programs in Algeria should follow a model created to pacify Mexico's indigenous populations in the decades after the 1910 Revolution.[65]

To implement a new educational program that would, according to Soustelle, "get rid of ignorance and indifference, sisters of poverty and inspirations of despair," he called upon fellow anthropologist and resistor Germaine Tillion.[66] Tillion had done fieldwork in the Aurès Mountains' Berber communities in the 1930s and worked with Soustelle at the Musée de l'homme before being sent to Ravensbrück (with her mother) in 1942 for resistance activities. In 1954, she returned to Algeria after a fourteen-year absence, in part because her mentor, Louis Massignon, "demanded" (*exigea*) she go.[67] He was certain Tillion had the moral and intellectual capital to investigate the allegations of violence and to protect "the civilian population."[68] Tillion initially hesitated when Soustelle asked her to construct what he called, in a speech to the Algerian Assembly, "cultural missions."[69] She eventually agreed, citing the deteriorating situation in Algeria—with police practices that reminded her of occupied France and living conditions that had spiraled into a crisis she famously described as the "pauperization" (*clochardisation*) of the Algerian people. For Tillion, the "destruction of rural structures and rapid urbanization" caused a "general and vertical drop in the standard of living."[70]

Tillion envisioned a series of new centers where the whole country, "thanks to its young people, could make up for the technical delay we call 'underdevelopment.'"[71] Her well-known assessment of the Algerian situation, *Algeria: The Realities*, first published in 1957, put most of the blame for Algeria's misery on rapid population growth, which could not be resolved with easy fixes—"food . . . birth control . . . or cholera" treatments. Instead, a shift in approach was needed, one that required a new way of thinking and a massive investment in Algeria's future. Unless France educated "*all the children*" and provided "a *trade* and a *job* for all adults," then the "unconditional revolt" underway would attract the most destitute, who are offered "no other alternatives"—no "hope."[72]

With support from the Algerian branch of the Education Ministry, Tillion set about creating the Social Center Service. She relied on the expertise of many of those already providing services to Algerians in Algeria and France. Charles Aguesse, a veteran educator, became the first director. Together, with Chéné, Forget, and Rabia Lacheref, a well-known Algerian midwife, they opened the first center in Hussien-Dey, making it a model and training center for the program.[73] In the first two years, Aguesse hired staff for thirty centers. At first, staff trained in France, some with the North African Family Social Service. In 1960, the Social Action Fund opened a home economics training center in Algiers that social center staff attended.[74]

Not ready to give up on the possibility of reconciliation, Tillion insisted it would be too easy to "put the blame for everything on that hoary scapegoat: colonialism."[75] The Social Center Service embodied her solution: bringing French and Algerian men and women together to solve the country's most dire problems. The Service integrated the staff, with mostly Algerian men (directors) and French women (social workers) working together. Crossing ethnic and gender lines, working in the poorest communities, and doing so without military oversight (unlike the Special Administrative Sections, which worked closely with the authorities), the Social Center Service quickly stirred up the colonial regime's ire. As Tillion recollected, "every Muslim was a suspect, every Frenchman who frequented Algerian Muslims was equally" suspect. In 1957, in the first of several raids on the social centers, authorities arrested seventeen staff members, including Forget.[76] Most were acquitted of charges and released, but nearly all—men and women—were abused or tortured and expected to leave Algeria. One young Algerian man "disappeared" while in custody.[77] Tillion used her connections—she had been at Ravensbrück with de Gaulle's niece—to play a vital role in the release of the Service's staff, as well as many others condemned to death.[78]

After the 1957 arrests, the Service continued its work, offering basic educational programs for children, gender-specific skills programs for adults, and help navigating the social services bureaucracy. According to Forget, the Service intended to "at once create elites and help the masses evolve" to a point where they could gain access to "modern life."[79] Programs for girls and women focused on "'domestic arts' and hygiene," with instruction in everything from child rearing to sewing (see Figures 5.2 and 5.3).[80] The metropole's North African Family Social Service, which Tillion helped Ghys create and on whose board she served, provided the model for the new services in Algeria.

To implement his integrationist reform agenda, Soustelle also created Specialized Administrative Sections. The social centers, which claimed to uphold "strict political neutrality,"[81] were punished for suspicion of sympathy for the FLN. The Specialized Sections, which provided the model for

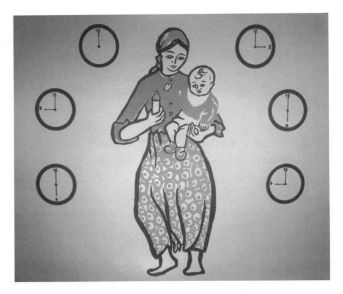

FIGURE 5.2. An example of classroom materials, including lesson plans, posters, printed booklets, and short films created by the Social Center Service for distribution in its centers. This poster was displayed in coordination with texts and films as part of a course on child care. It emphasized bottle-feeding at regular intervals.

Source: Reprinted with the permission of the Association Germaine Tillion.

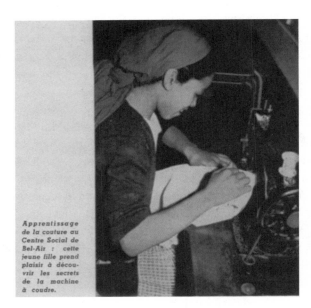

Apprentissage
de la couture au
Centre Social de
Bel-Air : cette
jeune fille prend
plaisir à décou-
vrir les secrets
de la machine
à coudre.

FIGURE 5.3. A sewing class student at the Bel-Air Social Center in Algiers. The caption reads, in part, "this young woman takes pleasure in discovering the sewing machine's secrets."

Source: Direction générale de l'éducation nationale en Algérie, Le service des centres sociaux en Algérie, 3. Reprinted with the permission of the Association Germaine Tillion.

the metropole's Technical Assistance Service and the Auxiliary Police Force, had dual "civil and military missions." Recruited from army officers and Algerian Affairs bureaucrats, these units had administrative, social, educational and economic goals.[82] To achieve its objectives, the Specialized Sections, like all the other programs, believed that women were at the heart of the battle since "ultimately, to promote the evolution of the woman was to promote the long-term evolution of their husband and their children [sic]." As a result, the Sections operated socio-educational centers where women learned practical skills—from knitting and sewing to child care—and could be "liberated" from what administrators imagined as their isolated, cloistered lives.[83] Like other colonial reforms, these programs functioned as a façade for the mission to collect information and to control the population.[84] Based on Soustelle's sense that Algeria's insufficient bureaucratic structures did not allow for accurate record keeping, which in turn fostered corruption, the Specialized Administrative Sections leaders would bring "order" to Algeria.[85] By enforcing civil codes, including the 1955 law that required all French citizens to obtain a national identification card,[86] these bureaucrats collected the most accurate census data to date (for the regions that had Specialized Sections), which in turn provided critical information the French army used in the war against Algerian nationalists.[87]

When de Gaulle announced his proposal for Algerian modernization, the state folded this and other programs into the new plan. In fact, the new government built the massive Constantine Plan, which the colonial administrators depicted as a way to provide Algeria with everything "modern civilization" had to offer,[88] on smaller-scale initiatives already underway.[89] It envisioned the Constantine Plan as a series of five-year plans that would allow Algerians to make up for their nation's "several centuries'" lag behind the West. Influenced by modernization theory and colonial discourses, the plan's architects depicted this far-reaching effort as one coherent endeavor that did "not dream of imposing technical or human progress from the outside, but will help them organize and give them the tools to do for themselves."[90]

In the first five years (1959–1963), the Constantine Plan's administrators promised to redistribute nearly 700,000 acres of land to Muslim farmers, begin exploiting the oil reserves of the Sahara desert, build heavy industries (including metallurgical and chemical plants), construct massive public works projects, create 400,000 jobs, house one million people, and provide basic education for the majority of Algeria's children (both boys and girls). An estimated four billion dollars would be needed to ensure success; programs underway in the first two years spent $450 million and $600 million, respectively.[91]

Housing occupied a key place in the Constantine Plan. According to Zeynep Çelik, authorities believed that "housing would cure the social ills of Algerian society and turn the local people into docile members of a French-dominated system." The plan concentrated on improving housing and schools because they were "the principle instruments for projecting Western consumer society onto Algerian society." Following this logic, the revolt would end if Algerians could be introduced and grow accustomed to the material benefits of France. Therefore, housing development received more funding than any other element in the social service portion of the Constantine Plan, with the exception of education. Between 1959 and 1962, it committed 2.6 billion francs to housing and the demolition of bidonvilles.[92]

The plan separated housing into two sections: rural and urban. Authorities estimated social housing construction companies would need to build about 56,000 residential units (new and renovated) in urban areas each year for ten years to solve the crisis and provide more homes as the population continued to expand. Work began in 1960 on a 25,000-unit project on the outskirts of Algiers and a 30,000-unit project in Bône, in addition to projects in smaller cities. By 1962, the plan had nearly reached its goal, having constructed or renovated 142,000 units—only 7,000 short of the objective—in urban centers. The urban development portion of the plan promised housing for low-, middle-, and higher-income families, of which up to ninety percent would be earmarked for Muslims.[93]

The vast majority of Algerians moved into apartments complexes for low-income families. In this respect, the housing program succeeded in increasing the standard of living for residents in these complexes by as much as thirty percent.[94] Yet, the material benefits did not seduce inhabitants into embracing French rule. Services had not worked before; this latest step could hardly transform Algerians into compliant subjects. In other words, de Gaulle's two-pronged approach—simultaneously increasing the social reform campaign (the Constantine Plan) and the military campaign (the Challe Plan)—failed to achieve its ultimate goals. No matter how the French government repackaged its presence in Algeria, General Challe's counterinsurgency operations did not succeed in destroying the Algerian army or in winning over the Algerian people.[95]

The scope of the urban housing projects paled in comparison to what the Constantine Plan claimed to offer Algeria's peasants. Challe made forced resettlement a strategic part of his strategy for people living in small towns and farming villages where FLN insurgents were believed to hide. Simultaneously, Paul Delouvrier, the technical consultant in charge of the rural resettlement and pacification programs, began to refer to the relocations as a "thousand 'new villages.'" Delouvrier believed resettlement could only be considered successful if it was "a step toward the village, viable sociological unity, and symbolic progress in the countryside." He promised to replace the temporary refugee camps with permanent villages. With the resources necessary for daily life and economic development, the New Villages, he claimed, would finally win over the peasantry.[96]

Officially, the Thousand New Villages project was a great success. It helped the military control the Algerian peasantry and led to "the permanent relocation of more than a million persons under better economic and social conditions than they had previously known"—or so it was portrayed to the international community. The New Villages program, co-opted by the Constantine Plan because of the prestige it would bring, seemed to be the perfect way to undercut FLN support in the countryside.[97]

French propaganda marketed all of these programs domestically and abroad as indicative of the government's altruism. The social centers were renamed "Centers for Social Education" to indicate their vital role in the Constantine Plan's promise to educate all Algerians. De Gaulle's initiative pumped in new funding, particularly from the Social Action Fund, and pressed for the construction of more centers—doubling the number to sixty in 1959 and again to one hundred and twenty by 1962.[98] While the social centers accepted the metropole's demands to expand their work, they continued to meet violent resistance from both the FLN and the ultras. Viewing them as symbols of "Franco-Muslim solidarity," the ultras mounted a campaign in the press against the centers, claiming the FLN and its sympathizers had infiltrated them to aid the enemy. This resulted in another wave of police harassment, arrests, torture, and convictions culminating in the OAS assassination of six of the Social Center Service's leaders, including novelist Mouloud Ferraoun and historian Max Marchand, the Service's third director, just three days before the signing of the Evian Accords, which led to Algeria's independence.[99]

The leadership of the Social Action Fund, which sponsored both the Social Center Service and Specialized Administrative Sections as part of the

Constantine Plan, had heated discussions with the colonial government's representative to the Fund's board of directors, Roger Gouinguenet, about where money went in Algeria. As head of social action in Algeria, Gouinguenet managed two-thirds of the Social Action Fund's budget (over 1.7 billion old francs in 1959). The Fund had significant sway over how its funds were spent in the metropole; in Algeria, local governmental offices allocated funds to specific projects.[100] When the Fund's board demanded "total assurance" about spending, Gouinguenet claimed that he could not provide "a detailed program" because the administration had not yet "elaborated" its plan.[101] In response, Massenet traveled to Algeria in December 1959 to see for himself how funds were allocated.[102] Unable to sway colonial officials, Massenet acquiesced to colonial authorities' stone walling. Throughout the final years of the war, Gouinguenet repeatedly requested and received more resources, even though the completion record for projects in Algeria continued to lag significantly behind that of projects in the metropole.[103] The Social Action Fund's board, apparently unable to address this relative lack of success, stopped pressing about exactly where the money (which came from deductions from Algerian migrant workers' salaries) went in Algeria.

Michel Cornaton's comprehensive study of the system of relocation camps vividly demonstrates the radical disconnect between the French government's claims of reform and investment and what the Algerian people actually endured. Even with the new packaging, "resettlement had only military objectives." The Thousand New Villages project, staffed by the Specialized Administrative Sections, was part of a massive military operation that began in 1955 when French forces began declaring towns and villages "prohibited zones." By the end of the war, Cornaton estimates the French had forcibly displaced several million Algerians. Any humanitarian concerns acted as a window dressing for camps that barely possessed the basic necessities for everyday life. The inhabitants moved under duress. They arrived in their homes in the New Villages the same way as those sent to temporary resettlement camps, following violent raids and forced marches that often left whole villages burned.[104] Women who escaped life in the camps for the bidonvilles of Paris described the ordeal as an exodus. "We had to abandon everything and leave on the back roads. Empty handed. Running, with a child on our backs, terrified we would be mowed down by machine gun fire or artillery shells."[105] In many ways the women who recounted their stories were the lucky ones. They managed to reach their husbands or other family members in France.

Those who did not die or escape faced life in places that looked more like military bases than country villages. The locations had been chosen with surveillance requirements rather than the inhabitants' living conditions in mind. Since low-lying, open areas with little vegetation made it easier to oversee the camps and to prevent inhabitants from having contact with FLN forces, the Special Administrative Services situated the villages in floodplains or in areas where nothing grew. The inhospitable concrete block constructions offered no relief from the extremes in weather, too hot when the sun beat down on them and freezing cold at night.[106]

Furthermore, although colonial civil servants in these new villages set up schools, artisan shops (blacksmiths, etc.), and systems for the distribution of food and other basic goods, the village administrators did not provide for the new residents' livelihoods. Those close to their homes tried to care for the livestock and crops left behind, but most had to abandon their old lives completely. Those who tried to cultivate the ground surrounding their new homes often found it could not support crops.[107] Dalila, a woman living near Paris, explained, "Soldiers chased my mother, brothers and sisters from their village. . . . Forced them to live in a camp [with the other villagers] and the officers refused to allow [them] to return home to feed their livestock. Abandoned, [the sheep] starved to death. Authorities even prohibited [her family] from cultivating their fields."[108] Dressed up for international observers as part of a massive development project that would bring Algeria into the civilized world, the Thousand New Villages program terrorized poor peasants who lost everything.

The ultimate goal, to break the rebellion and win over the rural populace, failed even as the French government kept up its rhetoric. In sheer numbers, the French claimed victory. From October 1959 to April 1960, the number of villages grew to 700, and the goal of 1,000 had been surpassed by January 1961. By the fall of 1960, over one million people lived in these villages, with another 650,000 still in temporary refugee camps.[109]

Algerian Responses in the Metropole

Migrating to metropolitan France became one Algerian response to the violence of the war. The 350,000 or more Algerian migrants reacted to new surroundings in a range of ways and the state's responses to their demands shifted with the phases of the war. Some came to protect themselves from the violence of the war with France and the civil war between nationalist factions, some for ideological reasons related to their nation's struggle for independence, and some for a combination of these reasons and to better their material conditions by demanding their rights as French citizens. All responses were complex, however, because the dual strong arms of the FLN and of the French police placed most Algerians in an impossible situation. On the one hand, the FLN, which had significant control in the bidonvilles, made contributions mandatory. On the other hand, police raids terrorized most of the population and sent those suspected of supporting the rebellion to internment camps.

Most accounts of Algerians' political action in France define it narrowly, focusing on FLN activities and on events like the protests of October 1961. Yet, for most Algerians, refusing to be invisible by making demands for a better life was an overtly political action. The archives demonstrate that throughout the last years of the war Algerians in France used the language of rights to demand what the state owed them as citizens. The struggle to gain the benefits of citizenship, however, should not be interpreted as a simple acceptance of French integrationist policy. Seeking to build a future in France by no means lessened Algerians' hope for or commitment to the end of French colonialism. Determining Algerians' intentions in the final years of the war is difficult, in large measure because of the high stakes associated with all behaviors. Paulette Péju, writing as a contemporary witness, argues that even the attitudes of the harkis, whose loyalties would at first glance appear straightforward, should not be oversimplified. Many contributed to the FLN while in the French military; some supported France but refused to reenlist even with incentives once they realized what they were expected to do.[110] One cannot, therefore, generalize about Algerians' responses during this volatile period, since self-preservation required navigating all sides of the conflict.

Conflicted or not, Algerians refused to accept isolation from French society and demanded the entitlements owed to them. As we have seen, thousands of Algerian families successfully claimed family allowance benefits, often with the help of social service organizations. By 1960, the Family Allowances Bureau in Lyon paid out benefits to 6,254 Algerian families, a startlingly large number since other statistics from the period estimated the Algerian family population in the Rhône region to be much lower.[111]

Whether helped by welfare organizations or via their own initiative, Algerians filed hundreds of requests and complaints about welfare benefits with the Muslim Affairs Bureau for the Prefecture of the Bouches-du-

Rhône. Some requested duplicate copies of their *livret de famille* (family record book), an indispensable document without which participation in the French welfare state is impossible. Others wrote to complain when family allowance checks arrived late or never came at all or requested emergency aid when the male head of household was recovering from injury or illness or died leaving a wife and several children. Still others sought assistance to bring family members to France or requested government funds to move back to Algeria. Correspondence generally had one thing in common: Algerians were well aware of their rights as citizens and used this language to claim benefits.[112]

In the case of the Ahmed family, Mr. Ahmed, a fifty-seven-year-old military veteran and agricultural worker employed by small farmers in the town of Auberts, wrote to the Muslim Affairs Bureau on 1 December 1958 explaining:

I am a Muslim with French nationality. . . . I do not receive family allowances, even though my large family gives me the right to them. This remains the case in spite of numerous complaints. My wife is expecting a baby in early January. She has taken all the steps to enroll and has completed all necessary appointments. She still has not received even a partial payment for her prenatal allowances. . . . [Therefore,] I respectfully ask why this honest, peace-loving, hardworking father of a family is ostracized in this way.

Within a month, the family received restitution in the amount of 81,900 francs for undistributed benefits, and his wife began receiving family allowances. "Thanks to you," Ahmed replied to regional officials, his family could live "a better life."[113] Mr. Ahmed clearly understood how the bureaucracy functioned, believing if he followed procedures, he would reap the rewards. Ahmed's frank approach, possibly influenced by his military service, demonstrated that he never doubted his right to settle with his family in France and to enjoy all the benefits of citizenship. Moreover, officials at the prefecture agreed and moved to rectify the situation in record time.

In another case, Mrs. Menebhi sent a letter on 14 September 1959 explaining that she was a single mother with two small children. After being abandoned by her second husband while pregnant, Menebhi moved into her parents' one-room apartment in Aix-en-Provence, which was unfortunately already overcrowded with four of her siblings, aged four to seventeen. The Muslim Affairs Bureau responded with much sympathy. Officials were concerned that "her husband left her without resources" and that since August she had not received family allowances—"the only salary she had a right to claim in the name of her two young children." As a result, Menebhi received an "exceptional subsidy" of 10,000 francs sent the following month to help her regain her independence and to live on her own with her children.[114]

As with the Ahmed family, Menebhi's appeal not only drew on the language of rights, but also was resolved rapidly. Unlike the other family's situation, here the bureaucrats provided additional financial support because the traditional family structure had been breached. Having first turned to her extended family, Menebhi fit into a category for which the French government had already set interventionalist precedents. The male head of household remained the undisputed norm. But building on the pronatalist tradition in French social policy, the government intervened as a surrogate husband and father to ensure the children's health.

This is particularly important since the French government did not have a consistent response to Algerian women who had been abandoned, widowed, or did not otherwise fit into the patriarchal family structure. In the early 1950s, concern about the drain on public resources made repatriation the official policy for indigent Algerians, male and female.[115] But there were exceptions, particularly when state agents approached an isolated case. Moreover, at the height of the war, Massenet argued the families of interned men needed to be cared for in order to prevent the FLN from taking control of them.[116] Many of these families stayed in France, but the police repatriated the families of some men deported in October 1961.[117]

The case of the Khaled family included an interesting twist on the desire to return to Algeria. Fahrat Khaled lived in Aubagne with his wife and seven children. He wrote to the authorities in Marseille about their impending eviction from a condemned structure. Khaled planned to return to Philippeville in Algeria, although his wife and two oldest daughters intended to remain in France. Authorities urged the family to remain together, explaining they "wished the party concerned would also take his wife and oldest daughters with him" and suggesting the women would be without resources. Undaunted by this possibility, the women told officials they considered themselves "independent." They had "no intention of following" the male head of household back to Algeria. These three women utilized the language of freedom and equality in ways French officials had not intended. Social workers espoused a particular kind of women's liberation—promoting freedom from so-called backward Muslim practices, but not from a primary, naturalized role as wife and mother. Mrs. Khaled and her daughters refused to be subordinates; they rejected the notion that a woman's place was inevitably within a traditional family governed by the male breadwinner.[118]

Other independent Algerian women also lived in France. Some of them fell into prostitution. Some found other ways to prosper in spite of patriarchal norms emanating from both French and Algerian society. Zorah, a woman interviewed by the Franco-Algerian filmmaker Yamina Benguigui for her 1997 documentary *Mémoires d'immigrés*, came to France with her cousin Radia in 1948 using money they acquired by stealing their mothers' jewelry. Zorah rejoined her father, who had been in France for many years, having fought in the World Wars and the Resistance, and even having spent time in Buchenwald for helping Jews escape raids in Bordeaux.

Zorah, encouraged by her father to be independent, worked for others, saving money to purchase a café in Paris near the Saint-Martin canal. She explained to Benguigui, many years later, that she opened the café because

I had ambitions! I wanted to live like the French, I wanted a beautiful dining room, a beautiful chandelier, a Phillips vacuum. . . . And at the same time, I raised my children. Seven in eight years! Of course, maybe because of the café I didn't spend enough time with them. But we all have to choose. I didn't want to spend my time watching my children and buying our bread on credit.[119]

Cases like Zorah's were rare. Men comprised the vast majority of Algerians approaching governmental and private welfare service providers. Moreover, as the war escalated, particularly in Paris and its environs, Algerians reacted to growing discrimination. Facing the increasingly well-orchestrated police repression, many Algerians stopped lodging official complaints, fearing they might be arrested or worse. Instead, they voiced their frustrations to a handful of trusted "priests, nuns, social workers, [and] teachers,"[120] whom the police also targeted. Among the most committed advocates were Brigitte Gall, who worked for North African Family Social Service, and Monique Hervo, who worked for Civil Service International. Algerians told Gall they fully expected the arrest and imprisonment of ordinary people to occur for no apparent reason in Algeria, but in France, they were shocked this could happen. Others, having become accustomed to discrimination, knew their complaints fell on deaf ears or they could be arrested and deported.[121] As a result, in some instances, Algerian men sent "the women" to file reports about missing relatives and to run household errands.[122]

In the summer of 1960, one Algerian confided to Hervo that the French police and the harkis regularly tortured Algerians and that "the police mock us, they are always looking to humiliate us."[123] A witness of many police raids, Hervo described one that took place in March 1961 this way:

Five inspectors broke down the door. They surrounded Jamâl . . . manhandling him, molesting him, knocking him off-balance . . . until he had trouble standing up. . . . The inspectors moved on to the home's interior. His wife, his children looked petrified as their husband and father went limp. Reunited, worry silenced them despite their young age. Fear was everywhere. The search began. Suitcases overturned with one swift kick. Clothes left in shreds. The couscous pot, where the evening meal simmered, knocked over: semolina, lamb, chick peas, carrots, a spicy red sauce, soaked into flowered dresses, children's clothes, a sport coat, a burnoose. Food covered the floor pell-mell. The children's beds flipped over. The mattresses slashed while Khadija and the children watched in horror. Tufts of white wool scattered everywhere. The red-hot stove emptied: cinders and glowing coals spilled across the cement floor. No weapons found.[124]

This scene was repeated countless times, often with little or no notice during the day when men were at work. The goal, Algerians insisted, was to "frighten our children, something we cannot forgive."[125]

Despite these risks, on numerous occasions Algerians came together to protest. Certainly, the FLN marches organized in October 1961 were the best-known overt protest against France's attempt "to hide us . . . to make us invisible."[126] Yet, there were other, smaller protests, such as an unsuccessful petition signed by 93 "heads of households" requesting the water company open a second spigot for the families in the rue de la Garenne bidonville.[127] The unwillingness of French authorities to respond to Algerians made them increasingly believe "some of them [including Gall and Hervo]" helped, but the "politicians, without exception, were against us."[128]

Social Services and the Escalating Violence

In this atmosphere, the social welfare network drew the attention of both the FLN and the French police. Unlike the employees of the Algerian Social Centers, people from North African Family Social Service and other associations working directly with Algerian clients were never systematically targeted, but they nonetheless got caught in the crossfire and occasionally became victims of mounting violence. The "extremists in both camps"[129]—the FLN on one side and the police and the OAS on the other—routinely insulted and threatened violence against direct service providers.[130] On several occasions "terrorist" attacks threatened or killed service providers.[131] Fearing for their lives or unable to do their work, some left their posts.[132]

Others became more militant. Gall decided on 17 October 1961 that she could no longer remain silent. After meeting with her supervisor, Renée Bley, who told her she could speak out as long as she did not do so as an employee of North African Family Social Service, Gall began to make her voice heard, even publishing articles in local papers with Hervo.[133] Hervo, initially inspired by a sense of social justice stemming from her Catholic faith, worked in the bidonvilles of Nanterre.[134] She did everything she could to improve conditions by intervening with governmental services, calling attention to Algerians' plight, and trying to bring to light the "injustice of the Algerian war." At the height of the violence, Hervo moved into a small trailer in the rue de la Garenne bidonville, even sleeping in the shanty of a very pregnant woman to protect her during the events of October 1961.[135]

They both worked closely with colleagues in their organizations and with other groups, including the North African Friendly Society of Nanterre and the Groupe d'étude et d'action pour les Nord Africains de la région parisienne, known as GEANARP. GEANARP, which began as a branch of Nanterre's North African Friendly Society, broke away from its parent organization in 1960 to focus on the bidonvilles. It brought together Pierre Lienart, an engineer with SNCF (France's national railway company), a couple of local restaurant owners, and graduate students from some of Paris' most prestigious institutions (ENA, the Ecole normale supérieur, and the Ecole des sciences politiques).[136] One of the ENA students, Jean-Paul Imhof, became a leading figure in the group and, like his colleagues, wrote about the injustices taking place during the war.[137]

Working directly with Algerian women and children through programs developed by the Friendly Society, North African Family Social Service, the SONACOTRAL, and others, GEANARP managed educational programs and summer camps and produced "sociological and statistical" studies to find a "global solution" to the problems Algerians faced.[138] Like

Gall and Hervo, its members often intervened directly, putting themselves at risk. Brahim Benaïcha, who spent his childhood among approximately 240 Algerian families in the rue des Pâquerettes bidonville in Nanterre,[139] remembered Claude, a young man who took "risks" to win Algerians' trust. Claude organized summer camps where Benaïcha and his brothers experienced "fresh air . . . [and] adventure." Benaïcha also remembered Claude putting himself between the shanties and the "steel monsters painted yellow" that bulldozed the bidonville, yelling "If you wish, you have only to crush me [first]!"[140]

Notwithstanding what Benaïcha called the "stubbornness and conviction" of some service providers,[141] the lines between services and discriminatory and repressive policies—particularly in regard to regular and police services—frequently blurred. For many in regular and Algerian services, only a fine line separated social action and repression. Although Algerians had already faced and frequently overcome discrimination when seeking government services, discriminatory practices increased at the height of the war. No national policy ever directed them to do so, but it is clear that both local governmental officials and low-level bureaucrats took matters into their own hands. Algerians and those working directly with them reported that local governmental offices practiced de facto discrimination. As early as 1956, when Algerians arrived in Nanterre seeking information about available housing, the mayor's office gave out the bidonville's address.[142] As the white population's disdain for Algerians grew, "racist" protests of all "social measures that benefited the Muslim population" became more frequent, and some elected officials felt emboldened to exclude Algerians openly.[143] By 1959, Nanterre refused to renew the North African Friendly Society's use of municipal facilities for its programs and expressed its desire to see dislocated Algerian families (who became homeless when the city condemned and demolished their shanties) settled in bidonvilles outside the city limits.[144] Other service providers, including medical clinics and other public agencies, began segregating their clients, reserving one day a week for Algerians so that metropolitans would not have to wait in long lines "with all these Muslim women."[145]

Both before and after October 1961, key actors in the welfare network worked to separate their services from the police and the war, arguing that the families and single men they served had "confidence" in them and insisting that "our goal is understood and our neutrality appreciated."[146] Nevertheless, civilian agencies cooperated with the military and continued to approach clients with the same paternalism as before. Not only the police, but the IGAMEs, technical consultants, and even some veterans' services collected information to break Algerian nationalism and participated directly in extralegal, repressive, and even military operations.[147]

Housing services, in particular, regularly discriminated against Algerians in several ways. Since most of the members of SONACOTRAL's board of directors had colonial experience, the board sought retired military officers and others who had experience in the colonies, believing their familiarity with "the Muslims' language and lifestyles" made them highly qualified housing managers.[148] From the FLN's perspective, managers were police agents, hired because of their willingness to monitor residents' behavior, file false reports in order to control tenants, or solicit bribes and turn suspected FLN supporters over to the police, all of which made them legitimate targets in the war.[149] In addition to monitoring Algerians, local officials also frequently either dropped or reassigned Algerian families to the bottom of HLM waiting lists, claiming that metropolitans (*de souche*) had been on the lists longer, that technical errors had been made on applications or, as the Prefecture of the Seine argued in 1961, that the "national economy's" need for flexible labor outweighed the need to make this "labor force sedentary."[150]

The Fifth Republic's decision to prioritize social services and police surveillance came, at least in part, from shared assumptions—that the FLN had to be routed from French soil and that the Algerian population had "to be definitively won over to our cause."[151] Both social service providers and the police believed Algerians were "essentially simple and good at heart," a quiet, hardworking, and apolitical people whose attempts to partake of the good life had been stifled by the FLN. Even though their tactics differed significantly and a "concealed tension" developed between 1958 and 1961,[152] both believed that direct intervention in Algerians' homes would counter the nationalists' message and would ensure the effective dissemination of official French propaganda. Even as social welfare administrators openly abhorred and criticized police repression, they maintained a paternalistic vision justified by a growing trepidation that the FLN's successes among average Algerian migrants disrupted their mission.

French authorities in all sectors believed that the control and use of propaganda was essential to destroying the nationalist threat and turning impressionable Algerians away from rebellion. Veterans' organizations, for example, argued from the early 1950s that their mission, in addition "to bringing material and moral aid" to veterans and "their families," was to "protect former North African soldiers from subversive influences and to let them know, through sympathetic affirmations, that their plight is understood, and give them a strong and precise idea of the grandeur and generosity" of France.[153] Fearing that the less than welcoming reception Algerian veterans received from their comrades-in-arms could make anti-colonial sentiment attractive even to those who had fought for the tri-color, the prefect for the Interior Ministry's Algerian Affairs Office asked the local veterans associations to use their influence to make a differ-ence in the lives of Algerian veterans and urged that, "in the spirit of the brotherhood of arms," these associations could encourage Algerians to adapt "to European life, thus removing [the attraction to] any subversive propaganda."[154]

This "fight against the subversive propaganda" intensified with the war,[155] even if service providers' attention to Algerians' "state of mind" re-mained firmly in place. Certain the majority of Algerians wanted nothing more than to live "in peace,"[156] the Muslim Affairs Service sent out a secret circular in early 1958 that articulated "the principles and methods" through which administrators could "discreetly, imperceptibly" implement "politi-cal and psychological action" in order "to neutralize" FLN propaganda.[157] The Interior Ministry also summarized new objectives for the IGAMEs and the technical consultants as the need:

1. to eliminate terrorism [and] to purify [*assainir*] Algerian migration by delivering it from the threats and extortion to which it is subjected;

2. to give new life to social, educative, cultural, professional and psychological ac-tion for migrants and their families;

3. to influence metropolitan opinion so that it separates troublemakers from the mass of wholesome [*saine*] migrants and can welcome them with comprehension and fraternity.[158]

Drawing on welfare network policies in place since the late 1940s and France's "project of redemptive hygiene,"[159] administrators used euphemis-tic language that often sanctioned violence by asking private associations to ensure they "coordinated with the cleanup project [*l'action d'épuration*] un-dertaken by police services."[160] And, even as some high-level administrators continued to argue that police and social services were most effective when they cooperated with one another but remained separate,[161] many others working in the social welfare network realized that the events in Algeria and "the fight against terrorism in the metropole" inspired the new infusion of governmental support and made their jobs much more difficult.[162]

Key welfare network administrators became persistent if ineffectual critics of police repression. Massenet learned about Papon's plans seven months into the new police chief's term. At a secret Interministerial Committee meeting held at the Hôtel Matignon in September 1959, Papon explained his plan to introduce the harki brigade to subdue the population, to destroy the bidonvilles in Nanterre, and to implement regulations that would further control Algerian migration by encouraging the apolitical to migrate and by turning away suspected nationalists. During the meeting it became clear to Massenet that the goal was to "quickly destroy" the FLN by inspiring "enough fear in French Muslims from Algeria to convince them not to blindly follow" the nationalist cause.[163] Massenet, who expressed his disapproval and stormed out of the meeting, quickly learned how the police responded to dissent. Within days anonymous sources fed sensitive information to the press and accused Massenet of being the leak. Although Massenet adamantly denied any wrongdoing,[164] this became one of many occasions when his protests against police violence "met a blank wall."[165]

Undaunted, Massenet, Claudius-Petit, and many others publicly expressed their horror following the events of October 1961. Many French papers, including *L'Humanité*, *France Observateur*, *Le Monde* and *L'Express*, carried articles for weeks, even months following the massacres. Aid organizations launched investigations and made inquiries on behalf of clients who had missing family members or asked about bodies found floating in the Seine.[166] It was not just socialist politicians and leftist political organizations that voiced their anger.[167] The SONACOTRAL's Claudius-Petit, concurrently a deputy from the Loire, used well-attended budget debates at the National Assembly as a platform to make an eloquent denunciation. Reminding the police that they were "not above the law," Claudius-Petit acknowledged that "a fratricidal struggle" had sparked the initial violence, but he condemned law enforcement for addressing the problem with extralegal and immoral solutions. This pitted French law enforcement against Algerians. Under the current structure,

guardians of the peace make determinations based only on the color of one's skin, the appearance of one's clothing, the neighborhood one lives in. The blond Kabyles have such luck! Following in the footsteps of the yellow star, will we now create a yellow crescent? And to think we like to pretend we cannot comprehend how the Germans lived with themselves after Hitler came to power!

Claudius-Petit closed his speech by declaring that "the hideous beast of racism has been unleashed" and, if it was not restrained, France could "lose its soul."[168]

In spite of the immediate attention, Papon colluded with Interior Minister Roger Frey to orchestrate a cover-up. With public opinion polls showing the French simply wanted to forget about Algeria and a lack of political will on the left, the story disappeared.[169] In a matter of months, one of the most egregious incidents of state violence against citizens in the nation's capital vanished nearly completely from the collective memory.[170]

The Social Action Fund also participated in military operations. In addition to sending resources to Algeria, the Fund supported programs intimately tied to waging the war in the metropole. In June 1960, for example, the Civil Action Service, a new association led by Colonel Terce, an inspector with the police's Technical Assistance Service, reported that it provided "professional and moral" skills needed "to improve Muslims' living conditions."[171] Despite several members of the Fund's board raising concerns about the association's activities and worthiness, Massenet urged that it approve a request for 50,000 new francs. The interior minister and the secretary-general for Algerian Affairs supported this "new initiative," and they hoped the Social Action Fund would make "a particular effort" in this case.[172]

As well, Massenet called for services to be provided to the internees in camps opened in 1957 to confine Algerians netted in police raids and sweeps of the streets. In the first year, the camps held men the state considered too "dangerous" for release, even after they had served their prison terms. In 1958, not long after he became the police chief, Papon expanded the parameters of internment, allowing the police to hold indefinitely anyone designated a threat.[173] By early 1959, the camps that had held Jews and others earlier in the century detained two thousand people.[174] The Muslim Affairs Service and the National Security Office, which jointly managed the camps, explained the goal: "preemptively neutralizing elements considered dangerous to public order even if there was insufficient proof to bring them before the courts." They also wanted to ensure that internees "do not keep, when circumstances permit their liberation, memories that generate hatred toward everything French."[175] Apparently, interning Algerians without a criminal record and re-incarcerating those who had already served a sentence, claiming that Algerians' unstable home life compromised the government's ability to monitor suspects, never seemed reason enough to hate France.[176]

Massenet, who called the camps "veritable management schools for the FLN," recommended services that would keep internees occupied during their incarceration and would allow them to be more closely monitored.[177] After dividing prisoners into three categories, "the unredeemables, the malleables, [and] the recoverables," the authorities provided several services—from language and job training classes to public address systems that piped in news and propaganda—to instill a "sense of human dignity" and to teach "a better comprehension of the real political situation, the intentions of France, and their own true best interests."[178]

Internees resisted in a variety of ways. They refused to participate in the installation of public address systems, to accept personal mail or newspapers distributed by social service personnel, or to enter the cafeterias. Many went on hunger strikes and practiced what authorities called "contact strikes" or "the politics of vacant looks," behaviors that involved essentially ignoring camp personnel at all times. Based on presumptions about Algerians supposed collective mentality, authorities stubbornly believed a few troublemakers instigated these unacceptable behaviors and that most Algerians could still be convinced that nationalism was not in their best interests.[179] When the initial attempt to overcome passive resistance failed, administrators isolated the supposedly unredeemable elements in one camp and redoubled efforts in the other camps by expanding services to include more classes, libraries, and radio programming for internees who might still be swayed.[180] The stalemate continued until a few months before the war ended. Only after 115 hunger strikes and the intervention of the United Nations were the camps closed down, at least in France.[181]

EVEN IN THE FINAL YEARS OF THE WAR, once negotiations that eventually culminated in the Evian Accords had begun, the leadership and many direct service providers in the Algerian welfare network remained committed to providing services to the Algerian community. Never deviating from their original mission, prominent voices still insisted that in addressing their "linguistic, social, professional and cultural handicaps . . . , permeable" Algerians could be convinced to turn away from the FLN and toward France.[182] They remained committed, as well, to ending the Algerian War. Yet, the climate of unrestrained violence greatly affected welfare services, clients, and providers. Key voices consistently denounced law enforcement's overtly racist policies and pushed back against the most overt repression. According to Father Ghys, who wrote several, rare pieces in the

Cahiers nord-africains at the height of the war, Algerians were not France's adversaries. Instead of vilifying them, Ghys urged his readers to convince their compatriots to pity these "poor working people, trapped by events, who then collide with impossible situations in the metropole." Ghys, like his colleagues, continued to believe that Algerians escaped the "suffering" of demographic and economic crises in Algeria in search of the "marvels" France promised. Worried that the climate had changed dramatically because of "events" in Algeria, Ghys admitted Algerians found more and more metropolitans "'no longer dare' help them."[183] As one Algerian put it, "it's always our fault. We're always held responsible, as if we chose to live like this."[184]

This sentiment, articulated by an Algerian who could have been facing severe racial discrimination or the open arms of a social worker, highlights assumptions shared by Algerians' vocal advocates and those promoting violence to crush the FLN. Most of Algerians' most eloquent advocates believed the heart of the problem was Algerians' mentality and their need to transform themselves in order to live in France. They feared FLN propaganda too easily swayed Algerians and that Algerians preferred life in segregated enclaves. "Muslims [needed to] overcome their difficulties," which included everything from "their anxieties . . . [and] timidities" to their struggle with the passage from traditional to industrial society.[185] Only France's "open friendship [and] active solidarity" could create in Algerians "a sense of probity, justice and equality."[186] The welfare providers trusted that their approach, which Ghys called "a broad and farsighted policy of hospitality [*accueil*] and education" seeking "harmonious human symbiosis,"[187] was the only effective weapon against the FLN.

Nevertheless, France's all-out war against the Algerian rebellion brought the civilian services and law enforcement closer together. The social welfare network supported the war in a myriad of ways. The line between assistance and surveillance, which was already blurred, became even more indistinct when monitoring moved beyond the realm of paternalistic assistance and into the realm of arbitrary arrests, detention in internment camps, torture, and even death. Welfare advocates increasingly recognized and spoke out against racial discrimination and police brutality. Yet, most were also, even if indirectly, a part of the state machinery that targeted Algerians.

As Chapter 6 will show, the decision to focus on the bidonville problem by funding housing and related services for Algerian families stemmed from experts' commitment to what they considered authentic family migration. Only it could provide the Algerian man with the "vocational and moral equilibrium" as well as the "material means" necessary to live normally.[188] Even in these exigent circumstances, the leadership of the welfare programs held onto a "profound sense of solidarity" that they insisted still existed between "two ethnic communities with a common destiny."[189]

6

The Great "Hope"
Housing Algerian Families
at the Height of the Algerian War

IN THE EARLY 1960S, the Algerian welfare network sponsored dozens of government-subsidized housing projects for Algerian families in France. Administrators imagined one of the first and largest of the SONACOTRAL and the Social Action Fund sponsored HLM projects, Canibouts, as more than just a shiny new apartment complex. Like many other complexes the French referred to as *grands ensembles*,[1] Canibouts was to be a community that would have "indispensable complements to social and economic life, including schools, cinemas, a shopping center, a swimming pool, parks, and parking lots."[2] Planners also envisioned a social center and even a church to help residents adjust to their new lives and quell any tensions.[3] Built on part of the razed bidonville in Petit Nanterre,[4] Canibouts, like a phoenix rising from the ashes, should have provided proof that France could win the war against the FLN by incorporating Algerians into the postwar expansion of the welfare state. The Interior Ministry led the assault on the bidonvilles, the symbol of the FLN's intractability. Using the police and welfare providers, the state infiltrated and destroyed Algerian enclaves to rout Algerian nationalists. Destroying the seemingly impenetrable shantytowns allowed the state to move Algerians into housing that separated them from nationalist influence and to place them under the panoptic gaze of social workers, housing managers, and neighbors. In short, housing offered the state a solution that appeared capable of making the so-called Algerian problem literally disappear.[5]

Planning for Canibouts began in 1959 and final approval came in August 1960. The original designs for this 800-unit complex included 230 units for single workers, some standard studio apartments and others five-bedroom apartments that would be converted into dormitories holding two adult men per room. The 570 family apartments, which ranged from one to five bedrooms,[6] would be issued according to each family's size following the guidelines used in all *grands ensembles*.[7] All units would have the modern conveniences: kitchens, bathrooms, living rooms, and separate bedrooms for parents and children. The layout of each unit would take into consideration contemporary notions of how space influenced the health and well-being of the nuclear family.[8] In addition, Canibouts needed to be a self-sufficient neighborhood because it was—just like the bidonville that preceded it—isolated from commercial centers and surrounded by an industrial zone, a military air base, Nanterre's municipal government building, and the Paris-Saint-Germain railroad tracks.[9]

The SONACOTRAL anticipated the cost of construction for Canibouts' dormitories as 834.2 million old francs, with 241.8 million old francs contributed from the Social Action Fund's budget. The family apartments would cost 1.6 billion old francs, eighty-five percent of which came from low-interest loans and the remaining fifteen percent from a Social Action Fund subsidy.[10] Despite several delays, by 1961 the SONACOTRAL had acquired three-quarters of the land planned for this massive undertaking.[11] The first phase included three sections, two for workers and one for families, scheduled to open in spring–summer of 1962. Construction on another section with 383 family apartments had just begun in the fall of 1961.[12] Ironically, Canibouts opened its doors just as the French and Algerian delegations drafted the Evian Accords outlining Algeria's independence.[13]

This chapter places the case of Canibouts in context. It explores why France invested more than ever before or since in housing for Algerian migrant families at the same time it negotiated with Algerian authorities to end the war. Of course, housing for male workers continued to garner significant attention and resources.[14] In sheer numbers, dormitories housed more people because they cost less per person than apartments for families. Nevertheless, family housing symbolized the "definitive solution."[15] In many respects policy makers' reasoning echoed what they had been espousing since the early 1950s. The Muslim Affairs Service called family housing the "most delicate" problem facing service providers because women, youths, and children represented the most important and growing segment of the population.[16] Whether in press accounts or in meetings at the Elysée Palace, those discussing the issue of Algerian migration argued that "more and more" families joined the head of household to settle "definitively" in France.[17]

As a result, family-housing services constituted a significant portion of all specialized services offered to Algerians in the Fifth Republic's first years. Dozens of organizations participated in housing programs for Algerians, from employers and local governments to the Construction Ministry and private associations.[18] In most cases these organizations worked with the two key players: the Social Action Fund and the SONACOTRAL. The former committed twenty-six percent of its first metropolitan operating budget (in 1959) to housing the over 8,000 Algerian families it estimated lived in substandard housing (1,800 in bidonvilles and 7,300 in other slums and rooming houses) in France. The Fund planned to contribute over 800 million old francs to social housing construction companies, the SONACOTRAL, the centers for Propaganda and Action against Slums, and local governments in subsequent years. Housing accounted for a significant portion of the budget, roughly fifty percent of the Social Action Fund's metropolitan expenditures for the war's final three years.[19] By 1961, the Fund had sponsored, in whole or in part, at least 2,500 family units in either transitional housing or permanent HLM complexes.[20] Its partner, the SONACOTRAL, despite initial hesitation, likewise took up its original mandate to house "not just workers from Algeria living alone, but also their families."[21]

The Interior Ministry's decision, in February 1958, to "evacuate" the bidonvilles and all other "insalubrious" housing motivated the early Fifth Republic's push for Algerian family housing.[22] Once the state prioritized the destruction of the bidonvilles, political pressures demanded it commit to rehousing the displaced. Initially key leaders in the welfare network rejected any discussion of creating separate, permanent housing for Algerian families. Yet, with the Interior Ministry pushing to empty the bidonvilles and advocates such as Jean-Paul Imhof calling the current housing situation "insoluble," something had to be done.[23] Given reports that moving families into HLM apartments would destroy communities because these families were not prepared for modern life and because their "failure . . . reinforced neighbors' hostility toward these 'strangers,'" administrators reluctantly agreed to implement what they believed was a temporary, separate housing policy.[24] To overcome racial discrimination, including Algerians' supposed "problems" and HLM mangers' "reluctance" to rent to Muslims,[25] the Interior Ministry requested that the Social Action Fund and the SONACOTRAL invest in a two-stage program: temporary, transitional projects followed by permanent HLM apartments. In the process Algerians would be segregated until someone within the network determined they were ready to live with the general population.[26]

The resulting policy created *cités de transit*, or transitional housing projects. According to numerous experts, including those with North African Family Social Service—the primary employer of social workers making decisions about Algerians' status—about seventy-five percent of families needed to spend time in transitional housing.[27] A great consensus, which brought together a variety of voices from noted experts in private associations to high-level ministerial officials, determined that Algerians needed this "intermediary step between the bidonville and the HLM complex" where it was easier for staff "to guide, monitor and supervise the population."[28] Then, once they completed an apprenticeship, Algerian families could move from what amounted to isolated mobile-home parks into HLM apartments.

Father Jacques Ghys referred to the HLMs as the great "hope,"[29] the Promised Land where well-adapted Algerians could embrace France. To fulfill this dream, the SONACOTRAL bought HLM companies to construct housing complexes. Yet, to prevent Algerians' permanent segregation in SONACOTRAL apartment complexes, advocates insisted on two policies, a quota system and an exchange program, to ensure a *brassage*, or mixing, of Algerians and the general population. The quota kept the housing complexes sponsored by the SONACOTRAL and the Social Action Fund from turning into segregated neighborhoods by limiting the number of Algerian families that could live in them and by offering most apartments to metropolitan families on regular HLM waiting lists. In exchange, the regular HLM companies agreed, in theory, to offer a limited number of apartments to Algerian families in their complexes. These programs intended to overcome discriminatory housing practices; for the most part they did not. In the turbulent final years of the Algerian War, housing advocates succeeded in assisting some families' transition to integrated housing, but failed in the larger task of overcoming widespread residential segregation.

Liquidating the Bidonvilles

Even at the highest levels of government, French officials had been well aware of Algerians' terrible housing conditions for years. Yet, a national plan for the "liquidation" of the bidonville problem began in earnest only after the interior minister issued a circular in February 1958 calling for "immediate solutions" to this "menace to public order."[30] Rooted in a long history of "creative destruction"—in which Haussmann's project is just one example of delivering Paris from "its illnesses, its cancers and epidemics" through an "act of surgery"[31]—the state instructed officials that these shantytowns had to be destroyed. They served as havens for Algerian nationalists that "escape all controls."[32] The timing of the decision reveals how the war, and in particular the desire to defeat the FLN, inspired the Interior Ministry's new policy. Within the welfare network, advocates made the bidonville crisis their top priority,[33] calling it everything from a national "shame" to a "cancer" that poisoned France with "de facto segregation."[34] Eliminating the bidonvilles became the only issue about which the Social Action Fund's board felt "a profound spirit of cooperation."[35] Rooted in the paternalistic approach that characterized the entire period, these experts concentrated on their ability "to penetrate" these ostensibly impenetrable areas and "to extricate" Algerians from the "misery of the bidonvilles," which would aid their transition "from an archaic and above all rural civilization" to one that is "technological and urban."[36]

Even though the vast majority of Algerians did not live in bidonvilles,[37] the shantytowns in France's three largest cities received the lion's share of attention both because of the abysmal conditions and because of the FLN's ability to portray them as its stronghold. Authorities confidently declared they could end the bidonville problem relatively quickly. In Lyon, a November 1959 headline announced, "All the bidonvilles of Lyon will have disappeared" by year's end.[38] Even though eliminating the bidonvilles in and around Paris would take time because of their sheer number, the destruction of those in Nanterre and nearby Gennevilliers had made so much progress that the prefect of the Seine assured Massenet they would reach their goal by October 1960.[39] And Marseille, which began the destruction more slowly, in part because of the number of people living in bidonvilles and in part because of the difficulty it had procuring land on which to resettle residents, nonetheless claimed to have emptied the three largest bidonvilles by 1960 and had ambitious plans for the others.[40] In fact, officials at the local and national level wrote on numerous occasions that they had "nearly finished the liquidation" in Lyon and Marseille and were on the way to solving the problem in Paris.[41]

A new law expanding the state's authority to "maintain order" in Algeria also quickened the pace.[42] When applied in the metropole, the

1960 law facilitated the "liquidation of the bidonvilles" by empowering authorities to confiscate the land under the shantytowns.[43] Despite growing state power, it soon became clear nothing would be resolved by the end of 1961, as the government had ordered.[44] Instead, the problem seemed to be growing, with one report estimating over 12,000 men and 3,500 families (numbering 18,000 people) lived in bidonvilles and other "unsanitary" dwellings in October 1961.[45]

Welfare administrators blamed Algerians, bureaucratic procedures, and police tactics for the failure to resolve the bidonville problem permanently. In some cases the prefect of the Seine insisted Algerians refused to move out of their shanties and in others they moved into bidonvilles in hopes of getting better housing.[46] The only way "to limit the problem," according to the director of the Muslim Affairs Service, was to control the "anarchy" of Algerian migration patterns.[47] Among a number of suggestions, Prefect Bénédetti argued for better controls: repatriation for those deemed inadaptable and measures limiting settlement to the families of men who had already migrated and found adequate housing.[48]

The migrants, however, did not shoulder all the blame. Massenet and others argued that there were also legal, technical, and financial obstacles, particularly when it came to delays in acquiring the land on which they planned to resettle families.[49] Simultaneously, welfare administrators both entreated the police to do more to prevent the creation of new bidonvilles and condemned the violent demolition of shanties before residents found alternative housing.[50] Acknowledging all these impediments in the "struggle against" the bidonvilles, the prefect of the Seine insisted the real issue lay not with "policing or good faith," but with a lack of money.[51] Only when the key players, including the Interior Ministry, the Social Action Fund, the SONACOTRAL, and other government offices at the national and regional level committed substantial resources to "improving Muslim housing by all means" at their disposal would France be able "to bleach" this "leprosy" ravaging its cities.[52]

More Attention to Families

At about the same time, Bénédetti enlisted the new Interior Minister Emile Pelletier and Construction Minister Pierre Sudreau to launch a massive housing revitalization and construction project to "return order" to Paris.[53] Algerian housing advocates insisted their clients be included in any "housing policy conceived of and implemented for all of the French popu-lation."[54] Specialized aid, from the Social Action Fund or any other source, needed to remain in the realm of complementary services that would con-tinue to lead Algerians to "normal social services."[55] When it came to hous-ing—the mark of integration—Algerian "families should be considered subject to civil law," allowing them the opportunity "to be awarded" an apartment in an HLM like any other family.[56] Separate housing, Ghys en-treated, was unthinkable for "intelligent and socially liberal men," implic-itly disparaging anyone that gave up on integration. He could not imagine French migrants to the United States or to China being segregated from the rest of the population. In making this comparison, Ghys unwittingly revealed that he viewed Algerians as foreigners, not as Frenchmen like all others. Despite an oblique warning that institutionalized separate hous-ing programs constituted a "public danger," he remained silent about the widespread residential segregation of American blacks or the Civil Rights movement. Instead, Ghys kept the comparison personal; he too might want to be with his compatriots if he lived abroad. He also emphasized his optimism, noting that Algerians were not so different; they had "the same needs, the same desires" as anyone else.[57] Even in the summer of 1961, several years into the state's decision to take "exceptional measures" to solve the bidonvilles crisis,[58] he had not given up hope. Algerians were not so "particular"; they could be part of the nation's universal solution to the housing crisis.[59] Ghys and his colleagues forced themselves to focus on the state's commitment to "the integration of these families in the French community"—which increased between 1958 and 1961 through the Social Action Fund, the SONACOTRAL, and other traditional organizations—to downplay the depth of racial discrimination and to ignore the violence and de Gaulle's overtures toward Algeria's self-determination.[60]

While contemporaries fixated on Algerians' desperate living condi-tions, reports also pointed out that some families found decent housing on their own or with the help of social services. This evidence reinforced Ghys' optimism about Algerians' ability to integrate into normal housing and legitimized the allocation of resources in this area. Experts tried to prove Algerian families could adapt by determining how many families had succeeded in acquiring the dream of "la petite propriété." In 1959, the director of the Muslim Affairs Service claimed that nearly a quarter of Algerian families had appropriate housing, with 2,000 families already liv-ing in HLMs and another 2,900 housed via employer or private association programs.[61] If we begin with one of the common estimates, that 20,000 Algerian families (about 93,000 people) resided in France,[62] the Muslim Affairs Service's figures seem too high. Given the overall tone of the report, this branch of the Interior Ministry provided figures that stressed the Herculean efforts already made to fix the problem. Instead, North African Family Social Service provided what seems to be a more realistic estimate by compiling records from its offices and from the agencies with which it worked closely in other regions. It determined that twelve percent of Algerian families were "sufficiently" housed.[63] Without exact numbers, since no one kept national residency records based on ethnicity, housing advocates used these statistics to tout their hard work and to plead for more funding.

These success stories also acted as proof Algerians could integrate if they tried hard enough. To underline the point, the propaganda mouthpiece *Messages d'Algérie* (a biweekly magazine) published a series of articles about Algerians in and around Lyon in 1960. The author emphasized how pleasantly surprised he was to find many Algerians felt more at home in Lyon than in their "birthplace." He was so impressed by the long-time residents' ability to become "totally integrated into the local population" that he ventured to call them "Algerian-Lyonese!" (*Lyonnais Algériens*).[64] By pointing out how much progress still needed to be made among newer arrivals, however, the author's overall intent was clear. If Algerians worked hard, they could become nearly the same as real Lyonese.

Despite success stories, the vast majority of Algerian families lived in tenements, other dilapidated dwellings, or the bidonvilles. Certain that Algerian families were the "unfortunate" victims of the FLN and that they were "more and more likely to accompany the head of household" in France, advocates expanded housing and related services even as they worried the growth in family migration exacerbated the problem.[65] To begin, Joseph Leriche noted in the *Cahiers nord-africains* their best figures represented a "minimum" estimate.[66] Families still constituted a minority of the overall Algerian population in the metropole, but they represented the largest growing segment of the population. At a time when male migration had "very much diminished," Massenet reported that family migration accounted for forty percent of total arrivals in 1959 (fifteen percent of which were Algerian women and twenty-five percent children).[67] Network officials reiterated again and again, with trepidation, that another 9,000 families arrived each year.[68] In addition, the demographic pattern made experts worry about the host of problems family migration

might engender.[69] Some pointed to a new trend: men returned from annual vacations with their families.[70] Others feared the long-term repercussions of the Constantine Plan's promise to create 800,000 jobs for
Algerians in ten years since it included 200,000 metropolitan positions.[71]

Even with the proliferation of anxiety about Algerian settlement, experts continued to argue the desire to settle "definitively" was "natural"
since men "were not made to live alone."[72] Two studies estimated fifty-
five percent of male migrants were married, about a third of whom had
brought their families to France. The authors of the first study defended
the demographic shift and recommended that men already settled in the
metropole send for their families since visiting loved ones during annual
vacations was not "sustainable" for "strictly humanitarian reasons." The second, released for limited circulation by the colonial government in 1960,
suggested it would be better to halt male migration altogether. Soliciting
family settlement would stabilize the population and ensure Algerians did
not intermarry with metropolitan women in large numbers. At the same
time, the article warned the government would have to take unprecedented
measures to deal with the current crisis as well as the expected growth.[73]

The views of government officials and experts on family migration
had much continuity from the Fourth to early Fifth Republic. They insisted men wanted to reunite their families in order to "conform to nature," end economic hardship, take advantage of the benefits of consumer
society, and escape often unnamed "circumstances of the political situation."[74] Unable to address the war directly, French officials nevertheless understood it played a central role in Algerian workers' desire to bring their
families to France. In one rare exception, a technical consultant explained
that two-thirds of the sixty men applying for family housing through their
employers in the Loire Valley did so because their families were in relocation camps in Algeria.[75] This type of detail appeared infrequently and was
never widely distributed; Algerian families' urgent need for housing and
related services, on the other hand, garnered more attention than ever before (or since).

Beliefs about women's vital role in stabilizing and depoliticizing
Algerian men carried over from the earlier period as well. Assumptions
about women's responsibility not only helped to explain the interest in
family housing, but also clarified the Interministerial Committee's recommendation that a "particular effort should be made in favor of Muslim
women."[76] A greater infusion of funds for women's services, welfare provid-

ers promised, would finally allow the Algerian man to find true happiness, the kind one felt when a nuclear family lived in a "normal" home.[77] The Public Heath and Population Ministry's Bureau 10, led by François Villey, continued to take the initiative in this area.[78] In 1960 it allocated over 890 million old francs to social programs.[79] This money, along with 70 million old francs from the Social Action Fund and other state agencies,[80] helped regional governments and associations like the North African Family Social Service expand services to save children and women in "moral danger," prevent adolescent delinquency, train women in home economics through classes and home visits, help the homeless, and provide training and scholarships for young men and women.[81] According to Villey, this social action was much more than just charity; the combined programs constituted a "vast ensemble" to help those in need with an eye toward the demands of "modern life." They acted as the "indispensable transitional step" in progressively integrating Algerians into French society and its economy.[82]

Experts, as we have already seen, feared many Algerian women were "totally ill-adapted to life in France."[83] Frequently age played a role; women who were "too old" were expected to return to Algeria at some point and younger women were expected to learn more quickly.[84] Young women, judged more amenable to a measure of "autonomy," would nevertheless have to learn everything necessary for keeping a home. Impediments from language barriers to unfamiliarity with bureaucracy and an inability to manage the household budget, it was argued, often impeded their adaptation.[85] And if they lived in the "conservative milieu" of the bidonville, GEANARP's Jean-Paul Imhof warned they could go "years without evolving."[86] Transforming Algerian women was tedious work. As Villey explained,

the evolution of the Muslim woman and her adaptation to the Western way of life requires enlightened patience, which is the work of specialized social workers . . . [particularly those from] North African Family Social Service. Their action is carried out over months, even years, and requires particular techniques and specialized personnel. This staff should allow the Muslim woman, who arrives from her village, to learn little by little, in a climate that encourages confidence, everything the lady of the house and mother of a European family needs to know.

If the Algerian woman worked hard and followed instructions, she could succeed by helping her "entire family to adapt."[87]

The same types of services implemented earlier in the decade continued as part of the new initiative. Office hours, home visits, and home economics courses provided the backbone of these organizations' work. Extra funding augmented current programs.[88] By 1961, North African Family Social Service had offices in twelve metropolitan departments and continued its partnerships with other agencies.[89] In many instances municipalities and small organizations used new funding to hire full-time social workers and buy new equipment.

One of the most novel ways that service providers tried to reach more people came in the form of mobile units. These involved vans, which the Social Action Fund subsidized for both North African Family Social Service and the Alliance Française, and which allowed social workers to reach Algerians in enclaves far from social program offices.[90] The Alliance Française, which also held courses for men and women in its offices on Boulevard Raspail and other locations in Paris, began using the vans in 1960. As always, carefully tailored services reinforced gender norms. Male instructors, working in regular classrooms or in mobile units that visited prisons, taught men French and showed films such as *Motorcycle Security* and the *Domestic Budget*. In developing a curriculum for women taught by women, the Alliance Française bought mobile kitchens and showed films such as *Baby Care, Hygiene and the Pregnant Woman*, and *Household Maintenance*.[91]

The mobile units represented a small innovation in educational services. Social centers, integrated into family housing complexes, were the newest and growing element of family services in the early 1960s. All over the country, organizations that provided transitional housing services for Algerian families opened on-site Social Intervention Centers in order to provide specially designed services for Muslim families.[92]

Transitional Housing Projects

The first transitional housing project jointly sponsored by the Social Action Fund and the SONACOTRAL received approval in October 1959.[93] Although it faced delays because of foot dragging in Nanterre's city hall,[94] it finally opened in January 1960 (see Figures 6.1 and 6.2). Claudius-Petit initially hesitated to support significant family housing,[95] but requests from numerous prefects, government agencies, and associations inspired the SONACOTRAL to invest in the construction of transitional housing.[96] Between 1960 and 1961, dozens of these "life preservers" (*logement de sauvetage*) opened in France's three largest cities as well as in smaller communities.[97] By December 1960, the SONACOTRAL had sponsored twelve transitional

FIGURE 6.1. Families moving from a bidonville into a *cité de transit* in Nanterre on 26 January 1960. In the background is a high-rise social housing apartment building (HLM).

Source: AN 770391/6, CAC Fontainebleau. Photograph no. 40121, by H. Guirard. Reprinted with the permission of the Archives nationales.

FIGURE 6.2. A French official shows new residents how the heating system in their mobile home works.

Source: AN 770391/6, CAC Fontainebleau. Photograph no. 40139, by H. Guirard. Reprinted with the permission of the Archives nationales.

housing projects totaling 423 family units. Together with the Social Action Fund, it cosponsored another five transitional housing projects totaling 165 units by the end of 1960.[98]

The Social Action Fund also collaborated with local organizations, regional governments, and other organizations to build transitional housing.[99] In Lyon, for example, two long-standing charitable organizations, Notre-Dame des sans-abris and La maison de l'Afrique du Nord, each built transitional projects for eighty families.[100] In all, the Social Action Fund cosponsored at least ten transitional housing projects with over 500 family units.[101] A report confirmed what Massenet had boasted at an Interministerial Committee meeting in the spring of 1961 that one thousand "educational" housing units were well underway.[102] The three largest cities would receive nearly two-thirds of the proposed units, or almost six hundred units. By 1961, Paris and its environs had nearly 300 units with 150 more expected by the end of the year. Marseille and Lyon each had at least 150 units, with more in the planning stages.[103]

Given the pedagogical goals of the transitional housing policy, social service providers recommended Algerians living in transitional housing have access to "social action centers" in or near the mobile-home parks.[104] Initially, local initiative and coordination within the welfare network linked transitional housing to services. In 1958 the SONACOTRAL constructed a one-hundred-unit project near the Aid to Overseas Workers' office in Marseille to make it easy for families to attend classes.[105] The following year a small organization in Valenciennes bought, with the help of Moral Assistance for North Africans, a "train car" that held organized activities for children as well as both breast-feeding consultations and basic skills classes for women.[106]

Before long, the initiative became a formal policy. From the planning stages, transitional housing projects began setting aside at least one trailer for an on-site social center. The detailed plans for one of these educational housing projects explained how the social center fit into the overall goals. Making the center a part of residents' everyday lives would facilitate social workers' efforts to help "Muslim families . . . succeed" in overcoming their profound inadequacy (*inadaptation*). The social center would provide a hands-on internship (*stage*) that gently helped residents make the transition from their "primitive" life to a "modern" one. It became a "human relations project" that succeeded when the staff knew how to be "discreet" and how to act as the intermediary with normal social services. Ultimately, the center was supposed to become the "motor, the soul of all life in the [housing] project." To reach these goals, educational programs targeted men and women separately. While claiming that gender separation was a response to Muslim customs, the goal was to reorganize family life and to provoke a voluntary "renovation of the Muslim family through an advancement of women."[107] As with other services, the centers sought to cultivate gender roles and skills based on normative understandings of men's and women's relationship to the nuclear family.

Services for men and boys focused on providing vocational training and leisure activities that addressed their "natural need" to relax after work.[108] In order "to overcome their suspicion" and prevent Algerians from congregating in venues that might offer a range of temptations, welfare providers depicted social center activities as healthy distractions, offering everything from ping pong tables and playing cards to radios, record players, and movies.[109] They also offered books, office supplies, and classroom space where men could acquire marketable skills by using the array of tools available in what GEANARP called its "manual labor room."[110] Ultimately, administrators designed the centers to replace the "Muslim cafés" found in the hotels, bidonvilles, and other Algerian enclaves that French authorities identified as the epicenter of Algerian nationalist activities and recruitment.[111] If the centers could provide a place where men enjoyed middle-class comforts while being inculcated with pro-French messages and without noticing or objecting to being monitored by staff, they could play a key role in defeating the FLN.

The bulk of the responsibility for remaking the Algerian family, as we have seen, fell on the Algerian woman's shoulders. Center proponents argued that if she encouraged her husband to spend time in the men's center while staff helped her create the ideal home, the whole family could achieve the good life France offered. As a result, the centers' most "essential" work was the "rapid training of women and young women."[112] The centers replicated other programs by offering home economics classes supplemented with home visits. Through constant "contact and comprehension," staff taught women how to keep a clean, orderly home, with "everything in its place." To give these women a sense of "autonomy in the tasks" of everyday life, they gave instructions about how to gain access to welfare benefits, use modern appliances, shop, and cook with "metropolitan recipes." The striking difference in the layout of the centers for men and women (see Figures 6.3 and 6.4) reflects the differentiated goals; only the women's center

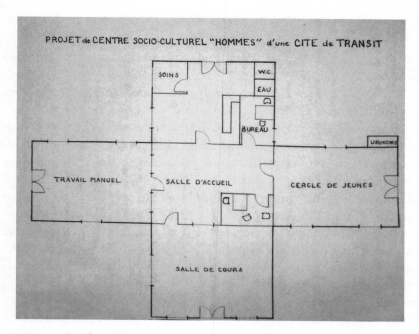

FIGURE 6.3. Plans for a men's center in a *cité de transit* in Nanterre. June 1960.
Source: AN 760140/1, CAC Fontainebleau. Reprinted with the permission of the Archives nationales.

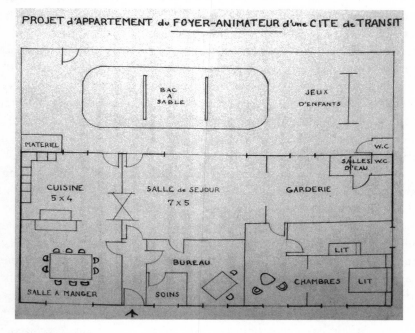

FIGURE 6.4. Plans for a manager's apartment and women's center in a *cité de transit* in Nanterre. June 1960.
Source: AN 760140/1, CAC Fontainebleau. Reprinted with the permission of the Archives nationales.

mimicked "family life." Just as in Algeria's social centers, staff often lived on-site to put the ideal model right "before their eyes."[113]

Local officials and association administrators anticipated that "less evolved" families—those who failed to meet social workers' expectations and to comply with their demands—would need to remain in this stage for between six months and one year before they could qualify for an HLM apartment.[114] Decision making relied almost exclusively on social workers. They determined which families could move directly from bidonvilles or other dilapidated housing directly into HLMs and which needed an "apprenticeship" in transitional housing first.[115] In 1961, the *Cahiers nord-africains* published the criteria that specialized services personnel used to determine whether a family would be "at ease" in an HLM. In its discussion of the conditions Algerian families had to meet, the *Cahiers* insisted Algerians' effort and not racism among service providers or HLM residents determined the outcome. In fact, the benchmarks for determining HLM residence worthiness rested on Algerian women's willingness to imitate the French. The stable employment of the "father" mattered, but each woman's "desire for evolution" and ability "to assume sole responsibility" for the household were paramount.[116] Social workers considered a woman's age and dress,[117] as well a number of other factors. These included her interest in learning French, sending children to school, adapting to European customs, balancing the budget, keeping her house clean, using household items (from furniture to appliances) properly, participating regularly in home economics and child-rearing programs, and having some level of "emancipation" (such as doing the household shopping).[118] All of these rested on assumptions about Algerians' backwardness and ignorance of the basic elements of modern family life and on the supposition that recalcitrant families would never make the transition.

A 1960 census of the 104 families (94 Muslim and 10 European) living in Marseille's La Timone bidonville offers additional insight into how social workers made decisions. The handwritten census recorded each family member's name, the year the family had arrived in France, the number of adults and children, and the male head of household's employment history and current salary. It also evaluated how well each woman maintained the current lodging as part of an overall appraisal of her degree of adaptation. The column that determined each family's overall "level of evolution" only correlated with factors that directly related to women's behaviors. The vast majority of women fell into the categories "evolved" or "sufficiently evolved," their homes judged "well kept" or "sufficiently well kept." This made them eligible for a social housing apartment in the future. In several cases the census report supported moving families into apartments when a family's wife/mother had completely adapted even when the husband/father was unemployed. The report also consistently recommended transitional housing for the families of women judged "un-evolved" or "less-evolved." Thus, women shouldered great responsibility in how social workers determined a family's well-being. The social workers involved in compiling the census recommended that the overwhelming majority of the families living in La Timone could move into an HLM apartment in the future.[119] While we do not know for sure, it is unlikely that most of these families actually moved into HLM apartments. Many complexes opened only after Algerian independence, when the commitment to housing Algerian citizens dwindled. At the same time, a growing number of repatriated colonists sought and received HLM housing ahead of Algerians.[120]

As we have seen, direct service providers, including the North African Friendly Society of Nanterre, had hope, even confidence, that Algerian women were capable of making the transition. Yet, they emphasized the slow, patient labor required to unearth the inherent qualities that Algerian women possessed but "generally ignore." If properly molded, Algerian women could better comprehend "their role as mother."[121] The experts at the *Cahiers nord-africains* also continued to urge welfare providers to act "with prudence" in order to prevent the grave consequences they imagined would result if a social worker made "an error in judgment" by moving an Algerian family into an HLM too early.[122] For the families in transitional housing, the material improvements that accompanied the move from shanties to new mobile homes came with significant trade-offs. They gave up a great deal of privacy and control over family life. While families likely appreciated having friends and relations as neighbors, transitional housing perpetuated the segregation that already existed in the slums and bidonvilles. It prolonged Algerians' isolation and facilitated state surveillance.[123]

HLMs

Families deemed ready, including those that had successfully completed the apprenticeship in transitional housing, were to be rewarded for their "success" (*réussite*) with an HLM apartment.[124] While no exact figures exist, we know some Algerian families moved into regular HLM apartment complexes. Given that some had moved in before the wide-spread use of the transitional housing programs, many Algerian residents of regular HLM complexes likely skipped the transitional step altogether. They made their way on their own or with the assistance of any number of organizations.

Nevertheless, Algerians faced a number of roadblocks when seeking rent-controlled apartments. Algerians and those working in the welfare network knew full well that many local governments and housing companies discriminated in a variety of ways. They refused to issue permits for everything from housing to water spigots and turned Algerians away even if they had been on housing lists longer than those awarded apartments. In one case the army refused to relinquish land on which part of Nanterre's La Folie bidonville sat, claiming it would be "dangerous" to have Algerians near a military installation.[125] Behind every justification, as SONACOTRAL director Jean Vaujour noted, stood local authorities' desire to prevent "these people" from mixing with the "local population."[126]

Keenly aware of "a certain racism . . . and indifference" among the general population and many of their colleagues,[127] social welfare administrators remained reluctant to build separate HLM-style housing for Algerians. Both Massenet and Claudius-Petit feared, with good reason, that once the Social Action Fund and the SONACOTRAL committed their funds to building permanent housing for Algerian families, regular HLM companies and regional governments would no longer feel any responsibility for housing Algerian families and would infer that only these specialized organizations needed to assist Algerian families. Massenet understood the severity of the situation, expressing his deep concerns to officials at the prime minister's office about setting a bad precedent. Families forced out of bidonvilles had no place to go; "the organizations that manage HLMs," Massenet complained, "refuse to provide them access to this type of housing, generally invoking the idea that they had too recently arrived in the area. In fact, severe racial discrimination is routinely being practiced by these organizations toward Muslim families."[128] For both Claudius-Petit and Massenet, the practice would not end unless the Construction Ministry required HLM construction companies around the country to accept "this category of Frenchmen" as it did all other citizens.[129]

Unable to acquire the government mandate they wanted, Massenet and other key administrators reasoned that a commitment to special, separate HLM complexes for Algerians offered the only short-term solution.

In fact, the SONACOTRAL's formal, legal status made it the perfect organization "to resolve this problem."[130] Initially, the SONACOTRAL and the Social Action Fund worked with existing HLM companies as well as regional governments and other institutions to help finance and construct housing with "a certain number of apartments" reserved for Algerian families.[131] By mid-1959, the Muslim Affairs Service reported that 1,950 Algerian families (9,200 people) lived in apartments at least partially sponsored by the SONACOTRAL.[132]

Nevertheless, it quickly became clear that the growth in Algerian family migration, coupled with HLM managers' continued unwillingness to accept Algerian residents,[133] required the SONACOTRAL to purchase or create its own HLM companies in regions with the worst housing problems. It made good financial sense for the SONACOTRAL to create distinct companies that benefited from special incentives reserved for HLMs.[134] Using an existing standardized business model known as Real Estate Management Companies, or LOGECO,[135] the SONACOTRAL's new HLM companies—LOGIREP (Paris), LOGIREL (Lyon), LOGIREM (Marseille), and LOGI-EST (Eastern departments)—remained separate, yet tightly connected to the parent corporation. They even shared one appointed administrator, Yves Jullien, who also served as a financial manager for the SONACOTRAL. In addition, the parent company's director, Jean Vaujour, followed by Henry Laborie in 1962, remained clearly in command of all branches.[136]

The bureaucratic processes necessary to create the SONACOTRAL's HLM companies took time. Planning began in 1959, but the first company, LOGIREP, did not start any projects until the Finance and Interior Ministries approved the deal in August 1960.[137] Canibouts was one of its first projects. The company also built a 130-unit complex on the Quai Saint-Denis in Argenteuil and a 48-unit apartment building in Aubervilliers, which was scheduled to house the approximately sixty Algerian families (260 people) living below the poverty line in that neighborhood.[138]

In Lyon the committee that oversaw all social housing construction companies in the Department of the Rhône region approved the SONACOTRAL's purchase of what became the LOGIREL in March 1960. Shortly thereafter, it broke ground on its first project, a 100-unit apartment building in the town of Vaulx-en-Velin.[139] In June the Bouches-du-Rhône and the surrounding coastal region also opened a social housing construction company for Algerian families. LOGIREM's first three projects produced 250 family units,[140] including a 70-unit structure built on part of Cap Janet in Marseille.[141] The last of these companies, LOGI-EST, which served the coal-rich departments of Meurthe and Moselle and to a lesser degree Alsace, started operations in October 1961.[142]

The HLMs initially expected to build only 1,100 family apartments over three years,[143] but authorities repeatedly revised the goals. With the help of the Social Action Fund, the SONACOTRAL's first three real estate management companies constructed nearly 2,200 permanent housing units by the end of 1960.[144] By early 1961 LOGIREP had either broken ground on or planned six more projects that would provide housing to 1,120 families, and the companies in Lyon and Marseille each had three projects underway, which would provide 670 and 250 units, respectively, to local families.[145] By the end of the year, each had made significant progress, with 431 apartments built in Paris and its environs, 243 in Lyon, and 190 in Marseille.[146] In total, by October 1961 the three companies had over 3,500 apartments either built or planned.[147]

In regions without a SONACOTRAL social housing company, other organizations continued the effort to relieve the housing crisis. Most prominently, the center for Propaganda and Action against Slums in the Nord worked with the Aid Association for French Algerians in the Region of Lille to build numerous transitional housing projects and half a dozen HLM complexes in the last years of the war. This local program, financed in large measure by the Social Action Fund, began in 1960. Although 240 HLM apartments were built,[148] they accommodated only a few dozen of the 1,000 Algerian families (which included over 2,000 children under the age of fifteen) estimated to be living in substandard conditions in the department. Admitting the larger problems could not be resolved "without first providing these families with decent housing," the Aid Association for French Algerians in the Region of Lille estimated the cities of Lille, Roubaix, and Tourcoing each required fifty more transitional and permanent housing units every year for the foreseeable future to begin to fulfill current needs.[149]

Despite the dozens of projects planned around the country, many of the SONACOTRAL's HLM complexes faced obstacles that stymied construction. In some cases land costs prohibited a particular purchase. To overcome this barrier, some localities contributed to the financing by deeding the land for a particular project. In many other cases, however, municipal governments or landowners thwarted projects. Some refused to sell land, and others agreed in principle, but held up construction with red tape. Some slowed or refused to issue permits using seemingly legitimate arguments, including that the new construction would put stress on sewers and other infrastructure.[150]

To facilitate the process, the state issued circulars and ordinances regarding the acquisition of land and the renovation of dilapidated housing. In addition to the circular that called for the liquidation of the bidonvilles, an ordinance issued in 1958 made it easier for all housing companies to confiscate land through eminent domain.[151] When this ordinance did not prove effective enough, the SONACOTRAL used two other policies to circumvent local obstacles. The first, an order issued by Construction Minister Sudreau, encouraged regular HLM housing companies to acquire and renovate older structures.[152] When the policy did not seem to be working, Construction Ministry officials recommended that the SONACOTRAL use these regulations to build less-expensive transitional housing for Algerian families.[153] Since even these policies did not prevent localities from keeping Algerians out of certain communities, Louis Joxe, the minister of state for Algerian affairs, issued another ordinance in February 1961 that authorized the temporary confiscation of land needed to build housing for "French Muslims."[154] These policies helped to free up land for construction, but it also seems clear the police and other local authorities used them to displace Algerians living in shanties before alternative housing became available.

Despite construction proceeding on dozens of projects, only a few Algerian families moved into the apartments built with money withheld from their paychecks. This arose for a variety of reasons. When authorities evicted Algerians from bidonvilles before construction began, families moved away, unable to wait for new, subsidized housing. Some officials tried to find solutions for homeless families; others were happy to rid themselves of the Algerian problem. According to the Muslim Affairs Service, "vehement" local protest with "racist" overtones spurred local political figures' actions.[155] The mayor of Nanterre, for example, argued that the destruction of bidonvilles should be used as an opportunity to disperse former residents among a number of communities, rather than expecting one city to shoulder the burden permanently.[156]

More-affluent communities tried to prevent an influx of Algerians into their towns. When the Social Action Fund proposed a worker dormitory in what one senator from the Seine called the "bourgeois" Parisian suburb of Rosny-sous-Bois, well-connected local leaders enlisted the support of high-ranking politicians, including Giscard d'Estaing, to make their case. The community declared it could accept a small but unspecified number of Algerian families, but it would not house 250 Algerian workers.[157] In making their case, community leaders used language inflected with both class- and race-based stereotypes. They insisted Rosny-sous-Bois had no industry, making it inconvenient for Algerians who would be too far from their place of employment. Leaders predicted that this demographic shift would be "disastrous" for the community's development.[158] They had been working on urban renewal projects and had thus far been able to stem the tide of "communist" influence. If constructed, the dormitory would "stifle the implementation of an improvement project" planned for the neighborhood.[159] Instead of upsetting the "psychological and sociological context" of the neighborhood, Senator Marette suggested Massenet relocate the project to a more appropriate "eastern suburb" of Paris.[160]

This case highlights growing fears about workers since leaders of a Parisian suburb of 19,000 thought they would be overrun by 250 single men (but could accommodate a smaller, less threatening number of Algerian families).[161] It does not mean, however, that communities embraced Algerian family settlement. The town of Villeurbanne (Rhône) tried to prevent the construction of apartment complexes that reserved some units for Algerian families.[162] In other cases, organizations applied for Social Action Fund monies to build family housing projects fully intending to place strict limits on the number of Algerian families that would have access to the apartments. When an HLM company in Le Havre applied for support, Social Action Fund board members voiced concerns about whether the Fund's contribution would achieve the desired results. Hopeful, the Fund's board approved the subvention, since the company promised to set aside 60 (or twelve percent of) apartments in two complexes that would eventually house 750 families.[163] In what Massenet referred to as one of "the most scandalous cases," a municipal HLM company in Saint-Etienne received Social Action Fund subsidies but accepted just two Algerian families in its nearly 4,000 completed apartments.[164]

The SONACOTRAL and Social Action Fund both anticipated and responded to these types of problems by sending a simple message: France needed to accept a mixture of Algerians and metropolitan families in all subsidized housing programs.[165] While they generally targeted people in the housing industry, including local government officials and HLM managers, leading advocates also appealed to the nation. In April 1960, Joseph

Leriche, the director of North African Social Studies, taped a radio address that aired twice on France II. He criticized the violent bulldozing of bidonvilles, calling it a "flagrant injustice." Moreover, he insisted that "real racism" did not exist in France, while nevertheless imploring the nation to unite in its condemnation of "all discrimination" by ensuring that subsidized housing incorporated "the broadest 'mixture'" of people possible.[166]

To ensure the mixing occurred, the SONACOTRAL and the Social Action Fund implemented two interrelated approaches: a quota system and a housing exchange program. These approaches developed together to balance the tensions between Algerians' needs and the general population's fears. When the SONACOTRAL reluctantly began to participate in the construction of Algerian family housing, Claudius-Petit proposed each complex reserve only between ten and fifteen percent of units for Algerian families to avoid "de facto segregation."[167] And although exact percentages were not codified in official policy, early on officials called for between ten and twenty percent of units and increasingly settled on reserving fifteen percent of units for Algerian families in order "to avoid segregation and to facilitate these families' integration into the French community."[168]

To ensure the quota would succeed in both preventing discrimination and housing a significant number of Algerian families, administrators linked it to "an exchange of apartments with other HLM companies."[169] The SONACOTRAL and the Social Action Fund believed this would prevent de facto segregation by limiting the number of Algerian families in their housing and by ensuring that Algerians moved into regular HLM complexes as well.[170] The program consisted of friendly agreements between regular HLM companies and the SONACOTRAL or the Social Action Fund. In each case a certain number of units in regular housing complexes would be accorded to Algerian families in exchange for placing metropolitan families into units built for Algerians. In theory, this would be to everyone's benefit. Regular HLMs received an incentive: if they housed some Algerian families, then a larger number of metropolitan families on their waiting lists could move into new complexes sponsored by the SONACOTRAL or the Social Action Fund. As housing companies became aware they could apply for money if they opened their doors to Algerians, the Social Action Fund experienced a sharp increase in applications.[171]

Algerian families moved into most housing sponsored by the SONA-COTRAL or the Social Action Fund, despite the kind of fraud in the "scandalous" example discussed above. Evidence strongly suggests housing complexes built with Algerian workers' money (through the one percent deduction) allocated about fifteen percent of units to Algerian families, with some variation in both directions. In a typical example, in the Department of the Bouches-du-Rhône a committee that included the prefect, Claudius-Petit, Vaujour, Louis Belpeer, the IGAME, a local technical consultant, and the head of the North African Dormitory Housing Association met to discuss the SONACOTRAL's "exceptional" involvement in a 750-unit HLM project in Marseille. The committee decided to set aside twenty percent (150) of the units for Algerian families. The remaining 600 apartments would go to metropolitan families already on waiting lists. As compensation, 225 apartments would be made available to Algerian families in the various HLM projects under construction throughout the region over three years.[172]

Enforcing the exchange policy with regular HLM companies proved difficult. Housing managers and local officials frequently refused to accept Algerians. As we have seen in other circumstances, they offered excuses legitimized by the widely accepted expert knowledge that framed Algerians' eligibility in a highly subjective evaluation of their supposed level of evolution. If social workers or housing managers rejected potential residents for being insufficiently evolved, they could justify their approval of only a very small percentage of Algerians. Housing advocates saw through the excuses. According to the SONACOTRAL's annual report for 1961, "too few HLM organizations" honored the agreements already in place for the reasons discussed above.[173] After numerous complexes accepted subsidies but refused to adhere to its policies, the Social Action Fund became more cautious. In one case the board postponed approval of financial support for a housing complex in the town of Salon-de-Provence because its plans indicated the segregation of Algerian families from the general population by reserving eighty percent of units in a Social Action Fund–supported complex for Algerians, without any indication of other HLMs' participation in an exchange. When Social Action Fund personnel made inquires, it became clear local HLM companies refused to accept Algerian families in exchange for apartments in the Social Action Fund subsidized complex.[174]

Right up until Algeria gained independence, administrators in the Algerian welfare network continued to voice their frustrations and condemn discriminatory housing practices as the biggest obstacle they faced.[175] They also implemented new techniques that might improve outcomes. The

SONACOTRAL studied contracts with regular HLM companies more closely before entering into exchange agreements.[176] The Family Housing Commission in the Seine took another step, compiling its own list of "future beneficiaries" that prioritized the neediest families. As part of it, Massenet insisted families whose homes had been destroyed to make way for HLM complexes not be placed at the bottom of the list.[177]

Despite disavowing racist practices and discrimination, little changed. In part this came from an inability or unwillingness to replace staff in the various agencies or to force housing managers and others to rethink how they made decisions. Massenet continued to worry that unless the Construction Ministry used its "authority," housing practices would not change.[178] Massenet, Claudius-Petit, and others had no power over those working in the regular HLM companies. The Social Action Fund tried to limit or even withdraw support from organizations that did not comply with agreements, but problems often surfaced only when complexes opened for business. And, as we have seen, contemporary experts believed former colonists' experience with Algerians' particular mentality made them well suited for these jobs. In the case of the SONACOTRA (the successor of the SONACOTRAL), as late as 1972 ninety-five percent of its dormitory resident directors had had a military career in Indochina, West Africa, or North Africa.[179] In other words, Algerian services' administrators fought discrimination and segregation even as they hired men whose primary experience and training had been in the bloody wars of decolonization.

The seeming contradiction in this practice is yet another reminder that Algerian advocates espoused and reinforced prejudicial stereotypes even as they criticized them. Experts continued to argue that only with the cooperation of local governments, state agencies, employers, and private associations could the "delicate task" of overcoming Algerians' "diverse linguistic, social and vocational handicaps" be accomplished without enflaming "social tensions."[180] Housing managers' experiences in the colonial context may have colored their views about Algerians' preparedness for life in HLMs, but welfare administrators' advice also legitimized their decisions. According to a technical consultant in the Loire, there were two types of Muslim families. The larger segment of the population had the "desire, above all, to live 'as Europeans.'" The rest preferred to live "with other families that have the same origins, so that they can reconnect tribal and family ties."[181] As Massenet pointed out in the *Cahiers nord-africains*, the best outcome that could be hoped for was to prove that "certain sufficiently evolved and stable families" could "benefit from HLM housing."[182] So, while advocates expressed frustration with the excuses that justified discriminatory practices, their own arguments legitimized, even buttressed, managers' reasoning for turning away Algerian families.

As hostilities associated with the war increased, so did concerns about the size of the Algerian population. Advocates more frequently distinguished between Algerians who had been in France for a long time and those who had arrived recently. Fears coalesced around claims that "less evolved" arrivals constituted a minority that "dominated" new migration patterns.[183] Even as those working in the welfare network continued to point out that many Algerian families had adjusted well, they also called for quality-control regulations for new migrants. In a meeting that brought together key officials in Marseille, the director of Aid to Overseas Workers proposed that Algerians in France "without work or housing" be issued a "repatriation ticket" and sent home.[184]

This request did more than foreshadow regulations implemented in the years following independence. In 1961, officials from Algerian Affairs informed regional prefects that families wishing to settle in France should complete a residency certification process. This policy directed local officials to determine a family's stability by collecting both the male head of household's work contract and a certificate proving he had found appropriate family housing. The housing certification also collected data about the size of the family and each member's relationship to the head of the household.[185] Implemented through a circular, the policy did not officially abrogate the freedom-of-movement clause of the 1947 law, but it became the first step in a series of regulations that intended to restrict Algerian family settlement after independence.[186]

Other changes taking place in the shadow of Algerian independence related to the network's allocation of resources. Some agencies earmarked funds for the "victims of North African terrorism in the metropole" and for French colonists fleeing Algeria.[187] For the latter, administrators reasoned that both "French Muslims" and "Algerians"—i.e., white colonists—were eligible for any services supported by the Algerian welfare network.[188] The Labor Ministry, the Muslim Affairs Service, the Social Action Fund, and the Aid Commission for North Africans in the Metropole all set aside part of their budgets to provide emergency aid for people fleeing the conflict. Recipients of cash payments included colonial bureaucrats of European and Algerian origin, Algerian veterans (harkis) and French colonists, referred to in documents as "French from Algeria," "repatriates," or "Algerians."[189] This practice continued and less than a month after the police massacre in October 1961, a Labor Ministry representative on the Social Action Fund's board voiced a widely held opinion. According to Chaulet, the Fund had to respect its original mission, but at the same time it needed to do all it could for the "French from Algeria" arriving in the metropole.[190]

These policy reinterpretations meant Algerians—French Muslims from Algeria—were no longer the exclusive recipients of the Algerian welfare network's services and aid. Instead, by arguing colonists had the same eligibility, a growing portion of welfare providers aided a group referred to pejoratively as *pieds noirs*. French colonists began fleeing in significant numbers in June 1962, when over 20,000 families fled Algeria. Between May and August 1962, more than 183,000 Europeans left the Department of Oran alone. By October 1962, only 200,000 French still lived in Algeria, most in the three major metropolitan areas of Algiers, Bône, and Philippeville. The provisional Algerian government—fearing a brain drain in the managerial sectors of government and business—and the Secret Army Organization tried to prevent the colonists from leaving. But no incentives, legal or otherwise, dissuaded them.[191]

This migration heaped more strain on the already overburdened housing system, especially when coupled with a massive increase in Algerian migration, including harkis, who faced summary execution if they remained in Algeria. As a result, former colonists and harkis moved into transitional housing and bidonvilles.[192] To ease the housing crisis and to prevent violent retribution between groups embittered by the long war, the state corralled harkis. Claiming safety precautions and the need to protect the French economy, military authorities placed the harkis and their families into austere camps previously occupied by prisoners of war and alongside Algerians suspected of FLN sympathies.[193] The camps, with barbed wire fences and armed guards, truly isolated their residents. No one left without special permission. French officials reconstructed each male resident's history and job skills to determine his employment prospects. They assigned most harkis to difficult, undesirable jobs. The National Forest Service employed many unable to find other work. Internees also included elderly pensioners and war widows thought to be incapable of integrating into French society. The camps even had separate schools for the children, who often remained in the camps with their families into their adolescence and beyond.[194]

Former colonists had a different experience. They too initially faced unsatisfactory conditions in transitional housing or slums,[195] but most eventually moved into permanent housing. Just as many newly constructed SONACOTRAL and Social Action Fund family housing projects began to accept residents, former colonists arrived in droves.[196] Since no one required former colonists to participate in the transitional educational programs, the SONACOTRAL immediately began assigning HLM apartments to them. By late 1962, the SONACOTRAL had developed an official policy to set aside 2,000 apartments for "repatriated" French citizens, 650 of which were already occupied.[197] Overall, as Marie-Claude Blanc-Chaléard has shown, the SONACOTRAL reserved up to thirty percent of apartments for repatriated French colonists.[198]

Given the acute housing shortages, former colonists often waited some time before permanent housing became available.[199] In SONACOTRAL-sponsored complexes, families on opposite sides of the conflict in Algeria frequently lived together. Housing former colonists, bitter about being exiled from their homeland, side by side with FLN adherents or average Algerians proud their homeland earned independence almost certainly aggravated tensions among people who perceived one another as adversaries. LOGIREM's La Busserine apartment complex provides a typical example. It allocated the first fifty apartments to open in its 288-unit complex to families it believed had the greatest need. "Algerian-Muslim families" that had already completed the training in Cap Janet and St. Barthélemy transitional housing moved into twenty apartments. Repatriated European families from Algeria and metropolitan families (all of whom had lived in Marseille's bidonvilles) evenly divided the other thirty apartments.[200] The case of La Busserine, like others, demonstrates that although Algerian families continued to move into HLM apartments several years after independence, housing officials also had great sympathy for colonists. Even though, presumably, Algerian families had lived in France and had been on waiting lists much longer, having European origins almost certainly played a role in how quickly families moved into HLM apartments. Thus, Algerian families more often languished in transitional housing complexes, sometimes for a decade or more.[201]

IN APRIL 1964, a social center for North African families opened on the grounds of the Canibouts apartment complex. The SONACOTRAL bemoaned the social isolation families faced. With no cafés or movie theaters nearby, families spent most of their time "isolated, huddled around their TVs."[202] To change this, the center targeted North African families (about twelve percent of residents).[203] The center's staff considered its services necessary because women moving from the transitional housing or the bidonvilles were "rarely prepared for the rational utilization of the [modern] comforts placed at their disposal." Even with "an array of educational, social, and sanitary services and communal programs" created to train them, Algerian women never met expectations. Officials apparently worried that without constant instruction and surveillance, Algerian women would not maintain their new apartments, even if the center's staff insisted its goal was to "help families and individuals blossom."[204]

Social workers continued to determine each woman's "level of evolution" using a placement exam, which in turn determined the kind of services she needed in her "adaptation . . . [to] the modern environment." Women scoring zero on the placement test had to attend remedial French language classes, while those with rudimentary language skills could participate in geography, history, and other courses. The center also offered babysitting and practical-skills training for all women which included dietary planning, budgeting, and coping with problems children might encounter. The local Family Allowance office also provided a social worker who taught women how to sew, cook, knit, mend and iron clothes, as well as how to clean under beds and behind curtains and to close window shutters properly.[205]

It became increasingly rare for Algerian families to receive this kind of attention after 1962. As part of a larger restructuring of the Algerian welfare network, in the spring of 1963 the Social Action Fund's board decided to change its policies. Family housing remained a priority, insofar as it facilitated the "liquidation" of the bidonvilles, but it no longer warranted "the very high priority that it had previously retained."[206] Thus, administrators anticipated a quick resolution of the bidonville problem, after which the rupture of "the unique connection uniting France and Algeria . . . no longer justified . . . a special effort in this area."[207] In early 1964, the Social Action Fund slashed spending on family housing from 8.5 to 1.5 million francs for that year.[208]

As priorities shifted, the aspiration that housing projects would become bustling neighborhoods vanished.[209] Planned communities like Canibouts that were supposed to have businesses, shops, parks, and transportation opened as unfinished, barren housing blocks. As a remedy, the state began using a new urban planning tool, the Prioritized Urban Zone (ZUP), to facilitate construction of its massive social housing complexes. A term also used in Algeria, the ZUPs in France, as Michael Miller has pointed out, "were less bereft of services and facilities than the earlier" social housing projects.[210] But by the end of the decade, ZUPs increasingly housed poor, minority communities; amenities were in disrepair if they existed at all. North African Family Social Service, one of the few organizations that continued to work with and keep track of Algerians long after Algerian independence, reported that residents in one ZUP felt "crushed" in the "15 story towers." Despite having lots of neighbors, the lack of privacy and the dearth of social spaces increased the sense of isolation.[211] Nearly twenty years after it opened, social workers at the oldest service organization for Algerian families in the metropole continued to blame circumstances, *not* Algerian women. No matter how hard Algerian women worked to maintain decent homes, these advocates warned that Algerians could never properly integrate into French society without adequate housing. While demanding that more be done to help clients left languishing in slums or in isolated projects, North African Family Social Service pointed to success stories. Even in the late 1960s, social workers helped families move into proper, large apartments or single-family homes.[212]

Algerian families also continued to move into SONACOTRAL and Social Action Fund housing after 1962. Taking LOGREM's estimates from 1967 as a snapshot of the situation in France's second largest city, Algerian families occupied twelve percent of its apartments, a figure only slightly lower than the optimal fifteen percent developed by the 1950s quota system. By 1970, SONACOTRA still reserved ten to fifteen percent of units for Algerian families.[213] At the same time, the exchange system had been an utter failure. Nearly all evidence suggests that regular HLM companies rarely accepted more than a handful of Algerian clients, even when hundreds of their own applicants moved into housing built for Algerians. In 1968, Algerians made up only one percent of residents in regular HLM complexes.[214] Instead of integrating into regular housing, Algerians as well as newer immigrant groups became increasingly crowded into bidonvilles, slums, and transitional housing projects.[215] According to the SONACOTRA's 1973 annual report, immigrant families inhabited fifteen percent of its HLM housing, whereas transitional units were often filled entirely by immigrants. Two-thirds of them came from North Africa.[216] A 1965 study of five transitional housing projects north and west of Paris indicated that the overwhelming majority of residents came from Algeria (ninety-one percent). On average, families lived in the transitional units for at least three years. Of the ninety-three families that moved out of these transitional housing complexes in 1964 and 1965, twenty-one returned to Algeria (twelve apparently voluntarily).[217] Some may have "integrated" into general housing, but the majority probably remained isolated from the general population.

Once Algeria gained independence, the state-led effort to resolve the Algerian problem through the integration of families vanished along with Algerians' visibility in France. Instead, a new narrative slowly developed in the last quarter of the twentieth century. It centered on the problem of immigration, ignored the history of colonialism and decolonization, and depicted Algerians as one of many unsolicited and unwelcome groups of foreign migrants invading France.

Conclusion

THE URBAN REBELLION that exploded in the suburbs north of Paris in October 2005 spread quickly, with images of burning cars in cities from Strasbourg to Toulouse flashing on media outlets around the world. One young man of Arab descent showed his French identity card to the television cameras, insisting "we are already French. We were born in French hospitals. Why do they talk about integration? We are French."[1] Most of the violence remained restricted to poor neighborhoods, where residents often lived in what had become dilapidated social housing. The HLMs Father Ghys considered the "hope" for Algerian migrants in the 1950s and 1960s became the site of violence after two young men were accidently killed fleeing the police. The boys' deaths symbolized frustrations about racial profiling, residential segregation, high unemployment, and hopelessness. Institutions examined in this book faced a barrage of criticism centered on the perceived failure of integrationist programs from housing to job training. Most pointedly, the FASILD—the updated acronym for the Social Action Fund—which had long been "on the side of the establishment,"[2] drew the ire of leaders in the affected communities. The mayors of Paris' burning suburbs claimed the FASILD turned its back on the minority populations in these marginalized areas; the void it left behind, they warned, had become increasingly filled by Muslim organizations.[3] Blaming an organization that supposedly abandoned its commitment to secular values by allowing confessional institutions to do the work of the Republic ignored the long history of the French state's use of private associations, which often had religious affiliations, in its civilizing project. Moreover, the Equal Opportunity law, the most prominent component of the state's response to popular unrest, renamed and repositioned the Social Action Fund once again, christening it the National Agency for Social Cohesion and Equal Opportunities.[4]

The events of 2005 as well as the ongoing Veil Affair demonstrate that while much has changed since the 1950s, many of the themes examined in this book still echo in the tensions, contradictions, and ambiguities of French social policy targeting citizens of color. Beginning in the 1970s, the Social Action Fund and the agencies with which it worked began committing resources to cultural programs, including the multilingual television program *Mosaïque*, which celebrated immigrant communities and traditions.[5] Nonetheless, multiculturalism—referred to with the pejorative "communitarianism"—and affirmative action remain, as Joan Scott has argued, anathema in France because of claims that they are contrary to universalism.[6] As this book has shown, France has a tradition of using specialized programs to help marginalized racial minorities "grasp equality." Tensions remain because France has not come to terms with the history of colonialism and the Algerian War. Moreover, what it means to be integrated into French society, who is considered truly French, and who is considered French with qualifications, is in part tied to the historical legacy of the services examined in this book. The ambiguous meanings of integration are largely the result of French welfare state policy and practice, which continue to weave together "compassion and repression,"[7] service and surveillance, paternalism and state aid. Social programs are blamed for failing to integrate French citizens of color even when these same citizens posses identity cards and social and cultural experiences they see as French. The tension originates in the transformative republican project's inherent conflict, which presupposes that citizens with names, religions, or other ethnic markers must relinquish their particularity and melt into the dominant, universal culture. The paternalistic approach of social programs continues to allow the mayors of Paris' suburbs to proclaim that integration has failed, even as young French citizens, products of the national education system and social services, declare they are integrated. The debate still revolves around the perceptions of government officials, social workers, and others, who judge if an individual or group has successfully become French.

The social policies and practices targeting minority populations from the former empire in the late twentieth and early twenty-first centuries are directly linked to the Algerian welfare network created during the era of decolonization. These links, however, have gone unnoticed because the origins of the Algerian welfare network fell victim to the amnesia about the Algerian War and the history of Algerian settlement in France. When the Social Action Fund celebrated its tenth anniversary in 1968, it published a glossy, thirty-page brochure—with a preface by Michel Massenet—for the occasion. Rather than providing a retrospective account of its creation at the height of the Algerian crisis and its work with Algerians in France, the brochure contained no references to either its history or original mission. Instead it discussed the Fund's efforts to help migrants—2 million Europeans, 800,000 Africans, and 100,000 from elsewhere. It highlighted the programs the Fund subsidized, nearly all of which were the same government projects and small charitable associations that it had funded since 1958.[8] Even though Algerians continued to receive aid, nothing in the brochure reminded readers that Algerians lived in France or that the entire system of services had been constructed in the midst of the Algerian War. Why, just six years after Algerian independence, did the Social Action Fund's anniversary publication make no reference to the minority population it was created to serve?

In one respect, Algerians living in France after 1962 continued to receive social services in much the same way they had before Algerian independence. Yet, the end of French rule in Algeria immediately changed their relationship to France. The Evian Accords afforded Algerians living in the metropole social but not political rights.[9] Algerians still had the right to claim welfare benefits, but they could no longer vote. In addition, Algerian migrants were physically and legal disconnected from their homeland (which could not extend control over them) and became foreigners that many people in France held responsible for a long and costly war.[10] Nearly all Algerian migrants continued to carry their French identity papers. It was not practical for most to request identity papers from the new Algerian Republic in the early 1960s. And, despite French laws that required Algerians in France to publicly assert their intention to remain French, most Algerians simply kept and continued to use the French papers they had.[11]

In response to all these changes, the Algerian welfare network also underwent a transformation between 1962 and 1966. French bureaucrats, program administrators, and other experts navigated a path that adapted the welfare network to the new political climate. The makeover shifted the network away from Algerians and instead established it as the foundation for all specialized services for immigrants and people of color in France into the twenty-first century. Algerians remained eligible for and continued to receive services, but the changes eclipsed their visibility in the system.

The transformation began just months after Algeria declared independence in July 1962. On 10 November 1962, the Social Action Fund's board of directors effectively cut support for programs in Algeria by delaying consent for their funding. Many board members did so reluctantly, worried about their decision's ramifications. The cuts, which amounted to roughly half of the Fund's annual budget, jeopardized the organizations it supported in Algeria, the people working in the network, and France's commitment to Algeria's "progress."[12] Board members also worried it was a first step in dismantling the Social Action Fund and the welfare network in the metropole. They were not alone. The *Cahiers nord-africains* dedicated its spring 1963 issue to the Fund's future, asking "Should we abolish the Social Action Fund?"[13] Its answer was an unequivocal no. The board of directors and other leading advocates made impassioned arguments that saved the network in the short term and led to its repositioning in the French bureaucracy.

Michel Massenet, as its highest-ranking official, became the most articulate voice for saving the welfare network. In a report that circulated among high-level administrators, he argued that services should be maintained for two overlapping reasons. First, "it is in our nation's own best interests for the French collectivity to uphold its responsibilities." If France abandoned these programs, solving the resulting problems would cost much more than was currently being spent. The second and perhaps most convincing justification hinged on the services' relationship to France's booming economy, which required labor. Algeria still offered a steady, unregulated supply.[14] Massenet both effectively defended the network and acknowledged that Algerian independence had "greatly modified the perspective through which these problems should be approached." He conceded that after July 1962, Algerians became foreigners. Laws governing other foreigners in France would determine their status as well. Henceforth, the new nation's consulates would mediate problems with its citizens. Immigration policy would be determined through bilateral agreements. The Algerian case, however, never proved simple, and Massenet and his colleagues understood its "particularities." He cited an unnamed study as a reminder that Algerian settlement in France represented one of the largest migratory movements in the world, and warned that because of "cultural" differences, Algerians risked permanent isolation from the rest of the population unless the welfare network, the "final link" between the two communities, continued to function.[15]

The *Cahiers nord-africains* made similar economic and "moral" arguments, urging the state to maintain the publicly and privately managed welfare programs. Not only did France need this indispensable and cost effective labor pool—when compared to European or other African workers (including Moroccans, Tunisians, and West Africans)—but it also had to help those "expelled from Algeria by misery and attracted to France because of a certain measure of contentment and freedom."[16] The government agreed; in early 1963 Prime Minister Georges Pompidou extended the Social Action Fund's mission in the metropole for at least three years.[17]

As a result, the Algerian social welfare network operated in much the same way it had before independence.[18] Despite cuts, the Social Action Fund budget distributed over twenty million francs to over one hundred fifty government agencies and private organizations.[19] It still supported services for women and children because, as Bernard Lory of the Public Health and Population Ministry explained, "the massive presence of these families" necessitated services in this area. In addition to supporting the Social Action Fund, Lory's department also continued its financial support of key welfare associations (including Moral Assistance for North Africans, North African Family Social Service, Aid to Overseas Workers, and the Aid Commission for North Africans in the Metropole) and subsidized social centers in HLMs and neighborhoods heavily populated by Algerian families.[20]

The administrators and advocates who protected the Social Action Fund and the associations it supported knew the future of their mission was uncertain. Prefects expressed great concern about continuing to support the growing Algerian population. The Interior Ministry's Jacques Aubert echoed Massenet. He admonished the prefects that despite their inclinations, "it is not appropriate to consider this particular problem resolved and [they should not] treat Algerians as ordinary foreigners." Aubert's advice acknowledged that everyone wanted to forget about decolonization, dismissed claims that Algerians received preferential treatment, and asserted that regional governors could not ignore the problems associated with Algerians. Navigating the realities of the post-independence situation, including the Evian Accords' extension of Algerians' right to circulate freely, meant that officials still had to consider Algerians' distinct status. Government officials outside Paris had to follow the national government's lead, which according to Aubert, meant continuing to provide social services.[21]

Even as the welfare network's administrators passionately argued for maintaining the status quo, they proposed ways to adapt to the new realities. Driven by a desire to prevent their own obsolescence and wanting to create new employment opportunities for the wave of former colonial bureaucrats reaching France, they began to search for long-term solutions.[22] Not wanting to throw away many years of experience that could be used in programs and controls for all immigrants, administrators made a compelling argument for the need to expand the network. Labor Minister Gilbert Grandval, himself a veteran of the colonial administration in Morocco,[23] worked to see the Social Action Fund's services expanded to immigrants from other countries. He emphasized that ties with Algeria were no longer "exclusive" and that Algerians could no longer "benefit from privileges" closed to other immigrants. Grandval hoped he and Massenet could cooperate to improve the quality of France's immigrant workforce. With the post–World-War II recovery expanding to other European nations, he warned of increased competition for foreign labor among industrialized nations. Social welfare programs could entice desirable workers. If France did not provide services to attract workers from Eastern Europe and the Iberian Peninsula, it would lose this productive labor force as Germany courted sought-after European workers.[24] For Grandval, expanding the client base made good sense. It allowed France to break its dependence on Algerian labor, forget about the colonial war, and hire white workers.

Most of the organizations in the welfare network, also wanting to cut their ties to the bitter war and to expand their mission and clientele, changed their names. The SONACOTRAL (Société nationale de construction de logements pour les travailleurs originaires d'Algérie et leurs familles) became the first major organization to redefine its mission and alter its title to reflect a new, broader clientele. In July 1963, a special gathering of the National Assembly introduced the SONACOTRA (Société nationale de construction de logements pour les travailleurs). The new legislation also specified that henceforth the SONACOTRA would concentrate on the production of housing for all "French or foreign workers . . . most notably those coming from overseas," i.e., non-European migrants from the former and remaining colonial possessions. When necessary, because of limited local resources or economic demands, the SONACOTRA also built housing for workers "already living in France" and for some students. Families remained one of the groups for which it could provide housing, but this category plummeted to the absolute last position in the ranking.[25]

Likewise, in the spring of 1964 the Social Action Fund changed its name, removing Algerians from its full title. Even if its acronym (FAS) did not change, its new mission made its resources available to all foreign workers in France.[26] Similarly, the Interior Ministry's Muslim Affairs Service extended its services and jurisdiction to all North and West Africans in France in 1964.[27] The following year it became the Liaison Service for Migrant Support—serving all migrants.[28] Once these key government agencies changed their names and constituencies, private organizations followed suit. Most notably, North African Social Studies published the final issue of the *Cahiers nord-africains* in the summer of 1964. It became *Hommes et Migrations*, France's premier migration studies journal.[29] Some organizations, known primarily by their acronyms, expanded their client base even if they did not change their names. For example, the Aid Association for French Algerians in the Region of Lille had served Algerians and their families in and around the Nord's largest city since 1953. Without changing its name, the association began shifting services away from Algerians in 1965. Until then, its correspondence with state agencies referred to Muslim clients, with clear indications that Algerians constituted the overwhelming majority of those it served. Starting in 1965, records stopped using the terms "Muslim," "Algerian," and "North African." From then on, the Aid Association, one of the largest private organizations in the Nord, referred to its clients as "foreigners," without reference to country of origin, ethnicity, or religion.[30] In all probability, the Aid Association in Lille, as well as similar organizations in other French cities, continued to serve Algerians, as well as Moroccans, Tunisians, and other immigrant groups. In the postcolonial era, however, categorizing clients by their relationship to the empire ceased being relevant or politically expedient.

The changes in these organizations' names symbolically captured the larger bureaucratic reorganization underway. When the 1964 interministerial decree reorganizing the Social Action Fund took effect, Algerians remained eligible for services provided by the agencies it funded.[31] Agencies and associations submitting annual reports and funding requests quickly learned, however, not to highlight Algerian clients. Instead, within a few years, reports from most organizations mirrored the new goals, using terminology that referred to immigrants from a variety of origins.

The Social Action Fund, like several other government agencies, also had to reposition itself when the state phased out all offices related to Algerian Affairs. Since its creation in 1958, the Social Action Fund reported to the prime minister's office via the secretary-general of Algerian Affairs. Following the initial restructuring, it reported directly to the prime minister. Likewise, it shuffled its board of directors to ensure representation of all agencies concerned with immigration. Massenet oversaw this transition and consolidated his power. He had ultimate control over the preparation of the Social Action Fund's annual programs, sat on the board of directors, acted as the organization's director, and continued to report directly to the prime minister. Several checks, however, prevented Massenet from making all decisions. Representatives from the prime minister's office, as well as from the Finance, Labor, and Public Health Ministries, reviewed each significant decision.[32]

In 1966, Massenet again took center stage as the state furthered its reorganization of the social service administration. Concerned that initial changes did not alleviate duplications in the system, the Pompidou administration created the Social Affairs Ministry, with Jean-Marcel Jeanneney, France's first ambassador to Algeria, at the helm. To streamline services, the administration consolidated key offices in several ministries and placed them, along with the Social Action Fund, under the new ministry. Its new Population and Migration Office (Direction de la population et des migrations, DPM) dealt with all aspects of the migratory process through its 3 sub-offices (Population Movements, Social Programs for Migrants, and Naturalizations). The national government's administrative leadership intended the Office of Population and Migration to play the central role in the politics of immigration, and none other than Michel Massenet became its first director. Jeanneney and Massenet filled the new administration with elite bureaucrats who had learned their management techniques during the Algerian crisis.[33] Not only had the leadership of the retooled immigrant service network come of age during the Algerian crisis, but the ministerial structures continued to support "the private initiatives of the earlier period."[34]

Immigration policy also reflected France and Algeria's complex relationship in the post-independence era. In 1964, the Neccache-Grandval Accords implemented a quota system based on unemployment in Algeria and underemployment in France.[35] These programs, like the recruitment programs established during the colonial period, had limited success.

Algerians avoided the procedures in place as part of the quota and instead used business and family connections. As a result, contemporary statistics remained as flawed as they had been in the 1950s, offering only global estimates of the size of the Algerian population in France.[36] What is clear: Algerians continued to migrate, the family population continued to grow, and social welfare organizations continued to provide Algerians' services.

The rhetorical place of Algerian women and children constituted one of the major differences between the two periods. Whereas family migration had been encouraged as part of war propaganda before 1962, Algerian women and children no longer had a place in post-independence French politics. Algerian family migration became a source of great anxiety, with multiple voices warning France would be overrun.[37] One of the Interior Ministry's concerns focused on the estimated 100,000 Algerian children who apparently posed "considerable social problems."[38] Continued migration and births (an estimated 25,000 children were born each year during the decade after Algerian independence) made officials increasingly worried about the impact of Algerian fecundity on France.[39] A report compiled for the Interior Ministry in 1965 indicated Algerians had the largest number of children among immigrant groups.[40] According to North African Family Social Service, after a dozen years in France, Algerian families had an average of seven children.[41] These figures, which indicated a much higher birthrate than that of the general population, amplified anxiety about Algerian families in a nation that had long worried about declining birthrates and demographic shifts that would change the nation's complexion.

These fears inspired officials to find new ways to curb Algerian family settlement and fecundity. Breaking with policies established during the Algerian crisis, new rules, based on the notion that large families took advantage of the social welfare safety net, tried to restrain family size. Algerian fruitfulness had to be reversed before it had a deleterious effect on France's future.[42] Officials repeatedly projected that the Algerian population in France, if allowed to reproduce unchecked, would reach as many as 1.3 million by the end of the century.[43] Massenet went even further, arguing in 1967 that Algerians' unrestrained migration and birthrates would lead to a population of 2.2 million by the end of the century, with "exponential consequences" for France.[44] The possibility that so many Algerians could call France home by the year 2000 seemed terrifying.

One of the first and most unambiguous steps the French government took to curb Algerians' apparently unrestrained population growth came in the realm of welfare services. In 1963, the state denied Algerian women prenatal and maternity benefits. Cognizant that Article Seven of the Evian Accords protected Algerians' right to social welfare benefits, a subcommittee of the Muslim Affairs Service nevertheless determined these allowances had "a more demographic character." Therefore, as foreigners, Algerian women could no longer claim eligibility—since the state created prenatal and maternity benefits to expand the national population, not foreign populations in France. The committee argued that Article 1519 of the Social Security Code, which indicated the explicit national purpose of prenatal and maternity services, was in place before the Evian Accords. Thus, Algerians could be denied the prenatal and maternity benefits that they had been eligible for as citizens. To avoid controversy, since immigrants from other nations were eligible for prenatal and maternity benefits, the committee recommended the Algerian government negotiate, like any other foreign government, to have these services reinstated for its citizens while they lived in France.[45]

At about the same time, North African Family Social Service began educating Algerian women about several forms of birth control—"sterilization, pills, injection." Although these programs, which encouraged Algerian women to curb or halt their fertility, invite questions about a neo-eugenic agenda, only the state's decision to cut prenatal and maternity benefits fits squarely into this category. As for birth control, limited evidence suggests Algerian women wanted better family planning techniques. Not only had Algerian women already been using traditional "recipes" to end unwanted pregnancies, but, North African Family Social Service reports also noted, Algerian men and women regularly initiated requests for family planning advice.[46]

Other policies, again building on initiatives from the 1950s, tried to ensure only whole families with a fully employed, male head of household and proper housing could settle in France. As during the war, administrators considered Algerian women and children living outside a male-headed household a drain on the welfare system. Reporting that Algerians represented thirty percent of residents in its women's emergency shelter, the largest among all immigrant groups, the Liaison Service for Migrant Support tried to force single mothers to return to Algeria.[47] These women, however, "absolutely refused" to go back—purportedly fearing they would face worse poverty and humiliation from family members who did not approve of their choices.[48]

Policy changes and programs cuts exemplified a shift in the way bureaucrats, experts, and the general population perceived Algerian families.
Even though policies that encouraged permanent family settlement had
never enjoyed unanimous support, the national crusade to save French
Algeria had made it possible for Algerian women and children to receive
state benefits tied to France's long-standing pronatalist agenda. After independence, motivations for integrating these families into French society
disappeared with the colonial empire.

At the same time, prominent organizations in the welfare network
continued to provide services to Algerians and to act as their advocates.
Hommes et Migrations rejected the commonly held notion that Algerians
caused more problems than other immigrants and instead insisted Algerians had become "the most disadvantaged" group among immigrants.
Algerian workers and families suffered immeasurable discrimination compared to other immigrants. An editorial in the journal exposed the contradictions of the post-independence narrative. France's prosperous economy
required immigrant labor, but France declared Algerians unfit after 1962.
Hommes et Migrations accused the state of abandoning a group that had
played an immeasurable role in the economic boom. Only after Algeria
gained independence had racial and religious differences appeared as insurmountable barriers to Algerian membership in the French nation.[49]

Similarly, North African Family Social Service rejected the commonly
held negative views of their clients and instead argued Algerians were still
capable of becoming model immigrants.[50] Its social workers and administrators insisted Algerian families showed "a real degree of adaptation," which
it defined as stable work for the male head of household, a well-furnished,
clean home, children attending school, and a "well-integrated mother."[51]
Even into the 1970s, North African Family Social Service contended that
its Algerian clients "progressed well" and that the problems they faced re-
sembled those of the majority population.[52]

Nonetheless, organizations that had tried to implement a new version of the civilizing mission in the metropole continued to perpetuate
long-held attitudes and beliefs about Algerian families that colored their
actions long after 1962. Contrary to most state-funded organizations,
North African Family Social Service continued to devote much of its attention to young Algerian women—touting them as the best way to remake
the Algerian population. Its staff and administration continued to assert
proudly that "we penetrate most deeply into these families" through edu-

cational programs teaching French models for hygiene, child rearing, and housekeeping. North African Family Social Service believed its programs instilled in these young women "moral principles of honesty, [a] sense of responsibility" and "tolerance and respect" for others.[53] By making these claims, the oldest private welfare organization dedicated to Algerian families in France implied that Algerians could not or did not learn these basic principles from their own families or cultural heritage. In other words, even though North African Family Social Service staff asserted that Algerians could adapt to life in France, they continued to perpetuate assumptions about Algerian inferiority. Its social workers and administrators spent a great deal of time grappling with Algerian cultural practices in an attempt to make this population compatible with French society.

Some of the specific ways North African Family Social Service approached its clients reflected changing preoccupations in the 1960s. Its staff worried much more than it had in the preceding decade about Algerians' fecundity, about the practice of "bigamy," and about the frequency with which Algerians brought multiple generations into apartments intended for nuclear families.[54] Certainly, overcrowding had been a concern in the 1950s, but in the 1960s inadequate housing and large, extended families became wholly interrelated problems. Concerned about Algerian birthrates, social workers responded to accusations from the general population that Algerian overcrowding ruined the HLMs for everyone by teaching Algerians how to adapt to French ways (including birth control).[55] Rather than pointing to structural discrimination, residential segregation, or practices and attitudes held by the public as at least a partial explanation of a range of problems, North African Family Social Service still traced the problems to Algerians' supposedly backward culture. Insistent that "too many Algerian families arrived with no aptitude for modern life,"[56] the staff generally blamed women for being unable or unwilling to adapt. As during the colonial era, women were criticized for not learning to speak French, not keeping a clean home, and not following social workers' recommendations. Algerian women's presumed inaptitude or resistance had lasting ramifications. They could be depicted as unfit for life in France, expected to adapt or return to Algeria.

French depictions of Algerians' actions can be read against the grain. Rather than evidence of backwardness, Algerians apparent recalcitrance can be interpreted as resistance to interference in family matters, as a desire to maintain religious and cultural traditions, and as an assertion of rights. In a case from the late 1960s, a social worker approached Milika, a sixteen-year-old girl raised by her mother and grandmother after her father's death, about attending home economics courses. Her family refused and announced Milika was getting married. North African Family Social Service concluded that it had failed Milika. She would not learn about the benefits of French society, social workers lamented, and therefore would not be prepared to assume her role as wife and mother. They could not imagine an alternative scenario, one that involved Milika's mother and grandmother preparing her for life and strategizing about how to keep social workers out of the family's affairs.[57]

Milika's case is part of a long tradition in the West of experts claiming to know what is in the best interests of women in both France and the empire. It is an example of the discourse that continues to echo in French debates about Muslims wearing the hijab. As Joan Scott reminds us, the public debate rarely takes women's voices into account even when sympathetic state officials—from high-level administrators to local teachers—weigh in. Instead, the discussion is framed in a series of oppositions reminiscent of those the Algerian welfare network implemented in the 1950s: particular/universal, Islam/France, oppression/emancipation, backward/modern.[58] The complex history of the Algerian welfare network provides context for better understanding these themes as well as the lasting legacies of decolonization.

Notes

GEANARP   Groupe d'étude et d'action pour les Nord Africains de la région parisienne

HLM   Habitat à loyer modéré

IGAME   Inspecteurs généraux de l'administration en mission extraordinaire

INED   Institut national d'études démographiques

INSEE   Institut national de la statistique et des études économiques

JO   Journal Officiel de la République Française

LOGI-EST   Logement et gestion immobilière pour la région de l'Est

LOGIREL   Logement et gestion immobilière pour la région lyonnaise

LOGIREM   Logement et gestion immobilière pour la région méditerranée

LOGIREP   Logement et gestion immobilière pour la région parisienne

MA   Ministère de l'Agriculture

MEN   Ministère de l'Education nationale

MI   Ministère de l'Intérieur

MNA   Mouvement national algérien

MR   Ministère de la Reconstruction

MSPP   Ministère de la Santé publique et de la Population

MTLD   Mouvement pour le triomphe des libertés démocratiques

MTSS   Ministère du Travail et de la Sécurité sociale

NF   New Francs

OAS   Organisation de l'armée secrète

OF   Old Francs

PACT   Propagande et action contre le taudis

PPA   Parti du peuple algérien

RTF   Radiodiffusion télévision française

SAMAS   Service des affaires musulmanes et de l'action sociale

SAS   Section administrative spécialisée

SAT   Service d'assistance technique

SLPM Service de liaison et de promotion des migrants

SONACOTRA   Société nationale de construction de logements pour les travailleurs

SONACOTRAL   Société nationale de construction de logements pour les travailleurs originaires d'Algérie et leurs familles

SSFNA   Service social familial nord-africain

UNAF   Union nationale des associations familiales

Introduction

1. "ATOM, Aide aux travailleurs d'outre-mer, historique," *Hommes et Migrations*, no. 110 (1968): 7.

2. Joseph Leriche, "Le logement familial," in "Le logement des Nord Africains (deuxième cahier)," *CNA* 35-6 (December 1953–January 1954): 33.

3. On the modernizing mission, see Chapter 1, and Shepard, *The Invention of Decolonization*, 6; Connelly, *A Diplomatic Revolution*, 27–34; Cooper, *Decolonization and African Society*, 277–322.

4. SSFNA, "Rapport moral," 1953, 2. SSFNA became ASSFAM in 1979.

5. Loi du 20 septembre 1947, portant statut organique de l'Algérie, *JO* 47-1853, 21 September 1947, 9470.

6. François Mitterrand, cited in Naylor, *France and Algeria*, 138.

7. Mitterrand, cited in Ageron, "L'opinion française devant la guerre d'Algérie," 260.

8. Wilder, *The French Imperial Nation-State*.

9. Herrick Chapman and Laura Frader, "Introduction," in Chapman and Frader, eds., *Race in France*, 3.

10. Brubaker, *Citizenship and Nationhood*.

11. Lewis, *The Boundaries of the Republic*; Weil, *Qu'est qu'un Français?*; Birnbaum, *Jewish Destinies*.

12. Frader, *Breadwinners and Citizens*, 104.

13. FAS, "Programme d'action sociale pour l'année 1959" (CAC 770391/2).

14. Pedersen, *Family, Dependence, and the Origins of the Welfare State*, 274.

15. Rager, "Les musulmans algériens," 126. As a student, Rager served in the cabinet of the governor-general of Algeria and by 1954 he was in the Labor and Social Security Department in Algiers.

16. The quotation is from Jean-Jacques Rager, "Evolution de la réglementation de la migration algérienne en France," in *Les migrations des populations* (Présidence du Conseil, Haut Comité de la population et de la famille, 1957), 69 (CAC 860269/5).

17. ESNA, "Situation et aspirations de la famille nord-africaine en métropole," *CNA* 49 (November–December 1955): 7. Whenever *CNA* articles provided authors, I have identified them. I have used ESNA as the author for introductions, editorials, or studies that either provide no author or for which ESNA appears as the author.

18. Emile Pelletier, *Accueil et hébergement des Nord Africains dans le Département de la Seine*, 15 March 1956, 5 (CIEMI 9/1/1).

19. J. Mathieu, "Les problèmes posés," in "Action et techniques sociales au service des familles nord-africaines en France," *CNA* 51 (March–April 1956): 8.

20. Lazreg, *The Eloquence of Silence*, 38.

21. Rager, "Les musulmans algériens," 275.

22. In addition to the rich welfare state literature cited throughout, see Davin, "Imperialism and Motherhood"; Auslander, *Taste and Power*; Tiersten, *Marianne in the Market*.

23. Camille Sabatier, a judge in Tizi Ouzou, and Hubertine Auclert, a feminist traveler, both quoted in Lazreg, *The Eloquence of Silence*, 49–50. According to Julia Clancy-Smith, mention of Arab women was rare in the early stages of colonialism. The status of women became important once "military domination gave way to civilian rule and moral subjugation after 1870." Clancy-Smith, "Islam, Gender, and Identities in the Making of French Algeria," in Clancy-Smith and Gouda, eds., *Domesticating the Empire*, 154.

24. Fanon, *A Dying Colonialism*, 37. François Maspero first published Fanon's work as *L'an V de la révolution algérienne* in 1959.

25. Stoler, *Carnal Knowledge and Imperial Power*, xxi.

26. S. Belpeer, "Note sur le problème des familles nord-africaines dans le Département des Bouches-du-Rhône en 1952," 1952 (CAC 860271/11).

27. Camiscioli, *Reproducing the French Race*, 32; Frader, *Breadwinners and Citizens.* Much of the rich historiography on the French welfare state has ignored the central role race played in its construction and implementation; these works are notable exceptions.

28. See, among others, Thébaud, *Quand nos grand-mères donnaient la vie*; Offen, "Depopulation, Nationalism, and Feminism"; Koven and Michel, eds., *Mothers of a New World*; Pedersen, *Family, Dependence, and the Origins of the Welfare State*; Nord, "The Welfare State in France"; Cole, *The Power of Large Numbers*; Schneider, *Quality and Quantity*; Dutton, *Origins of the French Welfare State.*

29. Camiscioli, *Reproducing the French Race*, 45; Stovall, "The Color Line behind the Lines"; Rosenberg, *Policing Paris*; Lewis, *The Boundaries of the Republic.*

30. Ross, *Fast Cars, Clean Bodies*, 71.

31. ESNA, "Le logement des Nord-Africains (deuxième cahier)," 29.

32. Direction des services de l'Algérie et des départements d'outre-mer, to the prefects of metropolitan departments, 28 February 1951 (AN F1a 5035). The archives in the F1a series that I consulted at the French National Archives are not available for open consultation. I applied for and received permission to examine these archives with the stipulation that I not reveal the name of any individual living or dead. Therefore, references to documents from this series throughout the book provide information about the job description, agency, and government ministry where appropriate without mentioning individual names.

33. Jacques Ghys, "La présence nord-africaine démure. Notre action sociale reste," in "Plus que jamais: Action sociale!," *CNA* 64 (April–May 1958): 3–5.

34. Rabinow, *French Modern*, 26. Among other works that are part of a literature examining the colonies as a site of social experimentation, see Abu-Lughod, *Rabat*; Wright, *The Politics of Design in French Colonial Urbanism*; Çelik, *Urban Forms and Colonial Confrontations*; Cooper and Stoler, eds., *Tensions of Empire*; Stoler, *Carnal Knowledge and Imperial Power.*

35. Conklin, *A Mission to Civilize*, 6; Keller, *Colonial Madness*, 4–5.

36. Conklin, *A Mission to Civilize*, 8.

37. According to Foucault, biopower refers to the "explosion of numerous and diverse techniques for achieving the [s]ubjugation of bodies and the control of populations." Foucault, *The History of Sexuality*, vol. 1: 140.

38. Donzelot, *The Policing of Families*, 7. His work is part of an extensive literature on welfare state protectionism. Among others, see Stewart, *Women, Work, and the French State*; Klaus, *Every Child a Lion*; Accampo et al., eds., *Gender and the Politics of Social Reform.*

39. Leriche, "Le logement des familial," 29.

40. Elisabeth Malet, quoted in ESNA, "Santé des Nord Africains en France (aspects médico-sociaux)," *CNA* 18–19 (October–November 1951): 21–23.

41. Spire, *Etrangers à la carte*, 15.

42. Lorcin, *Imperial Identities*, 220; Richard Fogarty and Michael Osborne, "Constructions and Functions of Race in French Military Medicine, 1830–1920," in Peabody and Stovall, eds., *The Color of Liberty*, 206.

43. Peabody and Stovall, "Introduction," *The Color of Liberty*, 4.

44. A growing literature critically examines the myths about racial discrimination in

contemporary France. See, among others, Wieviorka, *La France raciste*, and *La différence*; Todorov, *On Human Diversity*; Liauzu, *La société française*; Taguieff, *La couleur et le sang*; de Rudder et al., *L'inégalité raciste*; Bleich, "The French Model," and *Race Politics in Britain and France*; Fassin and Fassin, *De la question sociale à la question raciale*; N'Diaye, *La condition noire*. Two foundational texts in a growing body of scholarship that historicizes French racism are Cohen, *The French Encounter with Africans*, and Peabody, *There Are No Slaves in France*.

45. Etienne Balibar, "Racism as Universalism," in *Masses, Classes, Ideas*, 191–204.

46. Bourdieu and Sayad, *Le déracinement*, 38–40.

47. Scott, *Seeing Like a State*, 4, 88–89.

48. Algeria officially halted emigration to France in 1973 after dozens of racially motivated attacks against North African migrants resulted in fifteen deaths. Ben Jelloun, *French Hospitality*, 75. The French officially ended immigration following the economic downturn a year later.

49. For a survey of the early literature dedicated to the study of immigration, see Sayad, "Tendances et courants de publications en sciences sociales"; and Stora, *Aide-mémoire de l'immigration algérienne*. On the political context, see, among others, Georges Tapinos, "Pour une introduction au débat contemporain," in Lequin, ed., *La mosaïque France*, 432–33; Weil, *La France et ses étrangers*, 107–212; Hargreaves, *Immigration, "Race" and Ethnicity*; Témime, "La politique française." The quotation is taken from the title of a representative work, Zehraoui, *L'immigration*.

50. The thirty glorious years refers to the virtually uninterrupted economic expansion France experienced prior to the 1973 Oil Crisis. Jean Fourastié coined the term in his book *Les trente glorieuses ou la révolution invisible de 1946 à 1975*. This periodization provided a France-centric way to characterize the third quarter of the twentieth century as a coherent period, despite the Fourth Republic's collapse as a result of the Algerian crisis. It became shorthand for describing a period when France tried to navigate a path between the Cold War superpowers and the humiliating loss in 1940 by emphasizing the social, cultural, and economic renaissance France experienced and by ignoring the impact of decolonization on French society and culture. In terms of Cold War historiography, de Gaulle's notion of the "third way" dominated the narrative for many years. In much of this literature, the Algerian War is almost entirely absent. Among others, see Kuisel, *Seducing the French*. Others have analyzed the construction of this narrative. For an analysis of the Gaullist project to reassert France as a purveyor of culture in the world when it could no longer claim political, economic, or imperial dominance, see Lebovics, *Mona Lisa's Escort*.

51. Green, *Repenser les migrations*, 105–13.

52. Frederick Cooper and Ann Laura Stoler, "Between Metropole and Colony: Rethinking A Research Agenda," in Cooper and Stoler, eds., *Tensions of Empire*, 5–15; Scott, *Gender and the Politics of History*, esp. 42–45.

53. Gérard Noiriel led this group studying immigration in metropolitan France with *The French Melting Pot*. (His comment on "amnesia" appears on p. xii.) Among others on the early historiography of French immigration, see Milza, *Français et Italiens*; Schor, *L'immigration en France*; Green, *The Pletzl of Paris*; Ponty, *Polonais méconnus*. On modern colonialism as

a republican project, see Shepard, *The Invention of Decolonization*, 271. Shepard's work, a thoughtful exception, explores the post-1945 era rather than the interwar years. Other works in the more recent historiographical trend include Lebovics, *True France*; Blanchard and Lemaire, eds., *Culture coloniale*, and *Culture impériale*; Rosenberg, *Policing Paris*; Wilder, *The French Imperial Nation-State*; Lewis, *The Boundaries of the Republic*; Camiscioli, *Reproducing the French Race*; and Boittin, *Colonial Metropolis*.

54. Stora, *La gangrène et l'oubli*, 8, 13, and 220–26. In the decade following the war, the Gaullist agenda included a program of commemoration for all France had suffered since 1914—including the creation of forty-three museums—in part to ease the reconciliation with Germany and in part to obscure the unspeakable memory of the Fifth Republic's origins and replace it with a unifying memory of the republic's resilience and resistance in the face of war and loss in the first half of the twentieth century. The inability to come to terms with the loss in 1940 and the Vichy era also played a key role. See Rousso, *The Vichy Syndrome*.

55. A recent study referred to the Algerian War as "a relatively minor parenthesis" in an era affected more by economic forces than decolonization. Simon, ed., *L'immigration algérienne en France de 1962 à nos jours*, 11.

56. Stora, *La gangrène et l'oubli*, 284–87.

57. For detailed analyses of these issues, see, among others, Hargreaves, *Immigration, "Race" and Ethnicity*; Silverman, *Deconstructing the Nation*; Favell, *Philosophies of Integration*; Feldblum, *Reconstructing Citizenship*; Fysh and Wolfreys, *The Politics of Racism*; Freedman, *Immigration and Insecurity*; Silverstein, *Algeria in France*.

58. Stora, *La gangrène et l'oubli*, 284–87.

59. Ben Jelloun, *French Hospitality*, 9–10. The decades following independence witnessed an explosion in texts published on the Algerian War, with nearly a thousand in print. Yet, while a number of important books provided initial critical analyses, about two-thirds represented an apologist approach, written by those who bemoaned the end of French control in Algeria. See Stora, *La gangrène et l'oubli*, 238–41; and Stora, *Le dictionnaire des livres*.

60. Sayad, "Les trois 'âges' de l'émigration."

61. Much of Sayad's work appears in Sayad, *La double absence*. The collection appeared in English as *The Suffering of the Immigrant*. Sayad's influence is so great that the CNRS recently renamed its immigration documentation center for him. See the Centre de documentation Abdelmalek Sayad at the University of Paris-7, www.cdasayad.org (accessed 21 February 2011).

62. Abdelmalek Sayad, "L'immigration algérienne en France, une immigration exemplaire," in Costa-Lascoux and Témime, eds., *Les Algériens en France*, 21.

63. Ibid., 30–31.

64. See, among others, de Barros, "L'Etat au prisme des municipalités"; Hmed, "Loger les étrangers 'isolés' en France"; Byrnes, "French Like Us?"; Escafré-Dublet, "Etat, culture, immigration"; Laurens, *Une politisation feutrée*; Nasiali, "Native to the Republic."

65. Scott, *The Politics of the Veil*, 10. The emphasis is Scott's.

66. Ibid., 87.

67. P. Caltez, "Les trois étapes du contact," in "Contacts," *CNA* 10 (December 1950): 10.

68. Leriche, "Le logement familial," 29.

69. Excerpts of de Gaulle's speech are available through the Internet History Sourcebook, www.fordham.edu/halsall/mod/1958degaulle-algeria1.html (accessed 11 June 2010).

70. Darrouy, administrative secretary-general of CANAM, "Assemblée général du 6 juillet 1959: Rapport moral," 6 July 1959, 3 (CAC 770391/4).

Chapter 1

1. Cambon, *Le Gouvernement général d'Algérie*, 31.

2. Ibid., 129.

3. Rosenberg, "Republican Surveillance."

4. On the paradoxical nature of Algerian's citizenship, see Spire, "Semblables et pourtant différents."

5. Burke, "Theorizing the Histories of Colonialism and Nationalism in the Arab Maghrib," 19.

6. Cited in Lorcin, *Imperial Identities*, 113, 116. Lorcin examines the Saint-Simonian influence among the Polytechnique graduates working in Algeria. For more on the scientific project, see Pyenson, *Civilizing Mission*, 87–127; on Saint-Simonians, see Abi-Mershed, *Apostles of Modernity*.

7. Eighteenth-century philosopher Joseph Marie Dégérando, cited in Cohen, *The French Encounter with Africans*, 174–80.

8. Sessions, *By Sword and Plow*, 6.

9. *Discours et opinions de Jules Ferry*, 210–11. The editor noted that during Ferry's 1884 speech before the Chamber of Deputies representatives on both the far left and far right interrupted with shouting; they feared, respectively, that he had gone too far or that he failed to protect the role missionaries played in the colonies. See also, Ageron, "Jules Ferry et colonisation," 191–206. Despite the Third Republic's reputation for anticlericalism, religion still had a role in the colonial project. For more, see Chapter 2.

10. Sessions, *By Sword and Plow*, 177–211; Ruedy, *Modern Algeria*, 68–72; Stora, *Histoire de l'Algérie coloniale*, 29–34. In the nineteenth century, largely because of political instability in France, policy on Algeria was inconsistent and there was no consensus on how to bring about this new ideal colony. In the end, the majority of colonists came from outside France, even if the political upheavals of 1848, 1851, and 1870–1871 sent bursts of French citizens to Algeria and other parts of the empire.

11. Although the expropriation of land began in the early years of colonization, the pace expanded after settlers pressured the Third Republic to pass the Warnier law in 1873, which justified European control of land based on the presumption that only Europeans would properly exploit this natural resource. See Bourdieu and Sayad, *Le déracinement*, 15–16; Ageron, *Histoire de l'Algérie contemporaine, tome 2: De l'insurrection de 1871 au déclenchement de la guerre de libération, 1954*, 491; Stora, *Histoire de l'Algérie coloniale*, 27–28; Ruedy, *Modern Algeria*, 80–113.

12. Adas, *Machines as the Measure of Men*, 199–270.

13. Prochaska, *Making Algeria French*, 254.

14. The quotations are from Collot, *Les institutions de l'Algérie durant la période coloniale*,

7–9; and Pervillé, "La politique algérienne de la France," 27. See also Prochaska, *Making Algeria French*, 9–10. For the classic interpretation of assimilation, see Betts, *Assimilation and Association in French Colonial Theory*.

15. Fanon, *The Wretched of the Earth*, 182.

16. Alexandre de Laborde, speech to the Chamber of Deputies (1834), cited in Sessions, *By Sword and Plow*, 183. The French government took the first step to assimilate the Algerian and metropolitan territories in 1834. In 1848 the new republican government went a step further when its constitution made northern Algeria an integral part of France. Its three departments, Oran, Constantine, and Algiers, henceforth became like other departments in most ways. Barrière, *Le statut personnel des musulmans d'Algérie de 1834 à 1962*, 3; Ageron, *Modern Algeria*, 28–29.

17. Mignot (1887), cited in Kateb, *Européens, "indigènes," et juifs en Algérie*, 6.

18. From a report penned in 1841, cited in Kateb, *Européens, "indigènes," et juifs en Algérie*, 40. On Bodichon, see Brower, *A Desert Named Peace*, 166–70.

19. Benjamin Stora, preface to Kateb, *Européens, "indigènes," et juifs en Algérie*, xiii.

20. Kateb, *Européens, "indigènes," et juifs en Algérie*, 49–68. To these figures Kateb added population losses due to emigration. He estimated a decline of about two million people, approximately half the population. The first decades of conquest focused on the northern or Tell region. Later, the French set their sights on the southern Saharan region. On the conquest of southern Algeria, see Brower, *A Desert Named Peace*.

21. Eugène Daumus, cited in Yacono, *Les Bureaux arabes et l'évolution des genres de vie indigènes*, 15.

22. Ageron, *Les Algériens musulmans et la France*, vol. 1: 51–55.

23. Keller, *Colonial Madness*, 122.

24. Lazreg, *The Eloquence of Silence*, 55. See also Julia Clancy-Smith, "Islam, Gender and Identities in the Making of French Algeria," in Clancy-Smith and Gouda, eds., *Domesticating the Empire*, 154–74.

25. Kateb, *Européens, "indigènes," et juifs en Algérie*, 93–101.

26. Ferro, *Histoire des colonisations, des conquêtes aux indépendances*, 291–92. According to Ferro, at least 250 tribes, nearly half the population, participated in the last major rebellion before World War I. Lorcin, *Imperial Identities*, 46–47; Ageron, *Les Algériens musulmans et la France*, vol. 1: 3–36. On rebellions in 1876 and 1881 in the Aurès and Oran regions, see Ageron, *Les Algériens musulmans et la France*, vol. 1: 59–66.

27. From a settler brochure published in 1871, cited in Ageron, *Les Algériens musulmans et la France*, vol. 1: 52.

28. During the Affair, settlers stressed that Jews were "indigenous," and hence inferior. Stora, *Histoire de l'Algérie coloniale*, 21–22; Gallissot, *Misère de l'antiracisme*, 44–45.

29. The 1865 *sénatus-consulte* paved the way for discrimination against Algerians to become legal and systematic; it allowed indigenous subjects to be governed by Islamic or Jewish law in certain personal and religious matters including marriage, while imposing French civil law in all cases pertaining to property. See Blévis, "Sociologie d'un droit colonial."

30. Ageron, *Les Algériens musulmans et la France*, vol. 1: 168–76; Weil, *Qu'est qu'un Français?*, 223.

31. Weil, *Qu'est qu'un Français?*, 225, 231–32; Pervillé, "La politique algérienne de la France," 28. According to Weil, the 1891 census estimated Algeria had 267,672 French and 215,793 foreigners. By 1898, the governor-general estimated 384,000 French (Français d'Algérie), including 275,000 of French origin and 109,000 naturalized citizens (53,000 of whom were Jewish).

32. Gallissot, *Misère de l'antiracisme*, 45; Blévis, "Les avatars de la citoyenneté en Algérie coloniale ou les paradoxes d'une catégorisation."

33. Lorcin, *Imperial Identities*, 121.

34. Kateb, *Européens, "indigènes," et juifs en Algérie*, 98–101.

35. Stora, *Ils venaient d'Algérie*, 13; Massard-Guilbaud, *Des Algériens à Lyon*, 42.

36. Simon, *L'immigration algérienne en France*, 39. On the Kabyle myth, see Lorcin, *Imperial Identities*.

37. Simon, *L'immigration algérienne en France*, 40. The law of 15 June 1914, which replaced another in force since 18 June 1913, replaced a decree enacted in 18 May 1874.

38. On soldiers from the colonies, see Ageron, *Les Algériens musulmans et la France*, vol. 2: 1140–50; Andrew and Kanya-Forstner, "France, Africa, and the First World War"; Conklin, *A Mission to Civilize*, 142–73; Lunn, "'Les Races Guerrières'"; Stovall, "The Color Line behind the Lines"; Mann, *Native Sons*, 63–107; Fogarty, *Race and War in France*, 55–85, 96–142.

39. Camiscioli, *Reproducing the French Race*, 21–50. Experts included, among others, Fernand Boverat and Georges Mauco.

40. This included Ferhat Abbas' Young Algerians and Messali Hajj's North African Star. Stora, *Histoire de l'Algérie coloniale*, 75–76; Simon, *L'immigration algérienne en France*, 89–102. For more on Ferhat Abbas, Algerian nationalist leader and first president of the Provisional Government of the Algerian Republic, see Stora and Daoud, *Ferhat Abbas, une utopie algérienne*, and on Messali Hajj, the father of modern Algerian nationalism, see Stora, *Messali Hadj*.

41. Lewis, *The Boundaries of the Republic*, 189; Noiriel, *The French Melting Pot*, 5; Schor, *L'histoire de l'immigration en France*, 125. The foreign population went from 1.15 million in 1911, or nearly three percent of the total population, to 2.89 million in 1931, more than doubling to seven percent.

42. Italians, the largest and oldest immigrant population in France, made up thirty percent of the total, followed by Poles (eighteen percent), Spaniards (thirteen percent), and Belgians (over nine percent). Although the Italian population held relatively steady throughout the interwar years, Belgian immigration declined significantly, and Polish immigration grew substantially. Tapinos, *L'immigration étrangère en France*, 9. The census posed several questions pertaining to family settlement. The survey inquired if the head of household was married, if he was married to an indigenous Algerian or French woman, and, if he was married to an Algerian, did his family accompany him to France. Those who crafted the census questions justified these questions by noting that a few "entire families" had already been known to have migrated from Algeria. If this pattern continued, this segment of the population would need monitoring. See Massard-Guilbaud, *Des Algériens à Lyon*, 62–63.

43. Godin, quoted in Simon, *L'immigration algérienne en France*, 82.

44. Rosenberg, *Policing Paris*, 129–67. See also Derder, *L'immigration algérienne et les pouvoirs publics*, 108; MacMaster, *Colonial Migrants and Racism*, 153–71.

45. Sarraut, quoted in Lewis, *The Boundaries of the Republic*, 199.

46. Lewis, *The Boundaries of the Republic*, 188–215. On the Franco-Muslim Hospital, see Rosenberg, *Policing Paris*, 168–98.

47. Rosenberg, *Policing Paris*, 158.

48. Ibid., 74.

49. Louis Chevalier, cited in ESNA, "Les Nord Africains en France: Eléments de statistiques commentaires sociaux," *CNA*, 5–6 (May–June 1950): 12; MacMaster, *Colonial Migrants and Racism*, 76–77.

50. Le chargé des affaires Algériennes, Sous-direction de l'Algérie, section 1, "Recensement des indigènes nord-africains en zone occupée," 31 July 1942 (AN F1a 5046). The report determined 18,000 North Africans, of whom 14,000 were Algerian, remained in the occupied zone. Nearly all lived in the Department of the Seine: 12,000 North Africans, of whom 10,300 were Algerians. David Smith's new work sheds light on the low estimates. His dissertation, forthcoming from the University of Toronto, estimates about 30,000 Algerians lived in the occupied zone with another 20,000 or more in Vichy France. He estimates at least 50,000 North Africans lived in France, many working for the Germans. When the provisional government began collecting census data in 1945 it estimated as many as 80,000 North Africans, most of whom were Algerian, lived in France. Smith speculates the increase may be the result of poor record keeping, people coming out of hiding, people being released from German detention camps, and desertions from the army. On North African POWs, see Mabon, *Prisonniers de guerre "indigènes."*

51. Blévis, "Sociologie d'un droit colonial," 177–78.

52. Viet, *La France immigrée*, 62–63; Benjamin Stora, *Algeria, 1830–2000*, 19–20.

53. On the importance of the colonial empire during World War II, see Paxton, *Vichy France*, and Jennings, *Vichy in the Tropics*.

54. MTSS, Direction de la main-d'œuvre, "Les étrangers de l'assistance à la famille," *Bulletin de la Section d'information pour la main-d'œuvre étrangère* (May–June 1951): 18–19; Watson, "Population Policy in France." For more, see the section of Chapter 3 on the family allowances controversy.

55. See, among others, Wall, *France, the United States, and the Algerian War*; Connelly, *A Diplomatic Revolution*.

56. René Pleven, quoted in Betts, *France and Decolonization*, 63. The 1944 Brazzaville Conference sought to ensure French control through liberalized colonial policies. Pleven, unlike de Gaulle, continued to play an important role in the Fourth Republic, serving as legislator and minister. See Rioux, *The Fourth Republic*.

57. For more, see Spire, "Semblables et pourtant différents," 48–68.

58. Shepard, *The Invention of Decolonization*, 39.

59. The Commission de réformes musulmans du Conseil national de la résistance elaborated this reform before the Comité français de libération nationale, the future provisional government of the French Republic, which made it policy with the 7 March 1944

ordinance. Fortier, "L'indigène algérien." The same liberation committee reinstated Algerian Jews' citizenship in October 1943. Weil, "Histoire et mémoire des discriminations en matière de nationalité française," 10. For a reprint of the 1944 ordinance with commentary, see Pervillé, *L'Europe et l'Afrique*, 65–73.

60. Blévis, "Les avatars de la citoyenneté en Algérie coloniale ou les paradoxes d'une catégorisation," 557–80; Blévis, "Droit colonial algérien de la citoyenneté."

61. The one notable exception was the Blum-Viollette proposal made in 1936 that would have accorded citizenship to assimilated Algerians without requiring them to renounce their local civil status. This proposal, however, never became law and fell into oblivion with the demise of the Popular Front government. See Ruedy, *Modern Algeria*, 139–44. Blanchard points out that the Blum-Viollette proposal inspired the reforms of the mid-1940s. Blanchard, *La police parisienne*, 25.

62. Weil, "Histoire et mémoire des discriminations en matière de nationalité française," 8.

63. Loi du 20 septembre 1947, *JO* 9470.

64. In order to clarify voting rights, the fourth article of the 1947 law expressly provided that "women of Muslim origin" would have the right to vote based on parameters to be determined in the Algerian Assembly, a body divided into two houses based on racial and religious distinctions. When interpreting the 1947 law, political leaders effectively circumvented this provision and denied Algerian women access to the ballot, a right granted to them only after the creation of the Fifth Republic in 1958. See Elsenhans, *La guerre d'Algérie*, 724; Fortier, "L'indigène algérien," 53–61; Gros, "Sujets et citoyens en Algérie avant l'ordonnance du 7 mars 1944," 54–55; Weil, *Qu'est-ce qu'un Français?*, 240–46; Spire, *Étrangers à la carte*, 189–202; Shepard, *The Invention of Decolonization*, 43.

65. As before, Algerians had to declare their acceptance of French civil law over Islamic law to become citizens with equal footing. In essence, the new law obliged them to renounce Islam in order to achieve true legal equality, a provision that was apparently intended to dissuade large numbers of Algerians from seeking civil status. Most Algerian Muslims chose to maintain their personal status and not accept French civil law. Thus, despite the symbolic importance of achieving citizenship status, Algerians remained, effectively, second-class citizens.

66. Ruedy, *Modern Algeria*, 150–53; Collot, *Les institutions de l'Algérie*, 220–22.

67. Collot, *Les institutions de l'Algérie*, 19–20.

68. Roger Parant, "Le problème algérien," *CNA* 32 (July–August 1953): 35.

69. Ibid.

70. ESNA, "Guide de l'action sociale au bénéfice des Nord Africains en métropole," *CNA* 34 (October–November 1953): 9; MacMaster, *Colonial Migrants and Racism*, 76–77.

71. Numerous contemporary sources confirm this estimate. Chevalier, *Le problème démographique nord-africain*; Rager, "Les musulmans algériens," 102–77; ESNA, "L'immigration marocaine en France," in "A travers les 'Monographies,'" *CNA* 9 (October–November 1950): 12; ESNA, "Du Douar à l'usine," *CNA* 13 (March 1951): 12. Ageron put the figure at eighty percent. Ageron, *Histoire de l'Algérie contemporaine, tome 2*, 469–79.

72. Keller, *Colonial Madness*, 128–31.

73. See, among others, Maurice Vaussard, "Un péril national: L'immigration incon-

trôlée de travailleurs nord-africains," *Le Monde*, 7 December 1948, 4; "La criminalité nord-africaine soulève un problème national," *Le Monde*, 16 September 1949, 5; "Au barrage de Donzères-Mondragon des Nord-Africains attaquent un groupe de travailleurs," *Le Monde*, 30 March 1950, 8.

74. ESNA, "L'immigration marocaine en France," 12.

75. Assemblée nationale, no. 8377, "Proposition de résolution tendant à inviter le gouvernement à instituer d'urgence une commission pour étudier le problème de l'immigration des Nord-Africains dans la métropole et en proposer une solution ensemble," presented by Deputies Benchennouf, Lefebvre, Bentaieb, Reille-Soult, Chartier, and Fagon, 10 November 1949 (CAC 860269/7).

76. AUF, no. 177, "Proposition tendant à demander au gouvernement français de prendre plusieurs mesures en faveur du bien-être matériel et moral des travailleurs nord-africains en France," 28 April 1948 (CAC 860269/7). Abbé Catrice led this call in the Union Assembly; for more on Catrice, see the section Structuring a New Mission in the Metropole, below.

77. "Il faut mettre fin à la misère et à l'exploitation dont souffrent les travailleurs nord-africains nous déclare M. Martinaud-Déplat," *L'Aurore*, 28 April 1954, 3.

78. Camiscioli, *Reproducing the French Race*, 51–74.

79. See Note 73 above, and "Onze Algériens condamnes [*sic*] à la prison avec sursis à la suite des rafles de samedi soir," *Ce Soir*, 11 December 1951, 3; "M. Brune étudie une programme d'aide aux travailleurs algériens en France et demande que l'immigration soit réglementée," *Le Monde*, 12 December 1951, 8; "Le gouvernement voudrait fournir des emplois plus nombreux des logements plus sains aux 300.000 Algériens venus en France," *Le Monde*, 22 October 1954, 5.

80. Weil, *La France et ses étrangers*, 88–91.

81. Bensalem, delegate to the Algerian Assembly, quoted in "Main-d'œuvre algérienne, émigration des travailleurs algériens vers la France," report of a meeting presided over by Interior Minister Jules Moch, 4 June 1949 (CAC 860271/2).

82. Report "Sur le reclassement des travailleurs et des paysans dans la métropole," Governor-general of Algeria, secrétaire général du gouvernement, Direction des réformes, Service du plan des réformes, 3 May 1946 (AN F1a 5049).

83. MA, directeur des affaires professionnelles et sociales, "Reclassement de paysans musulmans dans la métropole," 15 April 1947 (AN F1a 5049).

84. French authorities developed similar programs to repopulate rural areas with immigrants from southern and eastern Europe in the interwar era. In 1939, Jacques Doublet argued that agriculture provided the best place for "the assimilation of foreigners." See Spire, *Etrangers à la carte*, 124; Rosental, *L'intelligence démographique*, 296n66. Initiatives targeted Polish immigrants. Ponty, *Polonais méconnus*, 241.

85. MI, préfet chargé de la Direction des services de l'Algérie et des départements d'outre-mer, Sous-direction de l'Algérie [in Paris] to the MA, "Situation dans la métropole des citoyens français musulmans d'Algérie," 11 April 1949 (AN F1a 5049).

86. Algerian Affairs to the MA, Sous-direction de la législation du travail et de la main-d'œuvre—2e Bureau, "Installation de paysans musulmans dans la métropole," 15 July 1947 (AN F1a 5049).

87. Lorcin, *Imperial Identities*, 146–66.

88. MI, "Installation de paysans musulmans dans la métropole."

89. MI, "Situation dans la métropole des citoyens français musulmans d'Algérie."

90. MI, directeur des affaires d'Algérie to the MA, "Implantation de familles algériennes sur les exploitations agricoles abandonnées en métropole," 21 November 1955 (AN F1a 5049).

91. Directeur des affaires d'Algérie, sous-directeur du Ministère de l'Intérieur, "Note sur le projet d'implantation de cultivateurs algériens sur les exploitations agricoles abandonnées de la Drôme, des Basses-Alpes et des Hautes-Alpes," 19 August 1955; Préfet des Basses-Alpes, "Implantation de familles rurales italiennes ou kabyles dans les Basses-Alpes," 14 January 1957; Minutes, Comité d'action interministérielle pour les affaires sociales musulmanes, 22 March 1957; Comité d'action interministérielle pour les affaires sociales musulmanes, "Projet d'implantation de familles kabyles rurales dans le Département des Basses-Alpes," 22 March 1957. All in AN F1a 5044. Citations from the January 1957 letter.

92. "Projet d'implantation de populations kabyles dans le Drôme, 1955," 28 February 1955 (AN F1a 5049).

93. MI, directeur des affaires d'Algérie, "Implantation en métropole de familles algériennes sur les exploitations agricoles abandonnées," 7 January 1956 (AN F1a 5049).

94. Directeur des affaires d'Algérie to the directeur du cabinet, secrétaire d'Etat à l'intérieur chargé des affaires Algériennes, "Installation d'agriculteurs musulmans dans les villages abandonnés de la métropole," 31 July 1957 (AN F1a 5049).

95. Governor-general of Algeria, Direction du travail et de la sécurité sociale, "Possibilités d'utilisation de la main-d'œuvre algérienne dans l'agriculture métropolitaine," 13 December 1954 (AN F1a 5049).

96. By 1961, the departments of Gard, Hérault, Bouches-du-Rhône, and Vaucluse had Algerian families living on farms receiving government aid through this program. Sous-préfet du Gard, "Implantation de familles d'ouvriers agricoles musulmans, compte-rendu," 21 December 1961 (AN F1a 5049).

97. Directeur des affaires d'Algérie, "Installation d'agriculteurs musulmans dans les villages abandonnés de la métropole."

98. Weil, *La France et ses étrangers*, 75–91; Viet, *La France immigrée*, 97–131.

99. Nord, *France's New Deal*, 173–76; Rosental, *L'intelligence démographique*, 21–34; Weil, *Liberté, égalité, discriminations*, 38–50; Weil, *La France et ses étrangers*, 77–78. The original members, Georges Pernot, Adolphe Landry, Philippe Serre, Frédéric Roujou, and Fernand Boverat, were joined by Jacques Doublet, Pierre de la Lande de Calan, and Alfred Sauvy. Mauco's publications from the interwar period include *Les étrangers en France*, and *L'assimilation des étrangers en France*.

100. Sauvy also sat on the National Economic Council and served as France's representative to the UN Commission on Population. On Sauvy and INED, see Rosental, *L'intelligence démographique*, 139–56; Nord, *France's New Deal*, 178–88; Reggiani, *God's Eugenicist*, 164–68.

101. Spire, *Etrangers à la carte*, 113.

102. Gallissot, *Misère de l'antiracisme*, 74.

103. Mauco, *Les étrangers en France*, quoted in Weil, *La France et ses étrangers*, 44.

104. For details, see Weil, *Liberté, égalité, discriminations*, 49–80.

105. Sauvy, *Bien-être et population*, 202.

106. Weil, *Liberté, égalité, discriminations*, 82–83.

107. Alfred Sauvy, "Rapport au ministre de la Santé publique et de la Population sur l'évolution de la population de L'Afrique du Nord," confidential report, n.d. (1956?) (CAC 860269/7).

108. On Boverat's extreme pronatalism during the interwar period, see Koos, "Gender, Anti-individualism, and Nationalism."

109. Fernand Boverat, "Gravité de la discordance entre les politiques de population convenant à la métropole, d'une part, à l'Algérie, aux Antilles et à la Réunion d'autre part," 20 May 1952 (CAC 860269/1); Fernand Boverat, "Le vieillissement de la population et ses répercussions sur la sécurité sociale," October 195[2?] (CAC 860269/1).

110. Rager, *L'émigration en France des musulmans algériens*, 121.

111. Alain Girard, "Introduction" to Claude Mothes, "Les familles algériennes musulmanes dans l'agglomération parisienne," in Girard and Stoetzel, eds., *Français et immigrés*, 96.

112. Boverat, "Le vieillissement de la population et ses répercussions sur la sécurité sociale."

113. On the history of colonial concerns about and approaches to miscegenation, see Stoler, *Carnal Knowledge and Imperial Power*, 77–111; White, *Children of the French Empire*; Saada, *Empire's Children*, 25–30. According to Saada, "there was no métis question in Algeria." The issue did not perplex colonial observers; they believed encounters between French men and Algerian women were infrequent if not impossible because of social/gender customs that cloistered women.

114. See, in particular, Fernand Boverat, "Note pour la Commission du haut comité de la population," 21 April 1959, and Emmanuel Rain to Georges Mauco, 27 October 1959 (both in CAC 860269/1).

115. Shunning the civilizing mission rhetoric, France (and Britain) repackaged their approach to emphasize the Western powers' commitment to providing everything—from infrastructures to social programs—needed to facilitate progress. See Frederick Cooper, "The Rise, Fall, and Rise of Colonial Studies," in *Colonialism in Question*, 36–37.

116. Shepard, *The Invention of Decolonization*, 59; Nord, *France's New Deal*, 184.

117. Michel, *Les travailleurs algériens en France*, 59.

118. Governor-general of Algeria, secretary-general of the Government of Algeria, MTSS, Direction de la main-d'œuvre, "Départ des travailleurs algériens pour la métropole," 3 June 1948 (AN F1a 5046).

119. Pelletier, "Les réalisations en faveur des Nord Africains dans le département," 121.

120. MTSS, Direction de la main-d'œuvre, "L'emploi de la main-d'œuvre nord-africaine en métropole, et les mesures prises pour son amélioration," 8 November 1953 (CAC 860271/3). On repatriation in the interwar period, see Lewis, *The Boundaries of the Republic*, 188–215.

121. Directive issued jointly by the Interior, Labor, Justice, and Public Health and Population Ministries, "Rapatriement des Français originaires des départements d'Algérie et se trouvant sans ressources sur le territoire métropolitain," circulaire no. 250, 13 July 1950

(AN F1a 5035). On the dismantling of the police surveillance system, see Blanchard, *La police parisienne*, 72–76.

122. ESNA, "Guide de l'action sociale," 18–19.

123. MTSS, "L'emploi de la main-d'œuvre nord-africaine en métropole."

124. On repatriations after Algerian independence in 1962, see Spire, *Etrangers à la carte*, 212–22.

125. Governor-general of Algeria to the MTSS, Direction de la main-d'œuvre, 13 November 1954 (CAC 860271/2).

126. Rosier, MTSS, Direction de la main-d'œuvre, "Organisation des visites médicales de travailleurs à Marseille," 3 March 1948; "Lutte antituberculeuse et antivénérienne—contrôle sanitaire des Nord Africains," 17 December 1948; Médecin inspecteur général du travail et de la main-d'œuvre, "Nomination de médecins inspecteurs divisionnaires," 5 March 1948. All in CAC 860271/2.

127. According to the historian Ralph Schor, Algerians were actually more likely to contract tuberculosis in France than to bring it with them. See Schor, *Histoire de l'immigration en France*, 216–17. Clifford Rosenberg's recent work has shown the movement of tuberculosis across the Mediterranean was complex. See, "The International Politics of Vaccine Testing in Interwar Algiers."

128. Governor-general of Algeria to the Labor Ministry, "Départ des travailleurs algériens pour la métropole"; MTSS, Direction de la main-d'œuvre, "Avis aux travailleurs désirant se rendre en métropole," poster printed by the colonial government in Algeria, marked for distribution 5 April 1950 (CAC 860271/2).

129. Michel, *Les travailleurs algériens en France*, 53–67.

130. Governor-general of Algeria to the Labor Ministry, "Départ des travailleurs algériens pour la métropole."

131. Among others, see Yacono, *Les Bureaux arabes*; Kadri et al., eds., *L'école dans l'Algérie colonial*; Abi-Mershed, *Apostles of Modernity*, 159–63; Fanny Colonna, "Educating Conformity in French Colonial Algeria," in Cooper and Stoler, eds., *Tensions of Empire*, 346–70; Curtis, *Civilizing Habits*, 101–30.

132. For a more detailed discussion of the immigration infrastructure, see Viet, *La France immigrée*, 164–230.

133. "Main-d'œuvre algérienne, émigration des travailleurs algériens vers la France," report of a meeting presided over by Interior Minister Jules Moch, 4 June 1949 (CAC 860271/2).

134. ESNA, "Guide de l'action sociale," 20.

135. Derder, *L'immigration algérienne et les pouvoirs publics*, 89–90.

136. SAMAS, "Action sociale en faveur des travailleurs algériens en métropole," 29 July 1959 (AN F1a 5056). It went through several incarnations, beginning as the Service des affaires indigènes nord-africaines (SAINA) in 1928. See Viet, *La France immigrée*, 168.

137. Minutes, Commission consultative nationale pour l'étude des questions nord-africaines, 13 February 1950 (CAC 860269/7). Bureau 10 was buried in the bureaucratic structures and reported to the Under Secretariat for Population, which itself fell under the General Secretariat for Population and Social Action.

138. Villey, *Le complément familial*, based on his doctoral thesis; and Villey, *Mémento pratique*, for which Paul Ribeyre, the minister of Public Health and Population, penned the preface.

139. Viet, *La France immigrée*, 177. The commission was known as La Commission sanitaire et sociale pour l'étude des problèmes nord-africains dans la métropole.

140. ESNA, "Guide de l'action sociale," 20.

141. Paul Bacon, MTSS to the président du Conseil des ministres, 9 October 1950 (CAC 860269/7). This included 12 million francs from the Interior Ministry for Labor Ministry programs, over 23 million for the upkeep and construction of housing, 12 million for managers' salaries, and 5 million to defray costs of repatriations (all from its own budget).

142. Michel, *Les travailleurs algériens en France*, 150; SAMAS, "Assistance aux citoyens français musulmans originaires de l'Algérie se trouvant en métropole—Attributions des contrôleurs sociaux de la main-d'œuvre nord-africaine et des services d'intervention," circulaire no. 348, 19 August 1952 (AN F1a 5035). See also the section on the family allowances controversy in Chapter 3. The Social and Sanitary Aid Fund was a precursor to the FAS; see Chapters 5 and 6.

143. See, among others, AUF, no. 177, "Proposition"; AUF, no. 231, "Proposition: Créer une commission interministérielle et une direction des Nord-Africains en France," 26 June 1949; Assemblée nationale, no. 8377, "Proposition de résolution." All in CAC 860269/7.

144. Frederick Cooper argues that the code, true to social Catholic form, was framed in the language of worker protection but actually "subordinated the workers to the *patronat*." Cooper, *Decolonization and African Society*, 290–91.

145. AUF, no. 230, "Améliorant pour les travailleurs algériens en France et leurs familles démurées en Algérie: Les prestations des assurances sociales et des allocations familiales," 1949 (CAC 860269/7); Michel, *Les travailleurs algériens en France*, 145.

146. AUF, no. 177, "Proposition."

147. AUF, no. 231, "Proposition."

148. Assemblée nationale, no. 8377, "Proposition de résolution." The Commission consultative nationale pour l'étude des questions nord-africaines was created by an "interministerial decree" on 30 May 1949. The commission had representatives from the colonial and metropolitan branches of the government, including a representative of the president, the French Union, the Algerian Assembly (both houses), the Interior Ministry's Algerian Affairs, the Foreign Ministry (to represent Moroccans and Tunisians in France), the Labor Ministry, the Patronat (employers association) and labor unions, and a French Muslim from Algeria living in France (who was never listed as in attendance in the minutes of any of the actual board meetings).

149. Ibid.

150. MTSS, préfet chargé de la Direction des services de l'Algérie et des départements d'outre-mer, Sous-direction de l'Algérie, "Crédits pour la main-d'œuvre nord-africaine," 16 December 1949 (AN F1a 5044).

151. MI, préfet chargé de la Direction des services de l'Algérie et des départements d'outre-mer, Sous-direction de l'Algérie to the MTSS, "Commission de coordination pour l'action à mener en faveur des algériens en métropole," 14 February 1950 (AN F1a 5044).

152. Minutes, Commission consultative, 13 February 1950. Cavaillon, an expert on venereal diseases, briefly worked in public health under the Vichy regime. He became part of a group of medical professionals, led by pediatrician Robert Debré, to implement postwar health policy. See Reggiani, "Birthing the French Welfare State," 365–68.

153. Minutes, Commission consultative, 13 February 1950.

154. The Comité d'action interministérielle pour les affaires sociales intéressant la population musulmane algérienne en métropole (1956–1958) replaced the Commission interministérielle de coordination pour les affaires sociales musulmanes (1952–1956) and had roughly the same duties. The minutes of the meetings for these committees and the decisions they made about funding programs and services are in AN F1a 5044.

155. Minutes, Commission interministérielle, "Pour l'action à mener en métropole en faveur des citoyens français musulmans originaires d'Algérie," 25 November 1952 (AN F1a 5044).

156. Piolet, "Compte rendu de la conférence sur le problème de l'utilisation de la main-d'œuvre nord-africaine en métropole" n.d. (1953?) (ADBR 138 W 56).

157. MI, préfet chargé de la Direction des services de l'Algérie et des départements d'outre-mer to all metropolitan prefects, "Assistance morale et matérielle aux citoyens français musulmans originaires d'Algérie," 26 June 1950 (AN F1a 5035).

158. Ibid.

159. Commission interministérielle, "Programme pour l'année 1955 des réalisations nouvelles en matière d'accueil et d'action sociale," 30 March 1955 (AN F1a 5044).

160. Bureau des affaires musulmanes, Nord, "Association d'aide aux Français d'Algérie de la région lilloise [ADAFARELI]," 14 June 1955 (AN F1a 5064).

161. MI, "Proposition de dépenses du programme 1956," 1956 (AN F1a 5044).

162. SAMAS, "Action sociale en faveur des travailleurs algériens en métropole."

163. CANAM, original mission statement reprinted in the minutes of the 1958–1959 annual meeting, 6 July 1959 (CAC 770391/4).

164. AUF, no. 231, "Proposition."

165. Secrétaire général administratif, CANAM, Assemblée générale, "Rapport moral," 8 July 1957 (AN F1a 5056).

166. Office algérien d'action economique et touristique du Gouvernement général de l'Algérie, 2 October 1948 and 19 July 1949 (CAC 860271/4). Morard led this office.

167. Minutes, Commission interministérielle, "Pour l'action à mener en métropole en faveur des citoyens français musulmans originaire d'Algérie."

168. Government-general of Algeria, Service des liaisons nord-africains, "Emigration des familles," in *Bulletin mensuel des questions islamiques*, March 1951 (AN F1a 5046); CANAM, "Rapport moral." As part of structural reorganization during the early Fifth Republic, representatives of the prefect of the Seine and the FAS were added as "consultants," not full members of the commission's board. See documents on CANAM, 1958–1961, in Michel Massenet's papers (CAC 770391/4).

169. CANAM, Conseil d'administration, 9e séance, 9 January 1951 (CAC 860271/4).

170. Guy de Serres-Justiniac, FAS director to prefect of the Bouches-du-Rhône, "Centre d'accueil nord-africaine," 16 October 1950 (ADBR 138 W 56).

Chapter 2

1. INED published several immigration studies between 1947 and 1955. Girard coedited *Cahiers* 19 and 20 with Jean Stoetzel in 1953 and 1954.

2. The report indicates it relied on studies by INED and ESNA as well by Jean-Jacques Rager—all of which are cited in this chapter. Girard and Leriche had access to the files of P. Rosier (assistant director of Algerian Affairs), A. Rosier (director of Unskilled Labor), Rain (director of Population and Social Aid), Piolet (Interior Ministry), Demondion and Romain (Labor Ministry), Wolff and Villey (Public Health and Population Ministry), and Malet (North African Affairs Bureau liaison to Social Security). Girard and Leriche, eds., *Les Algériens en France*, 9–10. The same report appeared as "Les Algériens en France: Etude démographique et sociale, ouvrage réalisé en collaboration avec l'Institut national d'études démographiques," *CNA* 43–44 (January–February 1955).

3. Girard and Leriche, eds., *Les Algériens en France*, 8.

4. Robert Laurette, "Conclusion," in "Aspects de la vie sociale en Petite Kabylie," *CNA* 17 (July–September 1951): 39; ESNA, "Perspectives de ce cahier," in "A travers les 'Monographies,'" (October–November 1950): 4.

5. Boltanski, *The Making of a Class*, 149.

6. Piolet, "Compte rendu de la conférence sur le problème de l'utilisation de la main-d'œuvre nord-africaine en métropole," n.d. (1953?) (ADBR 138 W 56).

7. Ibid.; P. Caltez, "Les trois étapes du contact," in "Contacts," *CNA* 10 (December 1950): 10.

8. ESNA, "Les Nord Africains en France: Le problème des cours du soir," *CNA* 1 (January 1950): 1.

9. For more on Le Play, see Note 25 below as well as the discussion in Chapter 4.

10. Caltez, "Les trois étapes du contact," 10.

11. Rabinow, *French Modern*, 105–10.

12. G. Pasquier, "Notre contact avec les Nord Africains," in "Contacts," *CNA* 10 (December 1950): 8; Georges Lamirand, *Le rôle social de l'ingénieur* (1932), cited in Boltanski, *The Making of a Class*, 80–82. On Moulay-Yousef and Lyautey, see, among others, Rabinow, *French Modern*; Segalla, *The Moroccan Soul*; Berenson, *Heroes of Empire*.

13. Caltez, "Les trois étapes du contact," 13; Girard and Leriche, "Les Algériens en France: Etude démographique et sociale."

14. Girard and Leriche, *Les Algériens en France*, 8; Girard and Leriche, "Les Algériens en France: Etude démographique et sociale," 159–66.

15. Piolet, "Compte rendu de la conférence sur le problème de l'utilisation de la main-d'œuvre nord-africaine en métropole."

16. Edmound Gorrier, "Par mode de conclusion," in "La famille patriarcale," *CNA* 7–8 (August–September 1950): 42. Gorrier not only contributed regularly to the *CNA*, but also worked directly with Algerians in France through AMANA. See his article "Les cours d'adultes, moyen de promotion des Nord Africains en métropole," *CNA* 40 (July–August 1954): 39.

17. Piolet, "Compte rendu de la conférence sur le problème de l'utilisation de la main-d'œuvre nord-africaine en métropole."

18. Pasquier, "Notre contact avec les Nord Africains," 8.

19. MI, Direction des services de l'Algérie et des départements d'outre-mer, Sous-direction de l'Algérie, "Situation actuelle de l'assistance aux Nord-Africains résidant dans la métropole," 25 October 1954 (AN F1a 5056).

20. Piolet, "Compte rendu de la conférence sur le problème de l'utilisation de la main-d'œuvre nord-africaine en métropole."

21. Ibid.

22. Paul Catrice, "Rapport: Contrôleurs sociaux," delivered at the French Union Assembly, 29 May 1952 (CAC 860271/2).

23. Horne, *A Social Laboratory*, 109–13.

24. Beale, *The Modernist Enterprise*, 104–44.

25. John Ambler, "Ideas, Interests, and the French Welfare State," in Ambler, ed., *The French Welfare State*, 9–11; Pedersen, *Family, Dependence, and the Origins of the Welfare State*, 62–68; Rabinow, *French Modern*, 86–97; Le Play, *On Family, Work, and Social Change*.

26. See, among others, Dutton, *Origins of the French Welfare State*, 6–7, 14–37, 97–130; Pedersen, *Family, Dependence, and the Origins of the Welfare State*, 227–36; Misra, "Mothers or Workers?"; Camiscioli, *Reproducing the French Race*, 32–40.

27. Nord, *France's New Deal*, 187. On social Catholics' anti-communist push among the working class, see Pulju, *Women and Mass Consumer Society*, 42–44.

28. Cohen, *The French Encounter with Africans*, 275–79.

29. Georges Goyau, cited in McCarthy, "French Native Policy," 73. On Lavirerie, see Lorcin, *Imperial Identities*, 177–81.

30. Daughton, *An Empire Divided*, 13–14.

31. Among others, see Abu-Lughod, *Rabat*, 136–51; Rabinow, *French Modern*, 277–319; Wright, *The Politics of Design in French Colonial Urbanism*, 85–160; Çelik, *Urban Forms and Colonial Confrontations*, 130–40; Colonna, "Educating Conformity in French Colonial Algeria," 346–70.

32. Julia Clancy-Smith, "Islam, Gender and Identities in the Making of French Algeria," in Clancy-Smith and Gouda, eds., *Domesticating the Empire*.

33. Jeanne Bowlan, "Civilizing Gender Relations in Algeria: The Paradoxical Case of Marie Bugéja," in Clancy-Smith and Gouda, eds., *Domesticating the Empire*, 175–92.

34. Clancy-Smith, "Islam, Gender and Identities," 154–74. See also Malek Alloula's classic work *The Colonial Harem*.

35. Beale, *The Modernist Enterprise*, 104–44.

36. Janet Horne, "In Pursuit of Greater France: Visions of Empire among Musée Social Reformers, 1894–1931," in Clancy-Smith and Gouda, eds., *Domesticating the Empire*, 30, 38.

37. MacMaster, "'A Demographic Time-Bomb.'"

38. Lamey, "Les Archives de la Société des Pères Blancs"; Cohen, *The French Encounter with Africans*, 276; Lorcin, *Imperial Identities*, 177–79.

39. ASSFAM, formerly SSFNA, and *Hommes et Migrations* relate Ghys' role as founder on their web pages. See "Qui sommes-nous?," at www.assfam.org/spip.php?article9; and a piece by Philippe Dewitte, editor of *Hommes et Migrations* until his death in 2005, at www.hommes-et-migrations.fr/index.php?id=5278 (both accessed 4 September 2012). Ghys continued to play an influential role in immigration politics in France until his death in 1991.

40. Most members of the National Advisory Commission for the Study of North African Questions held government posts (see Chapter 1, Note 148), but the board also invited Leriche, Dr. R. Barthe (president of SSFNA), and Renée Bley (director of SSFNA) to serve as members of the board for their expertise.

41. AMANA, Foyers de jeunes travailleurs, 21 October 1959 (CAC 760140/1).

42. Emmanuel Rain, MSPP, at the Interministerial Commission meeting, 11 December 1951 (CAC 860271/3).

43. Joseph Leriche, "Par manière de conclusion, rôle et place des ESNA dans cette action," in "Réfections sur notre action sociale," *CNA* 39 (May–June 1954): 57.

44. It also published the *Documents nord-africains* (*DNA*), which reprinted excerpts from the press, government documents, articles published by other experts, and any other materials ESNA considered especially important. In 1965, the *CNA* became *Hommes et Migrations*. *DNA* circulated into the 1980s. *Hommes et Migrations* and the Cité nationale de l'histoire de l'immigration has launched a project to digitize the CNA and make them available on line. To consult the collection visit www.histoire-immigration.fr/musee/collections/les-cahiers-nord-africains (accessed April 15, 2013).

45. ESNA, "A travers les 'Monographies,'" 3.

46. Joseph Leriche, "Pour un 'service social' ou une 'action sociale' adaptés," *CNA* 3 (March 1950): 7. Just one example of how influential this journal became: a 1956 Prefecture of the Seine circular quoted Leriche verbatim. Prefecture of the Seine, "Action sociale en faveur des Nord Africains dans la région parisienne, organismes concourant à l'action sociale—logement—cours d'enseignement," circulaire no. 40, December 1956 (AN F1a 5017).

47. Joseph Leriche, "La clientèle des 'Cahiers nord-africains' de leur origine à l'heure actuelle: Causes et conséquences de son évolution," unpublished report, May 1962. I am grateful to Patrick Simon for providing me a copy of this report from INED's archives. In addition to INED's complete collection, most of the archives I examined for this project held copies of some issues of the *CNA*. The *CNA* had significant influence on the Paris police. See Blanchard, *La police parisienne*, 223–25.

48. Minutes, Interministerial Commission, 30 October 1953 (CAC 860271/3).

49. Ibid.; Leriche, "La clientèle des 'Cahiers nord-africains' de leur origine à l'heure actuelle."

50. Leriche, "Pour un 'service social' ou une 'action sociale' adaptés," 7.

51. See the following *CNA* issues, among others: ESNA, "Les Nord Africains en France: Le problème des cours du soir"; Leriche, "Pour un 'service social' ou une 'action sociale' adaptés"; ESNA, "Les Nord Africains en France: Eléments de statistiques commentaires sociaux"; ESNA, "La famille patriarcale"; ESNA, "A travers les 'Monographies'"; ESNA, "Le logement des Nord Africains," *CNA* 11–12 (January–February 1951); ESNA, "Santé des Nord Africains en France (aspects médicaux)," *CNA* 14 (April 1951); ESNA, "Aspects de la vie sociale en Petite Kabylie"; ESNA, "La femme musulmane," *CNA* 27 (December 1952); and ESNA, "Essai de psychologie des travailleurs nord africains," *CNA* 31 (June 1953).

52. Patrick Simon, "L'immigration et l'intégration dans les sciences sociales en France depuis 1945," in Dewitte, ed., *Immigration et intégration*, 84.

53. Daughton, *An Empire Divided*, 227–59.

54. Girard and Leriche, *Les Algériens en France*, 159.

55. On the development of techniques for working-class families, see, among others, Stewart, *Women, Work, and the French State*; Fuchs, *Poor and Pregnant in Paris*; Accampo, et al., eds., *Gender and the Politics of Social Reform*; Clarke, *France in the Age of Organization*, 70–77. On the adaption of these techniques to the colonial setting, see Thompson, *Colonial Citizens*, and the essays in Clancy-Smith and Gouda, eds., *Domesticating the Empire*.

56. ESNA, "Contacts," 3–7.

57. "Aide aux Nord Africains," *La France catholique*, 26 October 1951, 3.

58. ESNA, "Les Nord Africains en France: Le problème des cours du soir," 1.

59. Gorrier, "Par mode de conclusion," 38–42.

60. Nord, *France's New Deal*, 22; Boltanski, *The Making of a Class*, 149.

61. A number of the *Population* articles covered parts of research done for the *Cahiers*, often published in advance of the full-length study.

62. Scott, *Seeing Like a State*, 2.

63. SAMAS, "Circulaires importantes concernant les affaires musulmanes 1943–1967" (AN F1a 5035).

64. Michel, *Les travailleurs algériens en France*, 58–59; MTSS, Direction de la main d'œuvre, Service du contrôle social nord-africain, "Statut des contrôleurs sociaux: Contrôle social nord-africain," n.d. (1950?) (CAC 860271/2).

65. *JO*, 20 June 1949, quoted in Catrice, "Rapport: Contrôleurs sociaux."

66. SAMAS, "Assistance aux citoyens français musulmans originaires de l'Algérie se trouvant en métropole—Attributions des contrôleurs sociaux de la main-d'œuvre nord-africaine et des services d'intervention," circulaire no. 348, 19 August 1952 (AN F1a 5035).

67. AUF, no. 177, "Proposition," 28 April 1948. Catrice recommended that the social inspectors be replaced with "North African assistants" from the indigenous population.

68. Directive issued jointly by the Interior, Labor, Justice, and Public Health and Population Ministries, "Rapatriement des Français originaires des départements d'Algérie et se trouvant sans ressources sur le territoire métropolitain," 13 July 1950, quoted in Catrice, "Rapport: Contrôleurs sociaux."

69. ESNA, "Guide de l'action sociale au bénéfice des Nord Africains en métropole," *CNA* 34 (October–November 1953): 23–24.

70. MI, "Situation actuelle de l'assistance aux Nord Africains résidant dans la métropole." The regions: 1–Seine (Paris); 2–Nord (Lille); 3–Calvados, Loire; 4–Indre and Loire, Gironde (Tours and Bordeaux); 5–Pyrénées Orientales; 6–Moselle, Rhin; 7–Doubs, Saône and Loire; 8–Savoie, Rhône (Lyon); 9–Bouches-du-Rhône (Marseille).

71. MI, préfet hors cadres, directeur du cabinet, "Affectation dans la métropole de fonctionnaires spécialisés dans les questions musulmanes," circulaire no. 54, 1 February 1952 (AN F1a 5035); SAMAS, "Assistance aux citoyens français musulmans originaires de l'Algérie se trouvant en métropole."

72. MI, "Affectation dans la métropole de fonctionnaires spécialisés dans les questions musulmanes."

73. Massenet served as Délégué à l'action sociale pour les Français musulmans d'Algérie en métropole and later as Directeur de la population et des migrations. As Laurens points

out, nearly 40 percent of administrators working in immigration in the 1960s—most of whom first passed through the Algerian services network—graduated from either ENA or the Polytechnique. See Laurens, *Une politisation feutrée*, 33, 92; Massenet, *Sauvage immigration*. On ENA's origins, see Nord, *France's New Deal*, esp. 147–48.

74. The National Assembly's famous special powers vote occurred on 12 March 1956.

75. Vann Kelly, "Papon's Transition after World War II: A Prefect's Road from Bordeaux, through Algeria, and Beyond, August 1944–October 1961," in Golsan, ed., *The Papon Affair*, 35–72. The quotation originally appeared in *Le Monde*, 26 April 1956, 6.

76. House and MacMaster, *Paris 1961*, 26.

77. Decree of 27 December 1951 from the governor-general's office in Algeria informed the IGAMEs of the new CTAMs. Many of the technical consultants continued in their posts until 1965. See de Barros, "Contours d'un réseau administrative 'algérien' en construction."

78. Interministerial Commission, "Coordination de l'action sociale en faveur des citoyens français musulmans résidant en métropole," 9 October 1953 (AN F1a 5044).

79. MI, "Affectation dans la métropole de fonctionnaires spécialisés dans les questions musulmanes."

80. SAMAS, "Note ayant pour objet l'inventaire critique des mesures prises ou en cours d'exécution au titre de l'action économique, politique, sociale, et psychologique auprès la population musulmane algérienne de la métropole," 30 May 1960 (AN F1a 5056); Derder, *L'immigration algérienne et les pouvoirs publics*, 95–96.

81. Piolet, "Compte rendu de la conférence sur le problème de l'utilisation de la main-d'œuvre nord-africaine en métropole."

82. Interministerial Commission, "Coordination de l'action sociale en faveur des citoyens français musulmans résidant en métropole."

83. "Commission consultative nationale pour l'étude des questions nord-africaines," *JO* 6101, 21 June 1949.

84. MI, "Affectation dans la métropole de fonctionnaires spécialisés dans les questions musulmanes."

85. SAMAS, "Assistance aux citoyens français musulmans originaires de l'Algérie se trouvant en métropole."

86. ESNA, "Guide de l'action sociale," 22–24.

87. Meeting at MI of the IGAMEs and the prefects of the departments in the metropole, "comptant une importante population musulmane originaire d'Algérie," 24 May 1951 (CAC 860271/2).

88. Blanchard, "Police judiciaire," 1; IGAME meeting, 24 May 1951 (CAC 860271/2).

89. Blanchard, *La police parisienne*, 72–76.

90. Ibid., 85–116; MacMaster, *Colonial Migrants and Racism*, 192. The rue Lecomte social services remained even if the invasive surveillance system no longer functioned as it had.

91. Blanchard, *La police parisienne*, 166–73; House and MacMaster, *Paris 1961*, 39–40.

92. Blanchard, "Police judicaire," 61–63.

93. *L'Algérie libre*, newspaper of the MTLD-PPA, 15 January 1954, quoted in Blanchard,

"La dissolution des Brigades nord-africaines"; available on-line at www.ihtp.cnrs.fr/spip.php
%3Farticle329&lang=fr.html (accessed 25 February 2010).

94. ESNA, "La famille patriarcale," 5–6.

95. Stora, *Ils venaient d'Algérie*, 13; Ministère secrétaire d'Etat à l'intérieur, le conseiller
d'Etat, secrétaire général pour la Police algérienne, "Demande de statistiques concernant
les Nord Africains," 2 February 1942; Chargé des affaires algériennes, "Recensement des indigènes nord-africains en zone occupée," 31 July 1942; "Renseignements concernant les travailleurs indigènes nord-africains dans la métropole," 10 September 1942. All in AN F1a 5046.

96. Henri Bourbon, "L'émigration nord-africaine en France," *Notes documentaires du
Secrétariat social d'outre-mer*, 12 (November 1953): 7 (INED P704).

97. For further discussion, see MacMaster, *Colonial Migrants and Racism*, 184–88; on
INSEE, see Kateb, *Européens, "indigènes," et juifs en Algérie*, 59, 216–56.

98. Despois, *L'Afrique blanche française*, quoted in ESNA, "A travers les 'Monographies,'" 6.

99. Roger Parant, "Le problème algérien," *CNA* 32 (July–August 1953): 18–36.

100. Alexandre Roche, "Mémoire de stage: Aspects de l'émigration algérienne," ENA,
January 1951 (INED A3355). Roche, one of many ENA graduate students interning in Alge-
ria, completed his report after doing fieldwork. The "service of the ideal" quotation is from
Parant, "Le problème algérien," 18–36.

101. Despois, *L'Afrique blanche française*, quoted in ESNA, "A travers les 'Monographies,'" 6; André-Jean Godin, *L'Afrique du Nord: Dernière chance de la France*, Exposé sur
la politique du gouvernement en Afrique du Nord, présenté au Congrès de l'action républicaine et sociale, 1954 (Paris: Corbière et Jugain Alençon, 1955).

102. Parant, "Le problème algérien," 18–36.

103. Roche, "Mémoire de stage."

104. INED's journal *Population* published parts of the study and the *CNA* reprinted
excerpts. For a critical examination of Chevalier, see Rosental, *L'intelligence démographique*.
Chevalier is best known for his work on nineteenth-century urban poverty, *Laboring Classes
and Dangerous Classes in Paris during the First Half of the Nineteenth Century*, first published in French in 1958. On Chevalier as an expert on North African issues, see Blanchard,
"Encadre des 'citoyens diminués,'" 357–60.

105. Chevalier, *Le problème démographique nord-africain*, 91–92.

106. Moch, "Main-d'œuvre algérienne, émigration des travailleurs algériens vers la
France," report of a meeting presided over by Interior Minister Jules Moch, 4 June 1949
(CAC 860271/2). Moch mentioned Chevalier.

107. Rager, *L'émigration en France des musulmans algériens*, 19. Rager noted the figures came from Jacques Breil, an administrator at INSEE. Rager's research on North
African workers in France began when the Interior Ministry, the Office of National Defense, and INED commissioned him to conduct a census in 1950. The governor-general's
office and the High Commission on Population and the Family also commissioned him
to conduct the previously cited studies published in 1956 and 1957.

108. Recent research estimates between the 1930s and the 1950s, Algeria's indigenous
population expanded by about 2.5 million people. The white settler population grew from

about 900,000 to one million. See Ganiage, *Histoire contemporaine du Maghreb*, 457, 530; Ruedy, *Modern Algeria*, 120–21.

109. Rager, *L'émigration en France des musulmans algériens*, 24.

110. The secrétaire d'Etat à l'intérieur chargé des affaires algériennes, "Action sociale sur le migrant algérien en métropole et sa famille," March 1957 (AN F1a 5055).

111. AUF, conseiller de l'Union française, reporting for the Commission des affaires sociales, "Compte rendu analytique," 27 July 1954 (AN F1a 5122).

112. Bourbon, "L'émigration nord-africaine en France," 7–8.

113. AUF, conseiller de l'Union française, "Compte rendu analytique."

114. ESNA, "Les Nord Africains en France: Eléments de statistiques commentaires sociaux," 14–16, and appendix. Other experts, including INED researchers, accepted and cited ESNA statistics, while acknowledging they were imprecise. See Girard and Stoetzel, eds., *Français et immigrés: Nouveaux documents*, 18n1; Girard and Leriche, *Les Algériens en France*, 6–10.

115. Piolet, "Compte rendu de la conférence sur le problème de l'utilisation de la main-d'œuvre nord-africaine en métropole"; Bourbon, "L'émigration nord-africaine en France," 5–9.

116. Rager, *L'émigration en France des musulmans algériens*, 72–73.

117. An industry report indicated that metallurgy, mining, and related fields accounted for 45 percent of Algerians' "stable employment." See Duron, director, l'Ecole industrielle de la Société des hauts-fourneaux de la Chiers, "La main-d'œuvre nord-africaine et son emploi dans les industries des métaux," report for the Union des industries métallurgiques et minières, 1952 (CIEMI XVI D 85).

118. Rager, *L'émigration en France des musulmans algériens*, 89; Piolet, "Compte rendu de la conférence sur le problème de l'utilisation de la main-d'œuvre nord-africaine en métropole." It seems clear the INED/CNA joint study had access to some of these sources and others cited in this section and used them as well, coming up with approximately the same results. Girard and Leriche, eds., *Les Algériens en France*, 63–83.

119. Minutes, Interministerial Commission, 30 October 1953.

120. Ibid.; Moch, "Main-d'œuvre algérienne, émigration des travailleurs algériens vers la France"; Piolet, "Compte rendu de la conférence sur le problème de l'utilisation de la main-d'œuvre nord-africaine en métropole."

121. Gilbert Marc, "L'Algérie devant les conséquences de son émigration," ENA, December 1953 (INED A3355). Marc cites Louis Chevalier, Jean-Jacques Rager, Alexandre Roche, Robert Montagne, and the ESNA *Cahiers*.

122. Minutes, Interministerial Commission, 30 October 1953. Simoneau was director of Algerian Affairs from 1955 to 1959.

123. Minutes, Commission consultative nationale pour l'étude des questions nord-africaines, 13 February 1950 (CAC 860269/7); Honorary governor-general of Algeria, president of CANAM, to an inspecteur de l'instruction publique, directeur des Services d'enseignement de la Seine, 28 July 1953 (AN F1a 5060).

124. Government-general of Algeria, "Emigration des familles." See also Roche, "Mémoire de stage." While Roche recognized many Algerians intended to return eventu-

ally to their homeland, he feared that two groups wanted to "assimilate": young men who arrived in France with limited family ties and thus would want to marry French women, and entire families, which would most likely become permanent settlers.

125. S. Belpeer, "Note sur le problème des familles nord-africaines dans le Département des Bouches-du-Rhône en 1952" (CAC 860271/11); Jean-Jacques Rager, "Evolution de la réglementation de la migration algérienne en France," in *Les migrations des populations* (Présidence du Conseil, Haut Comité de la population et de la famille, 1957), 69 (CAC 860269/5).

126. Louis Massignon (1932), quoted in Bourbon, "L'émigration nord-africaine en France," 5.

127. Belpeer, "Note sur le problème des familles nord-africaines."

128. Rager, "Les musulmans algériens," 262–64.

129. Mathieu, "Les problèmes posés," 8.

130. Belpeer, "Note sur le problème des familles nord-africaines."

131. Bourbon, "L'émigration nord-africaine en France," 7.

132. Zehraoui, *L'immigration*, 48; Girard and Leriche, eds., *Les Algériens en France*, 59.

133. Gillette and Sayad, *L'immigration algérienne en France*, 61. Their figures appear to come from Girard and Leriche, eds., *Les Algériens en France*, 60.

134. MI, Direction des services de l'Algérie et des départements d'outre-mer, Sous-direction de l'Algérie, "Enquête sociale sur la situation des musulmans originaires d'Algérie résidant en métropole," circulaire no. 310, 24 August 1953 (CAC 860271/3). This circular requested the survey of Algerian workers, women, and children. A conseiller de l'Union français delivered results to the AUF in a report from the Commission des affaires sociales, 10 June 1954 (AN F1a 5122).

135. MI, Direction des services de l'Algérie et des départements d'outre-mer, Sous-direction de l'Algérie, "Recensement numérique des Français musulmans originaires d'Algérie en résidence dans la métropole," 24 August 1954 (AN F1a 5056).

136. Ibid.

137. Elisabeth Malet, "Situation et problèmes des familles nord-africaines en Seine-et-Marne," in "Situation et aspirations de la famille nord-africaine en métropole," *CNA* 49 (November–December 1955): 35–42.

138. MI, "Recensement numérique des français musulmans originaires d'Algérie en résidence dans la métropole."

139. Ibid. The first of these was circular no. 120 of 19 March 1949. Girard and Leriche reiterated this point in *Les Algériens en France*, 58–59.

140. "Essai d'appréciation du nombre de familles nord-africaines en métropole," in ESNA, "Situation et aspirations de la famille nord-africaine en métropole," 35–42.

141. Girard and Leriche, eds., *Les Algériens en France*, 58–62.

142. SAMAS, "Problèmes sociaux concernant la population musulmane algérienne en métropole," October 1957 (AN F1a 5055). Again, some departments sent the figures too quickly or without changes.

143. G. Morlot, SAMAS, "Prise de participation par la SONACOTRAL dans le capital d'une société HLM," 28 May 1959 (CAC 770391/7).

144. INSEE, "Recensement des Hauts-de-Seine," 1962 (ADHS 1249 W 3 and 4).

145. Haut Comité consultatif de la population et de la famille, *La population française*, vol. 1: 292.

146. Bourbon, "L'émigration nord-africaine en France," 20.

147. Jeanine Roy's two-part series "Le Maroc vu par une femme," *La Dépêche du Midi*, 24 May 1953, 5, and 7 June 1953, 4. On fears about miscegenation during World War I, see Tyler Stovall, "Love, Labor, and Race: Colonial Men and White Women in France during the Great War," in Stovall and Van Den Abbeele, eds., *French Civilization and Its Discontents*, 297–321.

148. Chevalier, *Le problème démographique nord-africain*, 130.

149. Maurice Vaussard, "Un péril national: L'immigration incontrôlée de travailleurs nord-africains," *Le Monde*, 7 December 1948, 4.

150. See, among others, "Drame passionnel évoqué aux assises de Seine-et-Oise: Un algérien avait tué son amie qui refusait de l'épouser," *La Dépêche du Midi*, 18 February 1953, 1; "La jalousie, l'ivresse, ont fait germer la haine chez 3 couples tragiques," *L'Aurore*, 24 August 1953, 1, 8; "Avec un couteau à pain: Un cantonnier nord-africain tranche la gorge de sa jeune femme puis va se constituer prisonnier," *L'Aurore*, 30 September 1953, 1, 8; "Un tailleur algérien fou de jalousie tue son amie (16 ans et demi) à coups de couteau," *L'Aurore*, 4 December 1953; "Il m'a tuée! hurlait une jeune femme ses vêtements de nuit inondés de sang, mais le Nord Africain qu'elle accuse de l'avoir poignardée nie farouchement," *L'Aurore*, 7 May 1954, 1, 12.

151. Leo Bogart, "Les Algériens en France: Adaptation réussie et NON réussie," in Girard and Stoetzel, eds., *Français et immigrés: Nouveaux documents*, 19.

152. See the discussion of interracial marriage in Chapter 1, and ESNA, "Logement familial des Nord-Africains en France (quatrième cahier)," *CNA* 54 (September–October 1956): 9; Bogart, "Les Algériens en France," 31–32, 72; Claude Mothes, "Les familles algériennes musulmanes dans l'agglomération parisienne," 104–5, in Girard and Stoetzel, eds., *Français et immigrés: Nouveaux documents*.

153. Délégation générale du gouvernement en Algérie, "La migration algérienne en France," (diffusion restreinte) *La Semaine en Algérie* no. 98, 20–26 October 1960 (AN F1a 5017).

154. ESNA, "A travers les 'Monographies,'" 4.

155. Ibid.

156. Pasquier, "Notre contact avec les Nord Africains," 8.

157. ESNA, "Les Nord Africains en France: Le problème des cours du soir," 2.

158. Ibid.; A. Causy, "Les travailleurs nord-africains dans notre économie moderne," *CNA* 2 (February 1950): 8; ESNA, "Du Douar à l'usine," *CNA* 13 (March 1951): 36.

159. Sauvy, preface for Girard and Stoetzel, eds., *Français et immigrés: Nouveaux documents*.

160. Bogart, "Les Algériens en France," 23.

161. ESNA, "Les Nord Africains en France: Le problème des cours du soir," 2.

162. A. Morali-Daninos, "Les Nord Africains sont-ils différents des métropolitains?," in "Santé des Nord-Africains en France (aspects médicaux)" *CNA* 14 (April 1951): 11–13.

163. Causy, "Les travailleurs nord-africains dans notre économie moderne," 10; "Du Douar à l'usine," 28–29. Citations from Causy.

164. Bogart, "Les Algériens en France," 21.

165. ESNA, "Du Douar à l'usine," 27.

166. Reprint of the activities report of "Le Comité d'études et d'action nord-africaine de Lille et de sa banlieue," *DNA* 161 (30 November 1954): 6–8.

167. Caltez, "Les trois étapes du contact," 12.

168. ESNA, "Du Douar à l'usine," 32.

169. Caltez, "Les trois étapes du contact," 11.

170. Morali-Daninos, "Les Nord Africains sont-ils différents des métropolitains?," 13.

171. Ibid.

172. Causy, "Les travailleurs nord-africains dans notre économie moderne," 11.

173. Caltez, "La famille patriarcale en Afrique berbère," in "Problèmes familiaux," 13, and ESNA, "La famille patriarcale," 5–6, both in *CNA* 7–8 (August–September 1950).

174. Jean Fournier, "La famille patriarcale et nous métropolitains," in "Problèmes familiaux," *CNA* 7–8 (August–September 1950): 7–12.

175. ESNA, "La famille patriarcale," 5.

176. Caltez, "La famille patriarcale en Afrique berbère," 13.

177. ESNA, "Du Douar à l'usine," 10.

178. Caltez, "La famille patriarcale en Afrique berbère," 15.

179. Parant, "Le problème algérien," 18.

180. Bogart, "Les Algériens en France," 32.

181. Parant, "Le problème algérien," 18; Gorrier, "Par mode de conclusion," 36.

182. ESNA, "Les Nord Africains en France: Le problème des cours du soir," 2.

183. Ibid., 5; Laurette, "Conclusion," 39.

184. ESNA, "Les Nord Africains en France: Le problème des cours du soir," 4–5.

185. ESNA, "Logement familial des Nord-Africains en France," 9.

186. Gorrier, "Par mode de conclusion," 36. On the essential role wives played in caring for husbands, see Centre algérien de documentation et d'action familiale, "Les aspects familiaux de l'émigration nord-africaine," *DNA* 144 (10 July 1954): 3–12; ESNA, "Situation et aspirations de la famille nord-africaine en métropole," 8–9.

187. ESNA, "La femme musulmane," 5–18.

188. Ibid.

189. Girard and Leriche, eds., *Les Algériens en France*, 162–63.

Chapter 3

1. RTF, "Emission sociale: Conseils aux familles nouvellement arrivées dans la métropole," 27 April 1956 (CAC 860271/5).

2. Jean Fernand-Laurent, "Projet d'émissions radiophoniques pour les travailleurs algériens résidant en France," 27 May 1966 (CAC 760140/5).

3. Honorary governor-general of Algeria, president of CANAM to director of Algerian Affairs, 14 June 1955 (AN F1a 5057).

4. Weber, *Peasants into Frenchmen*.

5. The project was never completed since regional identities remained important. On the nineteenth century, see Rosental, *Les sentiers invisibles*; Moch, *Paths to the City*, and *The*

Pariahs of Yesterday. On André Malraux's project to create a shared cultural identity in the 1960s, see Lebovics, *Mona Lisa's Escort*, 109–31.

6. SSFNA, "Rapport moral," 1953, 2.

7. Frader, *Breadwinners and Citizens*, 9.

8. Among others, see Lazreg, *The Eloquence of Silence*, esp. 51–117; Julia Clancy-Smith, "La Femme Arabe," 52–64; Bowlan, "Civilizing Gender Relations in Algeria."

9. Housing for men, the other priority, is examined in Chapter 4.

10. On the state's quota system, see Spire, "Semblables et portant différents," 56; Shepard, *The Invention of Decolonization*, 50–51.

11. Directeur de la main-d'œuvre to the interministerial meeting, Algiers, "L'action du Ministère du Travail en faveur des travailleurs algériens," 5 June 1949 (CAC 860271/2).

12. "Enquête sur la stabilité d'emploi des travailleurs algériens dans la métropole," in *L'Emploi* no. 181–82 (January–February 1956), quoted in Michel, *Les travailleurs algériens en France*, 32.

13. Jean Verpraet, "Les institutions métropolitaines au service des Nord Africains," in "Réflexions sur notre action sociale," *CNA* 39 (May–June 1954): 26.

14. "Rapport préliminaire de l'inspecteur général du travail et de la main-d'œuvre Chaillé sur les conditions de travail et de vie dans la métropole des travailleurs nord-africains" (known as the Rapport Chaillé), 27 September 1954 (CAC 860271/2).

15. Michel, *Les travailleurs algériens en France*, 82.

16. ESNA, "Les Nord Africains et la psychotechnique," in "La psychotechnique au service des Nord Africains," *CNA* 20 (January–February 1952): 5–6.

17. See Camiscioli, *Reproducing the French Race*, 58–73; Carson, *The Measure of Merit*, 238–42.

18. Michel, *Les travailleurs algériens en France*, 79–86.

19. Ibid., 81.

20. ESNA, "Formation professionnelle des adultes nord-africains en métropole," *CNA* 42 (November–December 1954); Michel, *Les travailleurs algériens en France*, 84–86, 141–42.

21. Duron, director, l'Ecole industrielle de la Société des hauts-fourneaux de la Chiers, "La main-d'œuvre nord-africaine et son emploi dans les industries des métaux," report for the Union des industries métallurgiques et minières, 1952 (CIEMI XVI D 85). Michel reached similar conclusions in *Les travailleurs algériens*.

22. Michel, *Les travailleurs algériens en France*, 142.

23. Duron, "La main-d'œuvre nord-africaine."

24. Malet, "Jeunesse nord-africaine en France." According to Malet, the programs were open to anyone but more Algerian young men entered the specialized programs because they rarely had the education and language skills to enter directly into apprenticeship programs.

25. In 1959 the Education Ministry reported that 150,000 men and women attended night classes during the program's fifteen-year history. "Note sur le programme complémentaire du Ministère de l'Education nationale à financer par le Fonds d'action sociale," 1959 (CAC 760140/6).

26. MEN, Service de coordination de l'enseignement dans la France d'outre-mer, "Les centres d'éducation pour les travailleurs nord-africains de la métropole en 1950–1951," 16

November 1951 (AN F1a 5060). Of the 73 centers, 11 were in Paris, 19 in the Paris area (Seine), 1 in Seine-et-Marne, and 46 in other departments, including 2 in the Bouches-du-Rhône, 3 in the Nord, and 3 in the Rhône. By 1955, the Paris area had 27 centers with 12 in the following arrondissements: 4, 12, 13, 14, 15, 17, 18, 19, and 20. SAMAS, "Liste des centres ouverts—Paris banlieue," 29 September 1955 (AN F1a 5060).

27. MEN, "Les centres d'éducation pour les travailleurs nord-africains de la métropole en 1950–1951."

28. MSPP, Bureau 10, "Les cours privés en faveur des Nord Africains dans la métropole," November 1953 (CAC 860271/3).

29. ESNA, "Les Nord Africains en France: Eléments de statistiques commentaires sociaux," *CNA*, 5–7 (May–June 1950).

30. Bureau 10, "Les cours privés en faveur des Nord Africains dans la métropole."

31. MSPP, Bureau 10, "Action éducative et culturelle poursuivie sur le plan privé en faveur des Nord-Africains résidant dans la métropole," September 1953 (CAC 860271/3). This included eight "housekeeping courses reserved for women and adolescent girls."

32. Bureau 10, "Les cours privés en faveur des Nord Africains dans la métropole."

33. ESNA, "Les contacts au cours et au delà du cours," in "Enseignement, contacts et promotion: Expériences et témoignages," *CNA* 40 (July–August 1954): 30; ESNA, "Mémento de l'Algérien dans la métropole," *CNA* 28 (January–February 1953).

34. ESNA, "L'enseignement dans les cours d'adultes aux Nord Africains," in "Enseignement, contacts et promotion," *CNA* (July–August 1954): 11–13.

35. Bureau 10, "Les cours privés en faveur des Nord Africains dans la métropole."

36. Rohet, "Notice à l'attention des utilisateurs de ce fascicule en complément du précédent 'Ali apprend le français,'" in "Enseignement, contacts et promotion," *CNA* (July–August 1954), appendix, 3. Rohet also published *Ali écrit à ses parents, à ses amis, Ali progresse en français, J'apprends le français*, and *Je progresse en français*—all of which have been reissued multiple times. The most recent edition I have come across is *J'apprends le français*, 14th edition (Paris: AMANA-Hommes et Migrations, 1992). For more, see Escafré-Dublet, "Etat, culture, immigration," 57–60, 91–92.

37. Rohet, "Notice à l'attention des utilisateurs de ce fascicule"; ESNA, "Méthodes d'enseignement à l'usage des Nord Africains des 'cours d'adultes,'" in "Annexe aux méthodes d'enseignement à l'usage des Nord Africains dans la métropole," *CNA* 29 (March 1953): 6.

38. Scott, *Seeing Like a State*, 89.

39. ESNA, "Leçon 21," in "Annexe aux méthodes d'enseignement à l'usage des Nord Africains dans la métropole," March 1953, appendix, 21.

40. Rohet, *Ali apprend le français (Manuel élémentaire pour cours d'adulte nord-africain)*, 1953; reprinted in ESNA, "Annexe aux méthodes d'enseignement à l'usage des Nord Africains dans la métropole," appendix, 1–28.

41. Rohet, "Eléments de grammaire française par la lecture expliquée," in "Enseignement, contacts et promotion," appendix, 26–27.

42. Ibid., 38–39.

43. Rohet, *Ali apprend le français*, appendix, 29.

44. ESNA, "Mémento de l'Algérien dans la métropole," 22–23.

45. ESNA, "Petit manuel de sécurité: A l'usage des travailleurs nord-africains," in "Main-d'œuvre nord-africaine et sécurité dans le travail," *CNA* 33 (September 1953), appendix, 2–49.

46. On radio's central role in the modernizing mission, see Connelly, *A Diplomatic Revolution*, 28.

47. Governor-general of Algeria to the MTSS, "Départ des travailleurs algériens pour la métropole," 3 June 1948 (AN F1a 5046).

48. Minutes, Interministerial Commission, 30 October 1953 (CAC 860271/3); Director-general of la Sûreté nationale, le directeur des Renseignements généraux, "Emissions radiophoniques en langue arabe et les Nord Africains en métropole," 22 November 1955 (AN F^{1a} 5057).

49. Minutes, Interministerial Commission, 30 October 1953.

50. Governor-general of Algeria to the MTSS, "Départ des travailleurs algériens pour la métropole."

51. Minutes, Interministerial Commission, 30 October 1953.

52. René Grinda penned the preface to this collection of broadcast transcripts. Ouary, *Par les chemins d'émigration*, 9.

53. "Emissions radiodiffuse: Recommandations pratiques qui pourraient être utilement faites aux Français musulmans d'Algérie se trouvant en métropole par le service des émissions arabes de la radiodiffusion française," 1953 (CAC 860271/5).

54. RTF, "Emissions en langues arabe et berbère," 1959 (AN F1a 5057).

55. They also echoed themes from the early days of radio. See Neulander, *Programming National Identity*.

56. Eva Compain, *La science de la maison* (1959), cited in Duchen, *Women's Rights and Women's Lives*, 64. See also Pulju, *Women and Mass Consumer Society*, esp. 59–72.

57. CANAM, "Programme des émissions radiophoniques destinées aux Nord Africains travaillant dans la métropole," 12 February 1954 (CAC 860271/4). For transcripts of broadcasts from 1954 to 1958, see CAC 860271/4.

58. RTF, "Emissions en langues arabe et berbère."

59. RTF, "Emission sociale: Conseils aux familles nouvellement arrivées dans la métropole."

60. Each season addressed family allowances. In particular, see the three-part series "Emission éducative pourquoi la législation des assurances sociales et des allocations familiales présente des différences en France et dans les départements algériens," 12, 19, and 26 December 1956 (CAC 860271/4).

61. Director-general of la Sûreté nationale, "Emissions radiophoniques en langue arabe et les Nord Africains en métropole."

62. Rosental, *L'intelligence démographique*, 26. The other half included retirement and health care. The national system was not comprehensive; it excluded certain sectors, including agriculture.

63. Rager, "Les musulmans algériens," 231.

64. Michel, *Les travailleurs algériens en France*, 144–45.

65. Pedersen, *Family, Dependence, and the Origins of the Welfare State*, 224–85.

66. AUF, no. 230, "Améliorant pour les travailleurs algériens en France et leurs familles démurées en Algérie"; Michel, *Les travailleurs algériens en France*, 145. For more on Catrice, see Cooper, *Decolonization and African Society*.

67. "Le problème des allocations familiales," in *Bulletin Mensuel des Questions Islamiques*, marked "diffusion restreinte" (December 1954): 140 (AN F1a 5046); Pierre Laroque, in the preface to Michel, *Les travailleurs algériens en France*, 1–3; Michel, *Les travailleurs algériens en France*, 144–45.

68. AUF, no. 230, "Améliorant pour les travailleurs algériens en France et leurs familles démurées en Algérie"; Math, "Les allocations familiales," 38. Catrice and others countered that the children of Italian migrant workers were eligible due to a bilateral convention between France and Italy.

69. Rapport Chaillé.

70. Director-general of la Sûreté nationale, "Emissions radiophoniques en langue arabe et les Nord Africains en métropole."

71. Many migrated to flee the war as the state forcibly removed three million rural families from their homes. See Cornaton, *Les camps de regroupement*, 59–67; Hervo, *Chroniques du bidonvilles*, 56–66.

72. Centre algérien de documentation et d'action familiale, "Les aspects familiaux de l'émigration nord-africaine," *DNA* (10 July 1954): 7.

73. Claude Mothes, "Les familles algériennes musulmanes dans l'agglomération parisienne dans l'agglomération parisienne," in Girard and Stoetzel, eds., *Français et immigrés*, 120.

74. See Chapter 5.

75. Vogel, "Andrée Michel."

76. Michel, *Les travailleurs algériens en France*, 144–45. Laroque, in his preface to Michel's study, dismissively warned that Michel's "natural generosity" led her to highlight some of the problems Algerians faced while "underestimating" the efforts made on Algerians' behalf. In particular, Laroque took issue with her characterization of the family allowance program.

77. Rager, "Les musulmans algériens," 231.

78. S. Pivot and F. Pavard, "Les travailleurs nord-africains et la sécurité sociale," 6 December 1954 (Archive Laroque, ENTEX 89/001 carton 114).

79. Michel, *Les travailleurs algériens en France*, 145–47.

80. Rapport Chaillé.

81. Policy makers who favored family planning also realized it would not be possible to impose a policy that aggressively curbed Algerian fecundity. MacMaster, "'A Demographic Time-Bomb.'"

82. Rapport Chaillé.

83. "Le problème des allocations familiales"; Fernand Boverat, "Gravité de la discordance entre les politiques de population convenant à la métropole, d'une part, à l'Algérie, aux Antilles et à la Réunion d'autre part," 20 May 1952 (CAC 860269/1); Laroque, preface to Michel, *Les travailleurs algériens en France*, 1–4.

84. G. H. Bousquet, "L'Islam et la limitation volontaire des naissances: Brèves réflexions sur un grand problème social," *Population* 5, no. 1 (January–March 1950): 128. *Population*, INED's widely circulated journal, distanced itself from the author's views in a disclaimer preceding the article.

85. AUF, no. 230, "Améliorant pour les travailleurs algériens en France et leurs familles démurées en Algérie."

86. The Social Security Administration issued a circular indicating that 500 million francs would be allocated for male worker housing. Subsequent circulars allowed funds to go to others services as well. These circulars are reprinted in ESNA, "Le logement des Nord Africains (deuxième cahier)," *CNA* 35-6 (December 1953–January 1954): 19–22, 24–25. According to Michel, the total collected between 1946 and 1956 reached "about 60 billion" francs. Michel, *Les travailleurs algériens en France*, 145.

87. Michel, *Les travailleurs algériens en France*, 146; Rager, "Les musulmans algériens," 127.

88. The UNAF, "the official voice of families," conducted the survey in 1953. The president of UNAF, Mr. Guibourge, had a copy of the questionnaire sent, as a courtesy, to Louis Henry at INED in December 1953. I am grateful to Paul-André Rosental for providing me a copy of the questionnaire from the INED archives. The UNAF asked leading questions about the appeal of family migration as well as the following related issues: Should men come alone, initially, in order to secure work and lodging? And, were the key problems posed by family migration women's adaptation, the adaptation of children, health problems, or "family needs"? Finally, it asked respondents to indicate what they thought family aid associations could do in Algeria and in the metropole to improve the situation. I have been unable to find the original responses (see below). Apparently UNAF regularly asked leading questions; see Duchen, *Women's Rights and Women's Lives*, 106–7. On UNAF, see Pulju, *Women and Mass Consumer Society*, 99, 112.

89. Centre algérien de documentation et d'action familiale, "Les aspects familiaux de l'émigration nord-africaine," 3–4. The Centre documented social workers' responses in Algeria. It published a summary of the findings of its study and of the UNAF study in its internal journal in early 1954, which the *DNA* reprinted. UNAF respondents mentioned in the summary came from the Nord, Lyon, Le Havre, Arles, Haut-Rhin, and Alès.

90. J. Mathieu, "Les problèmes posés," in "Action et techniques sociales au service des familles nord-africaines en France," *CNA* 51 (March–April 1956): 8. In a note, Mathieu explained his work was based on reports by social workers in Douai. They had not written for a public audience; Mathieu sought their permission before publishing their words.

91. Centre algérien de documentation et d'action familiale, "Les aspects familiaux de l'émigration nord-africaine," 2–3.

92. Ibid., 2.

93. Ludovic Naudeau, cited in Camiscioli, *Reproducing the French Race*, 43–44.

94. Renée Bley, "Le service social 'spécialisé' pour les familles nord-africaines," in "Action et techniques sociales au service des familles nord-africaines en France," 24–28. Bley remained at the helm of SSFNA for twenty-five years. She had significant influence in the realm of Algerian welfare services, managing the largest private association, publishing, and

sitting on the Commission consultative nationale pour l'étude des questions nord-africaines.

95. Ibid.

96. "Rapport d'activité présenté par 'le Comité d'études et d'action Nord-Africains de Lille et de sa banlieue,'" *DNA* 161 (30 November 1954): 5.

97. "Statuts" established by the Assemblé générale constitutive, in "Accueil familial nord-africain," 10 March 1952 (CAC 850021/70).

98. Rachel Fuchs, "The Right to Life: Paul Strauss and the Politics of Motherhood," in Accampo et al., eds., *Gender and the Politics of Social Reform*, 82.

99. Offen, *Women and the Politics of Motherhood*, 2.

100. Ross, *Fast Cars, Clean Bodies*, 172.

101. Rager, "Les musulmans algériens," 218; Camiscioli, *Reproducing the French Race*, 17–21.

102. This program began in 1920 and continued under Vichy. See Offen, *Women and the Politics of Motherhood*; Muel-Dreyfus, *Vichy and the Eternal Feminine*; Pollard, *Reign of Virtue*. After 1945, see Duchen, *Women's Rights and Women's Lives*, 101–2.

103. Lamri, "'Algériennes' et mères françaises exemplaires."

104. S. Belpeer, "Note sur le problème des familles nord-africaines dans le Département des Bouches-du-Rhône en 1952" (CAC 860271/11).

105. S. Belpeer, "L'aide à l'adaptation des femmes: Quelques réflexions sur l'éduation des femmes musulmanes par l'ATOM," in "Action et techniques sociales au service des familles nord-africaines en France," 35.

106. Elizabeth Malet, "Familles algériennes musulmanes en France," in Girard and Leriche, eds., *Les Algériens en France*, 128. Also published as Malet, "Situation et problèmes des familles nord-africains en Seine-et-Marne," in "Situation et aspirations de la famille nord-africaine en métropole," *CNA* 49 (November–December 1955): 35–42.

107. M.-L. Tournier, "Les services sociaux 'de droit common' de France et les familles nord-africaines," in "Action et techniques sociales au services des familles nord-africains en France," 17. CANAM paid her social assistant's salary.

108. No documents gave her full first name, just the first initial, S. Reference to her origin appeared in Lucien Ferre, sous-préfet, "Extraits du compte-rendu de la mission effectuée par M. le Sous-préfet," 20 December 1951 (CAC 860271/2). See also, S. Belpeer, "Deux 'descriptions' typiques familles vivant en monde clos: des territoires du sud de l'Algérie installés à Marseille (Hiver 1953–1954)," in "Situation et aspirations de la famille nord-africaine en métropole," 16.

109. Belpeer worked with a local home economics school to develop classes. See Belpeer, "Note sur le problème des familles nord-africaines."

110. Belpeer, "Deux 'descriptions' typiques familles vivant en monde clos," 20. While she did not identify the exact number of families in Cap Janet, Belpeer noted that the first families arrived in 1949. Families had settled in Aix even earlier, with 83 families established there by 1948.

111. Ibid., 24. The same phrase appeared in S. Belpeer, "Les familles musulmanes habitant Aix-en-Provence originaires d'Hennaya (1954)," in Girard and Leriche, eds., *Les Algériens en France*, 148.

112. Pedersen, *Family, Dependence, and the Origins of the Welfare State*, 273–75. Also see Donzelot, *The Policing of Families*, 96–168; Downs, *Manufacturing Inequalities*, 14; Frader, *Breadwinners and Citizens*, 134–36.

113. Pulju, *Women and Mass Consumer Society*, 59.

114. Financed by the Conseil général de la Seine, the social counselors worked with the interministerial organizations and with the network of private associations. MI, Direction des services de l'Algérie et des départements d'outre-mer, Sous-direction de l'Algérie, "Situation actuelle de l'assistance aux Nord Africains résidant dans la métropole," 25 October 1954 (AN F1a 5056).

115. Prefecture of the Seine, Direction des affaires sociales, Service social nord-africain, List of Social Counselors, 1 April 1954 (AN F1a 5011); Prefecture of the Seine, "Action sociale en faveur des Nord-Africains dans la région parisienne, Organismes concourant à l'action sociale—logement—cours d'enseignement," circulaire no. 40, December 1956 (AN F1a 5017).

116. Prefecture of the Pas-de-Calais, Comité départemental d'aide aux Français d'Afrique du Nord, 25 March 1957 (AN F1a 5066); J. Bellanger, president, ANAN, "Rapport d'activités pour l'année 1956" (CAC 770391/4).

117. SSFNA, "Rapport sur l'activité du SSFNA, 1957–1958," 12; SSFNA "Rapport sur l'activité du SSFNA, 1958–1959," 5.

118. CANAM, minutes of the 1958–1959 annual meeting, 6 July 1959 (CAC 770391/4).

119. Belpeer, "Note sur le problème des familles nord-africaines."

120. SSFNA frequently provided space to other organizations. See, among others, "Rapport d'activité présenté par 'le Comité d'études et d'action Nord-Africains de Lille et de sa banlieue,'" 14.

121. SSFNA, "Rapport sur l'activité du SSFNA en 1954," April 1954, 41–45; Bley, "Le service social 'spécialisé' pour les familles nord-africaines," 25.

122. Prefecture of the Seine, Secrétariat général, Service départemental de coordination des services sociaux de la Seine, pamphlet entitled "Cours d'enseignement organisés dans la région parisienne pour les Nord Africains de la métropole," May 1956 (CIEMI VII B 57).

123. Malet, "Familles algériennes musulmanes en France," 134.

124. SSFNA, "Rapport sur l'activité du SSFNA en 1954," 44; M. H. Boyer, "Cours d'enseignement ménager, réunions de femmes par le service social familial nord-africain," in "Action et techniques sociales au services des familles nord-africains en France," (March–April 1956), 42.

125. Boyer, "Cours d'enseignement ménager," 41–43. The Red Cross classes had been around for about twenty years and served mostly Polish Jews and a few Algerian women in the early 1950s.

126. Lucien Ferre, sous-préfet, Services d'études des mouvements de main-d'œuvre et d'action sociale, "Extraits du compte-rendu," 20 December 1951 (CAC 860271/2); Belpeer, "Note sur le problème des familles nord-africaines."

127. ATOM social worker, "Les familles de l'agglomération marseillaise," in Girard and Leriche, *Les Algériens en France*, 144. Of the 101 families included in her report, only 50 women could sew and another 13 sewed poorly.

128. S. Bertholot, "Pour la formation ménagère des femmes nord-africaines en Moselle dans le cadre de la Commission d'aide aux Nord Africains dans la métropole," in "Action et techniques sociales au services des familles nord-africaines en France," 39.

129. Belpeer, "Les familles musulmanes habitant Aix-en-Provence originaires d'Hennaya," 148.

130. Belpeer, "L'aide à l'adaptation des femmes," 35.

131. "L'aide aux mères de familles," *Pour la vie*, no. 34 (1950), cited in Duchen, *Women's Rights and Women's Lives*, 67.

132. Prefecture of the Seine, "Cours d'enseignement organisés dans la région parisienne pour les Nord Africains de la métropole"; ATOM and Caisse d'allocations familiales, "Problèmes de l'immigration familiale nord-africaine en métropole: Convention enseignant ménager," *DNA* 172 (26 February 1955): 1–2. The latter specified that teachers must have the appropriate diploma. By 1953, the Paris office of Family Allowances already provided SSFNA three home economics teachers. R. Barthe, SSFNA, "Rapport moral, 1953," 6.

133. ATOM and Caisse d'allocations familiales, "Problèmes de l'immigration familiale nord-africaine en métropole," 1–2; Belpeer, "L'aide à l'adaptation des femmes," 37. It seems likely that the decision to provide state subsidies and to mandate that recipients participate in the Family Allowances program resulted from both the Family Allowances controversy and the desire to register (and to monitor) more families.

134. Barthe, "Rapport moral, 1953," 1–3.

135. SSFNA, "Rapport sur l'activité du SSFNA en 1954," 16.

136. ATOM, "Rapport d'activités pour la période du 1er juillet 1953 au 30 juin 1954," 13 (ADBR M14 5852).

137. Belpeer, "L'aide à l'adaptation des femmes," 37.

138. ATOM and Caisse d'allocations familiales, "Problèmes de l'immigration familiale nord-africaine en métropole," 1–2.

139. ATOM, "Rapport d'activités pour la période du 1er juillet 1953 au 30 juin 1954," 13.

140. Massenet, "Programme d'action sociale pour l'année 1959 (pour les Français musulmans d'Algérie en métropole)," 15 October 1959 (Archive Laroque, ENTEX 98/001 carton 114).

141. Tournier, "Les services sociaux 'de droit commun' de France et les familles nord-africaines," 15–23.

142. Sometimes these associations even worked together. CANAM, SSFNA, and AMANA jointly sponsored a program in Paris that taught other providers how to bring home economics instruction into individual homes. Bertholot, "Pour la formation ménagère des femmes nord-africaines en Moselle," 41.

143. SSFNA, "Intervention de Madame Bley à la réunion consultative pour la main-d'œuvre nord-africaine au Ministère du Travail," 28 June 1954 (CAC 860271/3).

144. Barthe, "Rapport moral, 1953," 3; Bley, "Le service social 'spécialisé' pour les familles nord-africaines," 24.

145. "Exposé de la conception du rôle général de l'assistante sociale," submitted to the Comité départemental d'aide aux Français d'Afrique du Nord, 25 March 1957 (AN F1a 5066). Report from a social worker assisted by a family worker. SSFNA paid her assistant's

salary. They tried to get a local organization, L'Union régionale des sociétés de secours minières, to pay three-quarters of her salary.

146. SSFNA, "Rapport sur l'activité du SSFNA, 1957–1958," 12–20; Barthe, "Rapport moral, 1953," 3; Mathieu, "Les problèmes posés," 13. Family Allowances paid interpreters' salaries.

147. CANAM, "Rapport moral," 8 July 1957 (AN F1a 5056); Malet, "Familles algériennes musulmanes en France," 134.

148. Tournier, "Les services sociaux 'de droit commun' de France et les familles nord-africaines," 17.

149. Malet, "Familles algériennes musulmanes en France," 135.

150. Belpeer, "Les familles musulmanes habitant Aix-en-Provence originaires d'Hennaya," 148.

151. Barthe, "Rapport moral, 1953," 3.

152. ATOM social worker, "Les familles de l'agglomération marseillaise," 136.

153. ATOM, "Rapport d'activités pour la période du 1er juillet 1953 au 30 juin 1954," 13.

154. Directeur départemental du travail et de l'emploi des Bouches-du-Rhône to the préfet des Bouches-du-Rhône, "Centre d'accueil nord-africain—Attribution d'une subvention départementale," 18 March 1964 (ADBR M14 5852).

155. SSFNA, "Rapport sur l'activité du SSFNA en 1954," 15.

156. SSFNA, "Rapport sur l'activité du SSFNA, 1957–1958," 16.

157. CANAM, "Rapport moral," 8 July 1957.

158. "Rapport d'activité de l'amitié nord-africaine de Nanterre pour l'année 1950" (CAC 860271/3).

159. SSFNA, "Rapport sur l'activité du SSFNA, 1957–1958," 13–15.

160. Donzelot, *The Policing of Families*.

161. Pedersen, *Family, Dependence, and the Origins of the Welfare State*, 273–75.

162. No program offered employment-oriented training for Algerian women migrants. The government did, however, develop programs that trained French and Algerian women to become social service workers in Algeria. As part of the program, the French government offered young Algerian women scholarships to metropolitan schools before returning to work in Algeria. See Chapters 5 and 6.

163. Clancy-Smith, "La Femme Arabe," 53.

164. "Rapport d'activité présenté par 'le Comité d'études et d'action Nord-Africains de Lille et de sa banlieue,'" 5; Mathieu, "Les problèmes posés," 11; Belpeer, "L'aide à l'adaptation des femmes," 35.

165. Mothes, "Les familles algériennes musulmanes," 107.

166. Centre algérien de documentation et d'action familiale, "Les aspects familiaux de l'émigration nord-africaine," 10.

167. Mathieu, "Les problèmes posés," 9.

168. Malet, "Familles algériennes musulmanes en France," 133.

169. Bley, "Le service social 'spécialisé' pour les familles nord-africaines," 27.

170. Tournier, "Les services sociaux 'de droit commun' de France et les familles nord-africaines," 22; Mathieu, "Les problèmes posés," 11.

171. Belpeer, "Deux 'descriptions' typiques familles vivant en monde clos," 16; Mathieu, "Les problèmes posés," 11.

172. Mothes, "Les familles algériennes musulmanes," 114.

173. Belpeer, "Note sur le problème des familles nord-africaines."

174. Bley, "Le service social 'spécialisé' pour les familles nord-africaines," 28.

175. Bertholot, "Pour la formation ménagère des femmes nord-africaines en Moselle," 40. CANAM volunteers provided these magazines.

176. Centre algérien de documentation et d'action familiale, "Les aspects familiaux de l'émigration nord-africaine," 9.

177. Mothes, "Les familles algériennes musulmanes," 102.

178. Malet, "Familles algériennes musulmanes en France," 131–32. See also Tournier, "Les services sociaux 'de droit commun' de France et les familles nord-africaines," 20.

179. Among others, see P. Bernard, "Rôle des travailleuses familiales au SSFNA," in "Action et techniques sociales au service des familles nord-africaines en France," 28–29; Verpraet, "Les institutions métropolitaines au service des Nord Africains," 29. The citation is from Bernard.

180. Belpeer, "Les familles musulmanes habitant Aix-en-Provence originaires d'Hennaya," 148; Mothes, "Les familles algériennes musulmanes," 121.

181. Centre algérien de documentation et d'action familiale, "Les aspects familiaux de l'émigration nord-africaine," 3–12; ESNA, "Situation et aspirations de la famille nord-africaine en métropole," 8–9.

182. Girard and Leriche, eds., *Les Algériens en France*, 144; "Un groupe d'émigrés des territoires du sud de l'Algérie installés à Marseille (Hiver 1953–1954)," study conducted by an "assistante sociale" doing an internship at ATOM, in Girard and Leriche, eds., *Les Algériens en France*, 155. The same report also appeared in Belpeer, "Deux 'descriptions' typiques familles vivant en monde clos," 16–24. Social workers clearly thought the North African diet was insufficient since canned milk, including "lait Mont-Blanc," was advertised during this period as being good for children.

183. Bertholot, "Pour la formation ménagère des femmes nord-africaines en Moselle," 40.

184. S. Belpeer, "Observation no. 1," attached to "Note sur le problème des familles nord-africaines." The gesture also resulted from the young woman's joy at having someone with whom she could speak Arabic in her home.

185. Belpeer, "Deux 'descriptions' typiques familles vivant en monde clos," 22.

186. Belpeer, "L'aide à l'adaptation des femmes," 34; Belpeer, "Note sur le problème des familles nord-africaines."

187. Belpeer, "Observation no. 1."

188. Mothes, "Les familles algériennes musulmanes," 122.

189. Belpeer, "Observation no. 1."

190. Observations of an ATOM social worker, appendix in Girard and Stoetzel, eds., *Français et immigrés*, no. 20: 146.

191. Bertholot, "Pour la formation ménagère des femmes nord-africaines en Moselle," 40; SSFNA, "Rapport sur l'activité du SSFNA en 1954," 40.

192. Mathieu, "Les problèmes posés," 11.

193. SSFNA, "Rapport sur l'activité du SSFNA en 1954," 37–40.

194. Centre algérien de documentation et d'action familiale, "Les aspects familiaux de l'émigration nord-africaine," 1.

195. Girard and Leriche, eds., *Les Algériens en France*, 144–46.

196. Bernard, "Rôle des travailleuses familiales au SSFNA," 28. See also Bertholot, "Pour la formation ménagère des femmes nord-africaines en Moselle."

197. Belpeer, "L'aide à l'adaptation des femmes," 36.

198. This story, or two strikingly similar cases, appeared in two documents. See SSFNA, "Rapport sur l'activité du SSFNA en 1954," 37; Bernard, "Rôle des travailleuses familiales au SSFNA," 28.

199. SSFNA, "Rapport sur l'activité du SSFNA en 1954," 37.

200. Mothes, "Les familles algériennes musulmanes," 144.

201. Observations of an ATOM social worker, appendix in Girard and Stoetzel, eds., *Français et immigrés*, no. 20: 145.

202. Government-general of Algeria, "Emigration des familles." On the history of child custody, see Fuchs, *Contested Paternity*, esp. 207–17.

203. For examples of voluntary and involuntary removal of children, see a number of cases in ADBR 138 W 73 and in Tournier, "Les services sociaux 'de droit commun' de France et les familles nord-africaines," 22; Belpeer, "Note sur le problème des familles nord-africaines"; Benaïcha, *Vivre au paradis*, 58–65.

204. Bley, "Le service social 'spécialisé' pour les familles nord-africaines," 25–26. In one documented case, SSFNA intervened to keep a family together when a doctor tried to separate a sixteen-year-old mother and her six-month-old child, both of whom had been hospitalized for malnutrition. Barthe, "Rapport moral, 1953," 1–2.

205. Belpeer, "Note sur le problème des familles nord-africaines."

206. Ibid.; Bley, "Le service social 'spécialisé' pour les familles nord-africaines"; Mothes, "Les familles algériennes musulmanes," 101, 109–10.

207. Malet, "Familles algériennes musulmanes en France," 133–34.

Chapter 4

1. On immigrants, see Blanc-Chaléard, "Les immigrés et le logement en France." On reconstruction in the postwar see, among others, Voldman, *La reconstruction des villes françaises*; Wakeman, *Modernizing the Provincial City*; Rudolph, "At Home in Postwar France"; Newsome, *French Urban Planning*.

2. Joseph Leriche, "Le logement familial," in "Le logement des Nord Africains (deuxième cahier)" *CNA* 35-6 (December 1953–January 1954): 33.

3. "Pour donner un logement décent aux travailleurs nord-africains en France M. Claudius Petit propose: Subvention des départements et communes, prêts des employeurs," *Journal d'Alger*, 11 February 1952 (AN F1a 5122).

4. For a depiction of life in these shanties, written by a Franco-Algerian who grew up in one, see Benaïcha, *Vivre au paradis*. The term originated in the colonial setting to describe the shantytowns that exploded on the edges of urban areas in the 1920s. For a discussion of Algiers' first bidonville, see Çelik, *Urban Forms and Colonial Confrontations*, 109–13.

5. ESNA, "Loger les Nord Africains: Devoir social majeur," in "Le logement des Nord Africains," *CNA* 11-12 (January–February 1951): 9.

6. ESNA, "L'hébergement en commun des travailleurs," in "Le logement des Nord Africains (deuxième cahier)," 11.

7. Leriche, "Le logement familial," 29.

8. Rager, *L'émigration en France des musulmans algériens*, 116.

9. Hmed, "Loger les étrangers 'isolés' en France," 14–18.

10. Michel, "La population des hôtels meublés à Paris," 635.

11. See, among others, Rabinow, *French Modern*; Flamand, *Loger le people*; Guerrand and Thibault, eds., *Cent ans d'habitat social*; Stébé, *Le logement social en France*; Jordan, *Transforming Paris*.

12. Blanchard, *La police parisienne*, 193–95.

13. Leriche, "Esprit et méthodes," in "Le logement des Nord Africains," 8.

14. Ibid., 16, 18.

15. For an overview of Algerian worker housing in the decade after World War II, see Hmed, "Loger les étrangers 'isolés' en France," 58–131.

16. MTSS, "Statut des contrôleurs sociaux: Contrôle social nord-africain," n.d. (1950?) (CAC 860271/2); SAMAS, "Assistance aux citoyens français musulmans originaires de l'Algérie se trouvant en métropole," circulaire no. 348, 19 August 1952 (AN F1a 5035).

17. ESNA, "L'hébergement en commun des travailleurs," 11.

18. ESNA, "Un 'cadre technique' supérieur, 'Témoignages et expériences,'" in "Le logement des Nord Africains," 38.

19. Rager, "Les musulmans algériens," 248–57.

20. "Etude d'une proposition de la confédération du patronat français pour la création en 1952 de cinq centres d'hébergement abritant un millier de lits" (AN F1a 5122).

21. Rager, "Les musulmans algériens," 242–43. In Paris, rue Lecomte had 100 beds; rue Tocqueville, 250; Gennevilliers, 170; Boulogne-Billancourt, 350; and Nanterre (the newest), 72. The Red Cross facility in the 15th arrondissement had 108.

22. Rager, "Les musulmans algériens," 239–43; D. Parker, "Conclusion générale," in "Le logement des Nord Africains," 43.

23. Lounici, "A propos de la main d'œuvre algérienne," 34–35.

24. Rager, "Les musulmans algériens," 258.

25. Conseil départemental d'hygiène, Prefecture of the Bouches-du-Rhône, Direction départementale de la santé, 28 October 1953 (ADBR 138 W 55).

26. While the initial circulars restricted money to housing, subsequent circulars allowed allocations to other services. See reprints in ESNA, "Le logement des Nord Africains (deuxième cahier)," 19–22, 24–25.

27. Ibid., 26.

28. MI, "Assistance morale et matérielle aux citoyens français musulmans originaires d'Algérie," 26 June 1950 (AN F1a 5035).

29. MI, "Hébergement et patronat français," 2 May 1952 (AN F1a 5122).

30. "Pour donner un logement décent aux travailleurs nord-africains en France M. Claudius Petit propose."

31. MTSS to the prefects, "Habitat des citoyens français musulmans en métropole," circulaire no. 281, 2 September 1954 (AN F1a 5035).

32. M. Burkhardt, "Rapport," circulaire no. 193, 10 June 1954 (CAC 860271/3).

33. SAMAS, "Admission dans les foyers d'hébergement construits pour les ouvriers français originaires d'Algérie d'ouvriers de souche métropolitaine ou étrangère," n.d. (1958?) (ADBR 138 W 58).

34. Ibid.; SAMAS, "Note au sujet de l'admission éventuelle d'ouvriers français de souche et étrangers dans les foyers de travailleurs français d'Algérie," 6 March 1959 (ADBR 138 W 58).

35. SAMAS, "Action sociale en faveur des travailleurs algériens en métropole," 29 July 1959 (AN F1a 5056).

36. Michel, *Les travailleurs algériens en France*, 150–51.

37. ESNA, "Guide de l'action sociale au bénéfice des Nord Africains en métropole," *CNA* 34 (October–November 1953): 49.

38. "Problèmes sociaux concernant la population musulmane algérienne en métropole," October 1957 (AN F1a 5055).

39. Burkhardt, "Rapport."

40. Hmed, "Loger les étrangers 'isolés' en France," 50–290. The *CNA* first proposed semi-public companies play a role in meeting Algerians' housing needs. See ESNA, "L'hébergement en commun des travailleurs," 12.

41. Interministerial Commission, "Programme pour l'année 1955 des réalisations nouvelles en matière d'accueil et d'action sociale," 30 March 1955 (AN F1a 5044).

42. Stora, *Ils venaient d'Algérie*, 151–84.

43. MI to MTSS, Direction de la main-d'œuvre, 27 September 1955 (CAC 870056/11).

44. For more on Eugène Claudius-Petit, see Pouvreau, *Un politique en architecture*; on his social Catholic roots, see Hmed, "Loger les étrangers 'isolés' en France," 20, 114–30.

45. Minutes, Comité d'action interministérielle pour les affaires sociales musulmanes, 22 March 1957 (AN F1a 5004).

46. MI on a Interministerial Commission meeting, 4 April 1956 (AN F1a 5044); Hmed, "Loger les étrangers 'isolés' en France," 109–12.

47. Bernardot, "Un politique de logement," 41–42. Law 56-780 of 4 August 1956 appeared in the *Journal Officiel Lois et Décrets*, no. 182, 7 August 1956. The implementation of the law followed decree 56-1097 of 13 October 1956, which appeared in the *JO* on 31 October 1956, 10433.

48. MacMaster, *Colonial Migrants and Racism*, 194. On the educational components relation to limiting FLN adherence, see Hmed, "Loger les étrangers 'isolés' en France," esp. 58–131.

49. Minutes, Interministerial Commission, 5 April 1956 (AN F1a 5044).

50. The Crédit Foncier is a semi-public, semi-private bank operating since the mid-nineteenth century. The finance minister appointed its directors, allowing it to serve "as the government's errand boy in the field of housing finance." It became an essential element of the housing boom in the 1950s and 1960s because it loaned money to individual citizens and to social housing construction companies and other organizations at below-market

rates. The Crédit Foncier, along with the cheap labor construction companies employed, made social housing profitable. Duclaud-Williams, *The Politics of Housing*, 18–22.

51. Minutes, Comité d'action interministérielle pour les affaires sociales musulmanes.

52. François Villey, "Constitution de la société SONACOTRAL (Société nationale d'économie mixte pour la construction de logements destinés aux Français musulmans originaires d'Algérie et à leurs familles)," 1 February 1957 (CAC 870056/11).

53. Ibid.

54. MTSS, la Direction de la main-d'œuvre, Sous-direction de l'emploi, 1er bureau, to Monsieur le Maître des requêtes au Conseil d'Etat, directeur général du travail et de la main-d'œuvre, "Conseil d'administration de la SONACOTRAL," 27 June 1957 (CAC 870056/12).

55. Claudius-Petit to the minister of Reconstruction and Housing, 22 January 1958 (CAC 870056/12).

56. Ibid.

57. SAMAS, "Logement des familles d'ouvriers algériens en métropole," circulaire no. 242, 12 May 1958 (AN F1a 5035).

58. Leriche, "Le logement familial," 29.

59. Social unrest, revolution, and recurrent cholera epidemics thrust the poor into the spotlight. On urbanization, migration, and disease, see, among others, Chevalier, *Laboring Classes, Dangerous Classes*; Kudlick, *Cholera in Post-Revolutionary Paris*; Rosental, *Les sentiers invisibles*.

60. On Frédéric Le Play, see Brooke, *Le Play*; Pitt, "Frédéric Le Play and the Family"; Rabinow, *French Modern*, 86–97; and a collection of Le Play's works edited and translated by Bodard Silber: Le Play, *On Family, Work, and Social Change*.

61. Roger-Henri Guerrand, "De Mulhouse à Passy-Auteuil, Les origines du 'pavillon,'" in Guerrand and Thibault, eds., *Cent ans d'habitat social*, 42–44; Stébé, *Le logement social en France*, 42–43. The Workers City opened in 1862, with 560 homes. By the end of the century, 10,000 people called it home. Intended to be a nearly self-sufficient village, it had everything Le Play imagined workers and their families needed, including shops, restaurants, homes for families, dorms for single men, and a medical clinic. Although not a company town in the strict sense since residents worked for a variety of companies, it housed over ten percent of Mulhouse's population.

62. Stébé, *Le logement social en France*, 44–45; Guy Delabre and Jean-Marie Gautier, "Godin, ou l'union du génie industriel et du militant social," in Guerrand and Thibault, eds., *Cent ans d'habitat social*, 32–41; Flamand, *Loger le people*, 33–34.

63. Ghorra-Gobin, "Implementation as a Social Learning Process," 3. Jules Siegfried, mayor of Le Havre and deputy representing Seine-Inférieure, who had grown up in Mulhouse and had seen how the workers' town operated, gave his name to the first social housing law in France.

64. Flamand, *Loger le people*, 85–139; Roger-Henri Guerrand, "La Construction du cadre législatif," in Guerrand and Thibault, eds., *Cent ans d'habitat social*, 62–71.

65. Stébé, *Le logement social en France*, 61–70; Flamand, *Loger le people*, 144–45, 209–15; Marie-Jeanne Dumont, "Le 'Louvre' de l'habitat social, le modèle Rothschild," in Guerrand and Thibault, eds. *Cent ans d'habitat social*, 77–88. On colonial housing, see Chapter 5.

66. Flamand, *Loger le people*, 194–95. World War II destroyed over twenty percent of French building stock, including over 250,000 housing units, and partially destroyed another one million structures.

67. Newsome, *French Urban Planning*, 84; Butler and Noisette, *Le logement social en France*, 69; Louis Houdeville, "Répondre à l'urgence," in Guerrand and Thibault, eds., *Cent ans d'habitat social*, 129. The proponents of single-family dwellings had a voice in the postwar period, but quantity and therefore collective housing prevailed in an era burdened with such a severe crisis. Collective housing offered a rapid solution and seemed more modern and therefore became the wave of the future.

68. Flamand, *Loger le peuple*, 194–99; Houdeville, "Répondre à l'urgence," 111–12; Stébé, *Le logement social en France*, 91–92. Between 1947 and 1952, France built 45,000 new apartments (compared with 450,000 in Germany). Flamand, *Loger le peuple*, 194–99.

69. Wakeman, *The Heroic City*, 131–45.

70. Houdeville, "Répondre à l'urgence," 120–21; Stébé, *Le logement social en France*, 95; Duclaud-Williams, *The Politics of Housing*, 132–33.

71. Wakeman, *The Heroic City*, 132–35.

72. Stébé, *Le logement social en France*, 102; Butler and Noisette, *Le logement social en France*, 70–82.

73. *Le Monde's* Gilbert Mathieu filed the report cited in Flamand, *Loger le people*, 295; Houdeville, "Répondre à l'urgence," 129.

74. Duclaud-Williams, *The Politics of Housing*, 131–32.

75. On the concept of minimum living space, see Simmons, "Minimal Frenchman."

76. According to Ralph Schor, 6.5 percent of HLM units were reserved for immigrants in the 1950s. This percentage jumped in the 1960s and '70s as the French moved out. This made room for more foreigners in social housing, but, at the same time, slum landlords took advantage of the situation in many cases, leaving residents in terrible conditions. Schor, *L'histoire de l'immigration en France*, 214–15.

77. Blanc-Chaléard, "Les immigrés et le logement en France," 20–34.

78. Caisse nationale de sécurité sociale, circulaire no. 126, 10 February 1953, cited in ESNA, "L'hébergement en commun des travailleurs," 24.

79. J. Chirouse, "L'Association des foyers nord-africains de la région parisienne," 21 November 1953, in "Le logement des Nord Africains (deuxième cahier)," 50.

80. Rager, "Les musulmans algériens," 262.

81. Claude Mothes, "Les familles algériennes musulmanes dans l'agglomération parisienne," in Girard and Stoetzel, eds., *Français et immigrés*, 129–44.

82. Malet, "Familles algériennes musulmanes en France," in Girard and Leriche, eds., *Les Algériens en France*, 128.

83. ATOM social worker, "Les familles de l'agglomération marseillaise," in Girard and Leriche, *Les Algériens en France*, 138–39.

84. Rager, *L'émigration en France des musulmans algériens*, 116. Rager counted just over 600 families out of 6,772 workers.

85. Leriche, "Le logement familial," 28–48; ESNA, "Logement familial des Nord Africains en France (quatrième cahier)," *CNA* 54 (September–October 1956): 32.

86. I found Stanley Lieberson, *A Piece of the Pie*, particularly helpful in thinking about issues related to housing discrimination.

87. S. Belpeer, "Note sur le problème des familles nord-africaines dans le Département des Bouches-du-Rhône en 1952" (CAC 860271/11).

88. R. Barthe, SSFNA, "Rapport moral, 1953," 3.

89. Belpeer, "Note sur le problème des familles nord-africaines."

90. ESNA, "Avant propos," 5; Leriche, "Le logement familial," 28–48. Both in "Le logement des Nord Africains (deuxième cahier)."

91. President of CANAM to the MR, 14 January 1954 (AN F1a 5122); Burkhardt, "Rapport."

92. Prefect of the Seine to the minister of Reconstruction and Housing, "Logement des familles musulmanes du Département de la Seine," 23 April 1954 (AN F1a 5122).

93. CANAM to the MR, 14 January 1954.

94. ESNA, "Logement familial des Nord Africains en France," 30.

95. J. Chirouse, "L'Association des foyers nord-africains de la région parisienne," 49.

96. ESNA, "Logement familial des Nord Africains en France," 31.

97. Pulju, *Women and Mass Consumer Society*, 119.

98. ESNA, "Logement familial des Nord Africains en France," 31.

99. See, among others, Barthe, SSFNA, "Rapport moral, 1953," 3; CANAM to the MR, 14 January 1954; Hervo and Charras, *Bidonvilles l'enlisement*, 83–55, 129–36, 159–63.

100. ESNA, "Logement familial des Nord Africains en France," 30.

101. Leriche, "Le logement familial," 31–39.

102. "Convention entre l'Office national des anciens combattants et victimes de guerre et la Société coopérative musulmane Algérienne d'habitation et d'accession à la petite propriété," 27 September 1955 (CAC 770391/6); Conseillers techniques, "Synthèse des rapports trimestriels établis par les conseillers techniques pour les affaires musulmanes," 1er trimestre 1958: 14–15 (AN F1a 5010).

103. ATOM, "Rapport d'activités pour la période du 1er juillet 1953 au 30 juin 1954," (ADBR M14 5852); ESNA, "Logement familial des Nord Africains en France," 34–35; Union franco-nord-africaine de Valenciennes, "Rapport Moral et d'activité de l'exercice 1956–1957" (AN F1a 5065).

104. On the North African Friendly Society of Roubaix-Tourcoing, see Comité d'amitié nord-africaine de Roubaix-Tourcoing, "Projet pour l'exercice 1955: Création d'une maison nord-africaine à Tourcoing," 1955 (AN F1a 5066). This organization, established in 1953, helped three Algerian families become "proprietors of small houses" after a fire destroyed everything they had. By 1954, only one of the three families had become a homeowner. The family had purchased an apartment above the Friendly Society's offices. After buying another building, the society allowed the other families to buy small apartments and used the rest of the site for a twelve-bed dormitory, a clothing distribution center, and a playground. On the Aid Commission for North Africans in the Metropole, see CANAM to the MR, 14 January 1954. CANAM's president indicated that for several years it had been providing families with funds to buy, rent, or renovate housing. On Moral Aid for North Africans, see ESNA, "Logement familial des Nord Africains en France," 34–35. AMANA, the umbrella

organization of all for Ghys' projects, created the CLFNA in February 1954. For a list of projects underway in the nine IGAME districts in the mid-1950s, see Conseillers techniques, "Synthèse des rapports trimestriels." On North African Family Welcome Group, see Interministerial Commission, "Subventions pour Région I (Paris)," 1953 (AN F1a 5044).

105. Conseillers techniques, "Synthèse des rapports trimestriels." For more on quotas, see Chapter 5. On the quota system in immigrant housing after 1962, see Blanc-Chaléard, "Les immigrés et le logement en France," 29.

106. Renée Bley, director of SSFNA, quoted in SAMAS, "Logement des familles d'ouvriers algériens dans le Département de la Loire," 20 September 1960 (CAC 770391/7).

107. Prefect of the Seine, "Logement des familles musulmanes du Département de la Seine."

108. Emile Pelletier, *Accueil et hébergement des Nord Africains dans le Département de la Seine*, 15 March 1956, 5 (CIEMI 9/1/1).

109. Leriche, "Le logement familial," 28–48.

110. Ibid.

111. RTF, "Emission sociale allocations—logement," 4 May 1956 (CAC 860271/5).

112. Pelletier, *Accueil et hébergement des Nord Africains dans le Département de la Seine*.

113. Pelletier, "Les réalisations en faveur des Nord Africains dans le département," 124.

114. D. T., "Note sur le logement des familles nord-africaines dans la région parisienne," in "Logement familial des Nord Africains en France (quatrième cahier)," appendix.

115. ESNA, "L'immigration des familles nord-africains en France est-elle souhaitable?," in "Logement familial des Nord Africains en France (quatrième cahier)," 8–34.

116. ESNA, "Comment 'en sortir'?," in "Logement familial des Nord Africains en France (quatrième cahier)," 34–35.

117. Leriche, "Le logement familial," 32.

Chapter 5

1. Press wire transmission of 14 May 1958, 2:45 pm, in Marc Ferro, "La situation à Alger analysée de Paris," in Ferro, ed., *Le 13 mai 1958*, 7. Among many others, see Thomas, *The French North African Crisis*, chap. 7; Wall, *France, the United States, and the Algerian War*, 134–56; Connelly, *A Diplomatic Revolution*, 168–80; Shepard, *The Invention of Decolonization*, 73–77.

2. Thody, *The Fifth French Republic*, 18.

3. Melnik, *Mille jours à Matignon*; Ambler, *The French Army in Politics*, 240–46; Ageron, *La décolonisation française*, 152.

4. For a succinct, recent analysis of de Gaulle's approach to Algeria, see Thénault, *Histoire de la guerre*, part 3: esp. 165–71, 198–218. The Fifth Republic simultaneously began secret negotiations with the FLN. On the peace negotiations, see Gallissot, ed., *Les Accords d'Evian*.

5. On torture, see Branche, *La torture et l'armée*.

6. Excerpts of de Gaulle's speech are available through the Internet History Sourcebook, www.fordham.edu/halsall/mod/1958degaulle-algeria1.html (accessed 11 June 2010).

7. SAMAS, "Note ayant pour objet l'inventaire critique des mesures prises ou en cours

d'exécution au titre de l'action économique, sociale, et psychologique auprès de la population musulmane algérienne de la métropole," 30 May 1960 (AN F1a 5056).

8. SAMAS, "Note concernant l'action sociale menée en faveur des Français de souche nord-africaine résidant en métropole," 2 June 1959 (AN F1a 5056); Attached report, "Création d'un climat favorable par l'action sociale," 2 June 1959 (AN F1a 5056). His response followed a request made at a Hôtel Matignon meeting he attended.

9. Darrouy, administrative secretary-general, CANAM, "Assemblée général du 6 juillet 1959: Rapport moral," 6 July 1959 (CAC 19770391/4).

10. SAMAS, "Note ayant pour objet l'inventaire critique des mesures prises ou en cours d'exécution."

11. See Connelly, *A Diplomatic Revolution*; Wall, *France, the United States, and the Algerian War.*

12. Blanchard, *La police parisienne*, 187–89.

13. The MNA, created in December 1954, brought together the older PPA and MTLD. On the MNA in France, see Stora, *Ils venaient d'Algérie*, 151–84.

14. Ibid., esp. 151–69, 203–21; Einaudi, *La bataille de Paris*, 30–31; Amrane-Minne, *Des femmes dans la guerre d'Algérie*, 173; Brunet, *Police contre FLN*, 35–36.

15. S. Pivot and F. Pavard, "Les travailleurs nord-africains et la Sécurité sociale," 2 (6 December 1954) (Archive Laroque, ENTEX 89/001 carton 114).

16. Amrane-Minne, *Des femmes dans la guerre d'Algérie*, 175.

17. Haroun, quoted in Einaudi, *La bataille de Paris*, 21. The remaining twenty percent came from the Arab League.

18. Viet, *La France immigrée*, 184–85.

19. Police powers were strengthened by, among others, a law of 26 July 1957 and an ordinance of 7 October 1958. According to Blanchard, police autonomy grew substantially between 1958 and 1962. *La police parisienne*, 291. On the metropolitan camps throughout the twentieth century, see Bernardot, *Camps d'étrangers*. On camps in Algeria, see Thénault, *Violence ordinaire*. On Papon's appointment as police chief, see House and MacMaster, *Paris 1961*, 61. Papon remained in office until 1967.

20. For the best-known account by an FLN leader, see Haroun, *La 7è wilaya.*

21. The Service d'assistance technique (SAT) was modeled on the Sections administratives spécialisées (SAS); see the section The Constantine Plan and Services in Algeria, below. On the SAT in France, see Thénault, *Histoire de la guerre*, 219–27; House and MacMaster, *Paris 1961*, 73–75; Spire, *Etrangers à la carte*, 202–5; Blanchard, *La police parisienne*, 319–22. Most research has focused on police practices in Paris, although, according to Thénault, the SAT also operated in the Rhône and the Bouches-du-Rhône.

22. MacMaster, *Colonial Migrants and Racism*, 197.

23. Debré's memoirs, quoted in Einaudi, *La bataille de Paris*, 25–26.

24. Blanchard, *La police parisienne*, 322–27. The harkis included Algerian veterans of the French military and members of auxiliary police regiments. Sometimes the term also referred to civil servants and elected officials of the colonial administration, as well as anyone who had acted as an intermediary between the French and the Algerian population. Hundreds of thousands of Algerians served in the French military during the

two World Wars and in various colonial conflicts, including the Algerian War. Recruitment of harkis for the Algerian conflict began informally in 1955. Within two years, and after formalizing their role, over 100,000 Algerians served the French on Algerian soil. Thousands of others served as armed and unarmed auxiliary police officers and members of elite organizations, including the Sections administratives urbaines (SAU), Groupes mobiles de sécurité (GMS), and SAS (which trained the harkis sent to Paris). See Pierre Vidal-Naquet's preface to Péju, *Ratonnades à Paris*, 11; Jordi and Hamoumou, *Les harkis*, 25; Mohand Khellil, "L'instillation des rapatriés d'Algérie en France," in Gallissot, ed., *Les Accords d'Evian*, 143.

25. Einaudi, *La bataille de Paris*, 83; Stora, *Ils venaient d'Algérie*, 303–6.

26. Amrane-Minne, *Des femmes dans la guerre d'Algérie*, 172.

27. Thénault, *Histoire de la guerre*, 226–27. The Goutte d'Or is a working-class, immigrant neighborhood in Paris' 18th arrondissement.

28. The curfew curtailed Algerian movements between 8:30 pm and 5:30 am. Anyone needing to travel to work during the curfew had to get the local SAT office to stamp paperwork from the employer. About 14,000 permits were issued in about six weeks. House and MacMaster, *Paris 1961*, 99–100.

29. Omar Boudaoud, who led the French Federation from Germany to protect himself from arrest, summoned Mohammedi Saddek, the coordinator of the FLN in Paris, to Belgium and ordered him to ensure the protest remain peaceful, even in the face of police attack. Boudaoud forbade protesters to defend themselves or to disobey FLN orders. Saddek, who personally objected to this approach, acquiesced to the will of the leadership and distributed flyers that made the directives clear: "We are not looking for a fight. We are protesting our indignation over Papon's measures." Einaudi, *Octobre à Paris*, 13–14, 94–95. For more on Mohammedi Saddek, see Anissa Mohammedi, his daughter, "Mohammedi Saddek, un combatant du FLN," in Le Cour Grandmaison, ed., *Le 17 octobre 1961*, 141–56. The FLN had previously used a nonviolent approach when it organized a general strike in Algiers in 1957 to bring the attention of the United Nations to its cause. See Connelly, *A Diplomatic Revolution*, 119–41.

30. Péju, *Ratonnades à Paris*, 137–42.

31. The FLN demanded that women and children either join the march or pay three hundred francs and threatened violence against those who refused. "Note concernant les modalités du maintien de l'ordre public," 1961 (CAC 770391/8); Benaïcha, *Vivre au paradis*, 56–58.

32. Ouanassa Siari Tengour, "Octobre 1961 dans les archives de la CIMADE," in Le Cour Grandmaison, ed., *Le 17 octobre 1961*, 42–45.

33. Much of the growing literature on the events of 1961 is cited in this chapter. For the earliest critical account, see Péju, *Ratonnades à Paris*. François Maspero published Péju's text in November 1961; censors immediately confiscated it—a common fate for materials exposing French atrocities. Journalist Jean-Luc Einaudi's exposé, *La bataille de Paris*, brought the events to national attention in time for the thirtieth anniversary.

34. "1000 Algériennes et 550 enfants raflés hier à Paris," *L'Humanité*, 21 October 1961, 5.

35. Tristan, *Le silence du fleuve*, 80–81.

36. Viet, *La France immigrée*, 135.

37. Ordinance 58-1381 of 29 October 1958 appeared in the *JO*, 1 January 1959, 3.

38. *JO* 59-559, 23 April 1959, 4468. For a summary of FAS structures and functions, see ESNA, "Le FAS de 1959 à 1961," *CNA* 95 (April–May 1963): 9–26.

39. In some cases the board invited representatives and in others government agencies demanded representation. In 1960, for example, the Agricultural Ministry threatened to withhold its approval of the FAS budget unless it was granted representation. See FAS minutes, 11 February 1960 (CAC 760140/1).

40. Massenet led the newly reincarnated Interministerial Committee created by decree no. 380-1148 on 1 December 1958. See the *JO* of 2 December 1958. Debré appointed Massenet Délégué à l'action sociale pour les Français musulmans de l'Algérie en métropole on 3 January 1959. For a detailed discussion of the Fifth Republic's reorganization of Algerian social services and Massenet's role, see Viet, *La France immigrée*, 190–203, and the chart on page 205. For a sketch of Massenet's career, see Laurens, "La noblesse d'Etat à l'épreuve de l'Algérie et de l'après 1962," 86–95.

41. Massenet, *Sauvage immigration*, 23–24.

42. Massenet repeatedly visited Nanterre to "keep abreast of activities [and] . . . to keep up with the evolution of the problem." Groupe d'étude et d'action pour les Nord Africains de la région parisienne (GEANARP), "Relations du GEANARP avec les services publics et semi-publics," n.d. (1961?) (AMH).

43. On Doublet's early career, see Rosental, *L'intelligence démographique*, esp. 21–53, 95–99; Nord, *France's New Deal*, 173.

44. Letters in CAC 760140 and 770391.

45. Jacques Doublet quoted in the FAS, minutes, 8 July 1961, 3 (CAC 760140/2).

46. The Labor Ministry continued to prioritize training and male housing and the Public Health and Population Ministry prioritized services for women and families. The Interior Ministry's SAMAS continued to sponsor about 150 organizations, about 200 social welfare intervention offices ("to help Algerians with all their administrative paperwork"), numerous educational programs, housing via the SONACOTRAL and its HLMs, radio propaganda and other types of "psychological" action meant to crush FLN support. SAMAS, "Sur l'utilisation des crédits mis à la disposition du Ministère de l'Intérieur en faveur des populations," 22 November 1961 (AN F1a 5010).

47. Massenet, "Projet de procès verbal de la réunion du Comité interministériel d'action sociale pour les Français musulmans d'Algérie en métropole (Application de l'article 9 du décret du 23 avril 1959)," 6 June 1961, 2 (CAC 760140/6).

48. Briefly, the controversy concerned the FAS's budget. The Social Security Administration retained 80 percent (and by 1960, 90 percent) of family allowance funds owed to Algerian migrants. Concerns centered on whether the monies would come directly from Social Security or whether they first had to pass through the Algerian government and then into FAS coffers. Despite FAS advocates' desire for the former, it proved more politically advantageous to demonstrate the funds came from Algeria. Its "80 percent" was funneled through the three departmental Family Allowance Bureaus in Algeria before coming back to the FAS. FAS concerns seemed justified when in late 1959 board members expressed

frustration about having not yet received any of the money. The funds were eventually transferred and once underway the process worked fairly well—even providing more revenue than expected in the early 1960s (resulting in the increase to 90 percent)—but board members continued to complain about the inefficiency of the bureaucratic procedures right up to the time Algeria gained independence. *JO*, 2 October 1959, 9475; FAS minutes, 21 October 1959 (CAC 760140/1, as well as other FAS meeting minutes in CAC 760140).

49. La documentation française, "L'action sociale en faveur des travailleurs musulmans algériens en métropole," *Notes et études documentaires* no. 2.765 (30 March 1961): 5 (Archives Laroque, ENTEX 89/001); Math, "Les allocations familiales," 35–44.

50. FAS, "Programme d'action sociale pour l'année 1959" (CAC 760140/2). Massenet reiterated the four areas of intervention at many FAS board meetings. See FAS minutes, 17 June 1959, 3; FAS minutes, 12 July 1960. Both in CAC 760140/1.

51. Délégation générale du gouvernement en Algérie, "La migration algérienne en France," in *Les migrations des populations* (Présidence du Conseil, Haut Comité de la population et de la famille, 1957), 19–24 (CAC 860269/5).

52. ESNA, "Le FAS de 1959 à 1961," 12.

53. "Analyse de la répartition des crédits décidée par le Conseil d'administration du Fonds d'action sociale," 1960 (CAC 760140/1). In January 1960, France introduced the new franc (NF). One new franc was worth 100 old francs (OF). Contemporary documents continued to give figures in OF to clarify values during the transition. For the same reason, I have indicated figures in OF or NF as appropriate.

54. "Analyse de la répartition des crédits décidée par le Conseil d'administration du Fonds d'action sociale"; FAS, "Programme d'action sociale pour l'année 1959."

55. The rest of SSFNA's annual budget totaled 680,000 NF. It received 250,000 NF from both the Public Health and Population Ministry and the Social Action Fund. The final 180,000 NF came from various sources on the local level—state agencies and private donations. Bernard Lory, minister of MSPP to the director of FAS, "Demande de subvention présentée par le 'Service social familial nord-africain,'" 25 July 1961 (CAC 760140/2).

56. FAS minutes, 17 May 1960, 17 (CAC 760140/1).

57. SSFNA, "Rapport sur l'activité du SSFNA, 1957–1958," 1–16. See also Mahjoub-Guelamine, "Le rôle des services sociaux spécialisés," 165–99.

58. "Rapport sur l'activité du SSFNA, 1958–1959," 5, 16.

59. On SSFNA's role in other organizations and in decision making, see Chapters 3 and 6. SSFNA trained twenty social work student interns each year. It sent staff to social work schools to provide expert advice about Algerians and to answer questions about these "problems." "Rapport sur l'activité du SSFNA, 1958–1959," 11–12.

60. The Social Action Fund always insisted organizations secure other sources of funding, including state agencies, the SONACOTRAL, local governments, associations, etc., to make money go further and to ensure local interests felt invested in the projects and services involved. It rarely fully funded any project.

61. FAS minutes 16 June 1961, 19–20 (CAC 760140/2). The quotes come from Villey (Population Ministry), who supported Marseille's request, and Gourgeon (Finance Ministry), who did not.

62. Forget, "Le Service des centres sociaux en Algérie," 38; See also "Nelly Forget," archives of the Service Civil International, www.service-civil-international.org/forget-nelly (accessed 18 May 2010); Dore-Audibert, *Des Françaises d'Algérie dans la guerre de libération*, 45–48; Lacouture, *Le témoignage est un combat*, 246–50; MacMaster, *Burning the Veil*, 77–78. The organizations that provided services in Algeria included the Association des travailleurs sociaux d'Hussien-Dey, Entraide populaire familiale, the Association de la jeunesse algérienne pour l'Action Sociale, the Scoutes musulmans algériens, and the Union générale des étudiants musulmans.

63. Direction générale de l'éducation nationale en Algérie, *Le Service des centres sociaux en Algérie*, 11–12.

64. Le Sueur, *Uncivil War*, 23–57.

65. Direction générale de l'éducation nationale en Algérie, *Le Service des centres sociaux en Algérie*, 15. See also Soustelle, "La famille otomi-pame du Mexique central"; Shepard, "Algeria, France, Mexico, UNESCO"; Sanders, *Gender and Welfare in Mexico*.

66. Le Sueur, *Uncivil War*, 57. On Soustelle's program to reform women's status, see MacMaster, *Burning the Veil*, 68–78; Sambron, *Les femmes algériennes*, 75–113.

67. Tillion, *A la rechercher du vrai et du juste*, 248.

68. Lacouture, *Le témoignage est un combat*, 233–35; Forget, "Le Service des centres sociaux en Algérie," 40.

69. Direction générale de l'éducation nationale en Algérie, *Le Service des centres sociaux en Algérie*, 15.

70. Lacouture, *Le témoignage est un combat*, 238–42. Tillion first used this expression in *L'Algérie en 1957* (Paris: Editions de Minuit, 1957), published in English as *Algeria: The Realities*.

71. Tillion, "La bêtise qui froidement assassine," *Le Monde*, 18 March 1962, cited in Benjamin Stora, "Les engagements algériens," in Todorov, ed., *Le siècle de Germaine Tillion*, 206–7.

72. Tillion, *Algeria*, 31–53, emphasis in the original.

73. Pierre Racine, cofounder of ENA and director of internships, collaborated with Tillion to set up the social centers and became president of SSFNA after Barthe's death in 1958. See www.assfam.org/spip.php?article9 (accessed 20 May 2010). My thanks to Forget for filling gaps in this history and for telling me about Lacheref, who was absent from written accounts.

74. Each social center had a staff of three: a director, an assistant director, and a "moniteur"—usually women providing direct services. On the home economics school, see ESNA, "Le FAS de 1959 à 1961," 19.

75. Tillion, *Algeria*, 17.

76. Thénault, *Histoire de la guerre*, 118.

77. Tillion, *A la rechercher du vrai et du juste*, 250.

78. Stora, "Les engagements algériens," 208. FLN filmmaker Yacef Saadi credits Tillion with saving his life and the lives of over two hundred others. To hear his audio homage to Tillion, visit www.yacefsaadi.com/2012/01/05/hommage-de-saadi-yacef-a-germaine-tillion (accessed 9 September 2012). Tillion also aided North African POWs in the 1940s; see Mabon, *Prisonniers de guerre "indigènes,"* esp. 81–83.

79. Forget, "Le Service des centres sociaux en Algérie," 40–42.

80. Shepard, *The Invention of Decolonization*, 191; Direction générale de l'éducation nationale en Algérie, *Le Service des centres sociaux*, 23–61.

81. Direction générale de l'éducation nationale en Algérie, *Le Service des centres sociaux*, 16–17.

82. Mathias, *Les sections administratives spécialisées*, 11–43. On the SAS, see also Johnson Onyedum, "Humanizing Warfare," esp. 21–63.

83. Mathias, *Les sections administratives spécialisées*, 67, 83–86. In some cases, all female Equipes médico-sociales itinérantes (EMSI) were attached to SAS units. According to Ginette Thevenin-Copin, who worked in an EMSI, they brought together the adjointe-sanitaire-sociale-rurale-auxiliaire (ASSRA) and the personnel féminine de l'armée de terre (PFAT) to help women and children "confronted with the events" in Algeria. Several of these women died, some at the hands of the FLN. On these programs, see also Faivre, *L'action social de l'armée*, 49–71; MacMaster, *Burning the Veil*, 245–70; Johnson Onyedum, "Humanizing Warfare," 23, 46–48.

84. Bourdieu and Sayad, *Le déracinement*, 40.

85. Mathias, *Les sections administratives spécialisées*, 21–22.

86. Spire, *Etrangers à la carte*, 201.

87. Mathias, *Les sections administratives spécialisées*, 46–47, 108–15.

88. Délégation générale du gouvernement en Algérie, Direction du plan des études économiques, *Plan de Constantine 1959–1963, rapport général*, 33. From the decree of 12 February 1959.

89. Elsenhans, *La guerre d'Algérie*, 705.

90. Délégation générale du gouvernement en Algérie, *Plan de Constantine*, 33.

91. The glossy French embassy brochure, printed in New York (for the UN), was in English with figures in dollars. Most of the money came from the French government, about $200 million from the Caisse d'équipement pour le développement de l'Algérie (CEDA), $40–$60 million from specially earmarked funds, $40–$50 million from loans, and finally about $40 million from the European Common Market. Ambassade de France, *The Constantine Plan for Algeria*, in-text citation from the inside front cover, figures page 10. The official descriptions of the project masked the gains French companies expected from contracts, including exclusive access to the Sahara's untapped oil reserves. The nearly five-hundred-page official description of the plan (cited in Note 88, above) never referred, obliquely or otherwise, to the bloody war or the plan's involvement in the war.

92. Délégation générale du gouvernement en Algérie, *Plan de Constantine*, chap. 7; Çelik, *Urban Forms and Colonial Confrontations*, 120–21, 174–81; Elsenhans, *La guerre d'Algérie*, 705. According to chapter 1 of *Plan de Constantine*, new schools increased the number of children in elementary education from 350,000 in 1951 to 900,000 in 1960. For older children, the plan relied on the social centers.

93. Ambassade de France, *The Constantine Plan for Algeria*, 9–13; Délégation générale du gouvernement en Algérie, *Plan de Constantine*, 337.

94. Ageron, *Modern Algeria*, 119.

95. Cornaton, *Les camps de regroupement*, 65–67. Tillion wrote the preface to Corna-

ton's book. On the Challe Plan, see Horne, *A Savage War*, 330–48; Ruedy, *Modern Algeria*, 174–75; Pervillé, *Pour une histoire de la guerre d'Algérie*, 164–65.

96. Cornaton, *Les camps de regroupement*, 69.

97. Ambassade de France, *The Constantine Plan for Algeria*, 26; Cornaton, *Les camps de regroupement*, 71.

98. Délégation générale du gouvernement en Algérie, *Plan de Constantine 1959–1963*, 84–88; Elsenhans, *La guerre d'Algérie*, 715.

99. Le Sueur, *Uncivil War*, 55–56, 63–67; Tillion, *A la recherche du vrai et du juste*, 252–53; James Le Sueur's introduction to Feraoun, *Journal, 1955–1962*. Once de Gaulle announced he would support Algerian self-determination, disaffected members of the colonial government and the French military formed the Organisation de l'armée secrète (OAS), which launched a campaign of terror to undermine the cease-fire and prevent a settlement. The ultras' refusal to recognize the peace settlement resulted in an unprecedented period of violence that has been described as a near civil war, punctuated by multiple failed attempts to assassinate de Gaulle. Bernstein, *The Republic of de Gaulle*, 71–73; Vinen, *France, 1934–1970*, 160; Ambler, *The French Army in Politics*, 251–65; Thénault, *Histoire de la guerre*, 214–18; Shepard, *The Invention of Decolonization*, 83–100. On de Gaulle and the OAS, see Harrison, *Challenging de Gaulle*; Delarue and Rudelle, *L'attentat du Petit-Clamart*; Delarue, *L'OAS contre de Gaulle*; Fleury, *Tuez de Gaulle!*. Many OAS leaders, including Challe, were arrested and convicted of crimes against France in the early 1960s, but by the end of the decade and into the early 1970s, a series of pardons allowed most of them to not only live out their retirement as free men, but reinstated their military and government pensions. Stora, *Algeria, 1830–2000*, 112–13.

100. FAS, "Dépenses décidées," 15 December 1959 (CAC 760140/1). The Comités techniques régionaux received about 1.1 billion OF and the Caisse d'équipement received about 600 million OF of the 1.7 billion Algerian budget.

101. FAS minutes, 17 June 1959; FAS minutes, 8 July 1959, 4; FAS minutes, 21 October 1959, 14. All in CAC 760140/1.

102. Massenet, "Compte-rendu du voyage effectué les 7 et 8 décembre 1959" (CAC 760140/1).

103. By August 1961, the FAS had completed 92 percent of metropolitan projects started in 1959 and 63 percent of those started in 1960. In Algeria only 73 percent of projects from 1959 and 37 percent from 1960 were completed. FAS minutes, 8 July 1961, 4. As of September 1961, 19 percent of metropolitan projects for that year were underway but only 0.6 percent of Algerian projects had begun. FAS minutes, 14 September 1961, 7 (CAC 760140/2).

104. Cornaton, *Les camps de regroupement*, 59–65, 70–74.

105. Hervo, *Chroniques du bidonville*, 114–15.

106. Cornaton, *Les camps de regroupement*, 81–91.

107. Ibid.

108. Hervo, *Chroniques du bidonville*, 126.

109. Cornaton, *Les camps de regroupement*, 77. According to Cornaton (iii), these camps were only one part of the massive forced relocation program France implemented beginning in 1955. He estimated that as of 1961, 26 percent of the population, or over 2.3 million

people, were in official relocation camps, with more than 1.1 million in unofficial camps. In all, the French forcibly displaced least 3.5 million Algerians during the war.

110. Péju, *Ratonnades à Paris*, 11.

111. "Synthèses des rapports trimestriels établis par les conseillers techniques pour les affaires musulmanes," Spring 1961, 10 (AN F1a 5010).

112. Bureau des affaires musulmanes, cabinet du préfet, Bouches-du-Rhône, ADBR 126 W 75, 138 W 72, 138 W 73, and 138 W 74, from 1958–1961. Each code had 1–4 boxes, and each box contained approximately 35 case files.

113. Bureau des affaires musulmanes, cabinet du préfet, ADBR 138 W 72. Since I was prohibited from disclosing the names that appeared in these sealed files, I have used pseudonyms for all people involved.

114. Ibid.

115. Single, widowed, and abandoned women were advised to return. The following are examples of cases of women who refused to follow this advice and of organizations that provided aid to single or abandoned women: SSFNA, "Rapport d'activité," 1954, 9; Raymond Blanc, "Note relative au centre d'hébergement pour travailleurs nord-africains de Besançon," 31 October 1956, appendix, 6 (CAC 860271/11); Association d'entraide aux travailleurs nord-africains de la région lyonnaise et à leurs familles, "Rapport moral," 12 June 1959 (AN F1a 5079); Organisation du Comité Lyonnais de secours d'urgence aux sans logis et du Foyer Notre-Dame des sans-abri, 18 October 1961 (AN F1a 5080); Bureau des affaires musulmanes, cabinet du préfet, ADBR 138 W 72.

116. Massenet, "Situation des musulmans internés dans la métropole," 17 March 1959 (CAC 770391/8).

117. Tengour, "Octobre 1961," 43.

118. Bureau des affaires musulmanes, cabinet du préfet, ADBR 138 W 72. Letters dated 22 and 26 April 1960.

119. Benguigui, *Mémoires d'immigrés*, 91–101.

120. Sayad and Dupuy, *Un Nanterre algérien*, 89.

121. Gall, cited in Einaudi, *Octobre 1961*, 207–8; Monique Hervo, *Journal I–IV, 1956–1961*, the archival collection of her complete diary, AMH. Parts of her diary were published as the *Chroniques du bidonvilles*.

122. Hervo, *Journal I–IV*.

123. Ibid.

124. Hervo, *Chroniques du bidonville*, 107.

125. Hervo, *Journal I–IV*. Hervo even recorded seeing children's toys with knife marks inflicted by the harkis. Sayad and Dupuy provide similar testimonies in *Un Nanterre algérien*, 101–2.

126. Sayad and Dupuy, *Un Nanterre algérien*, 88.

127. AMH, "Nanterre Boîte 2." This file had numerous letters, including the petition from Algerians to the Compagnie des eaux de la banlieue de Paris. According to Hervo, the water company only responded when she wrote asking for an explanation. The water company promptly informed Hervo that a second spigot would not be possible because the bidonville consumed too much water already and "degraded" the current water source.

128. Sayad and Dupuy, *Un Nanterre algérien*, 89.

129. An SSFNA social worker's recollections, quoted in Mahjoub-Guelamine, "Le rôle des services sociaux spécialisés," 201–2. She further explained that SSFNA staff was threatened in Lille and Metz, but that the situation was most difficult in Paris.

130. Brigitte Gall, diary excerpts, 1961, AMH; Monique Hervo, *Journal I–IV*. Only portions of Gall's diary from 1961 are in the AMH collection. Hervo had a complete copy, but as she moved over the years, she could not keep all the documents she had. Aware of their historic importance, but unable to find a repository, Hervo tried to keep as many documents as she could. Regrettably, she lost or threw out many documents, including parts of the diary Gall had entrusted to her. From interviews with Hervo in May 2007 and 2008. Many of the surviving passages of Gall's diary are in Einaudi, *Octobre 1961*.

131. "Note concernant la situation de la migration algérienne," attached to the Compte-rendu de la réunion des conseillers techniques pour les affaires musulmanes en métropole, 16 May 1961 (CAC 770391/2). This document noted several attacks: the deaths of three dormitory managers (between March and April 1960) and of three social counselors known for their "generosity" (since September 1960), as well as the abandonment of home economics and language classes for women in Marseille after "death threats." Although the author blamed the FLN, it seems equally plausible that attacks like these could have been orchestrated by the OAS.

132. According to Mahjoub-Guelamine, three of SSFNA's social workers quit at the height of the violence. "Le rôle des services sociaux spécialisés," 203.

133. Brigitte Gall, diary excerpts, 17 October 1961. Clippings of articles Gall and Hervo wrote are in AMH.

134. Hervo remembered losing her religious faith at the height of the war. She stopped attending mass because she felt surrounded by hypocrisy. She described the middle-class faithful as having no compassion for the plight of people living only a short distance from them. Hervo, still militant, is an advocate of immigrants and writes about her experiences. She lives in a tiny trailer, without running water, near Troyes. Despite the urging of friends, she refuses to move into an HLM apartment, insisting she will not cut ahead of others who have been on the waiting lists for years. Interviews, May 2007 and 2008.

135. Hervo, *Journal I–IV*, and *Chroniques du bidonville*.

136. GEANARP "Statuts," n.d. (1961?) (CAC 760140/2).

137. See Jean-Paul Imhof, "Le transit de réadaptation sociale," *Les cahiers du groupe Construire*, published by Centre d'études juridiques techniques et culturelle des problèmes de l'habitat, November 1959, in the AMH, and CAC 770391/4; Imhof, "L'immigration algérienne en France."

138. GEANARP, "Renseignements généraux sur l'association: Rapport d'activités pour 1960," n.d. (1961?) (CAC 760141/2).

139. Sayad and Dupuy, *Un Nanterre algérien*, 33.

140. Benaïcha, *Vivre au paradis*, 49–51. Benaïcha does not identify GEANARP, but given the details he includes it seems likely Claude worked with this organization.

141. Ibid., 49.

142. Hervo, *Journal I–IV*.

143. SAMAS, "Coordination de l'action psychologique sur la population musulmane," 3, 30 September 1958 (AN F1a 5057). Françoise de Barros has shown that in Roubaix, near Lille, a local politician defamed the incumbent in a municipal election by arguing he had allowed North Africans to hurt local business and to ruin the neighborhood. See de Barros, "Les municipalités face aux Algériens," 91.

144. GEANARP, "Relations du GEANARP avec les services publics et semi-publics."

145. Hervo, *Journal I–IV*.

146. ANAN, "Rapport d'activité, année 1960," in CAC 770391/4.

147. See, among others, Derder, *L'immigration algérienne et les pouvoirs publics*; Blanchard, "Police judicaire," 61–72; House and MacMaster, *Paris 1961*.

148. Marc Bernardot, "Une politique de logement," 62.

149. See an SSFNA social worker's recollections, quoted in Mahjoub-Guelamine, "Le rôle des services sociaux spécialisés," 201–2; and Jean Bénédetti, prefect of the Seine, Direction des affaires sociale, Sous-direction des affaires sociales musulmanes, "Attribution d'une prime de risque au personnel de la Préfecture de la Seine en contact avec les travailleurs nord-africains," 15 December 1960 (CAC 770391/9). According to Bénédetti, the FLN assassinated housing managers on several occasions.

150. Hervo, *Journal I–IV*; GEANARP, "Relations du GEANARP avec les services publics et semi-publics."

151. See Agenda, "Définition d'une politique d'ensemble," for a top secret Interministerial Committee meeting, Hôtel Matignon, 28 September 1959 (CAC 770391/2).

152. House and MacMaster, *Paris 1961*, 53, 144.

153. Armand Guillon, president of the Conseil d'administration en amitiés africaines, "Bulletin de liaison et d'information du Comité des amitiés africaines," 1st trimester 1951 (CAC 860271/4).

154. Préfet chargé de la Direction des services de l'Algérie et des départements d'outre-mer, "Assistance aux anciens militaires musulmans résidant dans la métropole," 28 February 1951 (AN F1a 5035).

155. Conseillers techniques, "Synthèse des rapports trimestriels établis par les conseillers techniques pour les affaires musulmanes," 1st trimester 1958.

156. Interior minister to the IGAME, "Programme d'action à l'égard de la population musulmane algérienne en métropole. Mission des administrateurs des services civils de l'Algérie affectés auprès des IGAMEs et des préfets en qualité de conseillers techniques pour les affaires musulmanes en métropole," 10 February 1958 (AN F1a 5010).

157. SAMAS, "Note ayant pour objet l'inventaire critique des mesures prises ou en cours d'exécution." Secret circular no. 65 was dated 17 February 1958.

158. Minister of the Interior to the IGAME, "Programme d'action à l'égard de la population musulmane algérienne en métropole."

159. Ross, *Fast Cars, Clean Bodies*, 75.

160. Conseillers techniques, "Synthèse des rapports trimestriels établis par les conseillers techniques pour les affaires musulmanes," 1st trimester 1958.

161. SAMAS, "Note ayant pour objet l'inventaire critique des mesures prises ou en cours d'exécution."

162. CANAM, "Rapport moral," 6 July 1959; SAMAS, "Action sociale en faveur des travailleurs algériens en métropole."

163. Meeting agenda, "Définition d'une politique d'ensemble," undated. Related documents indicate the meeting took place on 28 September 1959. In Massenet's papers, CAC 770391/2.

164. Both the unsigned note and Massenet's self-defense are undated documents in a file with press clippings from Le Monde and Le Canard Enchaîné of 30 September and 1 October 1959 indicating what had been discussed at the 28 September meeting (CAC 770391/2).

165. House and MacMaster, Paris 1961, 108.

166. See GEANARP to Massenet, 27 October 1961 (CAC 770391/8). This report, sent to Massenet, detailed each time GEANARP found bodies (14 in all) it wanted to identify and bury; it indicated local authorities had tried to confiscate its records. The Red Cross inquired with the police about dozens of missing people. In some cases, police responses confirmed an Algerian's arrest for having "excited his coreligionists to follow the FLN." In other cases, the police denied any involvement and implied the man in question must have returned to Algeria, abandoning his family. Due to the unresponsiveness of government agencies, the Red Cross spearheaded an investigation to help families find loved ones who had disappeared. See, among others, C. Lesage, Assistance sociale départementale de la Croix-Rouge française pour la Seine, to Massenet, 20 October 1961 (CAC 770391/8); Pierre Somveille, Préfecture de Police, in response to a telephone conversation and written correspondence with the secretary-general of the Red Cross, 10 November 1961 (CAC 770391/8).

167. House and MacMaster, Paris 1961, 211–38; Union régionale parisienne of the Confédération française des travailleurs chrétiens (CFTC) and France Observateur report, "Face à la répression" 30 October 1961 (CAC 770391/8).

168. André Ballet, "A l'occasion du vote du budget de l'Intérieur, débat à l'Assemblée sur la répression," Le Monde, 1 November 1961, 6.

169. On public opinion on the war, see Ageron, "L'opinion française devant la guerre d'Algérie."

170. For the left, the Charonne massacre in February 1962 eclipsed the memory of October 1961. See Dewerpe, Charonne, 8 février 1962. In March 1980, philosopher Etienne Balibar publicly accused the left in the Nouvel Observateur of elevating Charonne to legendary status while completely forgetting the massacres of October 1961. This resulted in his ejection from the Communist Party. See Etienne Balibar, "De Charonne à Vitry," in Les frontières de la démocratie, 19–34. House and MacMaster argue the October 1961 massacre was the "bloodiest" in modern European history, comparing it to other state-sponsored massacres dating to the eighteenth century. On the history and memory of the events, see also Cole, "Remembering the Battle of Paris."

171. Colonel Terce to Massenet "Subventions pour les associations dépendant du 'Service d'action civique,'" 11 March 1961 (CAC 760140/2).

172. FAS minutes, 17 May 1960, 16.

173. Blanchard, La police parisienne, 304–5.

174. The camps included Thol in the Ain, Vadenay in the Marne (both opened in 1957),

Saint-Maurice-l'Ardoise in the Gard, and Larzac in l'Aveyron (both in 1958). For more, see Bernardot, *Camps d'étrangers*, and Thénault, *Violence ordinaire*.

175. Pimont of the Direction général de la Sûreté nationale and Blanchard, SAMAS, "Centres d'assignation à résidence surveillée de la métropole," 15 December 1959 (CAC 770391/8).

176. Bureau des affaires musulmanes, cabinet du préfet, "Propositions assignations à résidence loi du 26 juillet 1957," contains individual files (ADBR 137 W 407); Tristan, *Le silence du fleuve*, 30.

177. Massenet, "Situation des musulmans internés dans la métropole." Massenet also feared Algerian families, destabilized by the loss of the male head of household, would become prey to the FLN, exacerbating the situation.

178. Tristan, *Le silence du fleuve*, 30; Pimont and Blanchard, "Centres d'assignation à résidence surveillée de la métropole."

179. Ibid.

180. Interministerial Committee, Hôtel Matignon, marked top secret, "Mesures d'action sociale," 21 January 1960 (CAC 770391/2); Confidential document from Pierre Chatenet of the Direction général de la Sûreté nationale, 12 January 1960 (CAC 770391/8); Direction général de la Sûreté national and SAMAS, "Centres d'assignation à résidence surveillée—Services d'action éducative et sociale," included among files from Interdepartmental Committee meetings, 12 January 1960 (AN F1a 5055).

181. Tristan, *Le silence du fleuve*, 30. According to Tristan, many internees were deported or transferred to camps in Algeria.

182. SAMAS, "Note ayant pour objet l'inventaire critique des mesures prises ou en cours d'exécution."

183. Jacques Ghys, "La présence nord-africaine démure. Notre action sociale reste," in "Plus que jamais: Action sociale!," *CNA* 64 (April–May 1958): 3–5.

184. Sayad and Dupuy, *Un Nanterre algérien*, 89.

185. CANAM, "Rapport moral," 6 July 1959; Equipe de travail au bidonville de Nanterre, "Note sur l'organisation du transit des familles nord-africaines vivantes en bidonville," March 1959 (AMH, "Nanterre Boîte 2").

186. CANAM, "Rapport moral," 6 July 1959.

187. Ghys, "La présence nord-africaine démure," 6.

188. Ibid.

189. CANAM, "Rapport moral," 6 July 1959.

Chapter 6

1. In addition to sources cited in Chapter 4, see Fourcaut, "Les premiers grands ensembles."

2. SONACOTRAL, "Rapport du Conseil d'administration à l'Assemblée générale annuelle des actionnaires sur la gestion et les comptes de l'exercice 1959," 17 (CAC 870056/16); FAS, "Liquidation du bidonville de Nanterre—Avance de 200 millions demandée par la SONACOTRAL destinée à l'opération de Nanterre, périmètre dit des 'Canibouts,'" 21 November 1959 (CAC 760140/1).

3. SONACOTRAL, "Note justifiant la création d'un centre sociale à Nanterre 'Canibouts,'" 1, 23 February 1962 (AN F1a 5120).

4. As the destruction of the bidonvilles began, the Social Action Fund promised it would provide 800 apartments with a total of 2,264 rooms for temporarily displaced residents. It is unlikely that all or even most of those left homeless received state-sponsored temporary or permanent housing. FAS, "Constructions en faveur des musulmans célibataires ou isolés," 21 October 1959, 2 (CAC 760140/1).

5. FAS, "Liquidation du bidonville de Nanterre."

6. Ibid.

7. On living space minimum standards, see Simmons, "Minimal Frenchman."

8. FAS, "Liquidation du bidonville de Nanterre." See also, Yves Jullien, l'administrateur-délégué de la LOGIREP, "Construction à Argenteuil (Seine-et-Oise) Quai Saint-Denis de 130 logements 'HLM' environ destinés à des familles," 9 November 1960 (CAC 770391/2).

9. SONACOTRAL, "Note justifiant la création d'un centre social à Nanterre 'Canibouts.'"

10. FAS, "Liquidation du bidonville de Nanterre."

11. "Procès-verbal de la réunion de coordination tenue au ministre d'Etat chargé des affaires algériennes, le lundi 13 mars 1961," 23 March 1961 (AN F1a 5056). Later that year Vaujour reported the SONACOTRAL received a total of 8.35 million NF from a variety of sources for Canibouts and had used 3.25 million of these funds. Jean Vaujour, director-general, SONACOTRAL to the FAS director, 27 November 1961 (CAC 760140/2).

12. Vaujour to FAS, 27 November 1961.

13. Ageron, *Modern Algeria*, 120. In the summer of 1960, French officials met with leaders of the new Algerian provisional government in Melun, south of Paris, opening what became a two-year journey toward a lasting solution. That fall de Gaulle announced preparations for a national referendum on the possibility of Algerian self-determination through what he called "association with France." On 8 January 1961, the French public voted overwhelmingly to support his plan. Even though the tenuous peace nearly unraveled several times, government representatives finally reached a settlement in Evian, France, in March 1962. The Evian Accords outlined the final details of Algerian independence. They specified the terms of the ceasefire, the amnesty for belligerents, the self-determination referendum, and the provisional government that would be in place until the installation of the Algerian Republic. The provisional government, made up of Europeans, members of the FLN, and other, non-FLN Algerians, oversaw the transition beginning on 17 April 1962. On the war's end and the peace settlement, see, among others, Helie, *Les accords d'Evian*; Pervillé, *1962*; Gallissot, ed., *Les accords d'Evian*; Monneret, *La phase finale*; Naylor, *France and Algeria*; and a collection of documents edited by FLN leader Ali Haroun, *L'été de la discorde Algérie 1962*.

14. On housing for Algerian men, see Tchibindat, *Le logement des Algériens*.

15. Massenet, "Rapport d'activité du délégué aux affaires sociales," 6, 28 May 1960 (CAC 770391/9).

16. SAMAS, "Action sociale en faveur des travailleurs algériens en métropole," 29 July 1959 (AN F1a 5056).

17. "La métropole compte 25.000 Algériens de plus qu'en 1959," *Paris-Presse*, 23 Janu-

ary 1960 (CAC 770391/2); Massenet, "Situation dans le domaine de l'action sociale pour la migration algérienne," 4 April 1960 (CAC 770391/2), a report Massenet sent to the Elysée Palace for an Algerian Affairs committee meeting.

18. For example, in 1959 the Council General of the Seine earmarked sixty million OF for family housing, and the Reconstruction and Urbanization Ministry contributed 1.5 billion OF to build apartments for Algerian families over three years. Procès-verbal of the interdepartmental meeting, 23 April 1959 (CAC 770391/2); FAS, "Programme 1959: Analyse de la répartition des crédits décidée par le Conseil d'administration du Fonds d'action sociale," 1960 (CAC 760140/1); FAS, "Programme d'action sociale pour l'année 1959" (CAC 760140/2).

19. Procès-verbal of the interdepartmental meeting, 23 April 1959; FAS, "Programme 1959: Analyse de la répartition des crédits décidée par le Conseil d'administration du Fonds d'action sociale"; FAS, "Programme d'action sociale pour l'année 1959"; CANAM, "Procès-verbal de l'Assemblée générale, 1958–1959"; Josset, "Le FAS," 14–17.

20. Michel Massenet, "Note sur les problèmes posés par l'habitat des familles musulmanes de souche algérienne," in "Pour le logement des Africains du Nord," *CNA* 85 (August–September 1961): 57. The prepublication version of the article is found in Massenet, "Note sur les problèmes posés par l'habitat des familles musulmanes de souche algérienne," 1961 (CAC 770391/6).

21. SONACOTRAL, "Rapport du Conseil d'administration à l'Assemblée générale annuelle des actionnaires sur la gestion et les comptes de l'exercice 1959."

22. Interior minister, circular no. 56 of 10 February 1958, quoted in Georges Martin, administrator of CTAM, "Rapport relatif aux opérations d'assainissement des hôtels, meubles, immeubles, et îlots insalubres où menaçants ruine réalisées dans l'agglomération lyonnaise," 1958–1959 (CAC 770391/6).

23. FAS, "Programme d'action sociale pour l'année 1959"; Claude Huet and Jean-Paul Imhof, "Note sur l'organisation du transit des familles nord-africaines vivant en bidonville," March 1959 (CAC 770391/4).

24. The mayor of Salon-de-Provence, 24 August 1960 (CAC 770391/7); Angès Pitrou, Centre de recherches et de documentation sur la consommation, "Conditions de logement et adaptation à la vie française," in "Le logement des Nord-Africains à Marseille," *CNA* 82 (February–March 1961): 26.

25. Etudes de Claude Perret, chargé de mission au Plan 1959, "Note sur la migration des travailleurs algériens en métropole," Commissariat général du Plan, Commission d'examen des "Perspectives décennales," 8, January 1959 (CAC 770391/4).

26. Of course some Algerian families already lived in HLMs during the Fourth Republic. As well, before the formal transitional housing policy, families lived in transitional projects. A number of organizations and the Prefecture of the Seine had transitional family housing in place before 1959. See Chapter 4, and Hmed, "Loger les étrangers 'isolés' en France," 94–97.

27. SSFNA, "Rapport sur l'activité du SSFNA, 1957–1958," 5. Twelve percent already had housing, fourteen percent were ready for HLMs, and seventy-four percent needed a *cité de transit* or other transitional program. Other documents offered similar percentages.

See, for example, "Conférence du 13 octobre 1960 concernant le relogement des Nord-Africains," October 1960 (AN F1a 5121).

28. FAS, "Projet de réalisations sociales au profit des travailleurs d'origine algérienne en métropole (article 9 du décret no. 59-559 du 23 avril 1959)," 1960 (CAC 760140/1); "Projet de procès-verbal de la réunion du Comité interministériel d'action sociale pour les Français musulmans d'Algérie en métropole en date du 6 juin 1961 (Application de l'article 9 du décret du 23 avril 1959)" (CAC 760140/6); "Conférence du 13 octobre 1960 concernant le relogement des Nord Africains." The interministerial meeting brought together Massenet, Doublet, the director of the FAS, and representatives from the army and the following ministries: Labor, Public Health and Population, Education, and Construction.

29. Jacques Ghys, preface to "Quelques familles nord-africaines en France," *CNA* 67 (October–November 1958): 3–4.

30. MI, circular no. 56 of 10 February 1958, quoted in Martin, "Rapport relatif aux opérations d'assainissement." Martin also mentioned two earlier circulars (September 1954 and December 1957) that pointed to the need to find solutions to the housing crisis Algerians faced in the metropole. Dozens of documents referred to the project as the "liquidation" of the bidonville problem. See, for example, CAC 760140, 860269, and especially 770391.

31. Harvey, *Paris*, 259–60.

32. MI, circular no. 511 of December 1957, quoted in Martin, "Rapport relatif aux opérations d'assainissement."

33. FAS, "Programme d'action sociale pour l'année 1959"; FAS, minutes, 17 June 1959 and FAS, minutes, 12 July 1960 (both in CAC 760140/1).

34. ESNA, "Avant-propos," in "Familles nord-africaines en 'bidonvilles,'" *CNA* 89 (April–May 1962): 5; G. Duchatelet, "Des chancres à extirper: Les quartiers réservés," in "Pour le logement des Africains du Nord," 28.

35. "Note à l'attention de Monsieur le secrétaire général pour les affaires algériennes," in FAS, minutes, 17 June 1959 (CAC 760140/1).

36. ANAN, "Rapport d'activités pour l'année 1956" (CAC 770391/4); FAS, "Programme d'action sociale pour l'année 1959"; Pitrou, "Introduction," in "Le logement des Nord-Africains à Marseille," 7. Other documents used similar language; see, for example, Jean-Paul Imhof, "Le transit de réadaptation sociale," in *Les Cahiers du groupe construire*, 11, November 1959 (CAC 770391/4).

37. Of the approximately 350,000 Algerians living in France, at least 150,000 had substandard housing. Of those, the FAS determined that 15,000 men and 1,800 families (with 10,000 members) lived in bidonvilles in 1959. See Viet, *La France immigrée*, 204; FAS, "Programme d'action sociale pour l'année 1959." Yet, contemporary estimates varied enough to call their accuracy into question. For example, reports issued in 1959 offered wildly different estimates about the number of Algerian families in Marseille's bidonvilles—with one putting the number at about 120 and the other at 750. Likewise, ATOM director Louis Belpeer warned that determining exact numbers was difficult because of these families' "mobility" and poor estimates. He pointed out that most reports estimated 120 families lived in the La Calade bidonville until a census revealed that it was home to 198 families. Similarly,

estimates of 70 families in the St. Barthélemey bidonville turned out to be low when an examination of aerial photographs brought the estimate up to 180 families. See, "Projets concernant la liquidation des bidonvilles en métropole," 1959 (CAC 760140/6); Massenet, "Programme d'action sociale pour l'année 1959 (pour les Français musulmans d'Algérie en métropole)," October 1959 (Archive Laroque, ENTEX 98/001 carton 114); Louis Belpeer in "Les familles nord africaines en France: Essai de mise au point," *CNA* 83 (April–May 1961): 28–29.

38. Robert Jasseron, "Avant la fin de l'année, tous les bidonvilles lyonnais auront disparu," *La Dernière Heure Lyonnaise*, 6 November 1959.

39. FAS, minutes, 28 September 1960, 23 (CAC 760140/1).

40. It was estimated that about 3,500 men and 800 families lived in the region's bidonvilles. See "Bouches-du-Rhône renseignements statistiques, 1958–1959" (ADBR 138 W 27). On Marseille's "ambitious" plans, see Massenet, "Rapport d'activité du délégué aux affaires sociales." The three bidonvilles Marseille claimed to have destroyed were St. Barthélemy, la Timone, and Boulevard de la Corderie.

41. For the quotation see, "Note relative aux actions en cours pour l'amélioration de l'habitat des travailleurs originaires d'Algérie et de leurs familles," 8 September 1960 (CAC 770391/6). See also SAMAS, "Note ayant pour objet l'inventaire critique des mesures prises ou en cours d'exécution"; Massenet, "Situation dans le domaine de l'action sociale pour la migration algérienne"; "Bilan de l'action entreprise en faveur de l'habitat des familles nord-africaines du 1er octobre 1959 au 1er octobre 1961," 1961 (CAC 770391/6); Internal document in Massenet's papers, "La lutte contre les bidonvilles en métropole," October 1961 (CAC 770391/6).

42. *JO* 60-101, 5 February 1960, 1178. Expanding on the 1956 special powers, the new law "authorized the government to take, on the authority of Article 38 of the Constitution, certain measures necessary to maintain order, to safeguard the state [and] to pacify . . . Algeria." See also Thénault, "L'état d'urgence," 69–70.

43. FAS, "Projet de réalisations sociales au profit des travailleurs d'origine algérienne en métropole." It was a precursor to the better-known Debré law passed in 1964. See Fourcaut et al., *Paris-banlieues*, 347.

44. "La lutte contre les bidonvilles en métropole." According to this document, the government issued an order on 6 March 1959 for the bidonville issue to be resolved by the end of 1961.

45. "Les problèmes de la liquidation des bidonvilles en France," October 1961 (CAC 770391/6).

46. Letter from the prefect of the Seine to SAMAS, 30 July 1960 (AN F1a 5120).

47. FAS, minutes, 9 November 1961 (CAC 760140/2).

48. J. Bénédetti, prefect of the Seine, to SAMAS, "Bidonvilles," 20 February 1959 (CAC 770391/7); FAS meeting, 9 November 1961. The quotation is from SSFNA, "Rapport sur l'activité du SSFNA 1957–1958," 2–3.

49. Massenet, "Rapport d'activité du délégué aux affaires sociales."

50. Massenet, "Note concernant les problèmes posés par l'habitat des familles musulmanes de souche algérienne," n.d. (1960?) (CAC 770391/6); Massenet, "Rapport d'activité

du délégué aux affaires sociales"; "Destruction des baraquements familiaux à Nanterre," 1960 (CAC 770391/7); Letter from the prefect of the Seine to SAMAS, 30 July 1960.

51. Bénédetti to SAMAS, "Bidonvilles"; Massenet, "Rapport d'activité du délégué aux affaires sociales," 4.

52. Bénédetti to SAMAS, "Bidonvilles"; Massenet, "Rapport d'activité du délégué aux affaires sociales"; "Une lèpre à 'blanchir': Les bidonvilles," in "Pour le logement des Africains du Nord," 24–27. The bidonvilles continued to garner national attention off and on into the early 1970s when the asphyxiation of several African workers reenergized the search for a solution to the housing crisis among poor immigrants. See Blanc-Chaléard, "Les trente glorieuses," 21–22.

53. Wakeman, *The Heroic City*, 321–25.

54. CANAM, "Rapport moral," 1959, 6.

55. François Villey, "L'action sociale en faveur des musulmans d'Algérie en France," September 1960 (CAC 770391/4).

56. Massenet, "Programme d'action sociale pour l'année 1959."

57. Jacques Ghys, "D'un point de vue . . . ," in "Pour le logement des Africains du Nord," 52–54.

58. SAMAS, "Action sociale en faveur des travailleurs algériens en métropole."

59. Ghys, "D'un point de vue . . . ," 52–54.

60. SAMAS, "Action sociale en faveur des travailleurs algériens en métropole." Aside from the Social Action Fund and the SONACOTRAL, the organizations involved included the Centres de propagande et d'action contre les taudis (PACT), the Comité interprofes-sionnel de le logement (CIL), the Caisses d'allocations familiales (CAF), the Construction Ministry, and regional governments. On de Gaulle's efforts from the 1959 "peace of the brave" to the January 1961 referendum, see Shepard, *The Invention of Decolonization*, 114–15.

61. SAMAS, "Note concernant l'action sociale menée en faveur des Français de souche nord-africaine résident en métropole" and attached report, "Création d'un climat favorable par l'action sociale," 2 June 1959 (AN F1a 5056).

62. G. Morlot, directeur-adjoint du cabinet, pour le ministre de l'Intérieur, affaires musulmanes, "Prise de participation par la SONACOTRAL dans le capital d'une société HLM," 28 May 1959 (CAC 770391/7).

63. SSFNA, "Rapport sur l'activité du SSFNA, 1957–1958," 5.

64. "23.000 Algériens: Comment sont-ils arrivés à Lyon?," *Messages d'Algérie* no. 69 (1 July 1960); "Lyon: Un effort social sans précédent," *Messages d'Algérie* no. 72 (1 September 1960) (CAC 770391/7).

65. "Aide aux Français musulmans d'Algérie," 1960 (CAC 770391/4); "La métropole compte 25.000 Algériens de plus qu'en 1959," *Paris-Presse*, 23 January 1960 (CAC 770391/2). Fifty courses opened for women as they "accompanied the head of household more and more often."

66. Leriche, "Essai d'estimation du nombre des familles nord-africaines en France," in "Les familles nord africaines en France," 7–29. In his report, Leriche explains that no national survey of Algerian families had taken place since 1954. Using a variety of sources, he estimated the 350,000 Algerians in France included 21,000 women and girls over sixteen,

8,850 European "concubines," and 70,500 children from Algerian and "mixed" families. In his footnotes, he cited SSFNA statistics that counted 28,000 families—over 20,850 in twelve departments where it had offices and another 7,200 in other regions. It is fairly clear, though, that even these numbers were low. Having been given an advance copy of Leriche's report, ATOM's director Louis Belpeer penned a letter—cited in Note 37 above—which ESNA published in the same issue. As part of his discussion of the bidonvilles, Belpeer argued it was difficult to get a "real census" of Algerian families. He insisted that SSFNA underestimated the number of families in the Bouches-du-Rhône, with 3,000 families (1,150 women and 2,060 children). Instead, he argued that the prefecture's statistics (2,450 women and 7,000 children) were more accurate. Belpeer in "Les familles nord africaines en France," 28–29. In addition to providing similar figures, the SAMAS estimated France had 13,000 Tunisians and 30,000 Moroccans by 1960. SAMAS, "Besoins en personnel," 7 March 1960 (AN F1a 5010).

67. Massenet, "Questionnaire relatif à l'état de la migration algérienne," 19 October 1960 (CAC 770391/2). Massenet further argued that the trend seemed to be holding in 1960.

68. See SAMAS, "Action sociale en faveur des travailleurs algériens en métropole"; Morlot, "Prise de participation par la SONACOTRAL dans le capital d'une société HLM"; Perret, "Note sur la migration des travailleurs algériens en métropole"; Massenet, "Note concernant les problèmes posés par l'habitat des familles musulmanes de souche algérienne."

69. François Villey, "La migration des familles musulmanes dans la métropole," *Actualités d'Outre-mer*, no. 6 (November 1958): 15; Pitrou, "La population musulmane de Marseille et son habitat," in "Le logement des Nord Africains à Marseille," 11.

70. Prefect of the Rhône to Michel Massenet, "A/S de l'arrivée probable des familles musulmanes en métropole," 12 July 1960 (CAC 770391/6).

71. *Messages d'Algérie*, 15 February 1961, quoted in Leriche, "Essai d'estimation du nombre des familles nord-africaines en France," 18.

72. Massenet, "Situation dans le domaine de l'action sociale pour la migration algérienne"; Perret, "Note sur la migration des travailleurs algériens en métropole."

73. Perret, "Note sur la migration des travailleurs algériens en métropole"; Délégation générale du gouvernement en Algérie, "La migration algérienne en France," 20. Both offered the same figures, with the latter possibly citing the former.

74. Leriche, "Essai d'estimation du nombre des familles nord-africaines en France," 24–25.

75. Bellot, administrator of SCAA [Service de coordination des affaires algériennes], CTAM, Prefecture of the Loire, "Note concernant le logement des familles musulmanes dans le Département de la Loire," 17 September 1960 (CAC 770391/7).

76. SAMAS, "Action sociale en faveur des femmes musulmanes d'origine algérienne résidant en métropole," circulaire no. 716, 12 December 1958 (AN F1a 5035). The circular notes the directive came from the Interministerial Committee.

77. Jacques Ghys, "La présence nord-africaine démure. Notre action sociale reste," in "Plus que jamais: Action sociale!," *CNA* 64 (April–May 1958): 6.

78. Massenet, "Programme d'action sociale pour l'année 1959."

79. "Note sur l'action sociale du Ministère de la Santé publique et de la Population susceptible de recevoir un financement complémentaire du Fonds d'action sociale," 31 December 1959 (CAC 770391/9). To cover the costs of running programs (including equipment) and for scholarships, 273 million OF were set aside. Another 400 million went to maternity hospitals, children's homes, family placement, and services for young adults and the mentally and physically handicapped. Adult educational and medical services received 177 million and "specialized" programs—run by two associations, the SSFNA and AMANA—42 million.

80. FAS, "Programme d'action sociale pour l'année 1959," 12. The CANAM, for example, increased spending on programs for women and youths from four to ten million OF between 1959 and 1960. CANAM, "Exercice 1958–1959, Assemblée générale du lundi 6 juillet 1959, Procès-verbal," 3, 6 July 1959 (CAC 770391/4).

81. FAS, "Projet de réalisations sociales au profit des travailleurs d'origine algérienne en métropole"; "Note sur l'action sociale du Ministère de la Santé publique et de la Population susceptible de recevoir un financement complémentaire du Fonds d'action sociale." The scholarships were largely for training young Algerian women as social work assistants working alongside metropolitans. Many returned to work in the social centers. FAS, minutes, 28 September 1960. According to Jaime Wadowiec, Forget participated in these trainings and provided expert advice. See "The Afterlives of Empire." Wadowiec cites "Stage des monitrices chargées d'enseignement aux femmes algériennes," 17 February 1962 (CAC 960221/1).

82. Villey, "L'action sociale en faveur des musulmans d'Algérie en France," 5.

83. Imhof, "Le transit de réadaptation sociale," 11.

84. Bellot, "Note concernant le logement des familles musulmanes dans le Département de la Loire."

85. Pitrou, "La population musulmane de Marseille et son habitat," 15.

86. Imhof, "Le transit de réadaptation sociale," 11.

87. Villey, "La migration des familles musulmanes dans la métropole," 14.

88. FAS, "Note sur le programme complémentaire du Ministère de l'Education nationale à financer par le Fonds d'action sociale," 1959 (CAC 760140/6). The FAS also helped to keep Education Ministry programs running. It had forty centers for men and four for women, some of which it had taken over from private charities in danger of closing. FAS subventions allowed them to stay open and participate in the ministry's plan to build another twenty centers for women by December 1959.

89. Leriche, "Essai de localisation par départements," in "Les familles nord africaines en France," 13n1. The departments: Nord, Moselle, Meurthe-Et-Moselle, Belfort, Doubs, Loire, Rhône, Isère, Savoie, Puy-de-Dôme, Seine, and Seine-et-Oise.

90. MSPP to the FAS director, "Demande de subvention présentée par le Service social familial nord-africain," 25 July 1961 (CAC 760141/2); FAS, minutes, 17 May 1960 (CAC 760140/1).

91. Stephane Hessel, minister of MEN, Direction de la coopération avec la communauté de l'étranger, Sous-direction de la formation et de la coopération, to the FAS director, 9 April 1960 (CAC 760140/1).

92. Association douaisienne pour l'habitat des travailleurs originaires d'Afrique du Nord, "Rapport d'activité pour l'année 1957," 17 April 1958 (AN F1a 5066). As with other organizations, this association in Douai had previously specialized in housing for Algerian men. It opened the center to offer instruction when it began to provide housing for families.

93. FAS, minutes, 21 October 1959 (CAC 760140/1); "Construction à Nanterre de 30 logements d'urgences destinés à des familles originaires d'Algérie," 1959 (CAC 760141/1).

94. The mayor complained both before and after it opened. See "Construction à Nanterre de 30 logements d'urgences destinés à des familles originaires d'Algérie"; letters between Bénédetti, prefect of the Seine, and Barbet, mayor of Nanterre, May–July 1960 (CAC 770391/9); Massenet, "Rapport d'activité du délégué aux affaires sociales."

95. Claudius-Petit to the minister of Reconstruction and Housing, 22 January 1958 (CAC 870056/12).

96. SAMAS, "Action sociale en faveur des travailleurs algériens en métropole."

97. "Le CLFNA, ses raisons d'être et ses buts," 1955 (AMH).

98. SAMAS, "Note sur l'activité du Service des affaires musulmanes du 1er janvier 1959 à décembre 1960," 5 December 1960 (AN F1a 5010).

99. See numerous FAS board meeting minutes, especially FAS, minutes, 8 July 1959 (CAC 760140/1). See also, Prefecture of the Rhône, "Note relative au problème du logement des musulmans (célibataires et familles) originaires de l'Algérie," 29 July 1960 (CAC 770391/7); "Bilan de l'action entreprise en faveur de l'habitat des familles nord-africaines du 1er octobre 1959 au 1er octobre 1961," 1961 (CAC 770391/6).

100. "Les problèmes de la liquidation des bidonvilles en France," October 1961 (CAC 770391/6).

101. Massenet, "Note sur les problèmes posés par l'habitat des familles musulmanes de souche algérienne." This included *cités de transit* in Nanterre, Lyon, Marseille, Gennevilliers, Roubaix, Saint-Etienne, and Salon-de-Provence.

102. Massenet in the Interministerial Committee meeting, 6 June 1961. For the report, see "Bilan de l'action entreprise en faveur de l'habitat des familles nord-africaines." It estimated 90 percent of 1,150 units under construction would be completed nationwide by the end of 1962. In addition to those cities mentioned in the preceding note, Creil, Toulouse, Chambéry, Metz, and Bordeaux had *cités de transit*. Similar figures are in the annex to FAS, minutes, 8 July 1961 (CAC 760140/2).

103. "La lutte contre les bidonvilles en métropole."

104. Letter by Claude Huet and Jean-Paul Imhof for the Equipe de travail au bidonville de Nanterre, 15 March 1960 (CAC 770391/4). Imhof recommended that the center work with bidonville and *cité de transit* residents.

105. Prefecture of the Bouches-du-Rhône, "Procès-verbal de la réunion qui s'est tenue le 24 octobre 1958 à la Préfecture des Bouches-du-Rhône en vue d'examiner le programme d'amélioration de l'habitat des travailleurs musulmans algériens à effectuer dans les Bouches-du-Rhône avec l'aide de la SONACOTRAL," 24 October 1958 (ADBR 138 W 58).

106. Madeline Henry, "Essai de centre social du Marais de C . . . ," in "Les Africains du Nord dans l'arrondissement de Valenciennes," *CNA* 81 (December 1960–January 1961): 41–43.

107. "Projet de centre d'adaptation à la vie moderne pour une cité de transit de 80 à 100 familles musulmanes," June 1960 (CAC 760140/1).

108. Ibid.

109. Ibid; ANAN, "Rapport d'activité, année 1958" (CAC 77031/4). Quote is from ANAN.

110. GEANARP, "Demande de subvention d'équipement centre socioculturel hommes, Cité des Grands Prés," n.d. (1961?) (CAC 76140/2).

111. "Projet de Centre d'adaption à la vie moderne pour une cité de transit de 80 à 100 familles musulmanes."

112. ANAN, "Rapport d'activité, année 1960" (CAC 770391/4).

113. "Projet de Centre d'adaptation à la vie moderne pour une cité de transit de 80 à 100 familles musulmanes."

114. See, among others, Prefecture of the Bouches-du-Rhône, "Procès-verbal de la réunion qui s'est tenue le 24 octobre 1958"; ADAFARELI, "Rapport de l'année 1959," 11 (AN F1a 5064). ADAFARELI estimated six months.

115. The quote comes from Huet and Imhof, "Note sur l'organisation du transit des familles nord-africaines vivantes en bidonville." Many social workers made these decisions, but the SSFNA probably played the largest role in this process nationwide. See, among others, "Logement des familles d'ouvriers algériens dans les départements de la Loire," 20 September 1960 (CAC 770391/7); "Note concernant la situation de la migration algérienne à Saint-Etienne," 26 September 1960 (CAC 770391/7).

116. Pitrou, "Indication des divers types de logement à envisager," in "Le logement des Nord Africains à Marseille," 36–39; SSFNA, "Rapport sur l'activité du SSFNA, 1957–1958," 6–7.

117. These two items did not appear in the *CNA* article, but they were important criteria in numerous documents that also included the other elements listed above. See SSFNA, "Rapport sur l'activité du SSFNA, 1957–1958," 6–7; GEANARP, "Eléments d'étude sociologique sur le bidonville du petit Nanterre (rue des Paquerettes)," 1959 (AN F1a 5120).

118. Pitrou, "Indication des divers types de logement à envisager," 36–39.

119. "Récapitulation des recensements effectués au 'Bidonville' de 'La Timone,'" 11 March 1960 (ADBR 138 W 55).

120. For example, according to a 1974 study, foreign-born residents in Saint-Etienne HLMs were "for the most part repatriated *pieds noirs*." See Vant, *Les grands ensembles*, 42.

121. ANAN, "Rapport d'activité pour l'année 1957" (CAC 770391/4); ANAN, "Rapport d'activité, année 1958."

122. Pitrou, "Indication des divers types de logement à envisager," 36–37.

123. On the kinds of surveillance, regime, and expectations of behavior that continued well into the 1970s, see Hmed, "Loger les étrangers 'isolés' en France," 101–7.

124. "Projet de centre d'adaptation à la vie moderne pour une cité de transit de 80 à 100 familles musulmanes."

125. The dispute was eventually settled and construction went ahead. "Note sur la construction d'un foyer provisoire de transit à Nanterre mise à la disposition du département

d'une parcelle de terrain située dans l'entrepôt de Nanterre 'La Folie,'" 7 January 1960 (CAC 770391/6).

126. Bernardot, "Une politique de logement," 73.

127. Imhof, "L'immigration algérienne en France," 89.

128. Massenet to Dulière, technical consultant for the prime minister, Hôtel Matignon, "Concernant le reclassement des familles musulmanes habitant en bidonvilles dans la métropole," 9 June 1959 (CAC 770391/6).

129. Claudius-Petit to the minister of MR, 22 January 1958; Massenet, "Rapport d'activité du délégué aux affaires sociales," 6. The quotation comes from Massenet.

130. FAS, "Programme d'action sociale pour l'année 1959," 4. See also "Note relative au logement des familles originaires d'Algérie," 1959 (CAC 770391/6); SAMAS, "Action sociale en faveur des travailleurs algériens en métropole."

131. Quotation from SAMAS, "Note sur le logement des travailleurs," 1959 (AN F1a 5056); "Note relative au logement des familles originaires d'Algérie."

132. SAMAS, "Action sociale en faveur des travailleurs algériens en métropole."

133. Perret, "Note sur la migration des travailleurs algériens en métropole."

134. SAMAS, "Note sur le logement des travailleurs"; "Note relative au logement des familles originaires d'Algérie"; Bernardot, "Un politique de logement," citing an interview with J. Alaux, 74. The SONACOTRAL's HLMs took advantage of tax breaks and supplemental funding from the Crédit Foncier reserved for the construction of family housing. To create its HLMs, the SONACOTRAL petitioned the Construction Ministry for permission to purchase existing social housing companies and transform them into subsidiaries under legal provisions dating back to 24 July 1867. Many documents mention the nineteenth-century law, including, Prefecture of the Rhône, "Note relative au problème du logement des musulmans."

135. Flamand, *Loger le peuple*, 199–200.

136. LOGI stands for *Logement et gestion immobilière*. Henry Laborie replaced Vaujour as director in 1962. See Bernardot, "Un politique de logement," 74–76; SAMAS, "Note sur le logement des travailleurs."

137. The authorization of the SONACOTRAL's purchase of an HLM company in Paris for 2.6 million OF first appeared in *JO* on 6 August 1959. It was signed by Antoine Pinay (Finance Ministry), Pierre Chatenet (Interior Ministry), and Michel Maurice-Bokanowski (secretary of the Interior Ministry).

138. Jullien, "Construction à Argenteuil."

139. Prefecture of the Rhône, "Note relative au problème du logement des musulmans." Even though work began in July, officials at the national level did not approve the SONACOTRAL's purchase of LOGIREL stock until December. See Michel Debré, Pierre Chatenet, and Wilfrid Baumgartner, "Décret autorisant la [SONACOTRAL] à prendre une participation financière dans le capital d'une société anonyme d'habitation à loyer modéré. LOGIREL," 12 December 1960 (CAC 870056/14).

140. SAMAS, "Note sur l'activité du Service des affaires musulmanes du 1er janvier 1959 à décembre 1960."

141. FAS, minutes, 9 November 1961.

142. Eugène Claudius-Petit, "Action de la SONACOTRAL dans le cadre des HLM prise de participation dans le capital d'une société d'HLM dont la vocation s'étendra aux départements industriels de l'Est—Application du décret du 9 août 1953," 25 May 1962 (CAC 870056/14).

143. SAMAS, "Note sur le logement des travailleurs."

144. SAMAS, "Note sur l'activité du Service des affaires musulmanes du 1er janvier 1959 à décembre 1960."

145. Ibid.; Jean Vaujour, SONACOTRAL director to the FAS director, 16 January 1961 (CAC 760140/2).

146. SONACOTRAL, "Rapport du Conseil d'administration à l'Assemblée générale annuelle des actionnaires sur la gestion et les comptes de l'exercice 1961."

147. "Programme prévisionnel des Sociétés d'HLM 'LOGIREP'—'LOGIREL'—'LOGIREM,'" October 1961 (CAC 770391/2).

148. Massenet, "Note sur les problèmes posés par l'habitat des familles musulmanes de souche algérienne," 57. Massenet listed PACT/HLM projects in Lille, Roubaix, Tourcoing, Valenciennes, Douai, and Dunkerque totaling 240 units. The FAS also funded HLM complexes in Le Havre, Firminy, Clermont-Ferrand, and Grenoble.

149. ADAFARELI, "Rapport de l'année 1960," 10–12 (AN F1a 5064).

150. Massenet, "Rapport d'activité du délégué aux affaires sociales"; La Société coopérative musulmane algérienne d'habitation et d'accession à la petite propriété, 8 June 1960 (CAC 770391/7); Jullien, "Construction à Argenteuil"; SAMAS, "Problème posé par le logement des familles de travailleurs algériens à Marseille," June 1961 (AN F1a 5121).

151. *JO* 58-997, "Portant réforme des règles relatives à l'expropriation pour cause d'utilité publique," 23 October 1958, 9694.

152. Pierre Sudreau, "Conversion et aménagement des locaux existants en vue de la réalisation des logements d'habitations a loyer modéré de transition," *JO*, 11 February 1960, 1389.

153. SAMAS to the IGAMEs and the prefects, "Conversion et aménagement des locaux existants en vue de la réalisation des logements d'habitations à loyer modéré de transition," circulaire no. 88, 29 February 1960 (AN F1a 5035); "Examen des possibilités de logement des familles musulmanes offertes par l'arrête du 9 février 1960 de M. le Ministre de la Construction permettant la transformation des locaux vacants en logements HLM de transition," 1960 (ADBR 138 W 55). According to this Construction Ministry report, most of the structures acquired were either too far gone and had to be condemned and razed or the residents of the dilapidated structures could not afford newly renovated apartments. This SAMAS directive coincided with a series of laws that purported to "maintain order" among Algerians in the metropole. See Note 43 above, and Thénault, "L'état d'urgence."

154. *JO* 61-106, "Autorisant la réquisition temporaire des terrains nécessaires à l'instillation provisoire de logement destinés aux personnes évacuées de locaux impropres à l'habitation situés dans des agglomérations des Français musulmans," 2 February 1961, 1267.

155. SAMAS, "Coordination de l'action psychologique sur la population musulmane," 30 September 1958 (AN F1a 5057).

156. J. Bénédetti and Nanterre's mayor, 11 July 1960 (CAC 770391/9).

157. Jacques Marette, senator of the Seine, to Massenet, 8 April 1960 (CAC 770391/6).

All documents regarding Rosny-sous-Bois contained similar information as various officials worked to develop a unified, clear case against the FAS project.

158. Mayor of Rosny-sous-Bois, "Implantation éventuelle des Nord Africains sur le territoire de Rosny-sous-Bois," 30 March 1960 (CAC 770391/6).

159. Giscard d'Estaing, prime minister, brief note to Massenet, 14 January 1960. Attached to it was a report by Mr. Lubot, assistant director in the prime minister's office, that summarized his meeting with Rosny-sous-Bois' leadership. The quotations are from the report. CAC 770391/6.

160. Marette, senator of the Seine, to Massenet, 8 April 1960.

161. Mayor of Rosny-sous-Bois, "Implantation éventuelle des Nord Africains sur le territoire de Rosny-sous-Bois."

162. Letters to IGAME and Massenet from la Société coopérative musulmane algérienne d'habitation et d'accession à la petite propriété, February and June 1960 (CAC 770391/7).

163. FAS, minutes, 12 July 1960.

164. Massenet, "Note sur les problèmes posés par l'habitat des familles musulmanes de souche algérienne." It seems clear Saint-Etienne complied with FAS policy by accepting repatriated colonists. See Note 120 above.

165. This idea of *brassage* appeared in hundreds of archival documents including those in CAC 760133, 760140, 770391, ADBR 138 W 55, and F1a 5035, 5056, and 5057.

166. Leriche, "L'essentiel: Logement familial pour tous," in "Pour le logement des Africains du Nord," 64–68. The broadcast was sponsored by the Public Health and Population Ministry. Imhof also wrote for a national audience; see "L'immigration algérienne en France."

167. Claudius-Petit to the minister of Reconstruction and Housing, 22 January 1958. For an example of an early informal quota that suggested limiting Algerians to 10 percent of housing, see Prefecture of the Bouches-du-Rhône, "Procès-verbal de la réunion que s'est tenue le 24 octobre 1958," 2–3, 24 October 1958 (ADBR 138 W 58).

168. SAMAS, "Action sociale en faveur des travailleurs algériens en métropole." The quota system was already in use in hospitals. See "Enquête sur l'admission et le séjour des Français musulmans d'Algérie dans les établissements hospitaliers publics et privés des Basses-Pyrénées," and "Enquête sur l'admission et le séjour des Français musulmans d'Algérie dans les établissements hospitaliers publics et privés," both 1960 (AN F1a 5060).

169. SAMAS, "Action sociale en faveur des travailleurs algériens en métropole."

170. The expression "de facto segregation" appeared frequently. See Notes 34 and 162 above, and ESNA, "Du logement mais lequel?," in "Pour le logement des Africains du Nord," 5.

171. Interministerial Committee, "Procès-verbal," 25 March 1960 (AN F1a 5045). See also FAS board meeting minutes in CAC 760140.

172. Prefecture of the Bouches-du-Rhône, "Procès-verbal de la réunion qui s'est tenue le 24 octobre 1958."

173. SONACOTRAL, "Rapport du Conseil d'administration à l'Assemblée générale annuelle des actionnaires sur la gestion et les comptes de l'exercice 1961."

174. See letters between FAS and other governmental officials about Salon-de-Provence between December 1959 and June 1961 (CAC 770391/7). The FAS insisted that Salon-de-Provence ensure a *brassage* of families receive funding. It is not clear what happened after the summer of 1961.

175. ESNA, "Du logement mais lequel?," 5–6.

176. SONACOTRAL, "Rapport du Conseil d'administration à l'Assemblée générale annuelle des actionnaires sur la gestion et les comptes de l'exercice 1959." Similar discussions are in SONACOTRAL board minutes for 1960 and 1961.

177. "Procès-verbal de la réunion sous la présidence de M. le Préfet Garnier, le 26 octobre 1961 au sujet de l'organisation d'une commission d'attribution des logements aux familles musulmanes" (CAC 770391/6). Committee members included Garnier and Massenet and representatives from the SONACOTRAL, Seine, Social Affairs, Construction Ministry, Housing Office, SAMAS, and CTAM.

178. Massenet, "Note sur les problèmes posés par l'habitat des familles musulmanes de souche algérienne."

179. Ginesy-Galano, *Les immigrés hors la cité*, 129. On the SONACOTRAL becoming the SONACOTRA, see the Conclusion.

180. SAMAS, "Politique sociale en faveur des Français de souche nord-africaine résidant en métropole," 11 April 1960 (AN F1a 5056); SAMAS, "Note ayant pour objet l'inventaire critique des mesures prises ou en cours d'exécution."

181. Bellot, "Note concernant le logement des familles musulmanes dans le Département de la Loire."

182. Massenet, "Note sur les problèmes posés par l'habitat des familles musulmanes de souche algérienne," 58.

183. Bellot, "Note concernant le logement des familles musulmanes dans le Département de la Loire."

184. "Conférence du 13 octobre 1960 concernant le relogement des Nord Africains."

185. Ministre de l'Etat, Chargé des affaires Algériennes, "Contrôle de la migration du travail d'Algérie en métropole," circulaire no. 565, 3 November 1961 (AN F1a 5035).

186. See circulars of 9 March 1965, 9 July 1965, and 16 August 1965.

187. SAMAS, "Note sur l'activité du Service des affaires musulmanes du 1er janvier 1959 à décembre 1960"; "Attribution de secours par le Secrétariat général pour les affaires algériennes," 7 July 1959 (CAC 770391/4). Both refer to victims of terrorism; the quote comes from SAMAS.

188. For examples, see the Labor Ministry archives labeled "Action en faveur des Français musulmans et des Algériens 1955–1968" (CAC 770391/4). State agencies attempted to provide jobs for fleeing *pieds noirs*. For an excellent study of the repatriated French, see Scioldo-Zürcher, *Devenir métropolitain*, esp. 123–29.

189. The CANAM had a tradition of giving out small sums of emergency aid, which helped to monitor recipients. The CANAM received money from the Algerian Affairs administration in Algiers for this purpose. Since 1956, the CANAM and the CTAM helped former colonists in "desperate situations." Before then, Algerian Affairs had not set aside money for colonists moving to the metropole because it claimed it was doing everything pos-

sible to allow them to stay in Algeria. Beginning in 1959, Algerian Affairs directed CANAM to divide the 6 million OF it received for this purpose evenly between "French Europeans" and "French Muslims." See "Attribution de secours par le Secrétariat général pour les affaires algériennes"; "Note," June 1959 (CAC 770391/4); Massenet's files in CAC 770391/9.

190. FAS, minutes, 9 November 1961.

191. Brandell, *Les rapports franco-algériens*, 24; Fouad Soufi, "Ils sont parties! Oran 1962, le grand départ des Européens," 81–86, and Jean-Louis Planche, "Français d'Algérie, Français en Algérie," 98–104, both in Gallissot, ed., *Les accords d'Evian*.

192. Some harkis escaped from the camps. In some cases departmental governments (usually in southern France, where officials settled most harkis) and the National Committee for French Muslims offered subsidies to ensure a certain number of dwellings be set aside for harkis. This committee also urged the SONACOTRAL and its HLMs to build more housing for harki families. The project allocated funds to a few families planning to renovate their homes. Others received supplemental monthly checks of 1,875 francs per principal room to help them pay rent. Yet this solution rarely proved sufficient and many more families lived for years in temporary dwellings described as "rustic." Comité national pour les musulmans français, "Aide au logement des réfugiés musulmans," 24 September 1963 (CAC 770391/8).

193. Exactly how many harkis fled Algeria is still unknown. The best estimates indicate that between 62,000 and 87,000 men arrived in France through official or unofficial means between 1962 and 1967. This translated into about 300,000 people if one includes all family members. Muller, *Le silence des harkis*, 14–15; Jordi and Hamoumou, *Les harkis*, 48–49; Khellil, "L'instillation des rapatriés d'Algérie en France," 144; Ageron, "Le 'Drame des harkis,'" 5.

194. Khellil, "L'instillation des rapatriés d'Algérie en France," 145–48; Muller, *Le silence des harkis*, 14–15. The camps (and the schools) remained in operation into the 1970s. One of the camps, Saint-Maurice-l'Ardoise, finally removed its barbed wire after residents revolted in 1977. For a moving personal account of the harki experience by a Franco-Algerian journalist, see Kerchouche, *Mon père, ce harki*. On the harki experience in France after Algerian independence, see Miller, "Algerian, French, Refugees, Repatriates, Immigrants?"

195. Scioldo-Zürcher, *Devenir métropolitain*, 161–209.

196. The Labor Ministry kept track of requests, which increased sharply in 1961. Applicants generally requested help finding or furnishing apartments, covering expenses, or bringing their families to France. Individuals contacted Villey, Massenet, or the CANAM directly and explained their predicament. Most called themselves refugees. The majority appeared to be of European origin, but some described themselves as "assimilated" Algerians who fled with few belongings. The latter often explained they feared for their lives and needed help getting settled. Generally, officials helped them find housing or allocated between several hundred and a thousand francs for other necessities. See Labor Ministry archives labeled "Action en faveur des Français musulmans et des Algériens 1955–1968," and Massenet's files in CAC 770391/9.

197. SONACOTRAL, "Rapport du Conseil d'administration à l'Assemblée générale annuelle des actionnaires sur la gestion et les comptes de l'exercice 1962," 10 (CAC 870056/16).

198. Blanc-Chaléard, "Quotas of Foreigners in Social Housing."

199. Scioldo-Zürcher, *Devenir métropolitain*, 161–209, 211–47.

200. A. Martin, director of LOGIREM to the FAS director, 1964 (CAC 760140/3).

201. Michel, *The Modernization of North African Families*, 23.

202. SONACOTRAL, "Note justifiant la création d'un Centre sociale à Nanterre 'Canibouts,'" February 1962.

203. FAS, supplement 9 July 1965 meeting, "SONACOTRA: Opération de Nanterre-Canibouts," 9 July 1965 (CAC 760140/4). The 12 percent (the vast majority of whom were Algerian) included the projected inclusion of thirty families that would move in when the final sections of the complex opened.

204. Centre social des Canibouts, "Rapport d'activités pour l'année 1964," 1965 (CAC 760140/4).

205. Ibid.

206. FAS, minutes, 19 April 1963, annex 2 (CAC 760140/3). The FAS reiterated this in 1964; see FAS, "Projet de réalisations sociales au profit des migrants algériens travaillant en France: Exposé des motifs," 1964 (CAC 760140/6).

207. FAS, "Projet de réalisations sociales au profit des migrants algériens travaillant en France."

208. FAS, minutes, 27 February 1964 (CAC 760140/3). Funding for male housing remained steady at 4.5 million and job-training programs were cut only one million francs. Despite recognizing that the bidonville problem remained unsolved, the majority of FAS board members conceded that in the new political climate the programs could no longer be justified. Some board members greeted Massenet's proposal to reevaluate the decision in favor of Algerian family needs with a measure of hostility. They insisted that available funds should be reserved for "repatriated French citizens." In the end, the board compromised, reinstating some funding for transitional and permanent housing to help Algerians escape the bidonvilles and directing other funds toward relocation programs for former colonists. FAS, "Procès-verbal de la réunion du Conseil d'administration des 8 et 9 juillet 1964" (CAC 760140/3).

209. Blanc-Chaléard, "Les immigrés et le logement en France," 20–34.

210. Miller, *The Representation of Place*, 49. On the term's use in the colonial setting, see Çelik, *Urban Forms and Colonial Confrontations*, 173.

211. SSFNA, "Rapport moral, 1968–69," annex 4: 1–3.

212. Ibid., 1966–67, 16.

213. Jacques Augarde, "La migration algérienne," *Hommes et Migrations, études* 116 (1970): 83, 106–7.

214. SLPM, "Rapport annuel de synthèse concernant la migration étrangère," 49, 1968 (AN F1a 5015).

215. See, among others, Michel, *The Modernization of North African Families*; Zehraoui, *Les travailleurs algériens*; Tchibindat, *Le logement des Algériens*.

216. SONACOTRA, "Rapport d'activité de l'année 1973" (CAC 870056/12).

217. J. Corréard, Centres de transit familiaux (CETRAFA) to Michel Massenet, 4 April 1966 (CAC 770391/6).

Conclusion

1. Terrio, *Judging Mohammed*, 10. For a critical assessment of reactions to the unrest, see Murphy, "Baguettes, Berets and Burning Cars."

2. Ben Jelloun, *French Hospitality*, 81. The FAS became le Fonds de soutien pour l'intégration et la lutte contre les discriminations (FASILD) in 2001.

3. Bertrand Bissuel, Michel Belberghe, and Béatrice Jérome, "La réduction des aides exaspère les maires de banlieue," *Le Monde*, 5 November 2005.

4. The FASILD became l'Agence nationale pour la cohésion sociale et l'égalité des chances (L'Acsé) as part of the Equal Opportunity law, "Loi no. 2006-396 du 31 mars 2006 pour l'égalité des chances," *JO*, 2 April 2006. For more on L'Acsé, see www.lacse.fr (accessed 28 August 2012).

5. Escafré-Dublet, "Etat, culture, immigration," 283–300.

6. Scott, *The Politics of the Veil*, 11 and 118.

7. Fassin, "Compassion and Repression." While Fassin examines immigration policy, his argument is inextricably linked to social services for immigrants and other minority communities.

8. It allocated nearly a third of its resources to housing male workers, nearly twenty-eight percent to family housing, and the rest to the same job training, educational, and social programs that have been the examined in this book. FAS, DPM, "Dix ans au service des étrangers et des migrants" (Ministère du Travail, de l'Emploi et de la Population, 1968).

9. Marshall, *Social Policy in the Twentieth Century*.

10. Stora, *Ils venaient d'Algérie*, 226.

11. A state ordinance issued in 1962 and a follow-up law in 1966 required Algerian migrants to claim their intention to remain in France in order to keep their papers.

12. FAS, minutes, 21 December 1962, 2–3 (CAC 760140/2). Not long after these cuts, de Gaulle publicly recommitted France to aiding Algeria as part of the shift from colonialism to the neocolonial development agenda. For de Gaulle and many French administrators steeped in the colonial tradition, France could never relinquish its moral and humanitarian mission. From the end of the war until 1969, the administration dedicated roughly twenty-two percent of annual funds for so-called third world countries to Algeria. Ageron, *La décolonisation française*, 159–60.

13. ESNA, "Faut-ils supprimer le Fonds d'action sociale?," in "Le Fonds d'action sociale," *CNA* 95 (April–May 1963): 35–39.

14. Massenet, "La migration algérienne et l'administration française," 1962 (CAC 770391/9). Parts of this text also appear in the first annex of the FAS meeting of 19 April 1963 (CAC 760140/3).

15. Ibid.

16. ESNA, "Faut-ils supprimer le Fonds d'action sociale?," 35–37.

17. The prime minister's decision formalized the suspension of services already in place in Algeria but left the metropolitan budget untouched. Georges Pompidou, to his Algerian Affairs minister, 16 February 1963 (CAC 760140/6). See also, Viet, *La France immigrée*, 221–26.

18. In 1962, FAS spent over 10 million francs on family housing, 2.5 million on hous-

ing for men, over 700,000 on foyers for youths, 5 million on educational and professional training, and 1.7 million on diverse programs of social assistance and promotion for families. ESNA, "Le Fonds d'action social en 1962," in "Le Fonds d'action sociale," 29.

19. FAS, minutes, 19 April 1963, 3 (CAC 760140/3).

20. Bernard Lory to Michel Massenet, "Le programme du FAS pour 1963," 6 March 1963 (CAC 760140/6). Some of the social centers are still open. For example, the city of Nanterre supports the center in Canibouts. It provides a day care center, programs for school-age children, "parenting support, socialization and literacy workshops," hotlines for legal services, employment assistance, and "leisure and cultural activities." www.nanterre.fr /Citoyens/Associations/Annuaire/14.htm (accessed 31 August 2012).

21. Jacques Aubert, director of the cabinet of the MI, Direction des affaires politiques et de l'administration du territoire, Services des affaires musulmanes, "Migration musulmane—rapport trimestriel," 28 December 1962 (ADBR M14 5852).

22. Laurens, *Une politisation feutrée*, 67–98.

23. Grandval, *Ma mission au Maroc*.

24. Viet, *La France immigrée*, 222.

25. "Décret du 27 juillet 1963 portant approbation de modifications aux statuts de la Société nationale de construction de logements pour les travailleurs originaires d'Algérie," *JO*, 30 July 1963, 7004.

26. "Décret no. 64.356 du 24 avril 1964 relatif à l'organisation de l'action sociale en faveur des travailleurs étrangers," *JO*, 25 April 1962, 3667. The title was changed from Fonds d'action sociale pour les travailleurs algériens et leurs familles to Fonds d'action sociale pour les travailleurs étrangers et leurs familles. On this transition, see Escafré-Dublet, "Etat, culture, immigration," 87–89.

27. SAMAS, "Etudes de coût et de rendement des services," 18 February 1964 (AN F1a 5010).

28. Jean Perrier, prefect of the Bouches-du-Rhône, "Substitution au services des affaires musulmanes d'un service de liaison et de promotion des migrants," 23 September 1965 (ADBR, Fonds Payan 22 J 9); Laurens, *Une politisation feutrée*, 85.

29. On *Hommes et Migrations*, see an article by the editor-in-chief, Marie Poinsot, at www.hommes-et-migrations.fr/index.php?id=5276 (accessed 19 September 2012).

30. See correspondence from ADAFARELI to FAS, SAMAS (later Service de liaison et de promotion des migrants, SLPM) and the prefect of the Nord (AN F1a 5064).

31. "Décret no. 64.356 du 24 avril 1964," *JO*, 25 April 1962.

32. Viet, *La France immigrée*, 223–24.

33. Tapinos, *L'immigration étrangère en France*, 69–71; Viet, *La France immigrée*, 254; Spire, *Etrangers à la carte*, 238–39; Laurens, *Un politisation feutrée*, 135–63.

34. Escafré-Dublet, "Etat, culture, immigration," 95–101.

35. "Relevé de décisions de la réunion interministériel du jeudi 2 avril 1964 au sujet de l'entrée des travailleurs algériens en France," 2 April 1964 (AN F 1a 5010); Tapinos, *L'immigration étrangère*, 63; Gillette and Sayad, *L'immigration algérienne*, 92–93.

36. Jacques Aubert, "Enquête sur les conditions de vie de la main d'œuvre étrangère en France," June 1965 (CAC 770391/5); FAS, Etudes et contrôles, "Enquête auprès des préfets

sur les conditions de vie et les besoins sociaux des travailleurs étrangers et de leurs familles," October 1965 (CAC 770391/5).

37. "Le FAS et l'action educative en faveur des travailleurs migrants," 8 December 1964 (CAC 760140/3); ESNA, "Le Fonds d'action sociale," 36.

38. SAMAS, Groupe d'étude chargé d'examiner le régime juridique applicable aux Algériens en France, response to a circular of the prime minister dated 13 February 1963, no. 2069, 24 October 1963 (AN F1a 5045).

39. On the numbers of births, see Gillette and Sayad, *L'immigration algérienne*, 87.

40. Aubert, "Enquête sur les conditions de vie de la main d'œuvre étrangère en France."

41. SSFNA, "Rapport annuel," 1966–1967, 6.

42. "Le sort des travailleurs étrangers en France," *Le Républicain-Lorraine*, 26 October 1965.

43. "Concernant le calcul de développement de la population algérienne en France," June 1967 (CAC 760135/2); Interministerial Committee, "Problèmes de l'immigration: Statut des immigrants contrôle de l'immigration familiale," 10 February 1970 (CAC 760133/1). The projections were not inaccurate. By the 1990s, the Algerian population in France reached about 1.5 million. Silverstein, *Algeria in France*, 4.

44. Michel Massenet, "Réouverture des négociations de main d'œuvre avec l'Algérie," July 1967 (CAC 760135/2).

45. SAMAS, Groupe d'étude chargé d'examiner le régime juridique applicable aux Algériens en France, 24 October 1963.

46. SSFNA, "Rapport annuel," 1962 and 1966–1967, 19.

47. SLPM, "Rapport annuel de synthèse concernant la migration étrangère," 1968 (AN F1a 5015). In 1967 its 100 beds had 1,037 visits, 148 of them foreigners. The three largest groups: Algerians (49), Italians (12), and Spaniards (13).

48. SSFNA, "Rapport annuel," 1966–1967, 19.

49. "Emigrés algériens et autres émigrés," *Hommes et Migrations*, no. 653 (30 June 1966): 1–3.

50. SSFNA, "Rapport annuel," 1966–1967, 4–7. The SSFNA provides a rare vantage point because it continued to work with and keep track of Algerian families into the 1970s. Not only did it keep its original name (until 1979), but Algerians remained its primary clients into the early 1970s: 90.5 percent in 1971, 88.2 percent in 1972, and 84.4 percent in 1973. The rest were Moroccans and Tunisians.

51. SSFNA, "Rapport annuel," 1963–1964, 2–5.

52. Ibid., 1971–1972, 69.

53. Ibid., 1966–1967, 32.

54. To end bigamy, SSFNA helped women make their marriages legal according to French civil code, barring others from claiming that status. Ibid., 1966–1967 and 1970–1971.

55. Ibid., 1971–1972, 5, 33; 73–74.

56. Ibid., 1966–1967, 4.

57. Ibid., 1968–1969, annex 2: 1.

58. Scott, *The Politics of the Veil*, 27–33.

Bibliography

Archival Series

ADBR: Archives départementales des Bouches-du-Rhône, Marseille
 Fonds Payan; M 14; 137 W; 138 W; 146 W
ADHS: Archives départementales des Hauts-de-Seine, Nanterre
 1249 W
AMH: Archives Monique Hervo, Institut d'histoire du temps présent, Paris
AN: Archives nationales, Paris
 Series F1a
Archive Laroque, Archives nationales, consulted at the Ministère de l'Emploi et de la
 Solidarité, Paris
 ENTEX 89/001
CAC: Archives nationales, Centre d'archives contemporaines, Fontainebleau
 19760133; 19760135; 19760140; 19770391; 19850021; 19860271; 19860269; 19870056;
 19880084; 19930417; 19940250; 19960405
CIEMI: Centre d'informations et d'études sur les migrations internationales, Paris
INED: Institut national d'études démographiques, Paris
SSFNA: Service social familial nord-africain; held by Association service social familial
 migrants (ASSFAM), Paris

Publications

Abi-Mershed, Osama. *Apostles of Modernity: Saint-Simonians and the Civilizing Mission in
 Algeria*. Stanford, CA: Stanford University Press, 2010.
Abu-Lughod, Janet. *Rabat: Urban Apartheid in Morocco*. Princeton, NJ: Princeton University Press, 1980.
Accampo, Elinor, Rachel Fuchs, and Mary Lynn Stewart, eds. *Gender and the Politics of
 Social Reform in France, 1870–1914*. Baltimore: Johns Hopkins University Press, 1995.

Adas, Michael. *Machines as the Measure of Men: Science, Technology, and Ideologies of Western Dominance*. Ithaca, NY: Cornell University Press, 1989.

Ageron, Charles-Robert. *Histoire de l'Algérie contemporaine*. 2 vols. Paris: Presses Universitaires de France, 1979.

————. "Jules Ferry et colonisation." In *Jules Ferry fondateur de la république*, edited by François Furet. Paris: Editions de l'école des hautes études en sciences sociales, 1985.

————. *La décolonisation française*. Paris: Armand Colin, 1991.

————. "Le 'Drame des harkis': Mémoire ou histoire?." *Vingtième Siècle. Revue d'histoire*, no. 68 (October–December 2000): 3–16.

————. "L'opinion française devant la guerre d'Algérie." *Revue française d'histoire d'outre-mer* 63, no. 231 (1976): 256–85.

————. *Les Algériens musulmans et la France (1871–1919)*. 2 vols. Paris: Presses Universitaires de France, 1968.

————. *Modern Algeria: A History from 1830 to the Present*. Translated by Michael Brett. London: Hurst, 1991.

Alloula, Malek. *The Colonial Harem*. Translated by Myrna Godzich and Wlad Godzich. Minneapolis: University of Minnesota Press, 1986.

Ambassade de France. *The Constantine Plan for Algeria: Opening New Frontiers in Development*. New York: Service de Presse et d'Information, May 1961.

Ambler, John. *The French Army in Politics, 1945–1962*. Columbus: Ohio University Press, 1966.

————, ed. *The French Welfare State: Surviving Social and Ideological Change*. New York: New York University Press, 1991.

Amrane-Minne, Danièle Djamila. *Des femmes dans la guerre d'Algérie*. Paris: Editions Karthala, 1994.

Andrew, C. M., and A. S. Kanya-Forstner. "France, Africa, and the First World War." *Journal of African History* 19, no. 1 (1978): 11–23.

Auslander, Leora. *Taste and Power: Furnishing Modern France*. Berkeley: University of California Press, 1998.

Balibar, Etienne. *Les frontières de la démocratie*. Paris: La Découverte, 1992.

————. *Masses, Classes, Ideas*. New York: Routledge, 1994.

Barrière, Louis-Augustin. *Le statut personnel des musulmans d'Algérie de 1834 à 1962*. Dijon: Editions Universitaires de Dijon, 1993.

Beale, Marjorie. *The Modernist Enterprise: French Elites and the Threat of Modernity, 1900–1940*. Stanford, CA: Stanford University Press, 1999.

Ben Jelloun, Tahar. *French Hospitality: Racism and North African Immigrants*. Translated by Barbara Bray. New York: Columbia University Press, 1999.

Benaïcha, Brahim. *Vivre au paradis: D'une oasis à un bidonville*. Paris: Desclée de Brouwer, 1992.

Benguigui, Yamina. *Mémoires d'immigrés: L'héritage maghrébin*. Paris: Canal+ Editions, 1997.

Berenson, Edward. *Heroes of Empire: Five Charismatic Men and the Conquest of Africa*. Berkeley: University of California Press, 2010.

Bernardot, Marc. *Camps d'étrangers*. Bellecombe-en-Bauges: Editions du Croquant, 2008.

———. "Un politique de logement: La SONACOTRA, 1956–1992." Thèse de doctorat, Université de Paris I, 1997.

Bernstein, Serge. *The Republic of de Gaulle, 1958–1969*. Translated by Peter Morris. New York: Cambridge University Press, 1993.

Betts, Raymond. *Assimilation and Association in French Colonial Theory, 1890–1914*. 1961. Reprint, Lincoln: University of Nebraska Press, 2005.

———. *France and Decolonization, 1900–1960*. London: Macmillan, 1991.

Birnbaum, Pierre. *Jewish Destinies: Citizenship, State, and Community in Modern France*. New York: Hill and Wang, 2000.

Blanc-Chaléard, Marie-Claude. "Les immigrés et le logement en France depuis le XIXe siècle." *Hommes et Migrations*, no. 1264 (2006): 20–34.

———. "Les trente glorieuses: Le temps des bidonvilles." *Cahiers de l'Institut CGT d'histoire sociale*, no. 103 (2007): 19–22.

———. "Quotas of Foreigners in Social Housing: A Legacy of the Algerian War? Les Canibouts, Nanterre (1959–1968)." *Metropolitics*, 11 April 2012, www.metropolitiques .eu/Quotas-of-foreigners-in-social.html.

Blanchard, Emmanuel. "Encadre des 'citoyens diminués': La police des Algériens en région parisienne (1944–1962)." Thèse de doctorat, Université de Dijon, 2008.

———. "La dissolution des brigades nord-africaines de la préfecture de police: La fin d'une police d'exception pour les Algériens de Paris (1944–1953)?." *Bulletin de l'Institut d'histoire du temps présent*, no. 83 (2004): 70–82.

———. *La police parisienne et les Algériens (1944–1962)*. Paris: Nouveau monde éditions, 2011.

———. "Police judiciaire et pratiques d'exception pendant la guerre d'Algérie." *Vingtième Siècle. Revue d'histoire*, no. 90 (April–June 2006): 61–72.

Blanchard, Pascal, and Sandrine Lemaire, eds. *Culture coloniale: La France conquise par son empire, 1871–1931*. Paris: Autrement, 2003.

———, eds. *Culture impériale, 1932–1961: Les colonies au cœur de la république*. Paris: Autrement, 2004.

Bleich, Erik. "The French Model: Color Blind Integration." In *Color Lines: Affirmative Action, Immigration, and Civil Rights Options for America*, edited by John David Skrentny, 270–96. Chicago: University of Chicago Press, 2001.

———. *Race Politics in Britain and France: Ideas and Policymaking since the 1960s*. New York: Cambridge University Press, 2003.

Blévis, Laure. "Droit colonial algérien de la citoyenneté: Conciliation illusoire entre des principes républicains et une logique d'occupation coloniale (1865–1947)." In *La guerre d'Algérie au miroir des décolonisations françaises: Actes du colloque en l'honneur de Charles-Robert Ageron, Sorbonne, novembre 2000*, 87–103. Paris: Société française d'Histoire d'Outre-mer, 2000.

———. "Les avatars de la citoyenneté en Algérie coloniale ou les paradoxes d'une catégorisation." *Droit et Société*, no. 48 (2001): 557–80.

———. "Sociologie d'un droit colonial. Citoyenneté et nationalité en Algérie (1865–

1947), une exception républicaine?." Thèse de doctorat, Institut d'Etudes Politiques, Aix-en-Provence, 2004.

Boittin, Jennifer Anne. *Colonial Metropolis: Urban Grounds of Anti-Imperialism and Feminism in Interwar Paris*. Lincoln: University of Nebraska Press, 2010.

Boltanski, Luc. *The Making of a Class: Cadres in French Society*. Translated by Arthur Goldhammer. New York: Cambridge University Press, 1987.

Bourdieu, Pierre, and Abdelmalek Sayad. *Le déracinement: La crise de l'agriculture traditionnelle en Algérie*. Paris: Editions de Minuit, 1964.

Branche, Raphaëlle. *La torture et l'armée pendant la guerre d'Algérie: 1954–1962*. Paris: Gallimard, 2001.

Brandell, Inga. *Les rapports franco-algériens depuis 1962 du pétrole et des hommes*. Paris: L'Harmattan, 1981.

Brooke, Michael. *Le Play: Engineer and Social Scientist*. New Brunswick, NJ: Longman Group, 1970.

Brower, Benjamin. *A Desert Named Peace: The Violence of France's Empire in the Algerian Sahara, 1844–1902*. New York: Columbia University Press, 2009.

Brubaker, Rogers. *Citizenship and Nationhood in France and Germany*. Cambridge, MA: Harvard University Press, 1992.

Brunet, Jean-Paul. *Police contre FLN: Le drame d'octobre 1961*. Paris: Flammarion, 1999.

Burke, Edmund III. "Theorizing the Histories of Colonialism and Nationalism in the Arab Maghrib." In *Beyond Colonialism and Nationalism in the Maghrib: History, Culture, and Politics*, edited by Ali Ahmida, 17–34. New York: Palgrave Macmillan, 2000.

Butler, Remy, and Patrice Noisette. *Le logement social en France, 1815–1981*. Paris: Editions la Découverte/Maspero, 1983.

Byrnes, Melissa. "French Like Us? Municipal Policies and North African Migrants in the Parisian Banlieues, 1945–1975." PhD diss., Georgetown University, 2008.

Cambon, Jules. *Le Gouvernement général d'Algérie*. Paris and Algiers: E. Champion, 1918.

Camiscioli, Elisa. *Reproducing the French Race: Immigration, Intimacy, and Embodiment in the Early Twentieth Century*. Durham, NC: Duke University Press, 2009.

Carson, John. *The Measure of Merit: Talent, Intelligence, and Inequality in the French and American Republics, 1750–1940*. Princeton, NJ: Princeton University Press, 2007.

Çelik, Zeynep. *Urban Forms and Colonial Confrontations: Algiers under French Rule*. Berkeley: University of California Press, 1997.

Chapman, Herrick, and Laura Frader, eds. *Race in France: Interdisciplinary Perspectives on the Politics of Difference*. New York: Berghahn Books, 2004.

Chevalier, Louis. *Laboring Classes and Dangerous Classes in Paris during the First Half of the Nineteenth Century*. Translated by Frank Jellinek. New York: Howard Fertig, 2000.

———, ed. *Le problème démographique nord-africain*. Cahiers d'INED, no. 6. Paris: Presses Universitaires de France, 1947.

Clancy-Smith, Julia. "La Femme Arabe: Women and Sexuality in France's North African Empire." In *Women, the Family, and Divorce Laws in Islamic History*, edited by Amira El Azhary Sonbol, 52–64. Syracuse: Syracuse University Press, 1996.

Clancy-Smith, Julia, and Frances Gouda, eds. *Domesticating the Empire: Race, Gender, and Family Life in French and Dutch Colonialism*. Charlottesville: University of Virginia Press, 1998.

Clarke, Jackie. *France in the Age of Organization: Factory, Home, and Nation from the 1920s to Vichy*. New York: Berghahn Books, 2011.

Cohen, William B. *The French Encounter with Africans: White Response to Blacks, 1530–1880*. Bloomington: Indiana University Press, 2003.

Cole, Joshua. *The Power of Large Numbers: Population, Politics and Gender in Nineteenth-Century France*. Ithaca, NY: Cornell University Press, 2000.

———. "Remembering the Battle of Paris: 17 October 1961 in French and Algerian Memory." *French Politics, Culture and Society* 3, no. 21 (2003): 21–50.

Collot, Claude. *Les institutions de l'Algérie durant la période coloniale (1830–1962)*. Paris: Centre national de la recherche scientifique, 1987.

Conklin, Alice L. *A Mission to Civilize: The Republican Idea of Empire in France and West Africa, 1895–1930*. Stanford, CA: Stanford University Press, 1997.

Connelly, Matthew. *A Diplomatic Revolution: Algeria's Fight for Independence and the Origins of the Post–Cold War Era*. New York: Oxford University Press, 2002.

Cooper, Frederick. *Colonialism in Question: Theory, Knowledge, History*. Berkeley: University of California Press, 2005.

———. *Decolonization and African Society: The Labor Question in French and British Africa*. New York: Cambridge University Press, 1996.

Cooper, Frederick, and Ann Laura Stoler, eds. *Tensions of Empire: Colonial Cultures in a Bourgeois World*. Berkeley: University of California Press, 1997.

Cornaton, Michael. *Les camps de regroupement de la guerre d'Algérie*. 1967. Reprint, Paris: L'Harmattan, 1998.

Costa-Lascoux, Jacqueline, and Emile Témime, eds. *Les Algériens en France: Genèse et devenir d'une migration*. Paris: Publisud, 1985.

Curtis, Sarah. *Civilizing Habits: Women Missionaries and the Revival of French Empire*. New York: Oxford University Press, 2010.

Daughton, J. P. *An Empire Divided: Religion, Republicanism, and the Making of French Colonialism, 1880–1914*. New York: Oxford University Press, 2006.

Davin, Anna. "Imperialism and Motherhood." *History Workshop Journal*, no. 5 (1978): 9–65.

de Barros, Françoise. "Contours d'un réseau administratif 'algérien' en construction d'une compétence en 'affaires musulmanes': Les conseillers techniques pour les affaires musulmanes en métropole, 1952–1965." *Politix* 19, no. 76 (2006): 97–117.

———. "L'Etat au prisme des municipalités: Une comparaison historique des catégorisations des étrangers en France (1919–1984)." Thèse de doctorat, Paris I–Panthéon–Sorbonne, 2004.

———. "Les municipalités face aux Algériens: Méconnaissances et usages des catégories en métropole avant et après la seconde guerre mondiale." *Genèses* 53 (December 2003): 69–92.

de Rudder, Véronique, Christian Poiret, and François Vourc'h. *L'inégalité raciste: L'universalité républicaine à l'épreuve*. Paris: Presses Universitaires de France, 2000.

Delarue, Jacques. *L'OAS contre de Gaulle*. Paris: Fayard, 1994.

Delarue, Jacques, and Odile Rudelle. *L'attentat du Petit-Clamart: Vers la révision de la constitution.* Paris: La documentation française, 1990.

Délégation générale du gouvernement en Algérie. *Plan de Constantine 1959–1963, rapport général.* Algiers: L'Imprimerie officielle, June 1960.

Derder, Peggy. *L'immigration algérienne et les pouvoirs publics dans le Département de la Seine, 1954–1962.* Paris: L'Harmattan, 2001.

Despois, Jean. *L'Afrique blanche française: L'Afrique du Nord.* Paris: Presses Universitaires de France, 1949.

Dewerpe, Alain. *Charonne, 8 février 1962: Anthropologie historique d'un massacre d'état.* Paris: Gallimard, 2006.

Dewitte, Philippe, ed. *Immigration et intégration: L'Etat des savoirs.* Paris: La Découverte, 1999.

Direction générale de l'éducation nationale en Algérie. *Le Service des centres sociaux en Algérie.* Algiers, n.d. (1959?).

Discours et opinions de Jules Ferry. Edited by Paul Robiquet. Paris: A. Colin, 1897.

Donzelot, Jacques. *The Policing of Families.* Translated by Robert Hurley. New York: Pantheon, 1979.

Dore-Audibert, Andrée. *Des Françaises d'Algérie dans la guerre de libération: Des oubliées de l'histoire.* Paris: Karthala, 1995.

Downs, Laura Lee. *Manufacturing Inequalities: Gender Division in the French and British Metalworking Industries, 1914–1939.* Ithaca, NY: Cornell University Press, 1995.

Duchen, Claire. *Women's Rights and Women's Lives in France, 1944–1968.* New York: Routledge, 1994.

Duclaud-Williams, Roger. *The Politics of Housing in Britain and France.* London: Heinemann, 1978.

Dutton, Paul. *Origins of the French Welfare State: The Struggle for Social Reform in France, 1914–1917.* New York: Cambridge University Press, 2002.

Einaudi, Jean-Luc. *La bataille de Paris: 17 octobre 1961.* Paris: Seuil, 1991.

———. *Octobre 1961: Un massacre à Paris.* Paris: Fayard, 2001.

Elsenhans, Hartmut. *La guerre d'Algérie 1954–1962: La transition d'une France à une autre, le passage de la IVe à la Ve république.* 1974. Reprint, Paris: Publisud, 1999.

Escafré-Dublet, Angéline. "Etat, culture, immigration: La dimension culturelle des politiques françaises d'immigration, 1958–1991." Thèse de doctorat, Institut d'études politiques de Paris, 2008.

Faivre, Maurice. *L'action social de l'armée en faveur des musulmans, 1830–2006.* Paris: L'Harmattan, 2007.

Fanon, Frantz. *A Dying Colonialism.* New York: Grove Press, 1965.

———. *The Wretched of the Earth.* Translated by Richard Philcox. 1963. Reprint, New York: Grove Press, 2004.

Fassin, Didier. "Compassion and Repression: The Moral Economy of Immigration Policies in France." *Cultural Anthropology* 20, no. 3 (2005): 362–87.

Fassin, Didier, and Eric Fassin. *De la question sociale à la question raciale: Représenter la société française.* Paris: La Découverte, 2006.

Favell, Adrian. *Philosophies of Integration Immigration and the Idea of Citizenship in France and Britain.* New York: Palgrave, 1998.

Feldblum, Miriam. *Reconstructing Citizenship: The Politics of Nationality Reform and Immigration in Contemporary France.* Albany: State University of New York Press, 1999.

Feraoun, Mouloud. *Journal, 1955–1962: Reflections on the French-Algerian War.* Lincoln: University of Nebraska Press, 2000.

Ferro, Marc. *Histoire des colonisations, des conquêtes aux indépendances (XIIIe–XXe siècle).* Paris: Seuil, 1994.

———, ed. *Le 13 mai 1958.* Paris: Documentation française, 1985.

Flamand, Jean-Paul. *Loger le people: Essai sur l'histoire du logement social en France.* Paris: Editions de la Découverte, 1989.

Fleury, Georges. *Tuez de Gaulle! Histoire de l'attentat du Petit-Clamart.* Paris: Grasset, 1996.

Fogarty, Richard. *Race and War in France: Colonial Subjects in the French Army, 1914–1918.* Baltimore: Johns Hopkins University Press, 2008.

Forget, Nelly. "Le service des centres sociaux en Algérie." *Matériaux pour l'histoire de notre temps,* no. 26 (1992): 37–47.

Fortier, Bénédicte. "L'indigène algérien: Du sujet au citoyen, 1944–1947." In "Juger en Algérie 1944–1962," 53–61. *Le genre humain* 32. Paris: Seuil, 1997.

Foucault, Michel. *The History of Sexuality.* 3 vols. New York: Vintage Books, 1990.

Fourastié, Jean. *Les trente glorieuses ou la révolution invisible de 1946 à 1975.* Paris: Fayard, 1979.

Fourcaut, Annie. "Les premiers grands ensembles en région parisienne: Ne pas refaire la banlieue?." *French Historical Studies* 27, no. 1 (2004): 195–218.

Fourcaut, Annie, Emmanuel Bellanger, and Mathieu Flonneau. *Paris-banlieues, conflits et solidarités: Historiographie, anthologie, chronologie, 1788–2006.* Paris: Créaphis Editions, 2007.

Frader, Laura Levine. *Breadwinners and Citizens: Gender in the Making of the French Social Model.* Durham, NC: Duke University Press, 2008.

Freedman, Jane. *Immigration and Insecurity in France.* Burlington, VT: Ashgate, 2004.

Fuchs, Rachel. *Contested Paternity: Constructing Families in Modern France.* Baltimore: Johns Hopkins University Press, 2008.

———. *Poor and Pregnant in Paris: Strategies for Survival in the Nineteenth Century.* New Brunswick, NJ: Rutgers University Press, 1992.

Fysh, Peter, and Jim Wolfreys. *The Politics of Racism in France.* New York: Palgrave Macmillan, 2003.

Gallissot, René, ed. *Les accords d'Evian: En conjoncture et en longue durée.* Paris: Institut Maghreb-Europe, 1997.

———. *Misère de l'antiracisme.* Paris: Editions Arcantère, 1985.

Ganiage, Jean. *Histoire contemporaine du Maghreb.* Paris: Fayard, 1994.

Ghorra-Gobin, Cynthia Marie-Françoise. "Implementation as a Social Learning Process: The Case of a French Housing Policy." PhD diss., University of California, Los Angeles, 1994.

Gillette, Alain, and Abdelmalek Sayad. *L'immigration algérienne en France*. 1976. Reprint, Paris: Editions Entente, 1984.

Ginesy-Galano, Mireille. *Les immigrés hors la cité: Le système d'encadrement dans les foyers, 1973–1982*. Paris: L'Harmattan, 1984.

Girard, Alain, and Joseph Leriche. "Les Algériens en France: Etude démographique et sociale." *Population* 10, no. 1 (1955): 159–66.

———, eds. *Les Algériens en France: Etude démographique et sociale, ouvrage réalisé en collaboration avec les "Etudes sociales nord-africains."* Cahiers d'INED, no. 24. Paris: Presses Universitaires de France, 1955.

Girard, Alain, and Jean Stoetzel, eds. *Français et immigrés: L'adaptation des Italiens et des Polonais. L'attitude française*. Cahiers d'INED, no. 19. Paris: Presse Universitaire de France, 1953.

———, eds. *Français et immigrés: Nouveaux documents sur l'adaptation: Algériens, Italiens, Polonais; le service social d'aide aux immigrants*. Cahiers d'INED, no. 20. Paris: Presse Universitaire de France, 1954.

Godin, André-Jean. *L'Afrique du Nord: Dernière chance de la France*. Exposé sur la politique du gouvernement en Afrique du Nord, présenté au Congrès de l'action républicaine et sociale, 1954. Paris: Corbière et Jugain Alençon, 1955.

Golsan, Richard J., ed. *The Papon Affair: Memory and Justice on Trial*. New York: Routledge, 2000.

Grandval, Gilbert. *Ma mission au Maroc*. Paris: Plon, 1956.

Green, Nancy. *The Pletzl of Paris: Jewish Immigrant Workers in the "Belle Époque."* New York: Holmes and Meier, 1986.

———. *Repenser les migrations*. Paris: Presses Universitaires de France, 2002.

Gros, Dominique. "Sujets et citoyens en Algérie avant l'ordonnance du 7 mars 1944." In "Juger en Algérie 1944–1962," 39–52. *Le genre humain* 32. Paris: Seuil, 1997.

Guerrand, Roger-Henri, and Christian Thibault, eds. *Cent ans d'habitat social: Une utopie réaliste*. Paris: Albin Michel, 1989.

Hargreaves, Alec. *Immigration, "Race" and Ethnicity in Contemporary France*. London: Routledge, 1995.

Haroun, Ali. *La 7è wilaya: La guerre du FLN en France, 1954–1962*. Paris: Seuil, 1986.

———, ed. *L'été de la discorde Algérie 1962*. Algiers: Casbah Editions, 2001.

Harrison, Alexander. *Challenging de Gaulle: The O.A.S. and the Counter-Revolution in Algeria, 1954–1962*. New York: Preager, 1989.

Harvey, David. *Paris: Capital of Modernity*. New York: Routledge, 2006.

Haut Comité consultatif de la population et de la famille. *La Population française, Tome I, France métropolitaine*. Paris: La Documentation française, 1955.

Helie, Jérôme. *Les accords d'Evian, histoire de la paix ratée en Algérie*. Paris: Olivier Orban, 1992.

Hervo, Monique. *Chroniques du bidonvilles: Nanterre en guerre d'Algérie 1959–1962*. Paris: Seuil, 2001.

Hervo, Monique, and Marie-Ange Charras. *Bidonvilles l'enlisement*. Paris: François Maspero, 1971.

Hmed, Choukri. "Loger les étrangers 'isolés' en France: Socio-histoire d'une institution d'Etat: La Sonacotra, 1956–2006." Thèse de doctorat, Université Panthéon-Sorbonne, 2006.

Horne, Alistair. *A Savage War of Peace: Algeria, 1954–1962.* 1977. Reprint, New York: New York Review of Books Classics, 2006.

Horne, Janet. *A Social Laboratory for Modern France: The Musée Social and the Rise of the Welfare State.* Durham, NC: Duke University Press, 2002.

House, Jim, and Neil MacMaster. *Paris 1961: Algerians, State Terror, and Memory.* New York: Oxford University Press, 2006.

Imhof, Jean-Paul. "L'immigration algérienne en France." *Esprit* (January 1961): 89–98.

Jennings, Eric. *Vichy in the Tropics: Petain's National Revolution in Madagascar, Guadeloupe, and Indochina, 1940–44.* Stanford, CA: Stanford University Press, 2000.

Johnson Onyedum, Jennifer. "Humanizing Warfare: The Politics of Medicine, Heath Care, and International Humanitarian Intervention in Algeria, 1954–62." PhD diss., Princeton University, 2010.

Jordan, David. *Transforming Paris: The Life and Labors of Baron Haussmann.* Chicago: University of Chicago Press, 1995.

Jordi, Jean-Jacques, and Mohand Hamoumou. *Les harkis, une mémoire enfouie.* Paris: Autrement, 1999.

Josset, Sophie. "Le FAS: 1958–1998, 40 ans d'histoire au service de l'intégration." Mémoire de stage Université de Paris VII, 1988.

Kadri, Aïssa, Guy Putfin, and Jean-Paul Roux, eds. *L'école dans l'Algérie colonial: Conformer ou émanciper? Les instituteurs et les professeurs en Algérie (1883–1962).* Paris: Sudel, 2002.

Kateb, Kamel. *Européens, "indigènes," et juifs en Algérie, 1830–1962: Représentations et réalités des populations.* Paris: INED, 2001.

Katz, Ethan. "Jews and Muslims in the Shadow of Marianne: Conflicting Identities and Republican Culture in France, 1914–1975." PhD diss., University of Wisconsin, 2009.

Keller, Richard C. *Colonial Madness: Psychiatry in French North Africa.* Chicago: University of Chicago Press, 2007.

Kerchouche, Dalila. *Mon père, ce harki.* Paris: Seuil, 2003.

Klaus, Alisa. *Every Child a Lion: The Origins of Maternal and Infant Health Policy in the United States and France, 1890–1920.* Ithaca, NY: Cornell University Press, 1993.

Koos, Cheryl A. "Gender, Anti-Individualism, and Nationalism: The Alliance Nationale and the Pronatalist Backlash against the *Femme moderne*, 1933–1940." *French Historical Studies* 19, no. 3 (1996): 699–723.

Koven, Seth, and Sonya Michel, eds. *Mothers of a New World: Maternalist Politics and the Origins of Welfare States.* New York: Routledge, 1993.

Kudlick, Catherine. *Cholera in Post-Revolutionary Paris: A Cultural History.* Berkeley: University of California Press, 1996.

Kuisel, Richard. *Seducing the French: The Dilemma of Americanization.* Berkeley: University of California Press: 1997.

Lacouture, Jean. *Le témoignage est un combat: Une biographie de Germaine Tillion*. Paris: Seuil, 2000.

Lamey, René. "Les Archives de la Société des Pères Blancs (Missionnaires d'Afrique)." *History of Africa*, no. 1 (1974): 161–65.

Lamri, Sophie. "'Algériennes' et mères françaises exemplaires (1945–1962)." *Le mouvement social*, no. 199 (April–June 2002): 61–81.

Laurens, Sylvain. "La noblesse d'Etat à l'épreuve de l'Algérie et de l'après 1962." *Politix* 19, no. 76 (2006): 75–96.

———. *Une politisation feutrée: Hauts fonctionnaires et immigration en France*. Paris: Editions Belin, 2009.

Lazreg, Marnia. *The Eloquence of Silence: Algerian Women in Question*. New York: Routledge, 1994.

Le Cour Grandmaison, Olivier, ed. *Le 17 octobre 1961: Un crime d'Etat à Paris*. Paris: La Dispute, 2001.

Le Play, Frédéric. *On Family, Work, and Social Change*. Edited and translated by Catherine Bodard Silver. Chicago: University of Chicago Press, 1982.

Le Sueur, James. *Uncivil War: Intellectuals and Identity Politics during the Decolonization of Algeria*. Philadelphia: University of Pennsylvania Press, 2001.

Lebovics, Herman. *Bringing the Empire Back Home: France in the Global Age*. Durham, NC: Duke University Press, 2004.

———. *Mona Lisa's Escort: André Malraux and the Reinvention of French Culture*. Ithaca, NY: Cornell University Press, 1999.

———. *True France: The Wars over Cultural Identity, 1900–1945*. Ithaca, NY: Cornell University Press, 1994.

Lequin, Yves, ed. *La mosaïque France: Histoire des étrangers et de l'immigration*. Paris: Larousse, 1988.

Lewis, Mary Dewhurst. *The Boundaries of the Republic: Migrant Rights and the Limits of Universalism in France, 1918–1940*. Stanford, CA: Stanford University Press, 2007.

Liauzu, Claude. *La société française face au racisme de la révolution à nos jours*. Paris: Editions Complexe, 1999.

Lieberson, Stanley. *A Piece of the Pie: Blacks and White Migrants since 1880*. Berkeley: University of California Press, 1980.

Lorcin, Patricia M. E. *Imperial Identities: Stereotyping, Prejudice, and Race in Colonial Algeria*. London: I. B. Tauris, 1995.

Lounici, Fathia. "A propos de la main d'œuvre algérienne en banlieue nord-est de Paris de 1945–1962, l'exemple des foyers." Paper presented at the conference "Association histoire et mémoire ouvrière en Seine-Saint-Denis," November 2000.

Lunn, Joe. "'Les Races Guerrières': Racial Preconceptions in the French Military about West African Soldiers during the First World War." *Journal of Contemporary History* 34, no. 4 (1999): 517–36.

Mabon, Armelle. *Prisonniers de guerre "indigènes": Visages oubliés de la France occupée*. Paris: La Découverte, 2010.

MacMaster, Neil. *Burning the Veil: The Algerian War and the "Emancipation" of Muslim Women, 1954–1962*. Manchester: Manchester University Press, 2009.

———. "'A Demographic Time-Bomb': Racial Containment and the Failure of Family Welfare Policy in Late Colonial Algeria, c. 1945–54." Unpublished paper.

———. *Colonial Migrants and Racism: Algerians in France, 1900–1962*. New York: St. Martin's Press, 1997.

Mahjoub-Guelamine, Faïza. "Le rôle des services sociaux spécialisés dans la gestion pratique et symbolique de l'immigration en France. L'exemple du SSAE et du SSFNA, 1920–1980." Thèse de doctorat, Université de Paris VIII, 1997.

Malet, Elisabeth. "Jeunesse nord-africaine en France." *Masses Ouvrières*, no. 112 (1955): 52–72.

Mann, Gregory. *Native Sons: West African Veterans and France in the Twentieth Century*. Durham, NC: Duke University Press, 2006.

Marshall, T. H. *Social Policy in the Twentieth Century*. 5th ed. London: Hutchinson, 1985.

Martin, Thomas. *The French North African Crisis: Colonial Breakdown and Anglo-French Relations, 1945–62*. New York: St. Martin's Press, 2000.

Massard-Guilbaud, Geneviève. *Des Algériens à Lyon: De la Grande Guerre au Front populaire*. Paris: L'Harmattan, 1995.

Massenet, Michel. *Sauvage immigration*. Monaco: Editions du Rocher, 1994.

Math, Antoine. "Les allocations familiales et l'Algérie coloniale: A l'origine du FAS et de son financement par les régimes de prestations familiales." *Recherches et Prévisions Revue de la CNAF*, no. 53 (1998): 35–44.

Mathias, Grégor. *Les sections administratives spécialisées en Algérie: Entre idéal et réalité, 1955–1962*. Paris: L'Harmattan, 1998.

Mauco, Georges. *L'assimilation des étrangers en France*. Paris: Institut international de coopération intellectuelle, 1937.

———. *Les étrangers en France: Leur rôle dans l'activité économique*. Paris: Armand Colin, 1932.

McCarthy, Sister Joan Marie. "French Native Policy and the Church in Algeria." PhD diss., University of California, 1937.

McDougall, James. *History and the Culture of Nationalism in Algeria*. New York: Cambridge University Press, 2006.

Melnik, Constantine. *Mille jours à Matignon: Raisons d'Etat sous de Gaulle, guerre d'Algérie 1959–1962*. Paris: Grasset, 1988.

Michel, Andrée. "La population des hôtels meublés à Paris: Composition et conditions d'existence." *Population*, no. 4 (October–December 1955): 627–44.

———. *Les travailleurs algériens en France*. Paris: Centre national de la recherche scientifique, 1956.

———. *The Modernization of North African Families in the Paris Area*. Hague-Paris: Mouton, 1974.

Miller, Janet. "Algerian, French, Refugees, Repatriates, Immigrants? Harki Citizens in Post-Imperial France (1962–2005)." PhD diss., Pennsylvania State University, 2012.

Miller, Michael. *The Representation of Place: Urban Planning and Protest in France and Great Britain, 1950–1980*. Burlington, VT: Ashgate, 2003.

Milza, Pierre. *Français et Italiens à la fin du XIXe siècle*. Rome: Ecole français de Rome, 1981.

Misra, Joya. "Mothers or Workers? The Value of Women's Labor: Women and the Emergence of Family Allowance Policy." *Gender and Society* 4, no. 12 (1998): 376–99.

Moch, Leslie. *The Pariahs of Yesterday: Breton Migrants in Paris*. Durham, NC: Duke University Press, 2012.

———. *Paths to the City: Regional Migration in Nineteenth-Century France*. Thousand Oaks, CA: Sage, 1983.

Monneret, Jean. *La phase finale de la guerre d'Algérie*. Paris: L'Harmattan, 2001.

Muel-Dreyfus, Francine. *Vichy and the Eternal Feminine: A Contribution to a Political Sociology of Gender*. Translated by Kathleen A. Johnson. Durham, NC: Duke University Press, 2001.

Muller, Laurent. *Le silence des harkis*. Paris: L'Harmattan, 1999.

Murphy, John. "Baguettes, Berets and Burning Cars: The 2005 Riots and the Question of Race in Contemporary France." *French Cultural Studies* 22, no. 1 (2011): 33–49.

N'Diaye, Pap. *La condition noire: Essai sur une minorité française*. Paris: Calmann-Levy, 2008.

Nasiali, Minayo. "Native to the Republic: Negotiating Citizenship and Social Welfare in Marseille 'Immigrant' Neighborhoods since 1945." PhD diss., University of Michigan, 2010.

Naylor, Philip C. *France and Algeria: A History of Decolonization and Transformation*. Gainesville: University Press of Florida, 2000.

Neulander, Joelle. *Programming National Identity: The Culture of Radio in 1930s France*. Baton Rouge: Louisiana State University Press, 2009.

Newsome, W. Brian. *French Urban Planning, 1940–1968*. New York: Peter Lang, 2009.

Noiriel, Gérard. *The French Melting Pot: Immigration, Citizenship, and National Identity*. Translated by Geoffroy de Laforcade. Minneapolis: University of Minnesota Press, 1996.

———. *Immigration, antisémitisme et racisme en France (XIXe–XXe siècle): Discours publics, humiliations privées*. Paris, Fayard, 2007.

Nord, Philip. *France's New Deal: From the Thirties to the Postwar Era*. Princeton, NJ: Princeton University Press, 2010.

———. "The Welfare State in France, 1870–1914." *French Historical Studies* 3, no. 18 (1994): 821–38.

Offen, Karen. "Depopulation, Nationalism, and Feminism in Fin-de-Siècle France." *American Historical Review* 89, no. 3 (1984): 648–76.

———. *Women and the Politics of Motherhood in France, 1920–1940*. Florence: European University Institute, Working Paper no. 87/293, 1987.

Ouary, Malek. *Par les chemins d'émigration*. Algiers: La Société algérienne de publications, 1955.

Paxton, Robert. *Vichy France Old Guard and New Order, 1940–1944*. 1972. Reprint, New York: Columbia University Press, 2001.

Peabody, Sue. *There Are No Slaves in France: The Political Culture of Race and Slavery in the Ancien Régime*. New York: Oxford University Press, 2002.

Peabody, Sue, and Tyler Stovall, eds. *The Color of Liberty: Histories of Race in France*. Durham, NC: Duke University Press, 2003.

Pedersen, Susan. *Family, Dependence, and the Origins of the Welfare State: Britain and France, 1914–1945*. New York: Cambridge University Press, 1995.

Péju, Paulette. *Ratonnades à Paris. Précédé de les harkis à Paris*. Paris: La Découverte, 2000.

Pelletier, Emile. "Les réalisations en faveur des Nord Africains dans le département." *La conjoncture économique dans le Département de la Seine*. Paris: Imprimerie municipale, Hôtel de Ville, 1st trimester 1956.

Pervillé, Guy. *1962: La paix en Algérie*. Paris: La Documentation française, 1992.

———. "La politique algérienne de la France, 1830–1962. In "Juger en Algérie 1944–1962," 27–37. *Le genre humain* 32. Paris: Seuil, 1997.

———. *L'Europe et l'Afrique de 1914–1974*. Gap: Ophrys, 1994.

———. *Les accords d'Evian: Succès ou échec de la réconciliation franco-algérienne (1954–2012)*. Paris: Armand Colin, 2012.

———. *Pour une histoire de la guerre d'Algérie*. Paris: Picard, 2002.

Pitt, Alan. "Frédéric Le Play and the Family: Paternalism and Freedom in the French Debates of the 1870s." *French History* 12, no. 1 (1998): 67–89.

Pollard, Miranda. *Reign of Virtue: Mobilizing Gender in Vichy France*. Chicago: University of Chicago Press, 1998.

Ponty, Janine. *Polonais méconnus: Histoire des travailleurs immigrés en France dans l'entre-deux-guerres*. Paris: Publications de la Sorbonne, 1988.

Pouvreau, Benoît. *Un politique en architecture: Eugène Claudius-Petit, 1907–1989*. Paris: Editions du Moniteur, 2004.

Prochaska, David. *Making Algeria French: Colonialism in Bône, 1870–1920*. New York: Cambridge University Press, 1990.

Pulju, Rebecca. *Women and Mass Consumer Society in Postwar France*. New York: Cambridge University Press, 2011.

Pyenson, Lewis. *Civilizing Mission: Exact Science and French Overseas Expansion, 1830–1940*. Baltimore: Johns Hopkins University Press, 1993.

Rabinow, Paul. *French Modern: Norms and Forms of the Social Environment*. Cambridge, MA: MIT Press, 1989.

Rager, Jean-Jacques. *L'émigration en France des musulmans algériens (principaux aspects démographiques, économiques et sociaux)*. Documents algériens: Service d'information du cabinet de gouverneur général de l'Algérie, no. 49. Algiers: Service d'information du cabinet du gouverneur générale de l'Algérie, 1956.

———. "Les musulmans algériens en France et dans les pays islamiques." Thèse de doctorat, Université d'Alger, 1950.

Reggiani, Andrés Horacio. "Birthing the French Welfare State: Political Crises, Population, and Public Health, 1914–1960." PhD diss., State University of New York at Stony Brook, 1998.

————. *God's Eugenicist: Alexis Carrel and the Sociobiology of Decline.* New York: Berghahn Books, 2007.

Rioux, Jean-Pierre. *The Fourth Republic, 1944–1958.* Translated by Godfrey Rogers. New York: Cambridge University Press, 1987.

Rosenberg, Clifford. "The International Politics of Vaccine Testing in Interwar Algiers." *American Historical Review* 117, no. 3 (2012): 671–97.

————. *Policing Paris: The Origins of Modern Immigration Control between the Wars.* Ithaca, NY: Cornell University Press, 2006.

————. "Republican Surveillance: Immigration, Citizenship, and the Police in Interwar Paris." PhD diss., Princeton University, 2000.

Rosental, Paul-André. *L'intelligence démographique: Sciences et politiques des populations en France (1930–1960).* Paris: Odile Jacob, 2003.

————. *Les sentiers invisibles: Espaces, familles et migrations dans la France du 19è siècle.* Paris: Editions de l'école des hautes études en sciences sociales, 1999.

Ross, Kristin. *Fast Cars, Clean Bodies: Decolonization and the Reordering of French Culture.* Boston: MIT Press, 1996.

Rousso, Henry. *The Vichy Syndrome: History and Memory in France since 1944.* Translated by Arthur Goldhammer. Cambridge, MA: Harvard University Press, 1994.

Rudolph, Nicole. "At Home in Postwar France: The Design and Construction of Domestic Space, 1945–1975." PhD diss., New York University, 2005.

Ruedy, John. *Modern Algeria: The Origins and Development of a Nation.* Bloomington: Indiana University Press, 1992.

Saada, Emmanuelle. *Empire's Children: Race, Filiation, and Citizenship in the French Colonies.* Translated by Arthur Goldhammer. Chicago: University of Chicago Press, 2012.

Said, Edward. *Culture and Imperialism.* New York: Vintage Books, 1994.

Sambron, Diane. *Les femmes algériennes pendant la colonisation.* Paris: Riveneuve Editions, 2009.

Sanders, Nichole. *Gender and Welfare in Mexico: The Consolidation of a Postrevolutionary State, 1937–1958.* College Station, PA: Penn State University Press, 2011.

Sauvy, Alfred. *Bien-être et population.* Paris: Edition sociale française, 1945.

Sayad, Abdelmalek. *La double absence: Des illusions de l'émigré aux souffrances de l'immigré.* Edited by Pierre Bourdieu. Paris: Seuil, 1999.

————. *L'immigration ou les paradoxes de l'altérité: L'illusion du provisoire.* Paris: Editions Raison d'Agir, 2006.

————. "Les trois 'âges' de l'émigration algérienne en France." *Actes de la recherche en sciences sociales,* no. 15 (1977): 59–79.

————. *The Suffering of the Immigrant.* Translated by David Macey. Malden, MA: Polity, 2004.

————. "Tendances et courants de publications en sciences sociales sur l'immigration en France depuis 1960." *Current Sociology* 2, no. 32 (1984): 219–304.

Sayad, Abdelmalek, and Eliane Dupuy. *Un Nanterre algérien, terre de bidonvilles.* Paris: Editions Autrement, 1995.

Schneider, William. *Quality and Quantity: The Quest for Biological Regeneration in Twentieth-Century France*. New York: Cambridge University Press, 2002.

Schor, Ralph. *L'histoire de l'immigration en France de la fin du XIXe siècle à nos jours*. Paris: Armand Colin, 1996.

———. *L'immigration en France 1919–1939*. Nice: Centre de la Méditerranée moderne et contemporaine, 1986.

Scioldo-Zürcher, Yann. *Devenir métropolitain: Politique d'intégration et parcours de rapatriés d'Algérie en métropole, 1954–2005*. Paris: Editions de l'école des hautes études en sciences sociales, 2010.

Scott, James C. *Seeing Like a State: How Certain Schemes to Improve the Human Condition Have Failed*. New Haven, CT: Yale University Press, 1999.

Scott, Joan Wallach. *Gender and the Politics of History*. New York: Columbia University Press, 1989.

———. *The Politics of the Veil*. Princeton, NJ: Princeton University Press, 2007.

Segalla, Spencer. *The Moroccan Soul: French Education, Colonial Ethnology, and Muslim Resistance*. Lincoln: University of Nebraska Press, 2009.

Sessions, Jennifer. *By Sword and Plow: France and the Conquest of Algeria*. Ithaca, NY: Cornell University Press, 2011.

Shepard, Todd. "Algeria, France, Mexico, UNESCO: A Transitional History of Anti-Racism and Decolonization, 1932–1962." *Journal of Global History* 6 (2011): 273–97.

———. *The Invention of Decolonization: The Algerian War and the Remaking of France*. Ithaca, NY: Cornell University Press, 2006.

Silverman, Maxim. *Deconstructing the Nation: Immigration, Racism, and Citizenship in Modern France*. New York: Routledge, 1992.

Silverstein, Paul A. *Algeria in France: Transpolitics, Race, and Nation*. Bloomington: Indiana University Press, 2004.

Simmons, Dana. "Minimal Frenchman: Science and Standards of Living, 1840–1960." PhD diss., University of Chicago, 2004.

Simon, Jacques. *L'immigration algérienne en France: Des origines à l'indépendance*. Paris: Editions Paris-Méditerranée, 2000.

———, ed. *L'immigration algérienne en France de 1962 à nos jours*. Paris: L'Harmattan, 2002.

Soustelle, Jacques. "La famille otomi-pame du Mexique central." Thèse de doctorat, Université de Paris, 1937.

Spire, Alexis. *Etrangers à la carte: L'administration de l'immigration en France (1945–1975)*. Paris: Grasset, 2005.

———. "Semblables et pourtant différents: La citoyenneté paradoxale des 'Français musulmans d'Algérie' en métropole." *Genèses* 53 (2003): 48–68.

Stébé, Jean-Marc. *Le logement social en France*. Paris: Presses Universitaires de France, 1998.

Stewart, Mary Lynn. *Women, Work, and the French State: Labor Protection and Social Patriarchy, 1879–1919*. Kingston, ON: McGill/Queens University Press, 1989.

Stoler, Ann Laura. *Carnal Knowledge and Imperial Power: Race and the Intimate in Colonial Rule*. 2nd ed. Berkeley: University of California Press, 2010.

———. *Race and the Education of Desire: Foucault's History of Sexuality and the Colonial Order of Things*. Durham, NC: Duke University Press, 1995.

Stora, Benjamin. *Aide-mémoire de l'immigration algérienne, 1922–1992: Chronologie, Bibliographie*. Paris: L'Harmattan, 1992.

———. *Algeria, 1830–2000: A Short History*. Translated by Jane Marie Todd. Ithaca, NY: Cornell University Press, 2001.

———. *Histoire de l'Algérie coloniale, 1830–1954*. Paris: La Découverte, 1994.

———. *Ils venaient d'Algérie: L'immigration algérienne en France, 1912–1992*. Paris: Fayard, 1992.

———. *La gangrène et l'oubli: La mémoire de la guerre d'Algérie*. Paris: La Découverte, 1991.

———. *Le dictionnaire des livres de la guerre d'Algérie: Romans, nouvelles, poésie, photos, histoire, essais, récits historiques, témoignages, biographies, mémoires, autobiographies, 1955–1995*. Paris: L'Harmattan, 1996.

———. *Messali Hadj: 1898–1974*. Paris: Hachette, 2004.

Stora, Benjamin, and Zakya Daoud. *Ferhat Abbas, une utopie algérienne*. Paris: Denoël, 1995.

Stovall, Tyler. "The Color Line behind the Lines: Racial Violence in France during the Great War." *American Historical Review* 103, no. 3 (1998): 737–79.

Stovall, Tyler, and Georges Van Den Abbeele, eds. *French Civilization and Its Discontents: Nationalism, Colonialism, Race*. Lanham, MD: Lexington Books, 2003.

Taguieff, Pierre-André. *La couleur et le sang: Doctrines racistes à la française*. Paris: Mille et une nuits, Fayard, 1999.

Tapinos, Georges, ed. *L'immigration étrangère en France, 1946–1973*. Cahiers d'INED, No. 71. Paris: Presses Universitaires de France, 1975.

Tchibindat, Sylvestre. *Le logement des Algériens en France: Historique et inventaire des problématiques actuelles*. Paris: L'Harmattan, 2005.

Témime, Emile. "La politique française à l'égard de la migration algérienne: Les poids de la colonisation." *Le Mouvement social*, no. 188 (1999): 77–88.

Terrio, Susan. *Judging Mohammed: Juvenile Delinquency, Immigration, and Exclusion at the Paris Palace of Justice*. Stanford, CA: Stanford University Press, 2009.

Thébaud, Françoise. *Quand nos grand-mères donnaient la vie: La maternité en France dans l'entre-deux-guerres*. Lyon: Presses Universitaires de Lyon, 1986.

Thénault, Sylvie. *Histoire de la guerre d'indépendance algérienne*. Paris: Flammarion, 2005.

———. "L'état d'urgence (1955–2005). De l'Algérie colonial à la France contemporaine: Destin d'une loi." *Le Mouvement social*, no. 218 (2007): 63–78.

———. *Une drôle de justice: Les magistrats dans la guerre d'Algérie*. Paris: La Découverte, 2001.

———. *Violence ordinaire dans l'Algérie colonial: Camps, internements, assignations à résidence*. Paris: Odile Jacob, 2012.

Thody, Philip. *The Fifth French Republic: Presidents, Policies and Personalities*. London: Routledge, 1998.

Thomas, Martin. *The French North African Crisis: Colonial Breakdown and Anglo-French Relations, 1945–62*. New York: St. Martin's Press, 2000.

Thompson, Elizabeth. *Colonial Citizens: Republican Rights, Paternal Privilege, and Gender in French Syria and Lebanon.* New York: Columbia University Press, 2000.

Tiersten, Lisa. *Marianne in the Market: Envisioning Consumer Society in Fin-de-Siècle France.* Berkeley: University of California Press, 2001.

Tillion, Germaine. *A la rechercher du vrai et du juste.* Edited by Tzvetan Todorov. Paris: Seuil, 2001.

———. *Algeria: The Realities.* Translated by Ronald Matthews. New York: Knopf, 1958.

Todorov, Tzvetan. *On Human Diversity: Nationalism, Racism, and Exoticism in French Thought.* Translated by Catherine Porter. Cambridge, MA: Harvard University Press, 1993.

———, ed. *Le siècle de Germaine Tillion.* Paris: Seuil, 2007.

Tristan, Anne. *Le silence du fleuve: Ce crime que nous n'avons toujours pas nommé.* Paris: Au nom de la mémoire, 1991.

Vant, André. *Les grands ensembles du sud-est de Saint-Etienne: Essai de géographie sociale,* Dossier 9. Université de Saint-Etienne: Centre interdisciplinaire d'études et de recherches sur les structures régionales, June 1974.

Viet, Vincent. *La France immigrée: Construction d'une politique, 1914–1997.* Paris: Fayard, 1998.

Villey, François. *Le complément familial du salaire: Etude des allocations familiales dans leurs rapports avec le salaire.* Paris: Editions sociales françaises, 1946.

———. *Mémento pratique des étrangers: Recueil des principales dispositions applicables aux étrangers en France.* Paris: La Documentation française, 1952.

Vinen, Richard. *France, 1934–1970.* New York: St. Martin's Press, 1996.

Vogel, Marie. "Andrée Michel, sociologue sans frontières." *Travail, genre et sociétés,* no. 22 (November 2009): 5–7.

Voldman, Danièle. *La reconstruction des villes françaises de 1940 à 1954. Histoire d'une politique.* Paris: L'Harmattan, 1997.

Wadowiec, Jaime. "The Afterlives of Empire: Race, Gender, and Citizenship in Decolonized France." PhD diss., State University of New York, Binghamton, forthcoming.

Wakeman, Rosemary. *The Heroic City, 1945–1958.* Chicago: University of Chicago Press, 2009.

———. *Modernizing the Provincial City: Toulouse 1945–1975.* Cambridge, MA: Harvard University Press, 1998.

Wall, Irwin. *France, the United States, and the Algerian War.* Berkeley: University of California Press, 2001.

Watson, Cicely. "Population Policy in France: Family Allowances and Other Benefits." *Population Studies* 1, no. 8 (1954): 46–73.

Weber, Eugene. *Peasants into Frenchmen: The Modernization of Rural France, 1870–1914.* Stanford, CA: Stanford University Press, 1976.

Weil, Patrick. "Histoire et mémoire des discriminations en matière de nationalité française." *Vingtième Siècle. Revue d'histoire* 4, no. 84 (October–December 2004): 5–22.

———. *La France et ses étrangers: L'aventure d'une politique de l'immigration de 1938 à nos jours.* Paris: Gallimard, 1991.

————. *Liberté, égalité, discriminations: L'identité nationale au regard de l'histoire.* Paris: Grasset, 2008.

————. *Qu'est qu'un Français? Histoire de la nationalité française depuis la révolution.* Paris: Grasset, 2002.

White, Owen. *Children of the French Empire: Miscegenation and Colonial Society in French West Africa, 1895–1960.* Oxford: Oxford University Press, 1999.

Wieviorka, Michel. *La différence.* Paris: Ballard, 2000.

————. *La France raciste.* Paris: Seuil, 1992.

Wilder, Gary. *The French Imperial Nation-State: Negritude and Colonial Humanism between the Two World Wars.* Chicago: Chicago University Press, 2005.

Wright, Gwendolyn. *The Politics of Design in French Colonial Urbanism.* Chicago: University of Chicago Press, 1991.

Yacono, Xavier. *Les Bureaux arabes et l'évolution des genres de vie indigènes dans l'Ouest du Tell algérois (Dahra, Chélif, Ouarsenis, Sersou).* Paris: Editions Larose, 1953.

Zehraoui, Ahsène. *L'immigration: De l'homme seul à la famille.* Paris: L'Harmattan, 1994.

————. *Les travailleurs algériens en France: Etude sociologique de quelques aspects de la vie familial.* Paris: F. Maspero, 1976.

Index